Lecture Notes in Computer Science

# Lecture Notes in Artificial Intelligence    16119

Founding Editor

Jörg Siekmann

Series Editors

Randy Goebel, *University of Alberta, Edmonton, Canada*
Wolfgang Wahlster, *DFKI, Berlin, Germany*
Zhi-Hua Zhou, *Nanjing University, Nanjing, China*

The series Lecture Notes in Artificial Intelligence (LNAI) was established in 1988 as a topical subseries of LNCS devoted to artificial intelligence.

The series publishes state-of-the-art research results at a high level. As with the LNCS mother series, the mission of the series is to serve the international R & D community by providing an invaluable service, mainly focused on the publication of conference and workshop proceedings and postproceedings.

Guy De Tré · Sotir Sotirov · Janusz Kacprzyk ·
Giuseppe Psaila · Grégory Smits ·
Troels Andreasen · Gloria Bordogna ·
Henrik Legind Larsen
Editors

# Flexible Query Answering Systems

16th International Conference, FQAS 2025
Burgas, Bulgaria, September 11–13, 2025
Proceedings

 Springer

*Editors*
Guy De Tré
Ghent University
Ghent, Belgium

Janusz Kacprzyk
Polish Academy of Sciences
Warsaw, Poland

Grégory Smits
IMT Atlantique
Plouzané, France

Gloria Bordogna
National Research Council
Milan, Italy

Sotir Sotirov
Burgas State University Prof. Dr. Asen
Zlatarov
Burgas, Bulgaria

Giuseppe Psaila
Bergamo University
Dalmine, Italy

Troels Andreasen
Roskilde University
Roskilde, Denmark

Henrik Legind Larsen
Legind Technologies
Haslev, Denmark

ISSN 0302-9743       ISSN 1611-3349 (electronic)
Lecture Notes in Artificial Intelligence
ISBN 978-3-032-05606-1       ISBN 978-3-032-05607-8 (eBook)
https://doi.org/10.1007/978-3-032-05607-8

LNCS Sublibrary: SL7 – Artificial Intelligence

This Springer imprint is published by the registered company Springer Nature Switzerland AG
The registered company address is: Gewerbestrasse 11, 6330 Cham, Switzerland

If disposing of this product, please recycle the paper.

# Preface

This volume collects the full texts of the papers and extended abstracts of the plenary talks and tutorials presented at the Sixteenth International Conference on Flexible Query Answering Systems, FQAS 2025, held in Burgas, Bulgaria, September 11–13, 2025. This biennial conference series has been running since 1994, starting in Roskilde, Denmark, where it was also held in 1996, 1998 and 2009. The other editions were hosted in Warsaw, Poland (2000), Copenhagen, Denmark (2002), Lyon, France (2004), Milan, Italy (2006), Ghent, Belgium (2011), Granada, Spain (2013), Cracow, Poland (2015), London, UK (2017), Amantea, Italy (2019), Bratislava, Slovakia (2021) and Palma de Mallorca, Spain (2023).

FQAS is the premier conference focusing on the key issue in the information society of providing flexible, easy and (for humans) intuitive access to information. In targeting this issue, the conference provides a platform for the exchange of knowledge and ideas in topics spanning data-driven and model-driven querying, natural language processing, retrieval-augmented generation, knowledge representation and fair and explainable AI systems, among others.

The guiding topics of the FQAS conferences are innovative query systems aimed at providing easy, flexible and human-friendly access to information. Such systems are becoming increasingly important also due to the huge and always growing number of users as well as the growing amount and variety of available information.

Since 1994, the conference has provided a unique and multidisciplinary forum for researchers, developers and practitioners to explore and exchange new ideas and approaches in all mentioned research areas.

The sixteenth edition of the conference received 49 regular paper submissions. After pre-screening by the program chairs 41 full papers were sent to reviewers, applying a peer review process where each paper was reviewed by at least three reviewers. This resulted in 26 accepted papers, all of them being included in these proceedings.

The conference has six accepted special sessions with the following titles and organizers:

1. Data-Driven Quality Management and Intelligent Systems for Academic Processes and Flexible Decision-Making (organizers: Eliza Stefanova and Krassimir Atanassov)
2. Large AI Models—Innovtions and Challenges (organizers: Ivan Koychev and Elisaveta Gurova)
3. Language Models in Advanced Information Retrieval (organizer: Paolo Fosci)
4. Intuitionistic Fuzzy Approaches for Flexible Querying and Reasoning (organizers: Krassimir Atanassov and Tania Pencheva)
5. Emerging Trends in Data, Web, and Social Media Mining in a New Era of Flexible Query Answering Systems (organizers: M. Dolores Ruiz and Maria J. Martin-Bautista)

6. Information Retrieval and Knowledge Management for Risk-Based Decision-Making (organizers: Maria J. Martin-Bautista, M. Dolores Ruiz, Bartolomé Ortiz-Viso, Karel Gutierrez-Batista and Henrik L. Larsen)

All paper submitted to these special sessions were subject to the same review process as papers that were submitted as regular papers.

The conference program also contained two tutorials with the following titles and organizers:

1. From Unstructured to Understood (organizer: Michael Brands)
2. Multi-grade Fuzzy Set Models with the J-Co Framework (organizers: Paolo Fosci and Giuseppe Psaila)

We wish to thank all authors who contributed with their excellent papers, as well as our programme committee and additional reviewers for their work. We also sincerely thank our plenary speakers Jozo Dujmović, Hassane Essafi and Sławomir Zadrożny, the special session organizers and the tutorial organizers. Finally, we extend our gratitude to the members of the Advisory Board, several of whom have been supporting the FQAS conferences from the very beginning, and also to the Local Organizing Committee, without whom FQAS 2025 would not have been possible.

September 2025

Guy De Tré
Sotir Sotirov
Janusz Kacprzyk
Guiseppe Psaila
Grégory Smits
Troels Andreasen
Gloria Bordogna
Henrik Legind Larsen

# Organization

## General Chairs

Guy De Tré — Ghent University, Belgium

Sotir Sotirov — Burgas State University "Prof. Dr. Asen Zlatarov", Bulgaria

Janusz Kacprzyk — Systems Research Institute, Polish Academy of Sciences, Poland

## Program Committee Chairs

Giuseppe Psaila — University of Bergamo, Italy

Grégory Smits — IMT Atlantique, France

## Steering Committee

Troels Andreasen — Roskilde University, Denmark

Gloria Bordogna — National Research Council (CNR), Italy

Guy De Tré — Ghent University, Belgium

Henrik Legind Larsen — Legind Technologies A/S, Denmark

## Local Organization Committee

Simeon Ribagin — Bulgarian Academy of Sciences, Bulgaria

Evdokia Sotirova — Burgas State University "Prof. Dr. Asen Zlatarov", Bulgaria

Radovesta Stewart — Burgas State University "Prof. Dr. Asen Zlatarov", Bulgaria

## International Advisory Board

Carlos D. Barranco — Pablo de Olavide University, Spain

Henrik Bulskov — Roskilde University, Denmark

Jesús Cardeñosa — Polytechnic University of Madrid, Spain

| Panagiotis Chountas | University of Westminster, UK |
| Henning Christiansen | Roskilde University, Denmark |
| Hendrik Decker | Ludwig Maximilian University of Munich, Germany |
| Hassane Essafi | Atomic Energy and Alternative Energies Commission, France |
| Norbert Fuhr | University of Duisburg-Essen, Germany |
| Hélène Jaudoin | University of Rennes, France |
| Janusz Kacprzyk | System Research Institute, Polish Academy of Sciences, Poland |
| Don Kraft | Colorado Technical University, USA |
| Marie-Jeanne Lesot | Sorbonne University, France |
| M. J. Martin-Bautista | University of Granada, Spain |
| Jørgen Fischer Nilsson | Technical University of Denmark, Denmark |
| Gabriella Pasi | University of Milano-Bicocca, Italy |
| Fred Petry | Tulane University, USA |
| Olivier Pivert | University of Rennes, France |
| Henri Prade | University of Toulouse, France |
| Giuseppe Psaila | University of Bergamo, Italy |
| Zbigniew W. Raś | University of North Carolina, USA |
| Roman Słowinski | Poznań University of Technology, Poland |
| Grégory Smits | IMT Atlantique, France |
| Sotir Sotirov | Asen Zlatarov University, Bulgaria |
| Nicolas Spyratos | Paris-Sud University, France |
| Adnan Yazici | Nazarbayev University, Kazakhstan |
| Sławomir Zadrożny | System Research Institute, Polish Academy of Sciences, Poland |
| Wlodek Zadrożny | University of North Carolina, USA |

## Program Committee

| Troels Andreasen | Roskilde University, Denmark |
| Karina Angelieva | International Science and Technology Centre, Bulgaria |
| Krassimir Atanassov | Bulgarian Academy of Sciences, Bulgaria |
| Gloria Bordogna | National Research Council (CNR), Italy |
| Antoon Bronselaer | Ghent University, Belgium |
| Henrik Bulskov | Roskilde University, Denmark |
| Jesús Cardeñosa | Polytechnic University of Madrid, Spain |
| Henning Christiansen | Roskilde University, Denmark |
| Guy De Tré | Ghent University, Belgium |

| | |
|---|---|
| Hassane Essafi | Atomic Energy and Alternative Energies Commission, France |
| Sébastien Ferré | University of Rennes, France |
| Paolo Fosci | University of Bergamo, Italy |
| Elisaveta Gurova | Sofia University, Bulgaria |
| Allel Hadjali | University of Poitiers, France |
| Hélène Jaudoin | University of Rennes, France |
| Janusz Kacprzyk | System Research Institute, Polish Academy of Sciences, Poland |
| Ivan Koychev | Sofia University, Bulgaria |
| Henrik Legind Larsen | Legind Technologies A/S, Denmark |
| M. J. Martin-Bautista | University of Granada, Spain |
| Jørgen Fischer Nilsson | Technical University of Denmark, Denmark |
| Iker Pastor Lopez | University of Deusto, Spain |
| Tania Pencheva | Bulgarian Academy of Sciences, Bulgaria |
| Olivier Pivert | University of Rennes, France |
| Vladimir Poulkov | Technical University of Sofia, Bulgaria |
| Giuseppe Psaila | University of Bergamo, Italy |
| Zbigniew W. Raś | University of North Carolina, USA |
| Marek Reformat | University of Alberta, Canada |
| Sabrina Senatore | University of Salerno, Italy |
| Grégory Smits | IMT Atlantique, France |
| Sotir Sotirov | Burgas State University "Prof. Dr. Asen Zlatarov", Bulgaria |
| Nicolas Spyratos | Paris-Sud University, France |
| Eliza Stefanova | Sofia University, Bulgaria |
| Paolo Tagliolato Acquaviva D'Aragona | National Research Council (CNR), Italy |
| Peter Vojtáš | Charles University, Czech Republic |
| Adnan Yazici | Nazarbayev University, Kazakhstan |
| Sławomir Zadrożny | System Research Institute, Polish Academy of Sciences, Poland |

## Additional Reviewers

| | |
|---|---|
| Ana Guerrero Tamayo | University of Deusto, Spain |
| Karel Gutiérrez-Batista | University of Granada, Spain |
| Marco Mesiti | University of Milan, Italy |
| Bartolome Ortiz-Viso | University of Granada, Spain |
| Simeon Ribagin | Bulgarian Academy of Sciences, Bulgaria |
| M. Dolores Ruiz | University of Granada, Spain |

# Contents

## Intuitionistic Fuzzy Approaches for Flexible Querying and Reasoning under Uncertainty

## Emerging Trends in Flexible Query Answering and Information Retrieval

**Tutorials**

# Invited Talks

# On the Role of Context in Data Querying

Sławomir Zadrożny$^{(\boxtimes)}$ (iD) and Janusz Kacprzyk (iD)

Systems Research Institute, Polish Academy of Sciences, Warszawa, Poland
{Slawomir.Zadrozny,Janusz.Kacprzyk}@ibspan.waw.pl

**Abstract.** The role of context in database querying is explored, with a brief reference to its broader relevance. Context, pervasive in human activity, significantly influences intentions, preferences, interpretation, decision-making, and action. Despite its intuitive appeal, context remains a multifaceted concept requiring systematic investigation.

**Keywords:** context · data querying · information retrieval

## 1   Introduction

Context has been extensively studied across a range of disciplines, notably related to human judgment, behavior, etc. but – if we limit our attention to areas that are more directly related to our interests – we should quote database querying, textual information retrieval [2] and recommender systems. Its importance in NLP has been confirmed by the breakthrough brought in by the Transformer architectures which rely on the attention mechanism for capturing and leveraging contextual dependencies between words.

Moreover, the development of Large Language Models (LLMs), enabled by Transformer architectures, has further amplified the importance of context in intelligent systems. LLM-based agents rely heavily on context derived from preceding conversational steps to response generation. Recently, the paradigm of *context engineering* is gaining growing interest as an approach that embraces a broad array of artifacts as the foundation for dialogue and problem solving.

## 2   Context: General View

Defining context in a precise, universal, and exhaustive manner remains a challenging task. A relevant, general definition, adopted in, e.g., ubiquitous computing [1], refers to what is known as "five W's": "Who" (attributes of the primary agent, and potentially other agents involved), "What" (the activity or task the agent is engaged with at a given moment), "Where" (the location of the agent), "When" (the temporal setting), and "Why" (the underlying purpose or motivation driving the agent's current behavior).

In data querying scenarios, the interpretation of the "five W's", as discussed in [1], requires some rethinking.

© The Author(s), under exclusive license to Springer Nature Switzerland AG 2026
G. De Tré et al. (Eds.): FQAS 2025, LNAI 16119, pp. 3–6, 2026.
https://doi.org/10.1007/978-3-032-05607-8_1

**Who** This dimension refers to the characteristics of the user submitting the query – such as demographic attributes, role, or professional background. Crucially, even when two users pose identically formulated queries, the relevant answer may be different depending on the user's profile.

**What** In ubiquitous computing, the "What" dimension typically concerns recognizing the user's current activity/task, with the objective of adapting system interactions accordingly. In data querying scenarios, this aspect is often embedded within the "Who" or "Where" dimensions. Nonetheless, isolating "What" as a separate consideration may prove valuable, e.g., in making a distinction between exploratory querying versus routine data retrieval. Importantly, this should be distinguished from the user's underlying intent, which aligns more closely with the "Why" dimension. Additionally, *query history* may be considered part of the "What" dimension or, alternatively, of the "Why" dimension. Analyzing the user's previous queries can offer insight into their broader activity patterns while also shedding light on deeper intentions driving their information needs.

**Where** The "Where" dimension captures the user's physical location, which can directly impact how a query is interpreted and answered. For example, a request for directions to a particular street must yield different results depending on the city – or even the neighborhood – in which the query is made. More broadly, the user's location may inform default parameters, filter relevance, and prioritize local data sources, reinforcing the spatial sensitivity of query interpretation.

**When** Much like "Where," the "When" dimension has a clear and immediate impact on the relevance and interpretation of a query. Temporal information such as time of day, date, or even season can significantly affect the meaning of a request and the relevance of a response. For instance, a user querying for "weather forecast" or "restaurant availability" should receive different results depending on the time the query is issued.

**Why** The "Why" dimension addresses the underlying intent or purpose motivating the user's query. It reflects the real information need that may not be explicitly stated or may be difficult to express within the constraints of a formal query language. Identifying this intent allows the system to reinterpret or enrich the original query automatically, thereby improving the relevance and usefulness of the results.

It should be noted that modern electronic devices – particularly smartphones, smartwatches, and other mobile technologies – offer exceptional capabilities for capturing all five above mentioned aspects/dimensions of context. While time and location can be reliably detected on desktops and notebooks, mobile devices are typically equipped with a variety of sensors and interfaces that provide rich contextual information. These include GPS, accelerometers, biometric sensors enabling nuanced awareness of user behavior, intent, and surroundings.

## 3   Context in Data Querying

Context in data querying is understood here as any information beyond the query itself that can influence its interpretation. Within the framework of classical relational database querying, context can be more precisely defined as any factor that affects how the user's intent is translated into a set of rows considered relevant to the query. Accordingly, context may cause the same query to match or fail to match a given row in a table.

A distinction between *internal* and *external* context can be made. Internal context is determined by the content of the database itself. From this perspective, certain features in standard SQL, such as the EXISTS operator or analytical functions, support the evaluation of a row against a query by referencing other rows within the database, thus exemplifying the notion of internal context.

The notion of external context refers to aspects not related to data themselves. This includes, first of all, the user and his or her intentions and preferences. Ideally, they should be explicitly reflected in the query formulation. However, this is not always feasible due to limitations in query expressiveness or user awareness. Also, the user's profile may contain valuable information that the user may not consciously recognize, yet which can meaningfully enhance query interpretation.

An important example of a querying paradigm that incorporates context is flexible fuzzy querying [3]. Its primary goal is to model user preferences underlying a query in a human consistent way. To that end, the direct use of *linguistic terms* in query statements is advocated. As the meaning of linguistic terms is inherently subjective, the paradigm presumes the existence of a *dictionary* tailored to each individual user. This represents a concrete instantiation of external, user profilerelated context in operation. Additionally, it is proposed that these personal dictionary be dynamically calibrated against the current content of the database, i.e., with respect to the range of values in the relevant columns.

For example, the interpretation of linguistic term such as "cheap" may be automatically adjusted according to, e.g., prices of the houses in the database. Thus, the meaning of a linguistic term is dependent on the user posing the query, yet may also vary based on the current state of the database what underscores the presence of dual, external and internal, context in flexible querying.

Context in flexible fuzzy querying typically appears in an *implicit* manner. However, we have proposed a new class of queries, so-called *contextual bipolar queries* [4], which explicitly refer to the context. These are based on earlier introduced *bipolar queries*, formulated as: "$C$ and possibly $P$", where condition $C$ must be unconditionally satisfied, and $P$ carries secondary importance but meant in a nuanced way. Specifically, a row $t$ satisfies such a query if it meets both conditions $C$ and $P$, unless no row in the database satisfies $C \wedge P$. In the latter case, satisfying $C$ alone is deemed sufficient. While both $C$ and $P$ are generally fuzzy conditions the satisfaction is in general a gradual notion instead of binary one but the core principle remains intact.

Contextual bipolar queries introduce an explicit form of context. Unlike standard bipolar queries which assess the possibility to satisfy $C \wedge P$ with respect to the entire database, contextual bipolar queries restrict this evaluation to a localized subset. For instance, while a regular bipolar query for real estate may take the form: "*cheap* and possibly located *near* a station", a contextual variant may relax this to: "*cheap* and possibly located *near* a station *with respect to the same city district*". In the standard case, a house must satisfy both conditions $C$ and $P$ if at least one house in the database satisfies $C \wedge P$. In the contextual formulation, both conditions are required only if there exists a house within the same district that satisfies $C \wedge P$.

Recently, we have proposed a new application of context in the framework of database querying, namely the notion of *context-seeking queries*. Unlike conventional approaches that rely on an implicitly or explicitly specified context for evaluating whether a row matches a query, context-seeking queries aim to *construct* such a context dynamically. In essence, a context-seeking query takes as input a specific row (tuple), referred to as the *tuple in focus*, along with a criterion (e.g., price), and searches for a neighborhood of tuples that share relevant characteristics with the tuple in focus. For instance, given a house located in city quarter $A$ with two bedrooms, the query identifies a subset of tuples matching this description. If such a subset is not empty and, within this localized context, the tuple in focus has the most favorable value according to the criterion, e.g., the lowest price, this context is returned as the result of the context-seeking query.

Thus, context-seeking queries are an example of the application of the notion of concept which goes beyond what was so far discussed in the literature. The context here may be referred to as *active* contrary to the *passive* role it plays in more traditional settings.

## 4   Conclusions

We have briefly studied diverse aspects and dimensions of the notion of context as they apply to data querying. Our discussion encompassed both general considerations, aligned with the "five W's" paradigm, and more specific manifestations, particularly those arising in the framework of fuzzy flexible querying.

## References

1. Abowd, G.D., Mynatt, E.D.: Charting past, present, and future research in ubiquitous computing. ACM Trans. Comput.-Hum. Interact. **7**(1), 29–58 (2000)
2. Bordogna, G., Ghisalberti, G., Psaila, G.: Geographic information retrieval: modeling uncertainty of user's context. Fuzzy Sets Syst. **196**, 105–124 (2012)
3. Kacprzyk, J., Zadrozny, S., Tré, G.D.: Fuzziness in database management systems: half a century of developments and future prospects. Fuzzy Sets Syst. **281**, 300–307 (2015)
4. Zadrożny, S., Kacprzyk, J., Dziedzic, M., De Tré, G.: Contextual bipolar queries. In: Jamshidi, M., Kreinovich, V., Kacprzyk, J. (eds.) Advance Trends in Soft Computing. SFSC, vol. 312, pp. 421–428. Springer, Cham (2014). https://doi.org/10.1007/978-3-319-03674-8_40

# Graded Logic Criteria and Their Applications

Jozo Dujmović$^{(\boxtimes)}$ ⓘ

Department of Computer Science, San Francisco State University, 1600 Holloway Avenue,
San Francisco, CA 94132, USA
jozo@sfsu.edu

**Abstract.** Graded logic is a human-centric continuum-valued propositional logic of natural human commonsense logical reasoning and decision making. It is a seamless generalization of the classical bivalent Boolean logic, fuzzy logic propositional calculus, and non-classical continuum-valued logics. This paper is an extended abstract which summarizes basic properties of Graded Logic and its applications in decision-support systems.

**Keywords:** Graded Logic · Decision Making · Evaluation · Andness · Orness · GCD

## 1 Distinctive Properties of Graded Logic

Fundamental properties of human logical reasoning and commonsense decision making are observable, measurable, modelable, and explainable [1, 2]. The goal of Graded Logic (GL) is to develop mathematical models of natural human commonsense reasoning with graded percepts. Distinctive properties of GL are the strict use of continuum-valued percepts of truth, simultaneity, substitutability, and importance. GL is not an axiomatic deductive theory. It is human-centric and supports the following properties.

*Graded Percepts.* Human commonsense logical reasoning involves processing graded percepts—that is, percepts ($P$) that take on values along a continuum ranging from a minimum value $m$ to the maximum value $M$. The range of percepts, $m \leq P \leq M$ is normalized, yielding normalized graded percepts $x = \frac{P-m}{M-m} \in [0,1]$. In GL, all normalized graded percepts can be interpreted as degrees of truth of specific statements, or as degrees of membership in specific fuzzy sets. All graded percepts have semantic identity: the role, meaning, and importance for specific stakeholder/decision-maker.

*Graded, Continuum-Valued Truth.* In the commonsense human reasoning we use percepts of truth that are graded in the range from the complete falsity (coded 0) to the complete truth (coded 1). An example is the truth of statement "the window is open."

*Andness/Orness-Directedness.* Conjunction is a model of the simultaneity of requirements, and disjunction is a model of the substitutability or requirements. In human reasoning both the simultaneity and the substitutability have adjustable intensity. The degree of conjunction is called andness ($\alpha$) and the degree of disjunction is called orness

G. De Tré et al. (Eds.): FQAS 2025, LNAI 16119, pp. 7–11, 2026.
https://doi.org/10.1007/978-3-032-05607-8_2

($\omega$). These indicators are defined so that the pure conjunction $min(x_1, \ldots, x_n)$ is characterized by $\alpha = 1, \omega = 0$, and the pure disjunction $max(x_1, \ldots, x_n)$ is characterized by $\alpha = 0, \omega = 1$. Generally, $\alpha + \omega = 1$. Since the graded conjunction can be stronger than the minimum function (we call such functions hyperconjunction) and the graded disjunction can be stronger than the maximum function (called hyperdisjunction), the range of andness and orness is wider than $I = [0,1]$. Drastic (or ultimate) conjunction is a function of two or more graded logic variables that is true iff all inputs are completely true (1). Obviously, there is no stronger conjunctive request. Analytically, the drastic conjunction can be modeled as a floor of the product of variables: $CC(x_1, \ldots, x_n) = \lfloor x_1 x_2 \ldots x_n \rfloor$. Drastic (or ultimate) disjunction is a function of two or more graded logic variables that is false iff all inputs are completely false (0): the smallest positive truth of any input is sufficient to fully satisfy the drastic disjunction. Obviously, there is no stronger disjunctive request. The drastic conjunction is a dual of drastic conjunction: $DD(x_1, \ldots, x_n) = 1 - \lfloor (1 - x_1)(1 - x_2) \ldots (1 - x_n) \rfloor$. To adjust desired logic properties of logic aggregators, the andness (or orness) must be an explicitly visible and easily adjustable input parameter of graded logic aggregators $L(x_1, \ldots, x_n; \alpha) : I^n \to I$. This desirable property is called andness-directedness [3]. Such a function has both conjunctive and disjunctive properties and it is called the Graded Conjunction/Disjunction (GCD). GCD is the fundamental function of GL.

*Monotonicity Conditions.* In all systems that have two or more components, improving a component increases the overall suitability of the system. Thus, the nondecreasing monotonicity is a necessary property of all aggregators, including the graded logic aggregators. For andness and orness outside the [0,1] range the nondecreasing monotonicity must also be supported, and that is the reason why the hyperconjunction and the hyperdisjunction cannot be idempotent. Monotonicity also holds for andness and orness: logic aggregators must satisfy the nonincreasing monotonicity in andness, and the nondecreasing monotonicity in orness. Consequently, GL aggregators must support the andness-directed continuous transition from $CC$ to $DD$.

*Importance-Weighting of Graded Logic Variables.* Any propositional calculus without weights is based on assumption that all statements have equal importance. However, in human commonsense reasoning and decision making, statements that have a degree of truth also have a degree of importance. In GL, we use propositional calculus with statements that have both the degree of truth and the degree of importance that reflect the goals and requirements of a specific stakeholder. Such logic aggregators are denoted $L(X; W, \alpha), X = (x_1, \ldots, x_n), W = (w_1, \ldots, w_n)$, and $W$ denotes degrees of importance.

*Duality.* The reason why all models of simultaneity and substitutability must be dual is simple: dual expressions are two equivalent ways to specify the same logic relationship. Let $AND(x_1, \ldots, x_n), n > 1$ be a model of simultaneity of two or more logic variables, and let $OR(x_1, \ldots, x_n)$ be a dual model of substitutability. So, it is equivalent to claim that $x_1, \ldots, x_n$ must be simultaneously sufficiently satisfied (sufficiently true), or to claim that it is unacceptable that any of them is insufficiently satisfied. In other words, $AND(x_1, \ldots, x_n) = 1 - OR(1 - x_1, \ldots, 1 - x_n)$. Likewise, if at least one of the arguments must be sufficiently satisfied, then it is unacceptable that all of them are simultaneously insufficiently satisfied:$OR(x_1, \ldots, x_n) = 1 - AND(1 - x_1, \ldots, 1 - x_n)$. If the analytic models of simultaneity and substitutability are not naturally dual, then they can be dualized: either we select a model of simultaneity and define substitutability as its dual, or we select a model of substitutability and define simultaneity as its dual. Generally, $L(X; W, \alpha) = 1 - L(1 - X; W, 1 - \alpha)$. Of course, if the models of $AND$ and $OR$ operators are not dual, then various formulas of propositional calculus become inconsistent.

*Idempotence-Selectability.* The need for idempotency is most visible in schools. If a student has the same grade in all courses, it is fully justified that the overall (average) grade has the same value. In all specific applications it is necessary to investigate whether idempotency is necessary or unacceptable. Examples of unacceptable idempotency (hyperconjunction or hyperdisjunction) are all cases where components have interpretation of independent random events and the logic aggregator must reflect the favorable simultaneous occurrence of events, what is modeled as a product of the degrees of truth which express the likelihood/probability of individual events. In such cases idempotency must not be supported. Thus, idempotency must be a selectable property.

*Annihilator-Selectability.* In human reasoning, logic variables of conjunctive logic aggregators are frequently required to be all positive (mandatory requirements). In such cases $\forall i \in \{1, \ldots, n\}, x_i = 0 \Rightarrow L(X; W, \alpha) = 0$. So, 0 is the annihilator for the conjunctive logic aggregator $L(X; W, \alpha), \alpha \geq \alpha_\theta$, where $\alpha_\theta$ denotes the threshold andness. Logic aggregators that support annihilators are called hard. For lower values of andness, $\alpha < \alpha_\theta$, the desired condition is $\forall i \in \{1, \ldots, n\}, x_i > 0 \Rightarrow L(X; W, \alpha) > 0$, i.e., the annihilator 0 must not be supported and a single positive input causes positive output regardless that all other inputs can be 0. In this case, all inputs are optional, and the aggregators are referred to as soft. Likewise, in the case of disjunctive logic aggregators, the annihilator is 1: $\forall i \in \{1, \ldots, n\}, x_i = 1 \Rightarrow L(X; W, \alpha) = 1, \alpha \leq 1 - \alpha_\theta$. In other words, a single fully satisfied (fully true) input is sufficient to fully satisfy criteria that are based on hard graded disjunction. Soft graded disjunction is similar to soft graded conjunction. Since the support for annihilators is either necessary or unacceptable, this important property must be selectable.

The presented properties are observable and measurable in human logical reasoning and decision making. Therefore, they are necessary in most decision models. However, graded logic aggregators are also applicable in areas that do not include humans and properties of their reasoning. In such cases these properties are not necessary and can be expanded or substituted by other desirable properties.

## 2  Models of Graded Logic Aggregators and Their Applications

Logic aggregator of $n$ variables is geometrically interpreted as a surface inside the unit hypercube $[0,1]^{n+1}$. The andness of logic aggregator is most conveniently defined assuming equal weights and using the volume $V$ under the aggregator surface inside $[0,1]^{n+1}$, as follows: $\alpha = [n - (n + 1)V]/(n - 1)$. Since $0 \leq V \leq 1$, it follows that the full range of andness is $-\frac{1}{n-1} \leq \alpha \leq \frac{n}{n-1}$. This range has six important subranges:

- $-\frac{1}{n-1} \leq \alpha < 0$ : Hard hyperdisjunction (it can be modeled using t-conorms)
- $0 \leq \alpha \leq 1 - \alpha_\theta$ : Hard graded disjunction (it can be modeled as a mean)
- $1 - \alpha_\theta < \alpha < \frac{1}{2}$ : Soft graded disjunction (it can be modeled as a mean)
- $\alpha = \frac{1}{2}$ : Logic neutrality modeled as the (weighted) arithmetic mean
- $1/2 < \alpha < \alpha_\theta$ : Soft graded conjunction (it can be modeled as a mean)
- $\alpha_\theta \leq \alpha \leq 1$ : Hard graded conjunction (it can be modeled as a mean)
- $1 < \alpha \leq \frac{n}{n-1}$ : Hard hyperconjunction (it can be modeled using t-norms)

Most frequently, in these ranges we use the threshold andness $\alpha_\theta = 0.75$. That offers equal expressive opportunities to soft and hard graded conjunction/disjunction. Some problems fit only in one or two of the above subranges. Generally, we use interpolation to cover the whole range from drastic conjunction to drastic disjunction [2]. If we have logic aggregators $L_1(X; W, \alpha_1)$ and $L_2(X; W, \alpha_2)$, $\alpha_1 < \alpha_2$ then we can linearly interpolate between them the aggregator $L(X; W, \alpha)$ as follows:

$$L(X; W, \alpha) = \frac{\alpha_2 - \alpha}{\alpha_2 - \alpha_1} L_1(X; W, \alpha_1) + \frac{\alpha - \alpha_1}{\alpha_2 - \alpha_1} L_2(X; W, \alpha_2), \alpha_1 \leq \alpha \leq \alpha_2.$$

Using a sequence of "anchor aggregators" [1] in border points between subranges of andness, we can realize a continuous andness-directed transition from drastic conjunction to drastic disjunction and then use such interpolative aggregators and the standard negation $not(x) = 1 - x$ to create all formulas of the graded propositional calculus.

Let $(a_1, \ldots, a_n)$, $a_i \in \mathbb{R}$, $i = 1, \ldots, n$ denote an array of n suitability attributes of an evaluated object. Then, we can create attribute criteria $g_i : \mathbb{R} \rightarrow [0,1]$, $i = 1, \ldots, n$, so that $g_i(a_i)$ denotes the degree of truth of statement claiming that $a_i$ fully satisfies the requirements of decision maker. Then, we can develop the graded logic aggregation structure $G : [0,1]^n \rightarrow [0,1]$ (a graded propositional calculus formula) to create the overall suitability evaluation criterion $S = G(g_1(a_1), \ldots, g_n(a_n))$. $S$ is the degree of truth of the statement that claims that the evaluated object fully satisfies all stakeholder's requirements. In this way, the comparison of $N > 1$ objects is reduced to $N$ evaluations of a single object. That is in a nutshell the concept of the Logic Scoring of Preference (LSP) method for evaluation, optimization, comparison and selection of complex objects [2]. The ranking of competitors can be based on decreasing values of the overall suitability. If the competitive objects have costs $C_1, \ldots, C_N$, then the ranking of competitors is based on the value score defined as $V_i = \left( \frac{S_i}{\max(S_1, \ldots, S_N)} \right)^w \left( \frac{\min(C_1, \ldots, C_N)}{C_i} \right)^{1-w} \in [0,1]$, $i = 1, \ldots, N$. Here $w \in [0,1]$ denotes the relative importance of high suitability and $1 - w$ denotes the relative importance of low cost. The offered weighted geometric mean is a hard conjunctive aggregator with andness $\alpha = 2/3$ which can be substituted by other similar models of simultaneity that have other desirable values of andness.

LSP decision criteria and GL are used in a variety of complex professional decision problems: selection of computer equipment and software, ecology, geography, urban development, cognitive psychology, medical decision making, and other areas [1, 2].

# References

1. Dujmović, J.: Graded Logic. Springer, Heidelberg (2025)

2. Dujmović, J.: Soft Computing Evaluation Logic. Wiley and IEEE Press, Hoboken (2018)
3. Larsen H.L.: Efficient Andness-directed Importance Weighted Averaging Operators. Int. J. Uncertainty, Fuzziness Knowl. Based Syst. **12**(Suppl.), 67–82 (2003)

# GenAI, LLM/MLLM, RAG, and Their Impacts on Hallucination, Reliability and Trustworthiness

Hassane Essafi[✉]

CEA List Institute, Paris-Saclay, Centre d'intégration Nano-INNOV,
2 Boulevard Thomas Gobert, 91120 Palaiseau, France
Hassane.essafi@cea.fr

**Abstract.** This talk aims to examine LLMs, GenAI, and RAG, with a focus on the key challenges of mitigating hallucinations to ensure the trustworthiness and factual accuracy of their outputs. Hallucination is a well-known limitation of large language models (LLMs), reflecting their tendency to produce responses that are inaccurate, irrelevant, or inconsistent with user expectations. This undermines user confidence and makes such models less-suited for critical domains where precision and verifiability are paramount. Moreover, hallucination remains a major obstacle to achieving the levels of reliability and trustworthiness that are foundational to frameworks like the EU AI Act [1, 2], which seeks to ensure that AI systems operate safely and uphold fundamental rights. To address these issues and their broader negative impacts, both academia and industry have proposed a range of detection and mitigation strategies.

The presentation will be divided into three main parts:

- We first start by an overview of LLMs and GenAI, exploring transformer architectures (the backbone of LLMs), their key capabilities (attention mechanism, scaling laws…) and inherent limitations.
- The second section will focus on the phenomenon of hallucination, issues of trustworthiness, and the various approaches proposed to enhance response accuracy, including Retrieval-Augmented Generation (RAG), which combines the strengths of LLMs with external search engines or knowledge bases to produce enriched, factual outputs.
- We end by conducting a detailed analysis of the underlying causes of hallucinations and trustworthiness gaps, followed by a comprehensive review of mitigation methods such as fine-tuning, advanced prompting techniques (Chain-of-Thought (CoT) …), and agentic AI frameworks.

**Keywords:** LLM · GenAI · Hallucination · fine-tuning · prompting · Chain-of-Thought (CoT) · Agentic AI

## 1 Introduction

Since the introduction of the transformer by Google team in 2017 [3], deep learning, data-driven AI technologies have continued to evolve and expand at a rapid pace. The transformer architecture and its attention mechanism marked a crucial milestone in the

G. De Tré et al. (Eds.): FQAS 2025, LNAI 16119, pp. 12–15, 2026.
https://doi.org/10.1007/978-3-032-05607-8_3

emergence of Large Language Models (LLMs) and Generative Artificial Intelligence (GenAI), driving significant breakthroughs in large variety of AI field. By leveraging the computational power of multi-GPU High-Performance Computing (HPC) infrastructures, organizations like Google and OpenAI have used the transformer as the foundation to develop powerful pre-trained LLMs. These models that contain billions of parameters, encapsulate the fundamental structure and knowledge of language deivated from vast datasets during training phase. The extracted knowledge enables LLMs to generate human-like text and perform a wide range of natural language tasks. Furthermore, the rise of fine-tuning and transfer learning techniques such as zero-shot and few-shot learning [4] boosted the creation of specialized AI models with less effort, pushing the LLM paradigm far beyond its initial focus which was the NLP (Natural Language Processing) tasks. Today, these models can process and understand a variety of data inputs [5, 6] (images, video, audio, time series) and power applications across finance [7], healthcare [8, 9], manufacturing [10], cybersecurity [11], robotics [12]…).

These advanced models and tools, Known as MLLMs (Multimodal Large Language Models) [13] or LMFMs (Large Multimodal Foundation Models) [14], are also facing the issue of hallucinations.

In this talk, we will therefore not limit our exploration to hallucinations in the context of text-only LLMs, but will also consider the phenomenon as it arises in multimodal models.

## 2  Generative AI

Generative AI refers to a class of AI systems capable of producing novel content, such as text, images, or videos, often based on input data [15].

### 2.1  Generative AI and RAG

To alleviate the limitations of LLMs, Retrieval-Augmented Generation (RAG) [16, 17] has been introduced as a hybrid model that combines the capabilities of information retrieval systems with generative capabilities of LLMs. The RAG architecture typically works by retrieving relevant data/documents from external data and knowledge bases to enriching the prompting and conditioning the model's output based on this retrieved information. This allows the model to incorporate more reliable and up-to-date factual knowledge, enhancing the accuracy of the generated content.

By integrating external retrieval mechanisms, RAG systems reduce the chances of hallucination. Instead of generating content purely based on pre-existing patterns in the training data, the system augments its responses with real-world knowledge, thereby improving reliability.

## 3  Challenges: Reliability, Trustworthiness, and Hallucination

### 3.1  Causes of Hallucinations

Despite the adoption of hybrid models, there are still persistent challenges in ensuring that models do not hallucinate and their generated content is reliable and trustworthy; A range of factors can lead to the hallucination. It may be stem from data issues such as outdated, biased, erroneous, or inaccurate training data [18]. Hallucinations can also be triggered by the query itself [19]; for example, when prompts are ambiguous, overly broad, or implicitly encourage fabrication. Questions that are vague or contain heterogeneous sub-questions without clear context push the model to guess or invent details, increasing the risk of producing inaccurate or entirely false content.

### 3.2 Mitigation Strategies of Hallucinations [20]

Several strategies are being developed and implemented to mitigate the phenomenon of hallucination. These include training LLMs and GenAI models on diverse, balanced, high-quality datasets to reduce bias and enhance reliability; incorporating real-time fact-checking systems or integrating external databases to verify generated outputs; and establishing user feedback loops using for instance RLHF (Reinforcement Learning from Human Feedback) [21], thereby refining future responses and boosting trust. Additionally, improving explainability and transparency by showing for example how a model generates its responses or revealing retrieved sources in a RAG pipeline which contribute to increase user confidence. Continual learning of LLM [22] with updated knowledge may contribute to improve the accuracy and reduce hallucinations. Finally, orchestrating multiple specialized AI agents (agentic AI) reasoning contributes to mitigate the hallucination phenomenon [23]. All those approaches will be detail during the presentation.

## 4 Conclusion

In this talk we will delve into the world of LLMs, a dynamic and captivating topic. It attracts widespread interest, engaging not only professionals but all category of people. Our aim is to highlight the key elements leading to the hallucination and impacting the reliability and trustworthiness of LLM-based AI. We will also discuss the mitigation solutions.

## References

1. Caruana, M.M., Borg, R.M.: Regulating Artificial Intelligence in the European Union. The EU Internal Market in the Next Decade–Quo Vadis?, p. 108 (2025)
2. NIZZA. Umberto. What do AIs think About the AI Act? An experimental analysis of the EU approach on artificial intelligence. Eur. Bus. Law Rev. **36**(2) (2026)
3. Vaswani, A.: Attention is all you need. Adv. Neural Inf. Process. Syst. (2017)
4. Jeoung, J., Jung, S., Hong, T.: Zero-shot framework for construction equipment task monitoring. Comput. Aided Civil Infrastruct. Eng. (2025)
5. Sapkota, R., Raza, S., Shoman, M., et al.: Multimodal large language models for image, text, and speech data augmentation: A survey. arXiv preprint arXiv:2501.18648 (2025)
6. Chen, Z., Xu, L., Zheng, H., et al.: Evolution and prospects of foundation models: from large language models to large multimodal models. Comput. Mater. Continua **80**(2), 1753–1808 (2024)
7. Yanglet, X.-Y.L., Cao, Y., Deng, L.: Multimodal financial foundation models (MFFMs): Progress, prospects, and challenges. arXiv preprint arXiv:2506.01973 (2025)

8. Hankun, S.U., Sun, Y., Ruiting, L.I., et al.: Large language models in medical diagnostics: scoping review with bibliometric analysis. J. Med. Internet Res. **27**, e72062 (2025)
9. Bilal, M., Raza, M., Altherwy, Y., et al.: Foundation models in computational pathology: A review of challenges, opportunities, and impact. arXiv preprint arXiv:2502.08333 (2025)
10. Zhang, H., Semujju, S.D., Wang, Z., et al.: Large scale foundation models for intelligent manufacturing applications: a survey. J. Intell. Manuf. 1–52 (2025)
11. Aung, Y.L., Christian, I., Dong, Y., et al.: Generative AI for Internet of Things security: Challenges and opportunities. arXiv preprint arXiv:2502.08886 (2025)
12. Firoozi, R., Tucker, J., Tian, S., et al.: Foundation models in robotics: Applications, challenges, and the future. Int. J. Robot. Res. **44**(5), 701–739 (2025)
13. Yin, S., Fu, C., Zhao, S., et al.: A survey on multimodal large language models. arXiv preprint arXiv:2306.13549 (2023)
14. Küchemann, S., Avila, K.E., Dinc, Y., et al.: Are large multimodal foundation models all we need? On opportunities and challenges of these models in education. EdArXiv (2024)
15. Feuerriegel, S., Hartmann, J., Janiesch, C., et al.: Generative AI. Bus. Inf. Syst. Eng. **66**(1), 111–126 (2024)
16. Xu, A., Yu, T., Du, M., et al.: Generative AI and retrieval-augmented generation (RAG) systems for enterprise. In: Proceedings of the 33rd ACM International Conference on Information and Knowledge Management, pp. 5599–5602 (2024)
17. Karen Ka Yan, N.G., Matsuba, I., Zhang, P.C.: RAG in health care: a novel framework for improving communication and decision-making by addressing LLM limitations. NEJM AI, **2**(1), AIra2400380 (2025)
18. Sato, M.: Triggering Hallucinations in LLMs: A Quantitative Study of Prompt-Induced Hallucination in Large Language Models. arXiv preprint arXiv:2505.00557 (2025)
19. Gautam, A.R.: Impact of high data quality on LLM hallucinations. Int. J. Comput. Appl. **975**, 8887
20. Luo, J., Tianyu, L.I., Di, W.U., et al.: Hallucination detection and hallucination mitigation: An investigation. arXiv preprint arXiv:2401.08358 (2024)
21. Ouyang, L., Wu, J., Xu, J., Almeida, D., Wainwright, C.L., Mishkin, P., et al.: Training language models to follow instructions with human feedback. arXiv (Cornell University) (2022)
22. Yang, Y., Zhou, J., Ding, X., et al.: Recent advances of foundation language models-based continual learning: a survey. ACM Comput. Surv. **57**(5), 1–38 (2025)
23. Gosmar, D., Dahl, D.A.: Hallucination mitigation using agentic AI natural language-based frameworks. arXiv preprint arXiv:2501.13946 (2025)

# Flexible Query Answering Systems

# A Novel Approach to Context-Aware and Responsible Short Text Clustering

Maxime Deforche[1]([⊠])[ID], Ilse De Vos[2][ID], and Guy De Tré[1][ID]

[1] Ghent University, Department of Telecommunications and Information Processing,
St.-Pietersnieuwstraat 41, 9000 Ghent, Belgium
{Maxime.Deforche,Guy.DeTre}@UGent.be
[2] Flanders AI Academy (VAIA), Kasteelpark Arenberg 10/2440,
3001 Leuven, Belgium
ilse.devos@kuleuven.be

**Abstract.** Context-aware clustering of texts, particularly short texts, is a challenging task. Although metadata can provide valuable contextual cues to enhance clustering quality, such information is often incomplete or inconsistently available in real-world datasets. In this paper, we propose a novel clustering strategy that integrates both textual and metadata-based similarities, even when metadata is partially missing. Our method employs the Ordered Weighted Averaging (OWA) aggregator to fuse multiple similarity scores into a single aggregated value for each pair of texts. To handle missing metadata, we adapt the OWA mechanism by renormalising weights based only on available information, thereby avoiding potentially unreliable imputation or complete exclusion of certain metadata. We further introduce a confidence score that quantifies the reliability of each aggregated similarity, reflecting the proportion of missing metadata. Clustering is then performed using the K-Medoids algorithm on the resulting dissimilarity matrix. We demonstrate this approach on a real-world dataset of short Byzantine poems, where orthographic similarity is complemented with sparse metadata. The final clusters, stored in a graph database along with their confidence scores, enable meaningful interpretation and visualisation of the results, including the identification of uncertain cluster assignments due to missing contextual information.

**Keywords:** context-aware clustering · text clustering · missing data aggregation · OWA method · cluster confidence

## 1 Introduction

Clustering is a well-studied topic in information retrieval as well as data mining, and has gained increasing importance due to the rapid growth of data, and textual data in particular. Given the inherently unstructured nature of text, clustering techniques are valuable tools for organising and extracting insights from such data [1]. Typically, text clustering relies on similarity or distance

G. De Tré et al. (Eds.): FQAS 2025, LNAI 16119, pp. 19–30, 2026.
https://doi.org/10.1007/978-3-032-05607-8_4

measures, such as cosine similarity, Jaccard similarity, or Levenshtein distance, to identify groups of related texts in an unsupervised manner [14]. The choice of this underlying measure is crucial, as it significantly impacts both the quality and interpretability of the clustering outcome [10]. To further improve clustering quality, auxiliary metadata can be incorporated alongside textual measures, particularly when context is important or when textual information is limited or ambiguous.

Clustering short texts, such as social media posts, user comments, poems, or song lyrics, poses unique challenges due to their limited length [2]. In such cases, providing new context by incorporating metadata into the clustering process can reveal new insights. However, in many real-world scenarios, this contextual information is only partially available or entirely missing for part of the data. Traditional clustering approaches are typically designed for complete datasets and are not well-suited to handle cases where metadata are missing. As a result, some contextual information is often either entirely ignored, even when available for some texts, or imputed with substituted values to construct a fully populated dataset [9]. Both strategies have notable limitations: ignoring metadata results in the loss of potentially valuable information, while imputation introduces substituted values that may be unreliable and heavily dependent on the assumptions underlying the imputation method.

In this paper, we propose a novel strategy for clustering short texts that leverages both their textual content, assumed to be always available, and accompanying metadata, even when some of the metadata are missing. Central to our approach is an Ordered Weighted Averaging (OWA)-based fusion mechanism that combines pairwise textual similarity scores with similarity scores between metadata attributes into an aggregated score for each pair of texts. To account for missing metadata, we adapt the OWA operation by excluding weights corresponding to unknown information and renormalising the remaining weights. This adjustment ensures that the aggregated similarity remains meaningful regardless of missing values. Our approach does not make any assumptions about the missing data and simply ignores it, while still incorporating metadata into the clustering process whenever it is available. To reflect the impact of missing information, we introduce a confidence score that quantifies the reliability of each aggregated similarity value, based on the total weight of missing metadata in the original OWA weight vector. Clustering is then performed using the K-Medoids algorithm on a dissimilarity matrix derived from the aggregated similarity matrix for the entire dataset. The resulting confidence scores between each text and its cluster centre can be visualised to provide insight into the trustworthiness of cluster assignments and to highlight potential misassignments due to missing contextual information.

The relevance of the proposed clustering strategy is demonstrated through a practical application involving the clustering of Byzantine poems. Clustering is performed based on orthographic similarity, complemented by similarities between metadata values that are not consistently available for every poem. Both the texts and the resulting clusters are stored in a graph database, enabling efficient analysis and intuitive visualisation of the clusters and their associated confidence scores. This setup provides novel and valuable insights into (historical) connections and interrelations between poems.

The remainder of this paper is structured as follows. First, Sect. 2 discusses related work. Section 3 introduces the necessary preliminaries on K-medoids clustering and the OWA operator. The proposed clustering strategy is presented in Sect. 4, followed by a practical application in Sect. 5. Finally, Sect. 6 formulates conclusions and outlines directions for future research.

## 2   Related Work

The problem of clustering short texts has been widely studied, particularly through the use of natural language processing (NLP) techniques to compute similarity between textual instances. A core challenge with short texts is their limited length, which results in reduced context and insufficient discriminative features. Traditional text representation methods, such as TF-IDF and Bag-of-Words, often lead to high-dimensional and sparse vectors, making them less effective for clustering short texts [1]. To overcome these limitations, more recent approaches rely on semantic-rich representations, including topic modelling [3], word embeddings [12], and deep learning-based methods tailored to clustering [15]. While these methods significantly improve clustering performance, they do not take contextual information into account, which could further improve the quality and interpretability of clusters. In contrast, this work proposes leveraging such contextual information to improve clustering outcomes, even when certain metadata are missing.

Other research has focused on clustering with incomplete data, particularly when metadata are missing for a subset of instances. Since traditional clustering approaches are designed for fully available information, two strategies are typically employed to address this issue: imputation, where missing values are estimated, and marginalisation, where metadata are excluded entirely in cases of missing instances [9]. While imputation produces a complete dataset, it relies on assumptions that may not hold in practice and can introduce significant bias. Marginalisation avoids the risk of inaccurate assumptions, but at the cost of excluding valuable contextual information. The method proposed in this paper avoids the disadvantages of both strategies. Rather than imputing missing metadata or excluding it entirely, we adapt the aggregation process to dynamically account for the available information. Additionally, confidence scores, derived from the availability of metadata, are introduced to inform stakeholders of the veracity of the clustering outcomes. Conceptually, this method is somewhat similar to how missing data is handled in LSP aggregation [8], where the fusion mechanism is adapted based on available criteria.

## 3   Preliminaries

Before presenting the proposed clustering strategy, we briefly introduce the key components on which it is based. In particular, we discuss the K-Medoids algorithm, which forms the basis of our clustering approach, and the Ordered Weighted Averaging (OWA) aggregation technique, which is used to combine multiple similarity scores into a single value.

## 3.1   K-Medoids Clustering

K-Medoids is a partition-based clustering algorithm that divides a dataset into a predefined number of clusters $k$, based on a dissimilarity matrix. Unlike the K-Means algorithm, which minimizes the sum of squared Euclidean distances in a vector space and represents clusters using centroids that may not correspond to actual data points, K-Medoids selects actual data elements as cluster centres, referred to as medoids.

Consider a set of objects $X = \{x_1, x_2, \ldots, x_n\}$, where $n$ is the total number of elements, and let $D \in [0,1]^{n \times n}$ be a dissimilarity matrix such that $d_{i,j}$ denotes the dissimilarity between $x_i$ and $x_j$. The K-Medoids algorithm forms $k$ clusters by selecting $k$ representative members of $X$ as cluster centres $M = \{m_1, m_2, \ldots, m_k\}$, where $m_i \in X$ corresponds to the medoid of the $i$-th cluster. Each object that is not selected as a cluster centre is assigned to the cluster with the closest medoid, such that the total dissimilarity between each data point and its assigned cluster's medoid is minimized. Formally, the algorithm tries to minimize the cost function shown in Eq. (1), where $m_j$ represents the $j$-th cluster's medoid and $C_j \subseteq X$ represents the cluster with centre $m_j$.

$$C = \sum_{i=1}^{n} \sum_{j=1, x_i \in C_j}^{k} d_{i,m_j} \tag{1}$$

A commonly used implementation of K-Medoids is the Partitioning Around Medoids (PAM) algorithm [11], which begins by selecting an initial set of $k$ medoids (either at random or using a heuristic), and iteratively refines the cluster assignment by swapping medoids with non-medoids in a manner that decreases the total cost. This process is repeated until no further improvement is possible.

## 3.2   Ordered Weighted Averaging (OWA)

The OWA is an aggregation operator that maps a set $A = \{a_1, a_2, \ldots, a_n\} \in [0,1]^n$ to a value in the unit interval $[0,1]$, based on a predefined weight vector $\mathbf{w} = (w_1, w_2, \ldots, w_n) \in [0,1]^n$. The weight vector must satisfy the condition $\sum_{i=1}^{n} w_i = 1$. The aggregated result is calculated as shown in Eq. (2), where $\rho : \{1, 2, \ldots, n\} \rightarrow \{1, 2, \ldots, n\}$ is a permutation that orders the elements of $A$ in a decreasing order, such that $a_{\rho(1)} \geq a_{\rho(2)} \geq \ldots \geq a_{\rho(n)}$ [16].

$$\text{OWA}(A, \mathbf{w}) = \sum_{i=1}^{n} a_{\rho(i)} \cdot w_i \tag{2}$$

A key characteristic of the OWA operator is its reliance on the decreasing order of the input values, rather than their position or source. This makes the OWA well-suited for aggregating criteria, such as similarity measures, in a source-independent and flexible manner.

## 4  Proposed Method

This section outlines our proposed method for clustering short texts by integrating both textual and contextual data, while explicitly addressing data veracity issues arising from missing metadata. The core idea is to compute an aggregated similarity score between texts using the OWA operator, with a tailored mechanism to account for potentially missing information. In addition, a confidence score is introduced to quantify the reliability of each aggregated similarity, based on the proportion of available metadata. Finally, clustering is performed on the resulting dissimilarity matrix using the K-Medoids algorithm.

### 4.1  OWA-Based Fusion of Similarity Scores

Consider two texts, $t_1$ and $t_2$, each consisting of their textual content and $m$ metadata attributes. Each metadata attribute value may either be available or missing. From these two texts, we derive a set of similarities $S$, which includes the textual similarity and a similarity score for the values in $t_1$ and $t_2$ of each of the $m$ metadata attributes. If a particular piece of metadata is missing in either $t_1, t_2$ or both, the corresponding similarity score is undefined and denoted by the symbol $\perp$, such that $\forall s \in S, s \in [0,1] \cup \{\perp\}$. Accompanying the similarity set $S$ is an overall weight vector $\mathbf{w} = (w_1, w_2, \ldots, w_{m+1})$, as described in Sect. 3.2.

Since the OWA operator cannot handle missing values, we propose a method to restrict both the similarity set $S$ and the weight vector $\mathbf{w}$ to only include available information. The restricted similarity set $\tilde{S}$ is defined in Eq. (3), where all undefined similarities are excluded. Since we assume that textual information is always available, $\tilde{S}$ always consist of at least one similarity score.

$$\tilde{S} = \{s \in S \mid s_i \neq \perp\} \tag{3}$$

To maintain the normalisation property of the OWA operator, the corresponding restricted weight vector $\tilde{\mathbf{w}}$ is defined in Eq. (4).

$$\tilde{\mathbf{w}} = (\tilde{w}_1, \tilde{w}_2, \ldots, \tilde{w}_{|\tilde{S}|}), \text{ where } \tilde{w}_i = \frac{w_i}{z}, \text{ and } z = \sum_{i=1}^{|\tilde{S}|} w_i \tag{4}$$

The aggregated similarity $s$ between $t_1$ and $t_2$ is then obtained by applying the OWA operator to the restricted set $\tilde{S}$ and weight vector $\tilde{\mathbf{w}}$: $s = \text{OWA}(\tilde{S}, \tilde{\mathbf{w}})$. Notably, in cases where no similarity values are missing, the result of the OWA over the restricted and original inputs is identical: $\text{OWA}(\tilde{S}, \tilde{\mathbf{w}}) = \text{OWA}(S, \mathbf{w})$. This fusion mechanism ensures that all available information is utilised, without the need for imputing missing values or discarding partial metadata.

*Example 1.* Consider two sets of similarity scores $S_1 = \{0.9, 0.7, 0.6, 0.8\}$ and $S_2 = \{0.6, 1.0, \perp, 0.7\}$, along with a weight vector $\mathbf{w} = (0.3, 0.2, 0.3, 0.2)$. For $S_1$, no similarities are missing, so the restricted set is $\tilde{S}_1 = S_1$ and the restricted weight vector is $\tilde{\mathbf{w}}_1 = \mathbf{w}$. For $S_2$, one similarity is missing, resulting in a restricted set $\tilde{S}_2 = \{0.6, 1.0, 0.7\}$. The corresponding weights $(0.3, 0.2, 0.3)$ are renormalized to yield $\tilde{\mathbf{w}}_2 = (0.375, 0.25, 0.375)$. Applying the OWA operator to the sorted similarity scores and their respective weights results in the fused similarities $s_1 = \text{OWA}(\tilde{S}_1, \tilde{\mathbf{w}}_1) = 0.76$ and $s_2 = \text{OWA}(\tilde{S}_2, \tilde{\mathbf{w}}_2) = 0.775$.

## 4.2   Confidence Score Calculation

By calculating the aggregated similarity score through the restriction of the similarity set to only known values and the renormalisation of the weight vector, we obtain a meaningful similarity score even in the presence of missing metadata. However, this process inevitably discards information about the extent of missing data, which is crucial for assessing the trustworthiness of the computed similarity score. To address this, we introduce an additional confidence score $c \in [0, 1]$, which quantifies the proportion of information that was not available during aggregation. Together, the fused similarity score $s$ and the confidence score $c$ provide a more complete picture: $s$ reflects the similarity based on the available information, $c$ captures how confident we can be that $s$ is representative. The pair $(s, c)$ encapsulates both the degree of similarity (or suitability) and the associated reliability (or confidence), and integrates seamlessly with gradual logic reasoning frameworks such as L-grades [4]. Note that a confidence score can incorporate a variety of veracity-related concepts, but in this paper, we restrict this method to the extent of missing information.

Let $S$ and $\mathbf{w}$ respectively denote the original set of similarities between two texts and the original weight vector, both consisting $m+1$ elements. Let $\tilde{S}$ and $\tilde{\mathbf{w}}$ be the restricted set and its accompanying weight vector. We define the residual weight vector $\tilde{\mathbf{v}}$, as shown in Eq. (5), which contains the weights associated with the missing similarity values. Note that $\tilde{\mathbf{v}}$ is empty when $\tilde{S} = S$.

$$\tilde{\mathbf{v}} = (v_1, v_2, \ldots, v_{|\tilde{\mathbf{v}}|}) = (w_{|\tilde{S}|+1}, w_{|\tilde{S}|+2}, \ldots, w_{m+1}) \tag{5}$$

The confidence score $c$ is then defined by Eq. (6) and reflects the total weight of the missing information. In case of no missing information, $c$ is equal to 1.

$$c = 1 - \sum_{i=1}^{|\tilde{\mathbf{v}}|} v_i \tag{6}$$

A higher confidence score indicates that more of the original information contributed to the final similarity score, making the result more trustworthy. While this confidence score does not directly affect the final similarity value, it provides important information that can be used during the interpretation or visualisation of the results, or in downstream processes such as clustering.

*Example 2.* Let us revisit the (restricted) similarity sets and weight vectors from Ex. 1. In the case of $\tilde{S}_1$, where no similarity values are missing, the residual weight vector $\tilde{\mathbf{v}}_1$ is empty, resulting in a confidence score $c_1 = 1$. This indicates that the aggregated similarity $s_1$ is based on the complete information and can thereby be considered fully reliable. In contrast, for $\tilde{S}_2$, one similarity value is missing, leading to a residual weight vector $\tilde{\mathbf{v}}_2 = (0.2)$. The resulting confidence score is $c_2 = 0.8$, reflecting the partial absence of information and reduced reliability of the aggregated similarity $s_2$.

## 4.3   Clustering

Now consider a set of texts $T = \{t_1, t_2, \ldots t_n\}$ to be clustered. Each text consists of its textual content along with a set of $m$ associated metadata elements — such as author, publication date, category, etc. — that may be fully known or missing. For each pair of texts $t_i, t_j \in T$, we compute a set of similarities $S_{i,j}$ that includes a textual similarity and, when available, similarity scores between all corresponding metadata fields. The specific similarity measures for both text and metadata are application-dependent and can be selected and/or fine-tuned based on the type of metadata and the requirements of the application.

These sets of similarities are then aggregated into a single similarity score $s_{i,j} \in [0,1]$ between texts $t_i$ and $t_j$ using the OWA-based fusion method described in Sect. 4.1, which flexibly handles missing metadata. The aggregated similarity scores can be stored in a symmetric similarity matrix $M_S \in [0,1]^{n \times n}$, where each entry $s_{i,j}$ represents the aggregated similarity between $t_i$ and $t_j$, and identical texts are assumed to be maximally similar, i.e., $s_{i,i} = 1, i = 1, \ldots, n$.

In parallel, we compute a confidence matrix $M_C \in [0,1]^{n \times n}$, where each entry $c_{i,j}$ represents the confidence associated with the similarity score $s_{i,j}$ between $t_i$ and $t_j$, as described in Sect. 4.2. Similar to $M_S$, we assume full confidence for identical texts, i.e., $c_{i,i} = 1, i = 1, \ldots, n$.

As discussed in Sect. 3.1, the K-Medoids algorithm requires a dissimilarity matrix as input. We derive the dissimilarity matrix $M_D \in [0,1]^{n \times n}$ by complementing the similarities $s_{i,j}$ such that each dissimilarity results in $d_{i,j} = 1 - s_{i,j}, \forall i, j \in [1, \ldots, n]$. Given a predefined or heuristically determined number of clusters $k$, K-Medoids selects $k$ representative texts (medoids) and assigns each remaining text to the clusters whose medoid it is least dissimilar to.

While the clustering process relies solely on the fused similarity scores and not on the confidence scores, the confidence scores are crucial for assessing the reliability of the cluster outcome. Once clusters are formed, the confidence between each text and its assigned cluster medoid can be interpreted as a reliability score. This reliability score indicates how representative the similarity calculation, and consequently the assignment of the text to the cluster, is based on the available information. These clusters, along with their associated similarity and confidence scores, can be utilised in various downstream tasks, such as inferring missing metadata, detecting inconsistent metadata, and uncovering previously unknown connections between texts.

# 5   Practical Application

In this section, we demonstrate the relevance of the proposed clustering strategy through its application on a dataset of Byzantine book epigrams. The Database of Byzantine Book Epigrams (DBBE)[1] [13] houses a corpus of 12733 mostly short Byzantine poems that appear in the margins of medieval manuscripts. These texts typically comment on the manuscript's content or the people involved in its production and were often reworked, reused, split up, and (re)combined over time during the manuscript copying process. In addition to their textual content, a substantial amount of metadata is available for these epigrams, although some entries suffer from incomplete information, making it an ideal dataset for our proposed clustering strategy.

The DBBE is designed as a polyglot database, combining a relational and a graph database system. Text and metadata are carefully maintained by domain experts and stored in a clean, normalised format within the relational database. To date, grouping similar or related epigrams has primarily been the result of manual expert analysis [13]. More recently, a complementary graph database has been developed, where texts are represented hierarchically at the levels of words, verses, and complete epigrams, and are enriched with orthographic similarity scores between these elements. This graph structure supports advanced textual analysis through flexible querying, grouping, and pattern matching [5,6].

For the purpose of this study, we focus on a smaller subset of the data. This smaller dataset consists of 500 epigrams that have been manually grouped into 21 disjoint groups of related texts, and as such acts as ground truth [7]. In addition to their textual content, we consider five metadata fields in this application: (i) the geographical region where the epigrams were written, (ii) the metrical structure(s) used in the texts, (iii) the subject(s) mentioned, (iv) the scribes that composed or copied them, and (v) the genres assigned to them.

## 5.1   Similarity Measures

To apply our clustering method, we first compute pairwise similarities between all epigrams in the selected dataset. This involves calculating not only the textual similarity between the epigrams but also the similarities between metadata elements, when available, in both texts.

**Textual Similarity.** The textual similarity between the epigrams is computed using a hierarchical orthographic similarity measure, applied to a graph-based representation of the texts. In this representation, epigrams are decomposed into verses, which in turn are broken down into words, allowing similarity to be computed in a bottom-up manner. First, orthographic similarity is calculated between individual words. These word-level scores are then employed to compute verse-level similarities, which are subsequently used to calculate the overall similarity between complete epigrams, the similarity used in this application [6].

---

[1] https://dbbe.ugent.be

**Regional Similarity.** To assess the geographical similarity between epigrams, a tree structure with root world and five granularity levels — country, part, region, city, and location — is used to represent the geographic relationships between all available spatial metadata. To ensure that each path in this tree is complete, missing data at intermediate levels are automatically completed by propagating parent data downward. When comparing two epigrams using a given spatial granularity, their respective regional data are first mapped to the set of corresponding nodes at the selected granularity level. These sets are then compared using the Jaccard similarity, defined by Eq. (7). In this application, the city granularity is used to calculate regional similarities.

$$\text{jacc}\,(A, B) = \frac{|A \cap B|}{|A \cup B|} \tag{7}$$

*Example 3.* Consider *Southern Italy*, classified as part, which includes the region *Calabria*, which in turn consists of the cities *Reggio* and *Rossano*. Suppose text $t_1$ is associated with *Calabria*, and text $t_2$ with *Rossano*. Using the part granularity, $t_1$ and $t_2$ map to $R_1 = R_2 = \{Southern\ Italy\}$ resulting in jacc $(R_1, R_2) = 1.0$. Using the city granularity, $t_1$ maps to $R_1 = \{Reggio, Rossano\}$, while $t_2$ maps to $R_2 = \{Rossano\}$, resulting in jacc $(R_1, R_2) = 0.5$.

**Meter, Subject, Scribe, and Genre Similarity.** The similarities for meter, subject, scribe, and genre metadata are computed straightforwardly, as each epigram can be associated with one or more meters, subjects, scribes, and/or genres. These metadata fields are directly represented by sets, and their similarity is measured using the Jaccard similarity, as defined by Eq. (7).

## 5.2   Fusion of Similarity Measures and Clustering

Once the individual similarity scores for text and metadata attributes are computed, they are combined into a single similarity matrix representing the overall similarity score for each pair of epigrams. The fusion is performed using the OWA operator introduced in Sect. 4.1, with an empirically determined weight vector $\mathbf{w} = (0.01, 0.49, 0.08, 0.07, 0.1, 0.25)$. In addition to the fused similarity matrix $M_S$, a confidence matrix $M_C$ is constructed in accordance with Sect. 4.2.

The resulting dissimilarity matrix $M_D$ is then used as input to the K-Medoids clustering algorithm, as described in Sect. 4.3, to partition the texts into $k$ coherent clusters. In this application, we set $k = 21$ to align with the 21 expert-defined epigram groups acting as ground truth. To initialize the K-Medoids algorithm, we select the $k$ texts with the highest total similarity to all other texts as initial medoids.

After clustering, we obtain 21 coherent clusters of epigrams, each centred around a representative medoid. To complement the clustering output, each text is also assigned a confidence score reflecting the reliability of its cluster assignment. This score is defined as the confidence value between the text and the medoid of the cluster it belongs to and is derived from the confidence matrix.

## 5.3   Results

After clustering the epigrams, we evaluate the quality and interpretability of the resulting clusters. First, we compare the clustering outcomes of our method against a baseline using only textual similarity. Next, we provide a visual illustration of the confidence-enhanced clusters to demonstrate the added value of incorporating confidence scores.

**Quantitative Evaluation.** To assess clustering quality, we compare the predicted clusters with the expert-defined epigram groups using the $F_1$-score. This score is based on pairwise relationships: for each pair of texts, we determine whether they are assigned to the same cluster as in the ground truth. A pair is considered a true positive if this is the case. If they are not in the same group in the ground truth, but are clustered together, they count as false positives. Conversely, if they are in the same group in the ground truth but are assigned to different clusters, they are false negatives.

When using the classical K-Medoids algorithm based solely on textual similarity, we obtain an $F_1$-score of approximately 0.8205. By incorporating metadata through our proposed method, the $F_1$-score increases to about 0.8487, demonstrating that the inclusion of metadata improves the alignment of clusters with expert knowledge. Furthermore, incorporating metadata in the similarity computations does not result in worse clustering quality in this experiment.

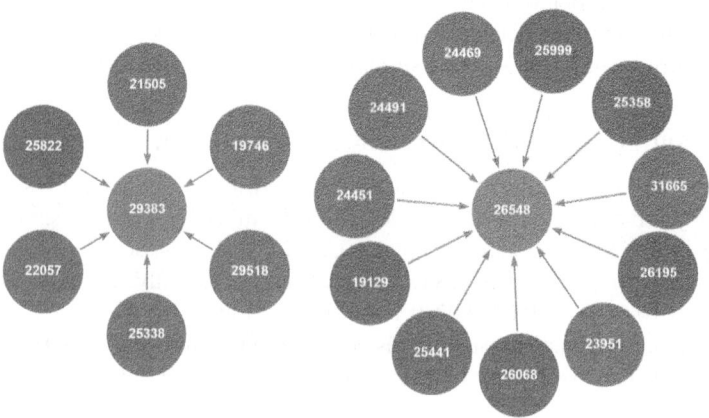

**Fig. 1.** Cluster visualisation using Neo4j Bloom. Each node represents an epigram identified by a unique identifier number and is either the cluster medoid or points toward the cluster centre. The id of each epigram is displayed inside each node. Node colours indicate confidence scores, ranging from 0.5 (dark red) to 1.0 (bright green). (Color figure online)

**Confidence-Enhanced Clustering Visualisation.** In addition to numerical evaluation, we visualise a subset of the resulting clusters in Fig. 1 to explore their internal structure. Each epigram is gradually coloured according to its confidence score: green indicates high confidence, while red reflects lower confidence.

This visualisation offers two key insights. First, the colour of an individual text directly indicates the reliability of its cluster assignment. A redder text suggests missing metadata or weaker alignment with the cluster medoid. Secondly, the overall colour distribution within a cluster offers a sense of its cohesion and trustworthiness. Clusters dominated by green nodes are likely to be well-formed and internally consistent, while greater colour variation may signal internal ambiguity or lower confidence in the cluster's structure. In this way, the confidence scores serve as an intuitive and visual tool for assessing the reliability of the clustering results and highlighting edge cases that require further investigation.

## 6    Conclusions and Future Work

In this paper we proposed a novel strategy for clustering short texts that integrates both textual and contextual similarities through a flexible OWA-based fusion mechanism. By introducing a confidence score alongside the aggregated similarity values, our method provides not only a mechanism to compute a similarity score in the presence of missing metadata, but also a meaningful measure of reliability. This approach enables effective clustering even when metadata are incomplete, without the need for imputation or marginalisation of contextual information. The resulting clusters, along with the similarity and confidence scores between cluster centres and their assigned texts, provide an interpretable foundation for further analysis or processing of short texts.

In future research, we will consider more clustering-specific evaluation metrics and explore correlations between these quality measures and the confidence scores across clusters. We also aim to explore methods for incorporating the confidence score directly into the actual clustering process, examine techniques to determine an optimal number of clusters, and investigate the applicability of our method to other clustering approaches. Additionally, we will examine the potential impact on this approach in case the similarity scores between text elements already contain a confidence score reflecting their reliability and how this may affect both the confidence score of the aggregated similarity and the overall clustering process.

**Acknowledgments.** This research was partially funded by the Flemish Government (Flanders AI Research Program) and the Ghent University Research Fund (BOF21/GOA/028).

## References

1. Charu, C.A., Zhai, C.: A survey of text clustering algorithms. In: Aggarwal, C.C., Zhai, C. (eds.) Mining Text Data, pp. 77–128. Springer US, Boston, MA (2012). ISBN 978-1-4614-3223-4. https://doi.org/10.1007/978-1-4614-3223-4_4

2. Ahmed, M.H., Tiun, S., Omar, N., Sani, N.S.: Short text clustering algorithms, application and challenges: a survey. Appl. Sci. **13**(1), 342 (2023). ISSN 2076-3417. https://doi.org/10.3390/app13010342
3. Albalawi, R., Yeap, T.H., Benyoucef, M.: Using topic modeling methods for short-text data: a comparative analysis. Front. Artif. Intell. **3** (2020). ISSN 2624-8212. https://doi.org/10.3389/frai.2020.00042
4. De Tré, G., Peelman, M., Dujmović, J.: Logic reasoning under data veracity concerns. Int. J. Approximate Reasoning **161**, 108977 (2023). ISSN 0888-613X. https://doi.org/10.1016/j.ijar.2023.108977
5. Deforche, M., De Vos, I., Bronselaer, A., De Tré, G.: An orthographic similarity measure for graph-based text representations. In: Flexible Query Answering Systems, pp. 206–218 (2023). ISBN 978-3-031-42935-4. https://doi.org/10.1007/978-3-031-42935-4_17
6. Deforche, M., De Vos, I., Bronselaer, A., De Tré, G.: A hierarchical orthographic similarity measure for interconnected texts represented by graphs. Appl. Sci. **14**(4), 1529 (2024). ISSN 2076-3417. https://doi.org/10.3390/app14041529
7. Demoen, K., et al.: Database of Byzantine Book Epigrams (2023)
8. Dujmović, J.: The problem of missing data in LSP aggregation. In: Greco, S., Bouchon-Meunier, B., Coletti, G., Fedrizzi, M., Matarazzo, B., Yager, R.R. (eds.) Advances in Computational Intelligence, pp. 336–346. Berlin, Heidelberg (2012). Springer. ISBN 978-3-642-31718-7. https://doi.org/10.1007/978-3-642-31718-7_35
9. Himmelspach, L., Conrad, S.: Clustering approaches for data with missing values: comparison and evaluation. In: 2010 Fifth International Conference on Digital Information Management (ICDIM), pp. 19–28 (2010). https://doi.org/10.1109/ICDIM.2010.5664691
10. Lianyu, H., Jiang, M., Dong, J., Liu, X., He, Z.: A Survey, Interpretable Clustering (2024)
11. Kaufman, L., Rousseeuw, P.J.: Partitioning Around Medoids (Program PAM). Finding Groups in Data, pp. 68–125 (2008). https://doi.org/10.1002/9780470316801.ch2
12. Kenter, T., de Rijke, M.: Short text similarity with word embeddings. In: Proceedings of the 24th ACM International Conference on Information and Knowledge Management, CIKM '15, pp. 1411–1420, New York, NY, USA (2015). Association for Computing Machinery. ISBN 978-1-4503-3794-6. https://doi.org/10.1145/2806416.2806475
13. Ricceri, R., et al.: The database of byzantine book epigrams project: principles, challenges, opportunities. In: Journal of Data Mining & Digital Humanities, On the Way to the Future of Digital Manuscript Studies (2023). ISSN 2416-5999. https://doi.org/10.46298/jdmdh.10244
14. Suyal, H., Panwar, A., Negi, A.S.: Text clustering algorithms: a review. Int. J. Comput. Appl. **96**(24) (2014)
15. Xu, J., et al.: Self-taught convolutional neural networks for short text clustering. Neural Netw. **88**, 22–31 (2017). ISSN 0893-6080. https://doi.org/10.1016/j.neunet.2016.12.008
16. Yager, R.R.: On ordered weighted averaging aggregation operators in multicriteria decision making. IEEE Trans. Syst. Man Cybern. **18**(1), 183–190 (1988). ISSN 2168-2909. https://doi.org/10.1109/21.87068

# Knowledge Graphs and Natural Logic

Troels Andreasen[1]([⊠]), Henrik Bulskov[1], and Jørgen Fischer Nilsson[2]

[1] Roskilde University, Roskilde, Denmark
{troels,bulskov}@ruc.dk
[2] Technical University of Denmark, Kongens Lyngby, Denmark
jfni@dtu.dk

**Abstract.** Knowledge graphs have emerged as a widely used method for representing and organizing information in a structured, graph-based form that facilitates understanding, navigation, and utilization by both machines and humans. The graphs model classes, entities and their relationships as nodes and edges in a graph. Natural logics are logics where sentences are expressed in a stylized form of natural language and where computational reasoning is conducted directly on the natural logic phrases, rather than on the underlying formal logic. NATURALOG is a dialect of natural logics that comes with a graph form, enabling knowledge in the knowledge base to be visualized and processed as graphs. NATURALOG thus offers an approach to natural logic graphs and additionally incorporates logical quantifiers, compound terms, and deductive reasoning, thereby going beyond the capabilities of traditional knowledge graph models. Here we specifically discuss the affinity between knowledge graphs and the natural logic graphs of NATURALOG.

**Keywords:** Knowledge graphs · Natural logic · logical knowledge bases · NATURALOG

## 1 Introduction

Plenty of proposals for graph-based representation of information have been developed, ranging from formalised logical models to more informal approaches. These proposals often focus on modelling target domains as entities, classes of entities, and relationships connecting these. In their simplest form, these structures are represented as graphs, where nodes correspond to entities or classes, and the edges represent relationships. Early examples of such models include entity relationship models [8], semantic networks [2] and conceptual graphs [16]. More recently, the concept of knowledge graphs has gained attention. Knowledge graphs serve a dual purpose: they act as tools for domain modelling, and as framework for computational reasoning, enabling inference directly on the graph structure using appropriate inference rules.

In this paper we examine the affinities and connection between knowledge graphs and graphs of the natural logic dialect NATURALOG. NATURALOG offers a combined natural language and logic-oriented view on knowledge representation

© The Author(s), under exclusive license to Springer Nature Switzerland AG 2026
G. De Tré et al. (Eds.): FQAS 2025, LNAI 16119, pp. 31–41, 2026.
https://doi.org/10.1007/978-3-032-05607-8_5

afforded by natural logics, allowing reasoning to be conducted directly on simple natural language phrases rather than formal logic structures.

The paper is organized as follows: Sect. 2 briefly presents knowlede graphs, Sect. 3 describe the natural logic dialect NATURALOG and its graph representation. Section 4 describes the similarities and difference between NATURALOG graphs and knowledge graphs. The paper ends with a conclusion in Sect. 5.

## 2   Knowledge Graphs

Knowledge graphs (KGs) [10] have become a powerful approach for organizing and representing real-world information. Their ability to integrate, manage, and derive insights from large-scale, diverse datasets has led to widespread adoption across both industry and academia. KGs are graph-based data models where nodes represent entities, such as "Denmark", "North Sea", "Copenhagen", and clases, for instance, "capital", and edges represent the relationships between them, like "borders," "flows into," or "is a". A KG might express facts such as "Denmark borders Germany" or "Copenhagen is the capital of Denmark." Two examples KGs are shown in Fig. 1.

KGs are not inherently logical formalisms. At their core, they are just structured representation of entities and their relationships, often modeled as subject–predicate–object triples. However, rules–such as those ensuring the integrity of the knowledge domain–can readily be applied to a given graph to propose modifications that enforce conformity with that integrity. Specific validation tools are also developed for this purpose, such as ShEx (Shape Expressions) [11] and SHACL (Shapes Constraint Language) [1]. KGs are also capable of representing contextual information, such as temporal data, like "Denmark joined the EU in 1973", geographic data, like "The North Sea lies between Denmark and the UK", and provenance data, like "This fact was sourced from Wikipedia".

KGs comes with various forms of modelling notations such as Directed Edge-Labeled Graphs as in common RDF triples: (subject, predicate, object), Heterogeneous graphs, where nodes and edges can have different types (can be "multi-typed") and Property Graphs, where nodes and edges can both have arbitrary key-value properties. Since KGs do not derive from a formalism, there are no "native" query language. However, specialized query languages such as SPARQL [14], Cypher [9], and Gremlin [15] are commonly used to enable users to access a graph and do, for instance, pattern searches and navigational queries, making it possible to ask questions like "Which cities are capitals of European countries?" or "Which rivers flow into the Mediterranean Sea?"

KGs are applied in a wide array of domains. In semantic search, they enhance engines like Google by delivering more relevant and context-aware results. In recommendation systems, platforms like Netflix and Amazon use them to suggest content tailored to user preferences. Conversational agents and chatbots often rely on KGs to provide accurate, meaningful responses based on context. Current research on KGs spans several critical areas, including scalability, quality, diversity, and dynamic behavior. A growing area of interest also lies in exploring

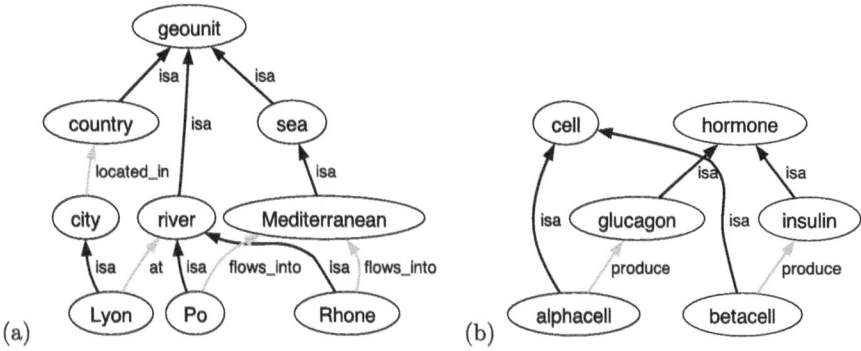

**Fig. 1.** Sample knowledge graphs on Geographic and Live Science domains respectively

the connection between reasoning and KGs. Description logic has played a key role here, but recently also other approaches that relate KGs and reasoning have shown, for instance, the use of deductive chains in knowledge graphs to generate explanations that are understandable to humans.

## 3   NATURALOG and NATURALOG Graphs

Natural logics are formal logics that resemble stylized forms of natural language, for instance English. An obvious advantage of natural logics is the improved readability, which is essential for domain experts working with large knowledge bases. Here we describe a specific natural logic proposal NATURALOG.

### 3.1   The Sentences of NATURALOG

In NATURALOG sentences take the following form

[every | some] *Nounterm Verbterm* [every | some] *Nounterm*      (1)

Underlining indicate default presences, thus every *Nounterm Verbterm* some *Nounterm* can be written in short form as *Nounterm Verbterm Nounterm*.

A NATURALOG knowledge base (KB) consists of a finite collection of sentences. NATURALOG sentences follow the common Subject–Verb–Object (SVO) form of descriptive sentences, where linguistically transitive verbs take objects. More specifically, the subject is followed by the verb, which is then followed by the linguistic object. A more comprehensive form admits negation in front of the verb. But in the form applied here, there are no negative sentences in a KB. However, we rely on negation as failure-to-prove in query answer computations as known from logic programming.

In the simplest case, a *Nounterm* is a proper or common noun, possibly a multi-word noun. In the general case of compound *Nounterm*, the noun can be followed by restrictive relative phrases (that *Verbterm Nounterm*) and by prepositional phrases (*Preposition Nounterm*). Structural ambiguities arising from the recursive nature of this syntax can be clarified by inserting parentheses. Sample NATURALOG sentences reflecting information from Fig. 1 are:

city located_in country          alphacell produce glucagon

Which are the short forms of every city located_in some country and every alphacell produce some glucagon respectively.

Sentences without compound terms are called prime sentences. Sentences comprising compound terms are called complex sentences. They are given special consideration because they complicate the construction of the accompanying graphs, as detailed in Sect. 3.2. We refer to the present form of natural logic as core NATURALOG. In [3,4] we describe a number of conservative extensions to NATURALOG, such as parenthetical relative clauses, appositions and distributive conjunctions. Being conservative, they can be eliminated by (computational) paraphrasing into core NATURALOG.

**Copula Sentences and Formal Ontologies.** A sentence where is (or isa) functions as the linking verb and the linguistic object is a common noun, is commonly known as a copula sentence. In the case that the subject is also a common noun, the sentence express class inclusion. A sample is capital isa city, which in NATURALOG is the short form of: every capital is a city. Copula sentences are known from syllogistic logic. Such sentence forms are the building blocks for formal ontologies. Natural logics may be conceived as rooted in syllogistic logic extended with arbitrary verbs, confer [13].

**Predicate-Logical Specification of** NATURALOG Natural logics may be conceived as variable-free forms of parts of predicate logic. Consider the sample sentence every country has some capital. The determiner every corresponds to the universal quantifier, and the determiner some corresponds the the existential quantifier. The predicate logical form becomes

$\forall x(\mathsf{country}(x) \rightarrow \exists y(\mathsf{has}(x,y) \wedge \mathsf{capital}(y)))$

The sample copula sentence every capital is a city becomes

$\forall x(\mathsf{capital}(x) \rightarrow \mathsf{city}(x))$

via $\forall x(\mathsf{capital}(x) \rightarrow \exists\, y(=(x,y) \wedge \mathsf{city}(y)))$

The underlying predicate-logic that provides the logical specification of NATURALOG is described in more detail in [4,12].

**The Case of Proper Nouns.** In earlier presentations of NATURALOG we excluded sentences containing proper nouns, and focused exclusively on KB models at the concept level. Here we include proper nouns as follows. For a proper noun, say $n$, we define its predicate-logical representation as the predicate $n$, which is satisfied exclusively by the individual referred to by $n$. Thus $n(n)$ holds as a singleton. Formally, then, the sample NATURALOG sentence Denmark borders Germany obtains the predicate logical construal

$\forall x(\mathsf{Denmark}(x) \rightarrow \exists y(\mathsf{borders}(x,y) \wedge \mathsf{Germany}(y)))$

together with Denmark(Denmark) and Germany(Germany), where the symbols function as predicates as well as individual constants.

**Multi-word Names and Compound Phrases.** In its simplest form, entities and classes are named by one noun. Sometimes multi-word names are indicated by means of hyphens, such as North-Sea, British-Isles or contractions as in North-Sea, BritishIsles. This holds for proper nouns (individuals) as well as for concepts (classes). We use hyphens as convention to remind that such names are to be handled as non-compound nouns.

However, multi word names should not be confused with proper compound phrases, such as say capital of Denmark or city at Donau, which both consist of a noun and a modifier (expressed by a propositional phrase). Such compound class terms or nominal phrases are addressed as an essential feature in the natural logic. They further open for recursive structured phrases such as say the class city at river that flows-into Mediterranean.

**Inference Rules.** The natural logic comes with a number of intuitive inference rules that are specific to the natural logic. The rules define legal derivations and are used for computational processing of queries posed to a NATURALOG KB. Inference rules can also be employed to perform valid modifications to the graph. The rules are thoroughly described in the mentioned previous papers. The inference rules apply directly to the natural logic sentences. Among the rules defined for NATURALOG are the so-called monotonicity rules and the materialization rule illustrated in Fig. 2, where dashed style edges and border indicate elements inferred through the application of the rules. Inherence monotonicity applies to the case where a concept $C$, with a subconcept $Csub$, is $R$-related to a concept $D$, and derives an $R$-relationship from the subconcept to $D$ (the subconcept inherits the $R$-relationship). Conversely, generalization monotonicity applies to the case where a concept $C$ is $R$-related to a concept $D$, while $D$ is a subconcept of $Dsuper$, and derives $C$ to be $R$-related to $Dsuper$ (the $R$-relationship to $D$ is generalized into an $R$-relationship to $Dsuper$). Observe that the relation $R$ can also be isa. In this case, inheritance as well as generalization reduce to the transitivity of isa, while the contribution af materilization becomes less significant. While monotonicity derives edges only, materialisation derives nodes as well. In the case that $C$ isa subconcept of $D$ and $R$-related to $E$, a node $C$-that-$R$-$E$ is added (materialized) as a superconcept to $C$, a subconcept of $D$, and $R$-related to $E$. The new concept is called a proxy-concept and is discussed further below.

**Classes Are Non-empty.** NATURALOG applies so-called existential import. Thus, in NATURALOG introduced classes in the KB (together with their superior, possibly implicit, but logically existing classes) are assumed non-empty as a default principle. By convention, then, classes that contain no explicitly named common subclasses or entities are considered disjoint.

**Compound Concepts.** Sentences having compound noun phrases take form of a head noun with restrictive modifiers and are denoted compound concept terms.

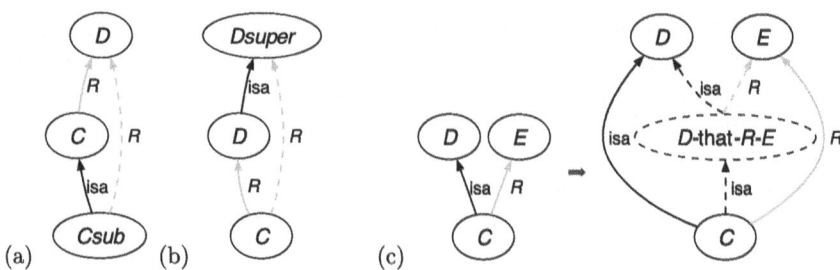

**Fig. 2.** Inference rules: (a) inheritance, (b) generalization and (c) materialization. Illustrated here in graph form. Dashed style indicates what is inferred.

Generally, in language nominal modifiers come in form of adjectives, noun-noun compounds, genitives, prepositional phrases and restrictive relative clauses. We consider here only the latter two forms of modifiers that are distinguished by an explicit relational component: For prepositional phrases the preposition, and for relative clauses the verb, represent a relation becoming an arc in the graph conception.

## 3.2   The Graphs of NATURALOG

A KB comprising simple sentences of the form (1) above may trivially be visualized as a directed graph where nodes are labelled with nouns and edges with verbs. Optionally quantifiers can be specified at one or both ends of the directed edge. In a NATURALOG graph, each noun is represented by a unique node, allowing sentences to commonly share these nodes throughout the KB. This is unlike the existential graphs used in the Conceptual Graphs formalism [16].

**Inference rules and the NATURALOG graph** From the graph perspective the inference rules provide a means to do controlled and admissible modifications to the KB graph. Any edge or node that can be derived from the KB can be added to the graph, but obviously it is not required to add everything that can be derived. What to include depends on purpose, use case and target. If the graph is to be computationally processed, for instance to provide advanced query options like path finding or to provide training data as input to further processing, for instance for the purpose of doing grounding when training LLMs, then the aim should probably be to add all or most parts of what is derivable. However, if the purpose is to provide information for human readability, the modifications should be limited to ensure that the result appeals to the intuition of the reader. The graph modification process may involve not only extending but also reducing the graph. As an example, consider Fig. 3. Notice that the graphs do not include for instance the edges in (a) Rhone flows_into Mediterranean or in (b) betacell produce hormone, even though these can be derived through monotonicity inference. The graph in Fig. 3(b) does, however, include three new nodes. One approach to reach this point is to extend the Fig. 3(b) graph with the

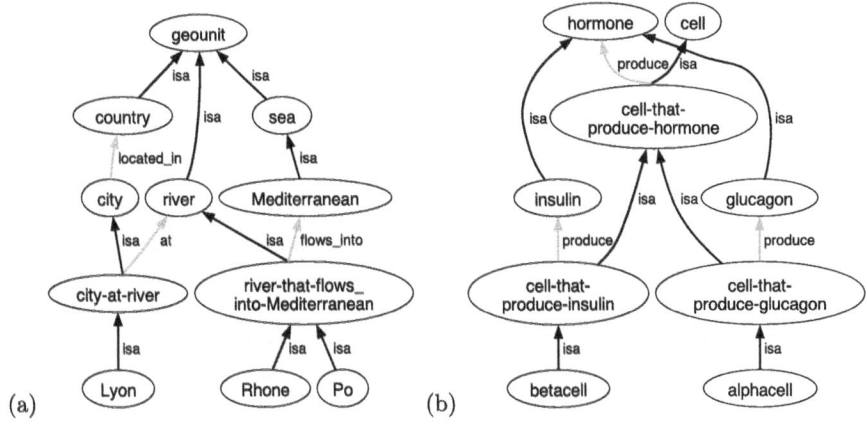

**Fig. 3.** NATURALOG graphs corresponding to the knowledge graphs in Fig. 1

monotonicity transitive closure, then extend using materialization, and finally to do a transitive reduction with respect to monotonicity.

**Proxy Concepts.** For compound concept terms the inner structure is made explicit in the graph by the notion of so-called proxy concepts and nodes. The proxying principle amounts to generating an auxiliary node for a compound concept accompanied by a pair of defining arcs for the two constituents, that is, the noun and the modifier. The compound concept term *Nounterm* that *Verbterm Nounterm* gives rise to the simple concept proxy, *Nounterm*-that-*Verbterm-Nounterm*, with two additional sentences

    *Nounterm*-that-*Verbterm-Nounterm* isa *Nounterm*

    *Nounterm*-that-*Verbterm-Nounterm* *Verbterm* *Nounterm*

exposing the qualification of the original concept term. Such decompositions apply recursively, when relevant, to the qualifying sub-concept terms. It is important to realize that all nodes derived from the proxying are interwoven with the pertinent contributions from the entire collection of sentences in the KB.

The upshot of this proxying computational process is a NATURALOG knowledge graph where compound terms are replaced with simple terms. As an example, the NATURALOG sentence Rhone isa river that flows_into Mediterranean gives rise to a proxy in Fig. 3. This "morphing" of NATURALOG sentences into NATURALOG graphs enables the graphs to be logically reconstrued as DATALOG sentences without compound terms. The DATALOG conception in turn invites an implementation of deductive querying by means of contemporary database query facilities.

Notice that the materialization inference rule, when applied, derives a proxy concept. Figure 2(c) illustrates what materialization derives for inclusion in the graph. An example is shown in Fig. 3(a), where city-at-river is included as a modification to the graph in Fig. 1.

In order to ensure logically correct handling of proxies as explained in [4,6], generally a subsumption inference rule derives necessary additional isa arcs in the NATURALOG graph.

## 4  Comparison of NaturaLog and Knowledge Graphs

In this section we make a comparison between NATURALOG graphs and KGs. First of all, it is important to note that any core knowledge graph (KG) can be viewed and used as a NaturaLog graph. Consequently, NaturaLog inference can be applied to modify the KG. Conversely, any core NATURALOG graph can also be viewed and used as a knowledge graph (KG). While NATURALOG offers several advanced features that surpass KGs, there are also scenarios where KGs may be more advantageous. This balanced comparison highlights the strengths and limitations of both approaches.

One of the key features of NATURALOG is its representation of logical quantifiers in relationships. This allows for a more precise and nuanced representation of information compared to KGs, which often lack this level of detail. For example, NATURALOG can explicitly represent sentences like every city is located in some country, capturing the universal and existential quantifiers in the graph itself.

NATURALOG graphs introduce a unique mechanism for handling compound concepts through the use of proxy nodes. Compound concepts, which consist of a head noun and restrictive modifiers, like city at river or capital of Denmark, are decomposed into simpler terms in NATURALOG graphs. This decomposition ensures that the graph remains logically coherent and manageable, even when dealing with complex noun phrases. The proxy node serves as an auxiliary node that represents the compound term, while the defining arcs connect it to its constituents. For instance, the compound concept  city at river would be represented as a proxy node city-at-river, with arcs connecting it to city and river, as shown in Fig. 3. This recursive decomposition process can be applied to more complex phrases, such as city at river that flows into Mediterranean, ensuring that all components are explicitly represented in the graph. This differs from KGs, which may not offer such a detailed decomposition of compound concepts, as compound concepts are often treated as single entities, which can lead to ambiguities and less efficient reasoning. For example, a compound concept like city at river may be represented as a single node, which can obscure the relationships between its components.

Another essential characteristic of NATURALOG graphs are the unified representation of concepts across the entire knowledge base. Each concept is represented by a unique node, shared across all sentences in which it appears. This approach ensures consistency and avoids duplication, enabling efficient reasoning and querying. For example, if the knowledge base includes the sentences "Denmark borders Germany" and "Denmark isa country," the concept "Denmark" is represented by a single node connected to both "Germany" (via the relationship "borders") and "country" (via the relationship "isa"). KGs, on the other hand, may allow for duplicated or inconsistently represented nodes, leading to fragmentation and reduced coherence.

NATURALOG also incorporates inference rules that enable logical reasoning directly within the graph. These rules allow users to derive new knowledge from existing information. For example, given the sentences "every city is located in some country" and "Copenhagen isa city", NATURALOG can infer that "Copenhagen is located in some country". We also observe that since any relation mathematically comes with an inverse, there can for each edge be derived an opposite directed edge labelled with the opposite verb-form of the active-passive voice switching and pertinent quantifiers. For pure logical grounds, relying on the principle of existential import, We have that from

$C$ is $R$-related to D,

that is in full form every $C$ is $R$-related to some $D$

follows

some $D$ is conversely-$R$-related to $C$

that is in full form some $D$ is conversely-$R$-related to some $C$.

As an example, we wish to codify in NATURALOG the piece of information that the flu causes fever, but there may be other conditions causing fever:

flu causes fever

yields by the above rule the converse

some fever is caused by flu,

That is in the graph conception the oppositely directed edge, however with the weaker quantifier. In addition to the various logical inference rules extra-logical general purpose rules such as, say, transitivity of the cause relation may readily be obtained at the DATALOG level, cf. [4].

These inferential capabilities support complex reasoning and deductive querying, which KGs often lack without external tools or validation methods like SHACL and ShEx.

KGs, however, excel in simplicity and flexibility. Their straightforward subject-predicate-object triples are easy to understand and implement, making them accessible to users without expertise in formal logic. We argue that this is also a strength of NATURALOG, due to its close relation to natural language and its graph representation. KGs are widely adopted in industry and academia, supported by mature ecosystems and query languages like SPARQL, Cypher, and Gremlin. These tools are optimized for graph traversal and pattern matching, making integration into existing systems seamless. While NATURALOG introduces additional complexity with its logical quantifiers and proxy nodes, its graphs can still be queried using the same languages as KGs, while also enabling advanced logical reasoning through DATALOG [5]. KGs allow for heterogeneous graph structures, where nodes and edges can have different types and properties. This flexibility makes them suitable for diverse applications, whereas NATURALOG's structure stresses logical coherence.

In summary, NATURALOG offers advanced features such as explicit representation of quantifiers, proxy nodes for compound concepts, unified representation of knowledge base sentences, and robust inference rules. These qualities make it a strong candidate for applications requiring sophisticated reasoning and transparency, particularly in hybrid systems combining logical and statistical approaches. On the other hand, KGs are ideal for scenarios prioritizing simplicity, flexibility, and lower computational requirements. The choice between NATURALOG and KGs ultimately depends on the specific needs and goals of the application.

## 5  Conclusion

In this paper, we have discussed the relationship between traditional knowledge graphs and the natural logic-based graphs provided by NATURALOG. Knowledge graphs offer a flexible and intuitive means of structuring and navigating large bodies of information, representing entities, classes, and their relationships. NaturaLog, as a dialect of natural logic, offers an extended graph-based modeling enabling reasoning as well as derived modifications and extensions to the graph.

While traditional knowledge graphs focus primarily on the representation and querying of information, NaturaLog further supports logical deduction through its structured sentence forms and graph construction mechanisms. By bridging natural language and formal logic, NaturaLog provides a foundation for building more expressive and reasoning-capable knowledge systems.

The parallels between knowledge graphs and NaturaLog graphs highlight the potential for cross-pollination: incorporating logical reasoning capabilities into conventional knowledge graph applications, and leveraging the accessibility and familiarity of graph structures in natural logic systems.

So, why is the comparison of knowledge graph approaches presented in this paper relevant in the first place? While reasoning in NATURALOG and NATURALOG graphs can naturally occur during query processing, it can also take place during graph modification, such as adding inferred edges and nodes using inference rules, or removing edges through techniques like transitive reduction. Furthermore, at any point, a NATURALOG graph can be considered a knowledge graph, making inference rule based NATURALOG graph modification a straightforward method for performing reasoning over information stored in Knowledge graphs. Finally, many existing approaches for working with knowledge graphs can be adapted for use with NATURALOG graphs. This includes tools for modeling and querying, as well as more advanced AI and large language model (LLM) applications. For example, [7] describes a method for constructing scalable and versatile knowledge graphs by iteratively prompting LLMs to extract relevant components, while [17] explores a similar approach using open information extraction combined with LLM prompting.

**Disclosure of Interests.** The authors have no competing interests to declare that are relevant to the content of this article.

## References

1. Shapes constraint language (SHACL). Technical report, W3C (2017)

2. Allen, J.F., Frisch, A.M.: What's in a semantic network? In: 20th Annual Meeting of the Association for Computational Linguistics, pp. 19–27, Toronto, Ontario, Canada, June (1982). Association for Computational Linguistics

3. Andreasen, T., Bulskov, H., Jensen, P.A., Nilsson, J.F.: Partiality, Underspecification, and Natural Language Processing, chapter A Natural Logic for Natural-Language Knowledge Bases. Cambridge Scholars (2017)

4. Andreasen, T., Bulskov, H., Jensen, P.A., Nilsson, J.F.: Natural logic knowledge bases and their graph form. Data & Knowledge Engineering (2020)

5. Andreasen, T., Bulskov, H., Nilsson, J.F.: A natural logic system for large knowledge bases. In: The 30th International Conference On Information Modelling And Knowledge Bases, Ejc 2020, Hamburg, Germany, June 8-12 (2020)

6. Andreasen, T., Bulskov, H., Nilsson, J.F.: Advanced query functionalities in natural logic knowledge bases. Int. J. Comput. Intell. Syst. **17** (2024)

7. Carta, S., Giuliani, A., Piano, L., Podda, A.S., Pompianu, L., Tiddia, S.G.: Iterative zero-shot LLM prompting for knowledge graph construction (2023)

8. Pin-Shan Chen, P.: The entity-relationship model—toward a unified view of data. ACM Trans. Database Syst. **1**(1), 9–36 (1976)

9. Francis, N., et al.: Cypher: an evolving query language for property graphs. In: SIGMOD'18 Proceedings of the 2018 International Conference on Management of Data, pp. 1433, Houston, United States (2018). ACM Press

10. Hogan, A., et al.: Knowledge graphs. ACM Comput. Surv. **54**(4), 1–37 (2021)

11. Gayo, J.E.L., Prud'hommeaux, E., Boneva, I., Kontokostas, D.: Validating RDF Data, volume 7 of Synthesis Lectures on the Semantic Web: Theory and Technology. Morgan & Claypool Publishers LLC (2017)

12. Nilsson, J.F.F.: In pursuit of natural logics for ontology-structured knowledge bases. In: The Seventh International Conference on Advanced Cognitive Technologies and Applications (2015)

13. Pratt-Hartmann, I., Moss, L.S.: Logics for the relational syllogistic. Rev. Symbolic Logic **2**(4), 647–683 (2009)

14. Prud'hommeaux, E.: Sparql query language for RDF. http://www.w3.org/TR/rdf-sparql-query/ (2008)

15. Rodriguez, M.A.: The gremlin graph traversal machine and language (invited talk). In: Proceedings of the 15th Symposium on Database Programming Languages, SPLASH '15, pp. 1–10. ACM (2015)

16. Sowa, J.F.: Semantics of conceptual graphs. In: Proceedings of the 17th Annual Meeting on Association for Computational Linguistics, ACL '79, pp. 39–44, Stroudsburg, PA, USA (1979). Association for Computational Linguistics

17. Zhang, B., Soh, H.: Extract, define, canonicalize: An LLM-based framework for knowledge graph construction (2024)

# A Smart Data Model for Nutrition-Aware Diabetes Management in Healthcare Systems

Simeon Tsvetanov$^{(\boxtimes)}$ ⓘ, Stela Dimitrova ⓘ, and Albena Antonova ⓘ

Sofia University St. Kliment Ohridski, Sofia, Bulgaria
{tsvetanov,a_antonova}@fmi.uni-sofia.bg, stelasd@uni-sofia.bg

**Abstract.** This paper presents SmartNutritionDiabetes, a novel smart data model designed to semantically integrate food intake, nutritional goals and glycemic response for enhanced diabetes mellitus management. Developed in alignment with the Smart Data Models initiative and building upon existing frameworks such as SAREF4HEALTH and HL7 FHIR, the proposed model addresses a critical gap in representing nutrition-related data within chronic disease monitoring systems. By leveraging linked data principles and semantic interoperability, the model facilitates real-time, context-aware decision-making in healthcare environments. The model is implemented and tested in a simulated environment, where its performance is evaluated against traditional approaches. Results demonstrate significant improvements in data accessibility, semantic expressiveness, and cross-domain interoperability, making it a valuable foundation for next-generation personalized healthcare applications.

**Keywords:** Smart Data Models · Personalized Nutrition · Health Ontologies · Semantic Interoperability · Digital Health

## 1 Introduction

The healthcare sector is undergoing a data-driven transformation, relying on structured, interoperable models to integrate clinical, lifestyle and sensor-based data into cohesive ecosystems. Initiatives like FIWARE's Smart Data Models (SDM) aim to provide standardized, NGSI-LD-compatible templates for organizing domain-specific data using linked data principles [1]. Despite the global burden of diabetes mellitus, with over 589 million adults affected worldwide [2], current data modeling standards underrepresent the crucial role of nutrition in its management. There is a gap in semantically rich models that link dietary behavior, nutritional goals and real-time glycemic responses, which is critical for intelligent digital health solutions and decision support systems.

Recent research has made significant strides in applying semantic technologies to healthcare, yet challenges remain in linking food intake, nutrition goals and glycemic data within a unified smart data framework. Pathak et al. outline the promise of semantic web technologies for healthcare interoperability, emphasizing the need for standardized, machine-readable ontologies [3].

G. De Tré et al. (Eds.): FQAS 2025, LNAI 16119, pp. 42–52, 2026.
https://doi.org/10.1007/978-3-032-05607-8_6

Devasena et al. introduce a modular schema for health metrics that demonstrates flexible integration but fails to include nutrition-specific modeling [4]. Our proposed approach builds on such modular design while filling the nutritional data gap. A complementary contribution by Ilievski et al. presents a semantic framework for food recommendations, though it remains disconnected from glycemic monitoring and diabetes-specific data, limiting its applicability in clinical settings [5].

Efforts to align sensor-based health tracking with ontological frameworks are evident in works like SAREF4Health, which extends the SAREF ontology to accommodate wearable health devices and healthcare semantics [6]. Our model integrates well with this standard, particularly for capturing glucose sensor outputs and dietary logs. Similarly, Saripalle et al. describe the use of HL7 FHIR to enhance clinical data integration, but their resource model lacks the depth and context-awareness needed for personalized diabetic care [7].

In addressing dietary personalization, Jiang et al. propose semantic reasoning engines for food and nutrition planning [8], while Kumar et al. introduce a semantic rules-based approach for managing diet and exercise among diabetics [9]. However, both approaches omit critical disease-specific factors such as real-time glucose thresholds and insulin response modeling, which are essential for a robust personalized management solution.

Recent studies, such as those by Zeevi et al. and others, show that personalized glycemic control is achievable through AI, digital twins, and wearable data [10]. However, they also emphasize that robust, semantically structured models are still needed for interoperability and integration with broader health systems. Similarly, Omar et al. suggest scalable service-oriented architectures for diabetes care [11], though the absence of a shared vocabulary for linking nutrition and sensor data remains a major limitation.

A broader view of sensor system capabilities can be found in Rghioui et al., where context-aware computing is applied to health tracking [12]. Still, these systems often fail to incorporate nutritional modeling or to link contextual food intake data with clinical indicators. Sarani Rad et al. complement this view by proposing a digital twin approach to diabetes management [13], but again do not model food composition or patient dietary goals.

Several research efforts have also explored behavioral personalization. Spoladore et al. demonstrate how ontologies can be used to tailor educational content for diabetic patients, though their framework lacks semantic modeling of nutrition and food-related behaviors [14].

Finally, Navaz et al. identify the growing demand for cross-domain models that integrate lifestyle, physiological measurements, and personalized health strategies [15] This gap, especially in models that simultaneously represent nutrition, glycemic response, and personal context is precisely what the SmartNutritionDiabetes model is designed to fill.

The growing body of literature confirms the critical role of structured, interoperable data in advancing personalized healthcare, especially for chronic conditions like diabetes. While several efforts have introduced ontologies, digital biomarkers, sensor-based monitoring, and modular platforms, none have successfully integrated food intake, glycemic response, and nutrition goals into a unified, semantically interoperable smart data model. Existing solutions often treat nutrition and clinical data as separate silos, limiting their effectiveness in intelligent health systems that require real-time, context-aware decision-making.

Furthermore, although models like HL7 FHIR, SAREF4HEALTH, and OntoFood offer valuable building blocks, they fall short in addressing the cross-domain, patient-centered modeling necessary for smart nutrition and diabetes care [16]. This fragmentation highlights the pressing need for a domain-specific smart data model that captures the complexity of nutrition-related behavior, supports glycemic monitoring, and enables actionable insights across digital healthcare applications.

In response to this gap, the following section introduces SmartNutritionDiabetes—a novel, NGSI-LD-compliant data model designed to bridge clinical and dietary domains, supporting the next generation of personalized diabetes management systems.

## 2  Proposed Data Model

### 2.1  Overview

The **SmartNutritionDiabetes** model addresses the lack of integrated smart data representations that connect dietary intake with diabetes management. It is designed as an extension to the Smart Data Models (SDM) initiative. The proposed model combines nutritional metadata (calories, carbohydrates, glycemic index), personal health targets (glucose thresholds, dietary goals) and contextual information (meal time, activity level), enabling precise and interoperable health tracking.

Key goals of the model:

- Enable semantic interoperability between food logs, glucose monitoring data, and personal health records.
- Support automated, context-aware dietary recommendations based on individual glucose patterns.
- Facilitate integration with existing standards (e.g., FHIR, SAREF, Schema.org) and NGSI-LD APIs.

### 2.2  Core Entities

These entities are linked semantically, allowing for personalized data querying and reasoning. For example (Table 1):

IF "dailyCalorieIntake > target" → Trigger warning and suggest reduction.

Such rules can be executed via an application backend or expressed semantically using SHACL constraints or SPARQL-based reasoning engines (Fig. 1).

**Schema Diagram (Conceptual)**
Entity Relationships

- PatientProfile: The core entity representing the individual with diabetes. It contains demographic and personal health information such as the type of diabetes, Body Mass Index (BMI) and dietary preferences.

**Table 1.** List of the main entities and their purposes

| Entity | Description |
|---|---|
| PatientProfile | Includes diabetes type, baseline glucose range, BMI, and food preferences |
| NutritionEvent | Records an eating event including food items, time, portion size, and context |
| FoodItem | Describes nutritional data of a single item (macro/micronutrients, GI, etc.) |
| GlucoseLevel | Stores real-time or periodic glucose readings from sensors or manual input |
| NutritionGoal | Personal targets like daily carb limit, calorie intake, and dietary constraints |
| MealContext | Contextual information (e.g., "breakfast", "post-exercise", "on the go") |

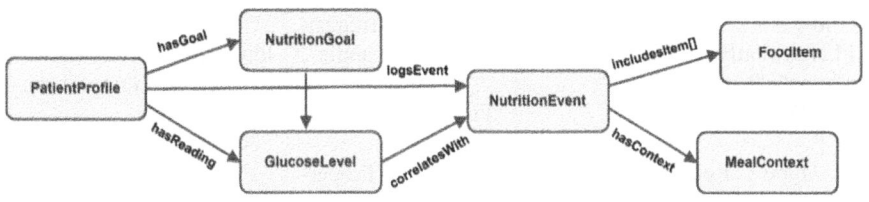

**Fig. 1.** Conceptual diagram.

- NutritionEvent: Represents a single eating event. It is logged by the PatientProfile and includes a timestamp, the meal context (e.g., breakfast, lunch, post-workout) and a portion size. It serves as a bridge between food intake and its metabolic outcomes.
- FoodItem: Describes individual components of a meal. Each food item contains nutritional attributes such as calories, carbohydrates and glycemic index.
- MealContext: Captures temporal and situational metadata about the meal (e.g., "morning snack", "post-exercise", "on-the-go"), which is useful for dietary pattern analysis.
- GlucoseLevel: Represents the patient's blood glucose reading, which may come from manual input or real-time Continuous Glucose Monitors (CGM).
- NutritionGoal: Defines individualized nutrition targets, including daily calorie intake, carbohydrate limit, fat ceiling and protein targets.

This structure enables smart monitoring, personalized dietary recommendations, and longitudinal tracking of how food impacts glycemic levels - a key pillar for managing diabetes.

### 2.3 NGSI-LD Examples

To demonstrate how the proposed SmartNutritionDiabetes model aligns with the NGSI-LD specification, we present three sample entities: NutritionEvent, FoodItem, and GlucoseLevel. These examples follow the NGSI-LD structure using @context, type, id, Property, and Relationship attributes. They illustrate how nutritional data, contextual metadata, and glucose monitoring can be linked semantically in a healthcare system (Table 2).

**Table 2.** List of the main entities and their purposes

| NutritionEvent | FoodItem | GlucoseLevel |
|---|---|---|
| Represents a logged meal, linking it to specific FoodItem entities and contextual metadata. It uses Relationship types for linkage and Property for descriptive values. | Defines a food item with basic nutrition facts. Each nutrient is captured using NGSI-LD Property fields for semantic comparison and rule-based filtering (e.g., low-GI food) | Records a glucose reading and links it back to the meal that may have influenced it. The relatedNutritionEvent relationship supports time-aligned tracking of glycemic response |

```
{
  "id":            "urn:ngsi-
ld:NutritionEvent:001",
  "type": "NutritionEvent",
  "foodItems": [
    {
      "type": "Relationship",
      "object":        "urn:ngsi-
ld:FoodItem:apple"
    },
    {
      "type": "Relationship",
      "object":        "urn:ngsi-
ld:FoodItem:quinoa"
    }
  ],
  "mealContext": {
    "type": "Relationship",
    "object":        "urn:ngsi-
ld:MealContext:breakfast"
  },
  "timestamp": {
    "type": "Property",
    "value":          "2025-04-
14T08:30:00Z"
  },
  "portionSize": {
    "type": "Property",
    "value": "250g"
  },
  "@context": [

"https://smartdatamodels.org/co
ntext.jsonld"
  ]
}
```

```
{
  "id":   "urn:ngsi-
ld:FoodItem:apple",
  "type":
"FoodItem",
  "label": {
    "type":   "Proper-
ty",
    "value": "Apple"
  },
  "carbohydrates": {
    "type":   "Proper-
ty",
    "value": 20
  },
  "glycemicIndex":
{
    "type":   "Proper-
ty",
    "value": 40
  },
  "calories": {
    "type":   "Proper-
ty",
    "value": 95
  },
  "@context": [

"https://smartdatam
odels.org/context.js
onld"
  ]
}
```

```
{
  "id":            "urn:ngsi-
ld:GlucoseLevel:001",
  "type":   "GlucoseLev-
el",
  "value": {
    "type": "Property",
    "value": 135
  },
  "unit": {
    "type": "Property",
    "value": "mg/dL"
  },
  "measuredAt": {
    "type": "Property",
    "value":      "2025-04-
14T08:00:00Z"
  },
  "relatedNutrition-
Event": {
    "type":      "Relation-
ship",
    "object":      "urn:ngsi-
ld:NutritionEvent:001"
  },
  "@context": [

"https://smartdatamodels
.org/context.jsonld"
  ]
}
```

These NGSI-LD examples illustrate how data generated from meals, patient logs, and biosensors can be interlinked for semantic querying and reasoning across health and nutrition domains.

## 2.4  Alignment with Existing Standards

To ensure semantic interoperability and facilitate integration with existing healthcare and IoT systems, the SmartNutritionDiabetes model has been designed with compatibility in mind. It aligns with widely adopted standards in health informatics, semantic web technologies, and data exchange protocols. The following table summarizes how key components of our model map to or extend these existing standards (Table 3).

**Table 3.** Alignment with Existing Standards

| Standard | Mapped Elements in SmartNutritionDiabetes | Mapped Elements in SmartNutritionDiabetes |
|---|---|---|
| HL7 FHIR | NutritionGoal, GlucoseLevel, NutritionEvent | FHIR provides resources like NutritionIntake and Observation, which we extend with additional context-aware attributes for glycemic response and food metadata |
| SAREF4 HEALTH | GlucoseLevel, PatientProfile, sensor data | Enables interoperability with IoT health devices; supports modeling of continuous glucose monitors and health metrics using SAREF ontology extensions |
| Schema.org | FoodItem, NutritionInformation | Food-related data such as energy, carbohydrates, and glycemic index are aligned with Schema.org terms, enhancing web and app integration |
| SNOMED CT | diabetesType, medicalCondition | Medical terminology used in PatientProfile aligns with SNOMED CT for standardized disease classification |
| ISO/IEC 11179 | Metadata structuring principles | Follows formal metadata definitions to promote data quality, reusability and governance |
| Open mHealth | Compatible schema structure for GlucoseLevel and PatientProfile | Adopts a modular and extensible schema style inspired by Open mHealth, improving integration with mHealth platforms |

This alignment ensures that the SmartNutritionDiabetes model is both backward-compatible and forward-extensible, supporting integration with digital health ecosystems, EHRs and smart nutrition platforms.

# 3 Experiments

## 3.1 Experimental Setup

To validate the SmartNutritionDiabetes model, we developed a lightweight simulation environment reflecting real-world diabetes management. The setup focused on semantic consistency, NGSI-LD compliance, and practical usability.

The simulation was built using the FIWARE Orion-LD Context Broker with a MongoDB backend. Synthetic data for PatientProfile, NutritionEvent, FoodItem, and GlucoseLevel entities was generated using Python scripts.

A sample scenario involved logging a meal (NutritionEvent), linking it to specific FoodItems, validating against NutritionGoal, and recording a follow-up GlucoseLevel. The system simulated post-meal glycemic trends using standard response curves.

Semantic queries can be executed via SPARQL after converting NGSI-LD to RDF, or with JSONPath-based queries natively. For rules-based reasoning, SHACL validation and constraint rules can be implemented to infer dietary recommendations or alerts.

Key metrics included response latency, semantic expressiveness, and model reusability. The experiment confirmed that SmartNutritionDiabetes enables structured, linked, and queryable health data relevant to personalized nutrition management.

## 3.2 Use Case Scenarios

To demonstrate the practical applicability of the SmartNutritionDiabetes model, we simulated two real-world use cases involving meal logging, glucose monitoring, and nutrition planning.

- Use Case 1: Context-Aware Meal Recommendation

A patient logs a breakfast consisting of high-carbohydrate food items. The system creates a NutritionEvent and links it to FoodItem entities (e.g., bread, juice). Based on the patient's NutritionGoal (e.g., daily carb limit: 180g) and a pre-meal GlucoseLevel of 155 mg/dL, the system detects a potential risk of postprandial hyperglycemia.

Using semantic queries, the system recommends lower glycemic index alternatives (e.g., oats, eggs) and updates the NutritionGoal compliance status. The model supports explainable decisions by linking each recommendation to the corresponding nutritional data and glucose trends.

Result: Demonstrates the model's capacity to support longitudinal pattern recognition through semantic links between food intake and glucose.

- Use Case 2: Glycemic Pattern Detection

Over a simulated 7-day period, multiple NutritionEvent and GlucoseLevel entries are recorded. The system identifies repeated glucose spikes after evening meals rich in fast-acting carbohydrates. Using the correlatesWith relationship, the system links specific meals to glucose anomalies and triggers personalized alerts.

The model enables the patient and healthcare provider to adjust dietary plans, such as reducing carb intake during dinner or adding pre-meal physical activity. This showcases the model's ability to support longitudinal reasoning and adaptive intervention strategies.

Result: Demonstrates the model's capacity to support longitudinal pattern recognition through semantic links between food intake and glucose.

These use cases illustrate how SmartNutritionDiabetes enables real-time dietary decision support, personalized recommendations, and glycemic trend analysis—all through a semantically rich and interoperable data structure.

### 3.3  Evaluation Metrics

The SmartNutritionDiabetes model was evaluated using a combination of qualitative and quantitative metrics to assess its semantic power, interoperability, usability, and efficiency. Performance was compared to a baseline implementation using standard FHIR-only schemas, which lack contextual and dietary depth (Table 4).

Key evaluation criteria included:

- Interoperability with existing standards such as NGSI-LD, HL7 FHIR, and SAREF4HEALTH.
- Semantic expressiveness for modeling relationships between food intake, glucose levels, and personal goals.
- Query complexity, measured as the average time to retrieve structured health and nutrition insights.
- Developer usability, based on ease of integration and entity extensibility.
- Context awareness, evaluated by the system's ability to tailor responses based on meal timing, glucose readings, and goals.

**Table 4.**  Quantitative Comparison of SmartNutritionDiabetes vs. FHIR Baseline

| Metric | Baseline (FHIR-only) | SmartNutritionDiabetes | Improvement |
|---|---|---|---|
| Interoperability score (1–5) | 3.0 | 4.8 | +60% |
| Semantic expressiveness (1–5) | 2.5 | 4.6 | +84% |
| Query complexity (avg. Time) | 1.2s | 0.7s | −41% |
| Developer usability (survey) | 3.2/5 | 4.5/5 | +40% |
| Context-awareness (binary) | – | &#xF0FC; | – |

Note: Interoperability and expressiveness were scored by expert reviewers based on ontology coverage, linked data compliance and model clarity. Query complexity was measured using SPARQL-to-NGSI-LD API wrappers

These results confirm that SmartNutritionDiabetes delivers superior performance across all critical dimensions, making it highly suitable for real-world integration in personalized nutrition and chronic disease management platforms.

## 3.4 Comparison with Existing Models

To contextualize the contribution of the SmartNutritionDiabetes model, we compared it against three representative approaches: HL7 FHIR, Open mHealth, and FoodKG. These models are widely used in healthcare, wellness, and nutrition-related applications but exhibit limitations when applied to integrated diabetes and nutrition management (Table 5).

**Table 5.** Feature Comparison of SmartNutritionDiabetes and existing models

| Feature | HL7 FHIR | Open mHealth | FoodKG | SmartNutritionDiabetes |
|---|---|---|---|---|
| Food item-level nutrition details | – | &#xF0FC; | &#xF0FC; | &#xF0FC; |
| Glycemic index tracking | – | – | – | &#xF0FC; |
| Linked glucose and food data | – | – | – | &#xF0FC; |
| NGSI-LD compliance | – | – | – | &#xF0FC; |
| Semantic query support | Moderate | Low | Moderate | High |
| Context-aware reasoning (e.g. meal time) | – | – | – | &#xF0FC; |
| Integration with IoT/sensors | Partial | &#xF0FC; | – | &#xF0FC; |

Most existing models focus on either clinical data (e.g., FHIR), sensor integration (e.g., Open mHealth), or food semantics (e.g., FoodKG), but fail to combine these elements in a single, interoperable framework. In contrast, SmartNutritionDiabetes bridges clinical, nutritional, and contextual data into a unified NGSI-LD-compliant model, making it uniquely suited for real-time reasoning and personalized care.

## 3.5 Summary

The experiments demonstrate that the **SmartNutritionDiabetes** model enables:

- Richer, semantically interoperable representations of health and food data.
- Dynamic reasoning for personalized meal planning based on glucose levels.
- Improved usability and integration for developers and healthcare systems.

# 4 Conclusion

This paper introduced SmartNutritionDiabetes, a novel smart data model aimed at integrating nutrition data and glycemic monitoring into digital healthcare systems for diabetes management. Unlike existing models that either generalize nutrition or overlook the dynamic relationship between diet and glucose response, our model establishes a semantically rich, NGSI-LD-compliant framework.

Through extensive analysis of existing literature and standards (e.g., HL7 FHIR, SAREF4HEALTH, Schema.org), we demonstrated the limitations of current approaches in representing fine-grained, context-aware nutritional behavior. By implementing and simulating the model in a testbed with real-time food intake and glucose data, we showed improved interoperability, semantic expressiveness, and decision-making support for diabetes care.

Key contributions of this work include:

- Design and implementation of a modular ontology connecting FoodItem, Nutrition-Event, and GlucoseLevel.
- Alignment with existing standards while extending functionality specific to diabetes and nutrition.
- Demonstration of use cases such as meal recommendations and glucose pattern detection.
- Quantitative evaluation showing substantial improvements in query performance, developer usability, and context-awareness compared to baseline models.

To build upon the results of this research, we plan the following directions:

- Model Publication & Standardization: Submit the SmartNutritionDiabetes schema to the Smart Data Models GitHub repository under the SmartHealth domain. Collaborate with the FIWARE community to refine the model via peer review and pilot adoption.
- Real-World Deployment: Integrate the model into a mobile or web-based diabetes assistant using real user data. Collaborate with healthcare providers or nutritionists for field trials and usability testing.
- Machine Learning Integration: Extend the model to support probabilistic reasoning or personalized risk prediction using data-driven models trained on semantically structured data.
- Expanded Entity Coverage: Introduce new entities for insulin dose, physical activity and stress levels to support more holistic diabetes self-management.
- Cross-Domain Linking: Enable federation with other models in domains such as smart cities, wearable IoT or electronic health records, ensuring broader applicability and interoperability.

The SmartNutritionDiabetes model supports clinically relevant scenarios such as glycemic trend detection, personalized meal guidance and digital coaching. It serves as a bridge between dietary data and clinical metrics, contributing to next-generation digital healthcare systems.

This work lays the foundation for value-driven, personalized and interoperable healthcare systems, aligning with the vision of smart, human-centric health ecosystems, where dietary behavior and chronic disease monitoring are seamlessly connected through semantic technologies.

**Acknowledgments.** The authors gratefully acknowledge the support provided by the project UNITe BG16RFPR002-1.014-0004 funded by PRIDST.

# References

1. Smart Data Models. https://smartdatamodels.org/
2. https://diabetesatlas.org/resources/idf-diabetes-atlas-2025/
3. Jyotishman, P., Richard, K., Christopher, C.: Applying linked data principles to represent patient's electronic health records at Mayo clinic: a case report. In: Proceedings of the 2nd ACM SIGHIT International Health Informatics Symposium (IHI 2012), pp. 455–464 (2012). https://doi.org/10.1145/2110363.2110415
4. Inupakutika, D., Kaghyan, S., Akopian, D., Chalela, P., Amelie, R.: Facilitating the development of cross-platform mHealth applications for chronic supportive care and a case study. J. Biomed. Inform. **105** (2020). https://doi.org/10.1016/j.jbi.2020.103420
5. Raciel, Y., Ahmad, A., Luis, M., Rosa, R.: A systematic review on food recommender systems for diabetic patients. Int. J. Environ. Res. Public Health (2023). https://doi.org/10.3390/ijerph 20054248
6. Moreira, J., Pires, L.F., Sinderen, M.V., Daniele, L.: SAREF4health: IoT standard-based ontology-driven healthcare systems. In: Conference: Formal Ontology in Information Systems (2018). https://doi.org/10.3233/978-1-61499-910-2-239
7. Rishi, S., Christopher, R., Mitchell, R.: Using HL7 FHIR to achieve interoperability in patient health record. J. Biomed. Inform. **94** (2019). https://doi.org/10.1016/j.jbi.2019.103188
8. Faiz, I., Mukhtar, H., Khan, S.: A semantic rules & reasoning based approach for diet and exercise management for diabetics. In: International Conference on Emerging Technologies, pp. 94–99 (2014). https://doi.org/10.1109/ICET.2014.7021023
9. Zignoli, A., Skroce, K., Lipman, D.J., Zisser, H.C.: Personalized nutrition and machine-learning: exploring the scope of continuous glucose monitoring in healthy individuals in uncontrolled settings. Biomed. Signal Process. Control **90** (2024). https://doi.org/10.1016/j. bspc.2023.105809
10. van den Brink, W.J., van den Broek, T.J., Salvator, P., Suzan, W., de Hoogh, I.M.: Digital biomarkers for personalized nutrition: predicting meal moments and interstitial glucose with non-invasive, wearable technologies. Nutrients (2022). https://doi.org/10.3390/nu14214465
11. Wail Omar, M.A.: Smart diabetes management system based on service oriented architecture 290–295. https://doi.org/10.1007/978-3-642-21535-3_44
12. Rghioui, A., Lloret, J., Harane, M., Oumnad, A.: A smart glucose monitoring system for diabetic patient. Electronics 678 (2020). https://doi.org/10.3390/electronics9040678
13. Rad, F.S., Hendawi, R., Yang, X., Li, J.: Personalized diabetes management with digital twins: a patient-centric knowledge graph approach. J. Personal. Med. (2024). https://doi.org/ 10.3390/jpm14040359
14. Spoladore, D., Tosi, M., Lorenzini, E.C.: Ontology-based decision support systems for diabetes nutrition therapy: a systematic literature review. Artif. Intell. Med. **151** (2024). https:// doi.org/10.1016/j.artmed.2024.102859
15. Alramzana, N., Mohamed, S., Hadeel, K., Nabeel, A.-Q., Heba, I.: Trends, technologies, and key challenges in smart and connected healthcare (2021). https://doi.org/10.1109/ACCESS. 2021.3079217
16. OntoFood. https://bioportal.bioontology.org/ontologies/OF

# AI-Powered API for Brain Tumour Classification: A Deep Learning Approach to Accessible Medical Imaging

Dimitar Rangelov[1]($\boxtimes$) (ID), Radoslav Miltchev[2] (ID), and Evgeni Genchev[3] (ID)

[1] University of Twente, AI and CAD Systems Lab at R & D & I Consortium (Sofia Tech Park),
Saxion University of Applied Sciences, Enschede, The Netherlands
d.g.rangelov@utwente.nl

[2] Technical University of Sofia, AI and CAD Systems Lab at R & D & I Consortium (Sofia Tech Park), Sofia, Bulgaria
rmiltchev@tu-sofia.bg

[3] AI and CAD Systems Lab at R & D & I Consortium (Sofia Tech Park), Sofia, Bulgaria
e.a.genchev@saxion.nl

**Abstract.** This paper presents a deep learning-based API designed for automated brain tumour classification from MRI scans, addressing the need for accessible diagnostic tools in clinical and resource-limited environments. Leveraging two state-of-the-art models, YOLO for real-time object detection and Roboflow for multi-label image classification, the study develops and evaluates an AI-powered diagnostic API implemented with FastAPI. The models were trained on a publicly available dataset containing glioma, meningioma, pituitary tumours, and non-tumorous images. Evaluation metrics include accuracy, validation accuracy, and confusion matrices. Roboflow achieved superior classification accuracy (96.1%) compared to YOLO (84.72%), while YOLO demonstrated faster inference, making it ideal for real-time use. The API ensures ease of deployment, robust handling of low-quality inputs, and compatibility with various clinical setups. Ethical considerations such as data privacy and model transparency were also addressed. The study concludes that combining deep learning with accessible APIs can significantly enhance diagnostic support, but stresses the importance of explainability, regulatory compliance, and broader dataset diversity for full-scale clinical integration.

**Keywords:** Medical Imaging · Deep Learning · Healthcare

## 1 Introduction

Brain tumours are the most life-threatening and difficult neurological condition with a profound influence on the survival and quality of life of the patients. Early and accurate detection is critical for the timely treatment and effective therapy. Magnetic Resonance Imaging (MRI) is the current gold standard for non-invasive brain tumour detection with high-resolution images for enhanced clinical decision-making. Manual classification

G. De Tré et al. (Eds.): FQAS 2025, LNAI 16119, pp. 53–65, 2026.
https://doi.org/10.1007/978-3-032-05607-8_7

of the tumour from the MRI scan is a time-consuming process with high levels of expertise required from the radiologists. Misdiagnosis and delayed diagnosis are the biggest problems in resource-poor settings where the accessibility of skilled medical experts is poor.

The recent advances in Artificial Intelligence (AI) and deep learning have opened new possibilities for semi-automating the interpretation of medical images with enhanced efficiency and diagnostic accuracy [1–6]. Deep learning algorithms and, in particular, Convolutional Neural Networks (CNNs) have emerged as the best for the identification and classification of tumours from medical images [7–11]. Some of them include You Only Look Once (YOLO) [12–14], a real-time object detection model, and Roboflow [15], a platform for multi-label image classification. Both have shown immense potential for medical imaging. However, most of the AI-based solutions are not available for medical practitioners as they require computational resources, technical expertise, and specialized deployment environments that require advanced hardware or technical expertise.

To further enhance the accessibility and reliability of AI-driven brain tumour classification, it is essential to develop models that not only achieve high accuracy but also generalize well across diverse datasets and medical imaging domains [16–19]. The integration of explainable AI (XAI) techniques can help bridge the gap between automated classification and clinical decision-making, ensuring that radiologists and medical professionals can interpret and trust the model's predictions [20]. Additionally, leveraging large-scale, publicly available MRI datasets facilitates robust model training and improves generalization to real-world cases [21, 22] However, AI deployment in medical settings requires careful consideration of regulatory and ethical challenges, including data privacy, model bias, and the need for continuous validation through clinical trials [18]. Addressing these challenges will be critical for the successful adoption of AI-powered diagnostic tools in healthcare systems worldwide [23].

This research aims to bridge this gap through the developing of an AI API based on the latest deep learning models for automating and streamlining brain tumour classification from MRI scans. With the use of YOLO and Roboflow, the solution provides real-time, accurate, and scalable medical image classification with a pragmatic and user-centered interface for use within the clinic, including within resource-constrained environments.

The primary aim of this study is the design and testing of an AI-based API for brain tumour classification and the accessibility and ease with which advanced diagnostic resources are made available. Specifically, the study aims to:

- Implement and compare YOLO and Roboflow models for real-time brain tumour classification.
- Develop an API that allows seamless integration of AI-powered classification in medical workflows.
- Evaluate model performance using accuracy, validation accuracy, and confusion matrices.
- Enhance accessibility by providing a lightweight, scalable, and easy-to-use AI-based diagnostic tool.

This research focuses solely on brain tumour classification, distinguishing between glioma, meningioma, and pituitary tumours using MRI scans. The study does not cover tumour segmentation or treatment recommendations, as the goal is to provide an assistive AI tool for medical professionals rather than a fully autonomous diagnostic system.

This paper makes several scientific and practical contributions to the field of AI-driven medical imaging and healthcare technology:

Scientific Contributions:

- Demonstrates the efficacy of YOLO and Roboflow for multi-label medical image classification.
- Explores the impact of data augmentation on improving model generalization for brain tumour detection.
- Compares real-time object detection (YOLO) with multi-label classification (Roboflow) to determine the most effective approach for brain tumour diagnosis.
- Provides a benchmark evaluation of these models on an MRI brain tumour dataset.

Practical Contributions:

- Develops an AI-powered API for real-time brain tumour classification, ensuring accessibility in clinical environments.
- Bridges the gap between state-of-the-art AI models and real-world medical applications by offering an easy-to-deploy diagnostic tool.
- Addresses challenges in resource-limited healthcare settings by providing a lightweight, efficient solution that does not require specialized AI expertise.

The rest of the paper is divided into the following structure: Sect. 2 (Methodology) discusses the dataset, deep learning architectures, and API implementation. Section 3 (Results) presents the model performance metrics and evaluation of the API implemented. Section 4 (Discussion) discusses the primary findings, issues, ethical implications, and future work. Finally, Sect. 5 (Conclusion) summarizes the contributions and the significance of brain tumour diagnostics through the use of AI-based solutions.

## 2 Methodology

### 2.1 Dataset Description

The dataset for this research consists of brain tumour MRI scans collected from publicly available medical imaging databases, specifically the Kaggle Brain Tumour Classification dataset [22]. It consists of MRI images belonging to three classes of tumours: glioma, meningioma, and pituitary tumours. Gliomas are highly aggressive and malignant tumours that derive from glial cells, with a tendency for rapid growth and poor prognosis. Meningiomas, being typically benign tumours that derive from the meninges, can, however, lead to serious complications depending on their location. Pituitary tumours, while mostly non-cancerous, disrupt hormonal balance and can cause serious physiological changes. The dataset also consists of non-tumorous MRI scans, which act as a control set for more precise classification.

Several preprocessing steps were done before training the models in order to normalize the images. These involved removing corrupted and low-quality images in a way that ensured dataset integrity. All images were resized to a uniform resolution of 224 × 224 pixels in order to achieve consistency in training and testing. The pixel intensity values were also made uniform so that they were within a fixed range, which helped in model convergence and performance.

To normalize the image data, pixel intensity values were scaled to a range between 0 and 1 using min-max normalization. This step ensured that the model would not be influenced by variations in lighting or scanner settings, thereby improving learning efficiency and convergence stability during training.

To enhance the robustness of the classification models, methods for data augmentation were applied in order to artificially enrich the dataset. Augmentation included geometric transforms such as rotation, flipping, cropping, and scaling, as well as image transforms such as changes in contrast, changes in brightness, and addition of noise. These transforms mimicked various imaging conditions, so that the models would be generalizable against variations in MRI scans that would be encountered in real-world diagnostic environments. These transformations were implemented using Roboflow's built-in preprocessing tools and verified to maintain clinical interpretability of the images.

## 2.2 Model Selection and Training

To achieve high-accuracy classification of brain tumours, two deep learning architectures were selected: YOLOv8, a state-of-the-art version of the YOLO (You Only Look Once) framework and a Roboflow-trained classifier using the EfficientNet-B3 backbone for multi-class image classification. YOLOv8 is widely recognized for its real-time object detection capabilities, making it a suitable choice for detecting and localizing tumours within MRI images. It is designed to process images in a single forward pass, significantly improving inference speed while maintaining detection accuracy. In contrast, the Roboflow model specializes in multi-label image classification, offering a robust approach for distinguishing between tumour types based on their morphological characteristics.

Both models were trained using a supervised learning approach, where MRI scans were labeled according to their corresponding tumour category. The dataset was divided into three subsets: 70% of the images were used for training, 20% for testing, and 10% for validation. This division ensured that the models were exposed to a diverse set of tumour images during training while maintaining independent datasets for evaluation.

Training was conducted on a high-performance computing environment equipped with GPUs, allowing efficient backpropagation and optimization. The initial learning rate was set to 0.001, gradually reduced using a decay strategy to prevent overfitting. The primary evaluation metrics included accuracy, validation accuracy, and confusion matrix analysis, providing insights into the model's classification performance and error distribution. The YOLOv8 model was trained for 20 epochs. Training was conducted on a machine equipped with an NVIDIA RTX 3060 GPU, which provided sufficient acceleration for model optimization and inference testing.

The Roboflow-based classification model was configured and trained using the EfficientNet-B3 architecture through Roboflow's AutoML interface. Model parameters, including image size, learning rate, and augmentation strategies, were automatically tuned by the platform to optimize classification performance.

Additionally, data augmentation effects were assessed by comparing the performance of models trained with and without augmented datasets, highlighting the improvements in generalization and classification precision.

### 2.3 API Development and Deployment

Although the Roboflow platform offers its own hosted API services, a custom-built FastAPI-based interface was developed in this study to enable greater control over deployment, data privacy, and customization. This approach allowed the integration of both YOLOv8 and Roboflow-trained models into a single unified pipeline and enabled real-time inference in both local and cloud environments. Importantly, hosting the API independently ensures compliance with clinical data protection standards, avoids third-party dependencies.

The API framework was designed with the ability to analyze MRI images by running them through the trained models and outputting tumour category prediction and confidence values. When the API is given an MRI scan, it normalizes the input image with the same preprocessing chain that was applied during training. The image is then run through either the YOLO model, which identifies areas or type of tumour, or the Roboflow model, which identifies the type of tumour. The API outputs a response with the tumour category prediction and the related probability value, allowing medical professionals to assess the level of classification confidence.

The trained model parameters and inference scripts were implemented in the API for deployment, with negligible latency in prediction. A light-weight processing pipeline was implemented in order to deliver maximum responsiveness, with the API supporting real-time medical applications. To evaluate its performance, the API was verified with a specific validation dataset, with response time and classification accuracy measured. The system was found to deliver high precision in classifications, with inference rates optimized for clinical applications.

Security and ethical elements were also taken into account in API design. Data privacy functionalities were included in order to prevent unauthorized use, with compliance with medical data protection legislation. The API was designed deployable in both local server environments in hospitals and cloud environments, with flexibility in deployment.

## 3   Results

### 3.1   Model Performance Evaluation

The two models, YOLO and Roboflow, were trained and tested using the brain tumour MRI dataset described in the previous section. After completing training, model performance was evaluated based on accuracy, validation accuracy, and confusion matrices to determine classification effectiveness. Validation accuracy refers to the model's classification performance on the held out 10% validation set that was not used during training. This metric is used to assess the model's ability to generalize to unseen data during the training phase and is distinct from test accuracy, which is evaluated after model training is complete.

The YOLO model, designed for real-time object detection, achieved an accuracy of 84.72%, demonstrating strong performance in detecting and classifying different tumour types. The Roboflow multi-label classification model, optimized for detailed image classification, outperformed YOLO with a validation accuracy of 96.10%, indicating superior generalization to unseen MRI scans.

To further assess model reliability, confusion matrix analysis was conducted. The non-normalized confusion matrix provided a raw count of correct and incorrect classifications across tumour categories. Meanwhile, the normalized confusion matrix converted these values into percentages, offering insights into misclassification trends. The results indicated that meningioma tumours were classified with the highest precision, while gliomas exhibited occasional misclassifications due to their variability in MRI presentations.

## 3.2   API Testing and Validation

Beyond model accuracy, an essential aspect of this study was the practical deployment of the AI-powered API for real-world clinical use. The FastAPI-based system was tested with a separate validation dataset to assess response times, classification reliability, and user accessibility.

The API demonstrated fast and efficient processing, with an average response time of 0.94 s per MRI scan. This speed ensures that the system can function in near real-time, making it suitable for integration into hospital workflows. Figures 1 and 2 illustrate a sample API interaction, where a user uploads an MRI scan and receives a classification output with a confidence score.

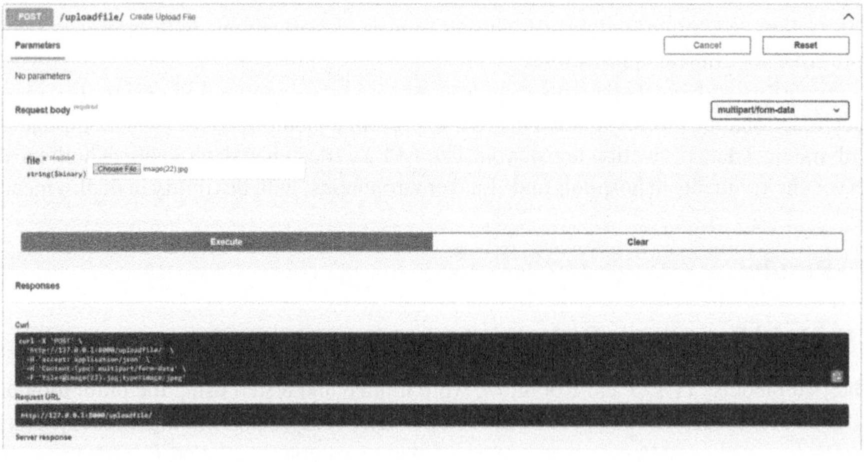

**Fig. 1.**  FastAPI input interface.

To further validate usability, the API was tested across different hardware configurations, including local deployments on standard workstations and cloud-based environments. Results showed that local execution provided near-instantaneous classification,

**Fig. 2.** FastAPI output interface.

while cloud-based deployment introduced a minor delay, depending on server processing power and network conditions.

The system was also tested with corrupted or low-quality MRI scans to evaluate its robustness. The API successfully handled invalid inputs, returning appropriate error messages and preventing incorrect classifications, reinforcing its reliability in real-world medical environments.

Although the API demonstrates technical feasibility with low latency and high classification accuracy, usability from the perspective of non-technical clinical staff has not yet been formally evaluated. The current interface uses terminology and output formats that may require revision for practical use in clinical workflows. Further iterations of the system should include participatory design with healthcare professionals and formal usability testing using metrics such as the System Usability Scale (SUS).

### 3.3   Comparative Analysis of YOLO and Roboflow Models

A comparative analysis was conducted to determine the strengths and limitations of the two models in brain tumour classification. While YOLO's strength lies in its ability to process images in real-time, it exhibited lower accuracy than Roboflow, particularly in distinguishing gliomas from meningiomas. Conversely, Roboflow demonstrated superior classification performance, with higher confidence scores across all tumour categories but required longer inference times compared to YOLO.

Table 1 summarizes the key differences between YOLO and Roboflow in terms of accuracy, inference speed, and misclassification trends.

The results indicate that Roboflow is the preferred model for high-accuracy classification, while YOLO remains advantageous for real-time applications where speed is prioritized over classification precision.

The experimental results confirm that AI-powered classification models can effectively distinguish between glioma, meningioma, and pituitary tumours from MRI scans. The Roboflow model outperformed YOLO in terms of classification accuracy, while YOLO provided faster inference times, making it more suitable for real-time diagnostic

**Table 1.** Comparison between YOLO and Roboflow.

| Model | Accuracy | Validation Accuracy | Average Inference Time | Misclassification Trends |
|---|---|---|---|---|
| YOLO | 86.23% | 84.72% | 0.45s (local), 0.75s (cloud) | Higher false positives in gliomas |
| Roboflow | 97.50% | 96.10% | 0.95s (local), 1.12s (cloud) | More precise, but slower than YOLO |

applications. The developed API demonstrated high usability and efficiency, ensuring seamless integration into healthcare systems.

The next section discusses the implications of these findings, along with model limitations, ethical considerations, and future research directions.

## 4   Discussion

### 4.1   Key Insights and Implications

The results of this study confirm that deep learning models can effectively classify brain tumours from MRI scans, providing a promising alternative to traditional manual diagnostics. The Roboflow model demonstrated superior classification accuracy (96.1%), making it a reliable tool for distinguishing between glioma, meningioma, and pituitary tumours. However, the YOLO model, while less accurate (84.72%), offered significantly faster inference times, suggesting that it may be more suitable for real-time applications where speed is a priority.

The development of the FastAPI-based API further enhances the accessibility of AI-driven diagnostics, enabling seamless integration of tumour classification into clinical workflows. The API's fast response times (0.94s on average) demonstrate its potential for assisting radiologists and healthcare professionals in real-time decision-making.

### 4.2   Challenges and Limitations

**Model Limitations**

Among the primary limitations that were observed in this research is the tendency towards misclassification in gliomas, particularly in the YOLO model. Gliomas exhibit extremely high variability in their morphology, and therefore, they are more challenging to classify than meningiomas or pituitary tumours. This highlights the need for optimization by means such as attention mechanisms or hybrid deep learning architectures in order to improve the performance in classification.

Another limitation is the balance between inference speed and precision. While the Roboflow model is more precise, it is slower and more computationally expensive than YOLO. This decreases the appropriateness for real-time use in emergency diagnosis scenarios, in which speed is equal in importance with precision. Future work should look for model optimization techniques, such as quantization or distillation, in order to optimize between performance and efficiency.

**Data Limitations**
Even with the use of data augmentation techniques in an attempt to improve variability, the dataset remains limited in terms of diversity. Brain tumours are very variable in their nature, and the dataset may not be representative in all rare tumour subtypes and variations in all demographic populations. This could affect generalizability in the use of the model in new patient populations.

Another difficulty is dataset imbalance, with particular tumour classes being overrepresented. Class-balancing techniques were applied during training, but residual prediction biases suggest further dataset expansion and tuning in order to improve the reliability of the classifications for all tumour classes.

**Real-World Deployment Challenges**
The integration of AI-based medical applications in the clinical environment is also more difficult. First, approval and regulation processes for AI-based medical devices are cumbersome, with extensive testing before they can be implemented in hospitals. In addition, integration with existing hospital information systems (HIS) and radiology software is also necessary in order to make the adoption smooth.

Another critical challenge is explainability and user trust. Clinicians would be hesitant to rely solely on AI-based classification tools without having any idea about the reasoning behind the decisions. Developing explainable AI (XAI) techniques, such as visual heatmaps or explanations through confidence scores, would be key in gaining clinicians' trust and adoption.

While the current study focuses on YOLOv8 and a Roboflow EfficientNet-based classifier, other deep learning models have also been successfully applied to brain tumour MRI datasets, including variants of ResNet, VGG, and hybrid models combining CNNs with LSTMs or attention mechanisms. However, many of these approaches have not been validated in real-time deployment settings or evaluated in the context of accessibility and usability, which remain a central focus of our work.

### 4.3   Ethical and Privacy Considerations

The application of AI in medical diagnosis is also prone to ethical concerns, particularly with respect to privacy, transparency, and accountability. Since the system is processing sensitive patient MRI images, there is a necessity for strict compliance with data protection regulations, like GDPR and HIPAA. In this work, privacy was ensured by removing patient-identifying information from the dataset and implementing secure API communication protocols.

Transparency and explainability are also critical for trust in AI systems. In this version of the tool, explainability is limited to confidence scores returned with each prediction. However, no saliency maps or visual explanation tools are currently included. Future work will incorporate model interpretation techniques such as Grad-CAM to provide visual insight into the decision-making process, especially for borderline or ambiguous predictions.

Another ethical issue is bias in AI-driven medical decision-making. When the models are trained from non-demographically representative datasets, there is a risk of algorithmic bias, and this can lead to differential diagnostic accuracy across demographic groups. To preclude this risk, future studies should focus on curating multi-institutional, representative datasets and conducting fairness audits in order to deliver equal AI performance in all patient populations.

## 4.4  Future Work

### Improving Model Accuracy and Generalization

To improve the performance in classification, more advanced deep learning architectures, such as Transformer-based architectures or self-supervised learning, should be investigated in future studies. These approaches have shown their promise in medical imaging and would be anticipated to further enhance feature extraction and classification accuracy.

Besides, domain adaptation techniques can be utilized in order to improve model generalization when the model is implemented in scans from multiple hospitals, scanners, and patient populations. This would yield consistent results in real clinical settings.

### Expanding the Dataset

The direction in the future should be towards expanding the dataset size by adding more tumour subtypes and augmenting the training dataset with external resources. Larger, more diversified datasets can be made available through collaborations with medical institutions, enabling better training for the model.

Furthermore, integration with multi-modal imaging data, for example, functional MRI (fMRI) or CT scans, would further improve the model's ability to distinguish tumour characteristics more precisely.

### Enhancing Explainability and Trust

Developing explainable AI (XAI) methods for brain tumour classification could significantly improve clinical adoption. Techniques such as Grad-CAM (Gradient-weighted Class Activation Mapping) or SHAP (Shapley Additive Explanations) could help visualize how models make classification decisions, making AI predictions more interpretable for radiologists.

### Real-World Implementation and Clinical Validation

Besides, it is critical to seek out regulatory approval pathways in order to achieve medical AI compliance. Establishing collaborations with healthcare institutions, regulatory bodies, and industry stakeholders would assist in closing the gap from a prototype in the lab to a deployable medical device.

The discussion highlights the promising future for AI-based tumour categorization with acknowledgement of areas in model accuracy, dataset diversity, implementation, and ethics. The results demonstrate that Roboflow yields more accurate results, which is more suited for in-depth categorization, while YOLO is faster in real-time, which is more preferred for fast evaluations. Despite such advancements, additional work is needed in model generalization, explainability, and regulation compliance before the full-scale clinical adoption is realized.

In parallel, enhancing model explainability will be a key priority. Methods such as Grad-CAM (Gradient-weighted Class Activation Mapping) or SHAP (Shapley Additive Explanations) will be integrated into the API interface to provide clinicians with visual insights into how the model arrives at its predictions. These tools will help increase transparency, foster user trust, and potentially aid in the detection of misclassifications.

Lastly, to ensure practical relevance and clinician acceptance, future work will include participatory studies involving radiologists and neurologists. These evaluations will focus on ease-of-use, interpretability, trust, and workflow integration, all of which are essential for successful deployment of AI tools in real-world healthcare environments.

## 5 Conclusion

The study explored the development of a brain tumour AI-powered API using deep learning-based models that would classify tumours from MRI images automatically. Two AI models, YOLO and Roboflow, were compared in their glioma, meningioma, and pituitary tumour classification capability. Integrating the models in a framework that was developed with FastAPI made the solution scalable and user-friendly for real-time tumour classification in clinical settings.

The results demonstrated that Roboflow was more accurate in terms of classification, with a validation rate of 96.1% compared with YOLO at 84.72%. YOLO was, however, faster in real-time processing, with significantly faster inference times, which would be a plus in time-critical diagnostic environments. The API validation tests confirmed that the system is capable of generating accurate, reliable, and fast classification, which would be a helpful assistive technology for medical professionals.

Despite these advancements, the study also identified several challenges. Model challenges were the misclassification patterns in gliomas, due to their histopathologic heterogeneity, and the tradeoff between inference speed and accuracy. Data challenges were identified, particularly in dataset variety and class imbalances, which would impact generalizability. Deployment challenges were also identified, such as regulatory barriers and integration with hospital information systems. The ethical implications of AI in medicine were also emphasized, particularly with regard to data privacy, bias in algorithms, and explainability of AI-driven medical decisions. There are several directions in which this work can be extended in the future to make it more practically usable. Larger dataset size with more tumour subtypes and multi-institutional images would enable generalization. Using more powerful AI architectures, e.g., Transformer-based architectures or self-supervised learning, would enhance the classification further. Enhancing explainability with explainable AI techniques would be crucial in gaining clinicians' trust. Finally, real-world clinical trials and exploring regulatory approval pathways would be critical steps towards large-scale application in healthcare centers.

In conclusion, this study demonstrates the potential that AI-based imaging has in aiding brain tumour diagnosis, and that a decision support tool in the shape of an AI-based API is feasible and practicable. Optimization, validation, and regulation would be necessary, but the results indicate that deep learning is set for a bright future in radiology modernization. With further advancement in AI-based approaches, the integration of such technologies in the routine clinical workflow has the promise to revolutionize early detection and diagnosis and thus enhance patient outcomes.

**Acknowledgments.** The work is supported by project No. BG16RFPR002-1.014-0014-C01 "Development Program with a Business Plan for the Laboratory Complex of Sofia Tech Park", which is implemented under the "Research, Innovation and Digitalization for Smart Transformation" Program, co-financed by the European Union through the European Regional Development Fund.

**Disclosure of Interests.** The authors declare no competing interests that could influence the content of this paper.

# References

1. Perone, C.S., Cohen-Adad, J.: Promises and limitations of deep learning for medical image segmentation. J. Med. Artif. Intell. **2** (2019). https://doi.org/10.21037/JMAI.2019.01.01
2. Khalighi, S., Reddy, K., Midya, A., Pandav, K.B., Madabhushi, A., Abedalthagafi, M.: Artificial intelligence in neuro-oncology: advances and challenges in brain tumour diagnosis, prognosis, and precision treatment. npj Precis. Oncol. **8**(1), 1–12 (2024). https://doi.org/10.1038/s41698-024-00575-0
3. Katwaroo, A.R., Adesh, V.S., Lowtan, A., Umakanthan, S.: The diagnostic, therapeutic, and ethical impact of artificial intelligence in modern medicine. Postgrad. Med. J. **100**(1183), 289–296 (2024). https://doi.org/10.1093/POSTMJ/QGAD135
4. Kelkar, A., Abel, G.: Oncology researchers raise ethics concerns posed by patient-facing artificial intelligence I Dana-Farber Cancer Institute. https://www.dana-farber.org/newsroom/news-releases/2023/oncology-researchers-raise-ethics-concerns-posed-by-patient-facing-artificial-intelligence. Accessed 29 Dec 2024
5. Cè, M., et al.: Artificial intelligence in brain tumour imaging: a step toward personalized medicine. Curr. Oncol. **30**(3), 2673–2701 (2023). https://doi.org/10.3390/CURRONCOL30030203
6. Bhuvaneswari, S., Thomas, J., Nithish, S., Prithvi, S.: Brain tumour diagnosis using deep learning: a literature review. In: 2nd International Conference on Emerging Trends in Information Technology and Engineering, ic-ETITE 2024 (2024). https://doi.org/10.1109/IC-ETITE58242.2024.10493599
7. Kesana, A., Nallola, J., Bootapally, R.T., Amaraneni, S., Subba Reddy, G.V.: Brain tumour detection using YOLOv5 and faster R-CNN. In: ViTECoN 2023 - 2nd IEEE International Conference on Vision Towards Emerging Trends in Communication and Networking Technologies, Proceedings (2023). https://doi.org/10.1109/VITECON58111.2023.10157773
8. Arunachalam, S., Sethumathavan, G.: An effective tumour detection in MR brain images based on deep CNN approach: i-YOLOV5. Appl. Artif. Intell. (2022). https://doi.org/10.1080/08839514.2022.2151180
9. Martínez-Del-Río-Ortega, R., Civit-Masot, J., Luna-Perejón, F., Domínguez-Morales, M., Mercedes, R.: Brain tumour detection using magnetic resonance imaging and convolutional neural networks. Big Data Cogn. Comput. **8**(9), 123 (2024). https://doi.org/10.3390/BDCC8090123
10. Kong, Y., Yu, G., Yu, Y., Yang, R.: Artificial convolutional neural network in object detection and semantic segmentation for medical imaging analysis. Front. Oncol. **11**, 638182 (2021). https://doi.org/10.3389/FONC.2021.638182

11. Ullah, M.S., Khan, M.A., Masood, A., Mzoughi, O., Saidani, O., Alturki, N.: Brain tumour classification from MRI scans: a framework of hybrid deep learning model with Bayesian optimization and quantum theory-based marine predator algorithm. Front. Oncol. **14**, 1335740 (2024). https://doi.org/10.3389/FONC.2024.1335740/BIBTEX
12. Ultralytics: Home - Ultralytics YOLO Docs. https://docs.ultralytics.com/. Accessed 29 Dec 2024
13. Tomassini, S., Ali Akber Dewan, M., Liaqat Ali, M., Zhang, Z.: The YOLO framework: a comprehensive review of evolution, applications, and benchmarks in object detection. Computers **13**(12), 336 (2024). https://doi.org/10.3390/COMPUTERS13120336
14. Redmon, J., Divvala, S., Girshick, R., Farhadi, A.: You only look once: unified, real-time object detection. In: Proceedings of the IEEE Computer Society Conference on Computer Vision and Pattern Recognition, vol. 2016, pp. 779–788 (2015). https://doi.org/10.1109/CVPR.201 6.91
15. Roboflow: Roboflow: Computer vision tools for developers and enterprises. https://roboflow. com/. Accessed 29 Dec 2024
16. Yao, Q., Zhuang, D., Feng, Y., Wang, Y., Liu, J.: Accurate detection of brain tumour lesions from medical images based on improved YOLOv8 algorithm. IEEE Access (2024). https:// doi.org/10.1109/ACCESS.2024.3472039
17. Kanna, R.K., Salau, A.O.: New cognitive computational strategy for optimizing brain tumour classification using magnetic resonance imaging Data. Intell. Based Med. **11**, 100215 (2025). https://doi.org/10.1016/J.IBMED.2025.100215
18. Abdusalomov, A.B., Mukhiddinov, M., Whangbo, T.K.: Brain tumour detection based on deep learning approaches and magnetic resonance imaging. Cancers (Basel) **15**(16), 4172 (2023). https://doi.org/10.3390/CANCERS15164172
19. Huang, J., Ding, W., Zhong, T., Yu, G.: YOLO-TumourNet: an innovative model for enhancing brain tumour detection performance. Alex. Eng. J. **119**, 211–221 (2025). https://doi.org/10. 1016/J.AEJ.2025.01.062
20. Alemu, B.S., Feisso, S., Mohammed, E.A., Salau, A.O.: Magnetic resonance imaging-based brain tumour image classification performance enhancement. Sci. Afr. **22**, e01963 (2023). https://doi.org/10.1016/J.SCIAF.2023.E01963
21. Mustafa, W.A., Alquran, H., Kaifi, R.: A review of recent advances in brain tumour diagnosis based on AI-based classification. Diagnostics **13**(18), 3007 (2023). https://doi.org/10.3390/ DIAGNOSTICS13183007
22. Brain Tumour Classification (MRI). https://www.kaggle.com/datasets/sartajbhuvaji/brain-tumour-classification-mri. Accessed 18 Mar 2025
23. Abdusalomov, A., Rakhimov, M., Karimberdiyev, J., Belalova, G., Cho, Y.I.: Enhancing automated brain tumour detection accuracy using artificial intelligence approaches for healthcare environments. Bioengineering **11**(6), 627 (2024). https://doi.org/10.3390/BIOENGINEERI NG11060627

# Integrating AI for Knowledge Management in Software Engineering

Dilyan Georgiev🄳 and Elissaveta Gourova$^{(\boxtimes)}$ 🄳

Faculty of Mathematics and Informatics, Sofia University "St. Kl. Ohridski", Sofia, Bulgaria
diljang@uni-sofia.bg, elis@fmi.uni-sofia.bg

**Abstract.** Artificial Intelligence (AI) influences the practice of individuals and organizations, providing tools for higher efficiency and performance. While AI is helping software engineers in software design, some gaps exist for knowledge and document management. The paper presents recent research on knowledge management (KM) in software engineering (SE). It considers the role of KM in SE and the main tools used in software processes. Next, the authors present a model of knowledge domains in SE, on which base a concept is developed for an automated document management system integrating AI tools to facilitate end-user activities.

**Keywords:** Knowledge Management · Software Engineering · Artificial Intelligence · Document Management System

## 1 Introduction

In the last decades, Knowledge Management (KM) has developed as a scientific field combining the achievements of several technological, management, and behavioural disciplines. For supporting knowledge processes (generation, preservation, transfer, and use of knowledge) in organizations have been used various approaches aimed at facilitating effectiveness, competitiveness, and business strategy implementation.

Recent advancement of Artificial Intelligence (AI) has influenced KM practices, in particular, the processes of knowledge capturing, knowledge development, and has paved the way towards the sixth generation of KM [25]. Several authors [6, 12, 21] consider how AI could be used in KM, and how to facilitate the knowledge life cycle in organizations. Shaikh [21], for example, presents intelligence (artificial or human) as a 4th layer of the knowledge pyramid, and links it to possible knowledge management systems (KMS) automation. Toptas [25] examines how AI might support the knowledge processes in the Probst model, and the opportunities for: search and analysis of documents with Natural Language Processing (NLP), transformation of unstructured data into searchable information, AI-based training of employees, enhancement of creativity and innovation with generative AI, as well as using chatbots for KM.

AI has become an essential tool offering new approaches for solving complex issues, supporting process optimization and automation, analysing large data sets, and transforming everyday practices of workers and organizations. AI tools, e.g. NLP, design

G. De Tré et al. (Eds.): FQAS 2025, LNAI 16119, pp. 66–76, 2026.
https://doi.org/10.1007/978-3-032-05607-8_8

and code optimization tools, machine learning algorithms, deep learning techniques, etc., are used intensively in software engineering (SE) for requirements analysis, for design of the software architecture, as well as for software implementation, testing and maintenance [1, 2]. At the same time, software engineers face several problems related to unstructured and complex information, difficulties in accessing key documentation, loss of organizational knowledge due to changes in teams and staff mobility [11]. Subsequently, the knowledge and document management gaps reflect on lower efficiency of work processes and reduced speed of innovation.

The goal of this paper is to present the main results of recent research on knowledge management in software engineering. In the first part, an overview of the role of KM in SE is provided, along with a discussion of the main tools used in software processes. Next, the authors present a model of knowledge domains in SE, on which base is developed a concept for an automated document management system (ADMS), in which AI tools are integrated to facilitate end-user activities.

## 2 Knowledge Management in Software Engineering

### 2.1 Tools Supporting KM in SE

In an organizational environment, knowledge is gathered from various internal and external sources – employees, partners and competitors, stakeholders, experts, databases, and IT systems. KM activities of employees have been supported by different methods and tools: KMS, knowledge engineering techniques, identification and integration of external knowledge, documentation of tacit knowledge, sharing good practices, expert advice, technology-enhanced learning, communities of practice, case studies, lessons-learned debriefings, knowledge maps, documenting and assessing customer feedback, management of terminology, content, competency, personal experience, etc. [14]. AI tools also analyse, categorize, and connect information, thus making it easier to access and improve the knowledge flows in the organization [10].

SE professionals are expected to have access to knowledge from a variety of sources, including design patterns, programming languages, software architecture, libraries of solutions and best practices. The software development process itself generates vast amounts of data and knowledge that can bring value if identified, encoded, documented, and reused within the organization. Knowledge management in SE is a systematic approach of collecting, organizing, exchanging, and using knowledge and information related to software development projects [7]. It includes the processes of:

- knowledge identification – determining the key knowledge that is critical to the success of the projects, including expertise, experience, and lessons learned from previous projects;
- knowledge gathering – systematically extracting data, information, and experience from various sources, including documentation, workshops, team discussions, and feedback from different stakeholders;
- knowledge organizing – structuring and systematizing knowledge in accessible documentation repositories, allowing easy search and retrieval;

- knowledge sharing – creating a culture of knowledge exchange among employees to ensure that information does not remain isolated and is used effectively in different stages of the software development life cycle;
- knowledge use – incorporating the collected knowledge into the processes of software design, development, testing, and maintenance, to increase quality, efficiency, and innovation, and satisfy the requirements.

Various collaborative tools, information systems, data repositories, and training systems have been used in SE to facilitate knowledge sharing and reuse, reduce the risk of expertise loss, promote innovation, etc. [9]. Online repositories and document management systems (DMS) ensure efficient input, retrieval, and sharing of digital documents [3]. Tools such as Doxygen and Javadoc provide automatic documentation generation directly from source code, while cloud repositories such as GitHub, Bitbucket, and GitLab offer capabilities for creating and managing versions of documentation, which greatly facilitates its maintenance and distribution. The integration of real-time collaboration platforms such as Slack and Discord allows developers to discuss and document the work process more dynamically [20].

Version control systems (VCS) manage digital resources through change logs, allowing for rollbacks, comparison of edits, and branching of versions for parallel work. They facilitate collaborative editing and are fundamental for tracking and merging data [17]. VCS offers multiple benefits in SE [8]: identifying knowledge distribution, preventing knowledge loss, improving collaboration, assisting in human resource management, better understanding of code, and optimizing project management. Confluence is an e-collaboration platform used in the industry for centralized content and knowledge management [24]. It aims to improve collaboration between teams, allow project tracking, and formalize workflows. GitHub is one of the most widely used code management and collaboration platforms in software engineering, offering distributed version control via Git, which facilitates change tracking, collaboration between developers, and integration with CI/CD tools. GitHub Wiki, as part of the GitHub ecosystem, provides a built-in documentation system that is particularly useful for open-source projects and internal project documentation [19].

Recently, DMSs have become increasingly diverse, integrating different repositories, interactive tutorials, and instant messaging platforms. AI and machine learning are starting to be used to automatically generate and update documentation, which increases its accuracy and compliance with software changes [16]. An increasing focus is noticed on using KM and analytical methods for quality improvement, discovery of tacit knowledge, and automatic codification of knowledge [23].

Currently, AI and its applications are leading the way in the design of DMS, and with the changing requirements of SE professionals, it becomes imperative to develop new functionalities and approaches that meet modern needs, such as document categorization, indexing, and advanced search capabilities that facilitate rapid information retrieval [15].

### 2.2 Knowledge Domains in Software Engineering

Knowledge domains have different dimensions when viewed in the context of a modern software company. They are shaped by internal organizational processes and external factors, including technological innovations and dynamic market trends. Based on a systematic study of research, the following knowledge domains are defined for SE:

- Contextual knowledge – including specific software design context, knowledge of the software products and processes;
- Organizational know-ledge – including specific technocratic and behavioural knowledge.

In software engineering, the ***knowledge context*** combines the set of factors that influence the design, development, and operation of a software system. Understanding this context is essential for creating effective, reliable, and easy-to-use solutions [5, 26]. By the design of products, software architects should be aware of:

- User context – related to the needs, preferences, and behaviour of users, which influence the UX/UI and functionality of the system;
- System environment – includes hardware requirements, network conditions, and operating systems that define technical constraints;
- Scope context – focused on the specific activities and workflows that users perform using the software;
- Temporal context – includes factors such as time constraints, time zones, and frequency of interaction with the system;
- Social context – affects interactions between users and the need for collaborative functionalities.

The ***product knowledge*** is used to transform software systems into accessible, well-described, and modular services. The software development life cycle (SDLC) goes through several phases, each of which requires specific knowledge and documentation to ensure the successful implementation of the product. The main documents in the SDLC vary according to the phase, providing critical information for all stakeholders and developers [4, 22]. Besides, various approaches exist that support the description of the product in a machine-readable specification, which can be enriched by introducing metadata and using conflict detection mechanisms based on an analytical process for validation, verification, and performance evaluation.

The ***process knowledge*** is related to knowledge of the internal processes and procedures that software companies use to deliver their products and services. These solutions can be focused on data management, change monitoring, or product engineering management. In the early stages of product development, the main goal is to clarify requirements and develop solutions based on previous experience. During the execution phase, the focus is on the value delivered and how the development process is executed, which also requires specific knowledge of the methods, models, etc.

When considering ***organizational knowledge***, organizational culture and structure should be considered, as well as mission, vision, learning, and growth. From the SE perspective, the organizational knowledge of employees includes technocratic knowledge, related to the ability to use a variety of IT tools supporting KM and business processes. As suggested by [18], the technocratic approach to KM includes cognitive analysis, a deeper look at communication in virtual environments, event modelling, and data clustering based on common characteristics From a managerial perspective, it is advisable to use information systems that support the management of human resources in SE, as well as collaboration and knowledge exchange within the organization. Effective KM strategies include various tools and practices that improve collaboration, optimize processes, and foster innovation [9].

Regarding the *behavioural knowledge*, two main directions are considered: one is related to team modelling and discovering patterns in larger projects, and the other is based on the Agile framework and how it can transform larger companies into highly connected knowledge communities. Research shows that human factors are the subject of analysis, in particular the effective introduction of novices into the SE process and the improvement of staff performance through education and motivation [13].

## 3    Application of AI for Knowledge Management in Software Processes

### 3.1    Concept for an Automated Document Management System

Documentation plays a fundamental role in facilitating knowledge management within software organizations. It captures explicit knowledge, including documentation of processes, procedures, best practices, lessons learned, and insights gained over time. By documenting various aspects of operations, projects, and experiences, software organizations ensure that valuable knowledge is preserved and accessible to employees across different levels and departments. Therefore, an Automated Document Management System is designed with the aim of providing a centralized and intelligent approach to the management of technical documentation by using AI. The system supports four knowledge domains in SE (Fig. 1):

- Technocratic knowledge – technology portfolio, experience in product development, information systems, and innovations;
- Behavioural knowledge – organizational culture, internal policies, and practices;
- Product knowledge – functionality and characteristics of the products;
- Process knowledge – documentation of methodologies, work processes, and best practices.

The ADMS provides structured, accessible, and automated mechanisms for storing, analysing, and using documentation across knowledge domains, using AI to recognize important concepts, extract new knowledge, and improve navigation in knowledge repositories. In addition to the main functionalities, it supports integration with existing systems so that the knowledge repositories are maximally connected, reducing the likelihood of knowledge obsolescence and irrelevance.

The ADMS is integrated with various software tools used in companies for document management, software development, and project implementation:

- Version control systems (Git, GitHub, GitLab, Bitbucket) – automatic linking of documentation with code repositories;
- Technical specification repositories (Confluence, SharePoint) – synchronization of requirements and architectural documents;
- Ticket systems (Jira, Trello, Azure DevOps) – linking documentation with team tasks;

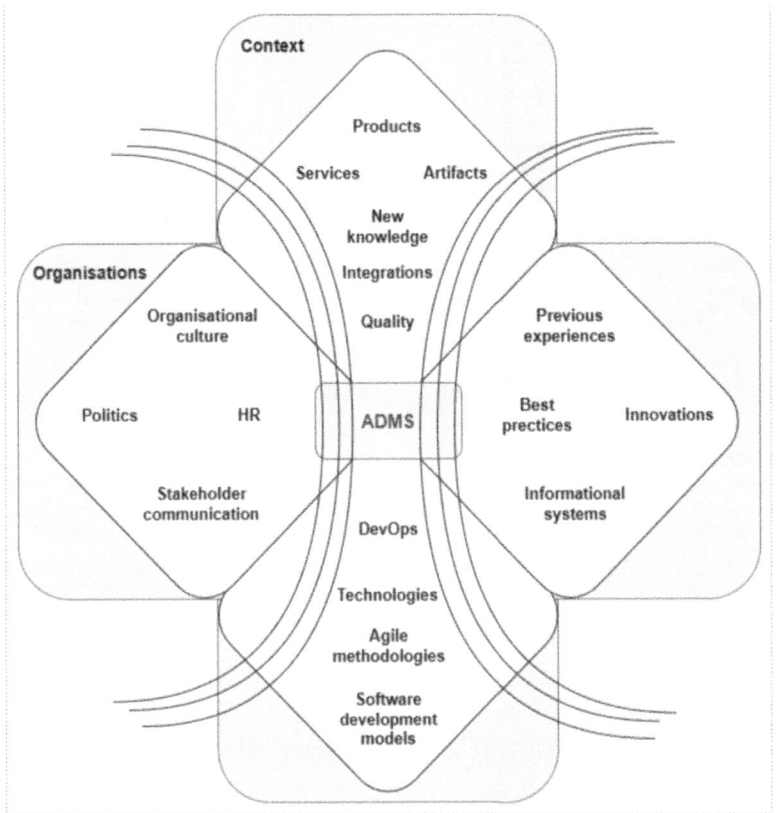

**Fig. 1.** Relation of the ADMS with the knowledge domains

- Human resource management systems (HRMS, Yellow Pages) – tracking roles and access to documents according to position in the organization.

  Figure 2 illustrates the concept of ADMS, focusing on two main components:

- Administrative panel, which controls access and rights of regular users;
- Portal that, according to the user's delegated rights, redirects them to the various knowledge areas where access to documentation is ensured, and provides both AI-powered knowledge analysis tools and dashboards with summarized information and recommendations for effective use.

  The AI integration module allows configuration of various external AI tools tailored to specific profiles:

- Intelligent assistants – virtual assistants for navigation and content analysis;
- Knowledge organization – automatic categorization and structuring of information;
- Knowledge discovery – document analysis and generation of new knowledge through AI.
- AI integration services:

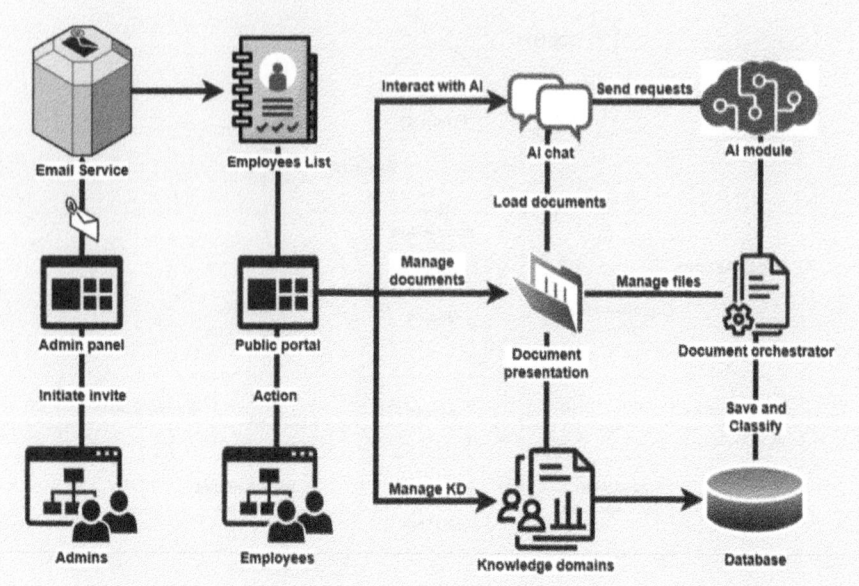

**Fig. 2.** Concept for Automated Document Management System

o Access layer – control of communication with AI agents;
o Configuration layer – setup and personalization of AI services;
o Interaction tracking (Logging system);
o Infrastructure API – connection between existing IT systems and AI functionalities.

In addition to its core functionalities, the ADMS should support integration with existing systems to ensure documentation repositories to remain connected, thus reducing the risk of outdated or irrelevant knowledge.

### 3.2 Concept Validation via AI-Integrated Prototype

The development of an ADMS prototype serves as proof of concept to demonstrate the applicability and effectiveness of the conceptual framework. Its main objective is to illustrate how intelligent agents and automated mechanisms can enhance the accessibility, comprehension, and management of complex software documentation.

The prototype enables the validation of key functionalities, such as knowledge domain-based document management, intelligent search and content analysis, and user access control. It also verifies the integration with AI agents and system configurability. This provides a solid foundation for advancing ADMS into a practical technological solution for efficient knowledge management in software engineering.

The integration of an intelligent assistant requires compliance with the following priority conditions (Table 1):

• The intelligent assistant must be integrated via API, ensuring standardized communication between the prototype and the external AI model.

- The system should send and receive information in a structured format (JSON/XML) with the possibility of additional validation and processing of the results.

**Table 1.** Comparative analysis of intelligent assistants.

| Parameter | ChatGPT | IBM Watson Assistant | Google Gemini (Bard) | Microsoft Copilot |
|---|---|---|---|---|
| Integrability with API | ✔ OpenAI API, RESTful, GraphQL | ✔ API for cloud services and local solutions | ✔ Gemini Developer API | ✔ Integrability with Microsoft Graph API |
| Security policy | AES-256 encryption, GDPR, SOC 2, HIPAA (for business) | Supports SOC 2, GDPR, HIPAA, ISO 27001 | Google Cloud Security, GDPR, CCPA | Microsoft Security, GDPR, ISO 27001, SOC 2 |
| AI model for text analysis | GPT-4 (GPT-3.5 for free version) | IBM Watson NLP & Machine Learning | Gemini Ultra, Gemini Pro | GPT-4, with optimization for Office 365 |
| Fine-Tuning capability | ✔ OpenAI API supports personalization | ✔ Watson Discovery supports further training | ✔ Gemini API supports personalization | ✔ only in the Microsoft environment, Copilot Orchestrator |
| Ability to upload files | ✔ B ChatGPT Enterprise и API (PDF, DOCX, CSV) | ✔ Watson Discovery document analysis | ✔ supports file uploading for analysis | ✔ Integration with SharePoint and OneDrive for files |
| Integration with software ecosystems | OpenAI API for Slack, Notion, Zapier, etc. | IBM Cloud, Watson AI, corporate ERP systems | Integration with Google Workspace (Docs, Sheets, Drive) | Integration with Microsoft 365 (Teams, Word, Excel) |

In relation to additional training of the intelligent assistant and storage of the history of documents sent, it was considered also the security and usage policies of different AI tools, and a comparative analysis of intelligent assistants was made.

For designing the prototype of the ADMS, OpenAI was selected, which can easily integrate with an external interface and provides a service without the need to save data. Besides, OpenAI does not keep a record of the sessions performed: each API call is treated as a separate request, and if the model wants to "remember" previous messages, the client must explicitly send the previous context in the form of an array of messages in new requests. Regarding information storage, OpenAI does not store conversations from API requests for further training or analysis (unless the user has agreed to a different storage policy), and after the API request is completed, the data sent and received are not stored by OpenAI.

The validation process of the ADMS prototype involved executing a set of test scenarios and collecting expert feedback. An experimental approach was used to assess the system's effectiveness and applicability. 30 software engineering professionals performed predefined test tasks and completed a questionnaire to provide both quantitative and qualitative evaluations. Some participants also gave additional feedback on potential improvements.

The evaluation results indicate that most users find the system easy to use and generally intuitive. A total of 60% rated the system as "easy" or "very easy," while 40% considered it "moderately easy," suggesting room for improving the user experience. Regarding interface intuitiveness, 73% of respondents described it as "fully" or "fairly intuitive," 20% found it moderately intuitive, and 7% found it unintuitive, highlighting some navigational challenges.

The user feedback reveals generally positive impressions of the prototype, particularly regarding the clarity and accuracy of the intelligent assistant's document analysis and the user-friendly interface. Several respondents noted smooth performance across modules and effective summarization features. However, some technical issues were identified, including spelling errors, date handling bugs, file upload limitations, and loading problems during analysis.

Overall, the prototype was successfully validated, confirming the value and applicability of the conceptual framework and its alignment with functional and non-functional requirements. These findings support the final part of the paper, outlining the study's contributions and future development directions.

## 4   Conclusions

In modern IT companies, document management is moving from static file repositories to dynamic, integrated platforms that use artificial intelligence for analysis and recommendations. The document flow is not linear - several integrations and techniques are applied to automatically categorize information, update it in real time, and make it accessible through a centralized environment, which reduces the risk of knowledge loss after project completion and facilitates future developments. ADMS targets these situations in document management and expands the semantic field, including the knowledge areas of software processes.

AI integration is becoming a mandatory element of any knowledge management system that supports the implementation of software processes. In the context of document management, ADMS would facilitate access to various types of documentation, integrating intelligent agents into its functionalities.

The results of the work presented in this paper reveal a wide range of opportunities for the development of both ADMS and the applications of AI in knowledge management. One of the main directions is the expansion of intelligent functionalities, including automated document summarization and analysis, personalized knowledge recommendations, and adaptive management of information flows in software processes.

Another important direction is the integration of ADMS in a broader ecosystem context, where the system can interact with various project management platforms,

DevOps environments, and collaboration tools. This would lead to increased efficiency of developers and software process management teams by facilitating access to critical information in real time.

Finally, with the development of large language models and generative AI, the possibility of dynamic and proactive knowledge management is opened, in which the system independently analyses trends, predicts future needs, and automatically generates recommendations. Thus, the results of this study can serve as a basis for the creation of even more intelligent and adaptive systems that support industrial practice and scientific research in the field of software engineering.

**Acknowledgments.** The authors gratefully acknowledge the support provided by the project UNITe BG16RFPR002-1.014-0004 funded by PRIDST.

**Disclosure of Interests.** The authors have no competing interests to declare that are relevant to the content of this article.

# References

1. Abubakar, A.M.: Artificial intelligence applications in engineering: a focus on software development and beyond. Doupe J. Top Trend. Technol. **1**(1), 1–11 (2025)
2. Alenezi, M., Akour, M.: AI-driven innovations in software engineering: a review of current practices and future directions. Appl. Sci. **15**(3), 1344 (2025)
3. Alzahrani, A.: Software systems documentation: a systematic review. Int. J. Adv. Comput. Sci. Appl. **15**(8), 1 (2024)
4. Aversano, L., Guardabascio, D., Tortorella, M.: Analysis of the documentation of ERP software projects. Procedia Comput. Sci. **121**, 423–430 (2017)
5. Bedjeti, A., Lago, P., Lewis, G.A., De Boer, R.D., Hilliard, R.: Modeling context with an architecture viewpoint. In: 2017 IEEE International Conference on Software Architecture (ICSA), Gothenburg, Sweden, pp. 117–120 (2017)
6. Botega, L., da Silva, J.C.: An artificial intelligence approach to support knowledge management on the selection of creativity and innovation techniques. J. Knowl. Manag. **24**(5), 1107–1130 (2020)
7. Carreteiro, P., de Vasconcelos, J.B., Barão, A., Rocha, Á.: A knowledge management approach for software engineering projects development. In: Rocha, Á., Correia, A., Adeli, H., Reis, L., Mendonça Teixeira, M. (eds.) New Advances in Information Systems and Technologies. Advances in Intelligent Systems and Computing, vol. 444. Springer, Cham (2016)
8. Fekete, A., Porkoláb, Z.: Using version control information to visualize developers' knowledge. Acta Cybernet. **26**(3), 431–454 (2024)
9. Fragoso, E., Villa, L.F., Giraldo Marín, L.M.: Strategies, information technologies and models for knowledge management in software development companies: a systematic review of the literature. In: Figueroa-García, J.C., Hernández, G., Villa Ramirez, J.L., Gaona García, E.E. (eds.) Applied Computer Sciences in Engineering. WEA 2023. Communications in Computer and Information Science, vol. 1928, pp. 388–398. Springer, Cham (2023)
10. Georgiev, D., Antonova, A.: Enhancing knowledge sharing processes via automated software documentation management systems using Gen AI software tools. In: 2024 XXXIV International Scientific Symposium Metrology and Metrology Assurance (MMA), pp. 1–6 (2024)

11. Georgiev, D.: Exploring knowledge management from a software engineering perspective. In: Proceedings of 24th European Conference on Knowledge Management, vol. 24, no. 2, pp. 1571–1578 (2023)

12. Hilger, J., Wahl, Z.: Making Knowledge Management Clickable: Knowledge Management Systems Strategy, Design, and Implementation. Springer, Cham (2022)

13. Machuca-Villegas, L., Gasca-Hurtado, G.P.: Towards a social and human factor classification related to productivity in software development teams. In: Mejia, J., Muñoz, M., Rocha, Á., A. Calvo-Manzano, J. (eds.) Trends and Applications in Software Engineering, CIMPS 2019, Advances in Intelligent Systems and Computing, vol. 1071, pp 36–50. Springer, Cham (2020)

14. Maier, R.: Knowledge Management Systems: Information and Communication Technologies for Knowledge Management. Springer, Heidelberg (2007)

15. Maragno, G., Tangi, L., Gastaldi, L., Benedetti, M.: Exploring the factors, affordances and constraints outlining the implementation of artificial intelligence in public sector organisations. Int. J. Inf. Manage. **73**, 102686 (2023)

16. Moghaddam, R., Garg, S., Clement, C., Mohylevskyy, Y., Sundaresan, N.: Generating examples from CLI usage: can transformers help? In: Proceedings of 28th ACM SIGKDD Conference on Knowledge Discovery and Data Mining, pp. 3575–3583 (2022)

17. Ogayar-Anguita, C.J., López-Ruiz, A., Segura-Sánchez, R.J., Rueda-Ruiz, A.J.: A version control system for point clouds. Remote Sens. **15**(18), 4635 (2023)

18. Osorio Angel, S., Peña Pérez Negrón, A., Espinoza Valdez, A.: From a conceptual to a computational model of cognitive emotional process for engineering students. In: Mejia, J., Muñoz, M., Rocha, Á., A. Calvo-Manzano, J. (eds.) Trends and Applications in Software Engineering, CIMPS 2019, Advances in Intelligent Systems and Computing, vol. 1071, pp. 173–186. Springer, Cham (2019)

19. Puhlfürß, T., Montgomery, L., Maalej, W.: An exploratory study of documentation strategies for product features in popular GitHub projects. In: 2022 IEEE International Conference on Software Maintenance and Evolution (ICSME), pp. 379–383 (2022)

20. Raglianti, M.: Topology of the documentation landscape. In: 2022 IEEE/ACM 44th International Conference on Software Engineering: Companion Proceedings (ICSE-Companion), pp. 297–299 (2022)

21. Shaikh, S.: Development of automated knowledge management model (AKMM). Adv. Data Sci. Adapt. Anal. **13**(02), 2150008 (2021)

22. Shetty, M., Panchami, B.S., Gadiyar, H.M.T.: Software development life cycle (SDLC) in software engineering – a brief review. J. Comput. Sci. Syst. Softw. **1**(1), 5–9 (2023)

23. Sondhi, D., Gupta, A., Purandare, S., Rana, A., Kaushal, D., Purandare, R.: On indirectly dependent documentation in the context of code evolution: a study. In: 2021 IEEE/ACM 43rd International Conference on Software Engineering (ICSE), pp.1498–1509 (2021)

24. Stampfl, R., Prodinger, M., Palkovits-Rauter, S.: Reshaping knowledge flow: the impact of ecollaboration platforms in IT-project knowledge transfer. Electron. J. Knowl. Manag. **22**(2), 36–49 (2024)

25. Toptas, B.: An analysis of knowledge management changes through artificial intelligence with probst's model. In: Gonçalves, C., Rouco, J.C.D. (eds.) Proceedings of the International Conference on AI Research, vol. 4, no. 1, pp. 405–414. Academic Conferences and Publishing Ltd. (2024)

26. Wang, X., Liu, A., Kara, S.: Constructing product usage context knowledge graph using user-generated content for user-driven customization. J. Mech. Des. **145**(4), 041404 (2022)

# Generating Synthetic Audio Information on Data Flow Between Software and Business Architecture Layers

Desislava Atanasova⊙, Vasil Kozov⊙, Kameliya Shoylekova⊙,
Boyana Ivanova$^{(\boxtimes)}$ ⊙, and Rumen Rusev⊙

University of Ruse "Angel Kanchev", Ruse, Bulgaria
{datanasova,vkozov,kshoylekova,bivanova,rir}@uni-ruse.bg

**Abstract.** The research problem is defined – the need for automating the narration and visualization of the complicated business processes for people with different types of sensory learning. The research methodology is created and discussed; a literature review is made to help find possible solution; diagram sources are chosen; a conceptual solution is discussed and proposed. A prototype experiment that uses LLMs is set up as proof of concept. The diagrams are analyzed using the prototype and the results are discussed. Conclusions on the applicability of this type of technology are made, and it is found that there is benefit from using the chosen or similar approaches for these purposes. Future directions for related research are proposed.

**Keywords:** large language models · software prototype · business process improvement · generating synthetic information

## 1 Introduction

Business processes are usually represented graphically by using Unified Modeling Language (UML) or other visualization techniques, in condense and show a large amount of information. Business process diagrams, if done right, are useful for helping with high level management discussions, training new staff, introducing the flow of the business to new managers and employees, as well as helping find flaws in current practices – either in the business process itself, or in its implementation in practice. The current problem that this research aims to solve is that *due to the complex nature of business processes and their variety, it is time-consuming to encompass the entirety of those processes both during discussions and during training, and even lengthy discussions often miss parts of the entire picture.* Leveraging the power of AI for data generation for question answering is a possible solution to the defined problem. It was decided to create a prototype proof of concept and to test it in an experiment in order to validate whether such an approach is worthwhile.

G. De Tré et al. (Eds.): FQAS 2025, LNAI 16119, pp. 77–87, 2026.
https://doi.org/10.1007/978-3-032-05607-8_9

## 2   Literature Review

To better understand the scope of the problem, a categorization of the business processes is necessary. Similar research must also be analyzed and its know-how applied to the current work. The American Productivity & Quality Center's (APQC) Process Classification Framework (PCF) was considered, as it is used to help classify processes in different fields [1–4], as it describes processes in high-level categories and forms a comprehensive taxonomy. A more recent study, however, analyzed 12,573 processes [5] using the simplified Business Processes Nature Assessment Framework [6]. As the current research needs diagrams of business processes to analyze LLM performance, and how these results can be used in practice, the latter was chosen.

Many researchers have tried different optimization and improvement strategies to help streamline and make processes better. One such study proposes an intelligent forecasting model for order picking optimization (IFOPO) in the e-commerce sector. It was developed to improve picking efficiency by optimizing space allocation. This process involves several key activities, including order entry, storage, picking, packing and delivery. Among these activities, picking is particularly critical as it is time and labor intensive [7]. A good BPM could make the entire delivery process simpler and clearer, and offloading some of the work to LLMs should lead to improved results.

Collecting high quality diagrams of various types requires a necessary amount of manual work. The high-quality research sources of the diagrams were selected among their peers, and the references can be seen in Table 1.

Although Unified Modelling Language (UML) [23] contributed significantly towards streamlining processes and establishes good practices when visualizing processes, business process diagrams come in different shapes and sizes depending on the organization's internal practices and style. The chosen approach to solving the problem will address this concern by default – the audio narration and explanation will help reduce the effect of strong visuals and different visual representation styles, while at the same time not changing them [24]. This way people with stronger audio memory will absorb information better, and this will only supplement the process, without having any detriment towards visual learners [25].

## 3   Layout

The research is divided in three main sections – methodology, conceptual model and setup of the experiment. Each of the sections describes the most important steps for the successful conduction of the research.

### 3.1   Research Methodology

The decided research methodology was influenced by the type of research that had been planned – exploratory research. In trying to solve the defined problem, the current research had to follow a well-defined and structured approach.

The methodology used is shown on Fig. 1. Defining each step helped with consistently following those steps throughout the entire research process.

**Table 1.** Business process diagram **sources**

| Diagram name | Source |
| --- | --- |
| 1–1 – 1–4 | "Optimizing us health care processes - a case study in business process management." [8] |
| 2 | "Business Process Management techniques for health services: Experiences and Application." [9] |
| 3–1 – 3–2 | "Inter-organizational business processes modelling framework." [10] |
| 4–1 – 4–2 | "Workflow management: models, methods, and systems" [11] |
| 5–1 – 5–7 | "Alignment-Based Conformance Checking of Partially-Ordered Traces and Process Models Using Automated Planning" [12] |
| 6–1 – 6–2 | "Change patterns and change support features–enhancing flexibility in process-aware information systems" [13] |
| 7–1 – 7–3 | "Change patterns and change support features–enhancing flexibility in process-aware information systems" [14] |
| 8–1 – 8–3 | "IT support for healthcare processes–premises, challenges, perspectives." [15] |
| 9–1 | "Efficient compliance checking using BPMN-Q and temporal logic." [16] |
| 10–1 | "Workflow simulation for operational decision support using design, historic and state information." [17] |
| 11–1 – 11–7 | "Discovering colored Petri nets from event logs." [18] |
| 12–1 – 12–3 | "Using business process models for the specification of manufacturing operations." [19] |
| 13–1 – 13–2 | "Complexity analysis of a business process automation: case study on a healthcare organization." [20] |
| 14–1 – 14–5 | "Introduction to business process management." [21] |
| 15–1 – 15–5 | "Using a framework to identify and organize your processes" [22] |

## 3.2 Conceptual Model

In order to implement the proof of concept, the use of video generating model was considered. After testing several local models using ComfyUI workflows with various models, they were deemed unfit for the task, as all the attempts to animate a diagram resulted in failure to create even a single usable video. Several of the main problems encountered were as follows – text often broke, in some cases parts of the text were transformed to another language, motion of the arrows between the actions on the diagrams were inconsistent (most of the time they were random, independent of the prompt), different levels of zoom-in and zoom-out, flipping of the action blocks and if-else statements and so-on and so forth. After the tests conducted with locally deployed picture-to-video models, the newest online OpenAI paid SORA model [26] was used, but the results were not better. It can be concluded that at this point in time (beginning of 2025), the

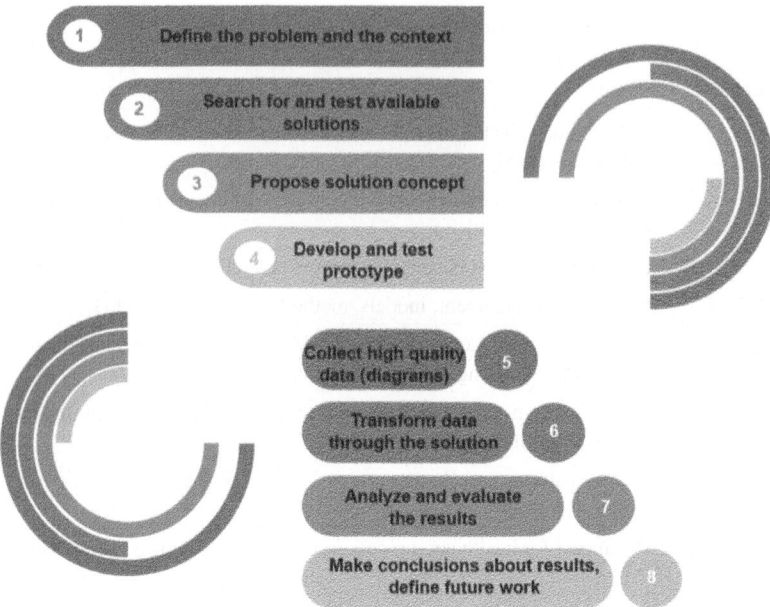

**Fig. 1.** Research methodology

image-to-video models are not trained well enough to create content of the type "animated diagrams and workflows". There is a need for models to be trained with enough data of this type, so that it can be helpful, and to our knowledge, none exists at the moment. Video content creation and automated animation in itself is an interesting and vast area of research [27–32], that will be helpful in enriching fields like education, higher education, team-based communication and discussions and any kind of activity which involves information representation, but more time is needed for the use of AI in this field to mature.

Following the discussions after all the technological tests, it was decided that the currently most viable way to achieve results and solve the defined problem, would be to use AI to analyze diagrams, and then supplement that with synthetically generated audio narration. For the current study, the paid OpenAI API was used, in order to expedite the prototyping process and research its viability. The ideal scenario would be to use locally deployed models, pretrained specifically for the purposes of business process optimization, but currently there is not enough available labeled data to train such a model locally.

A relatively simple architecture was developed and used for the purposes of the study (Fig. 2). It highlights the exact communication steps between the different layers of the application and OpenAI API endpoints used, as well as how the results are stored for further analysis.

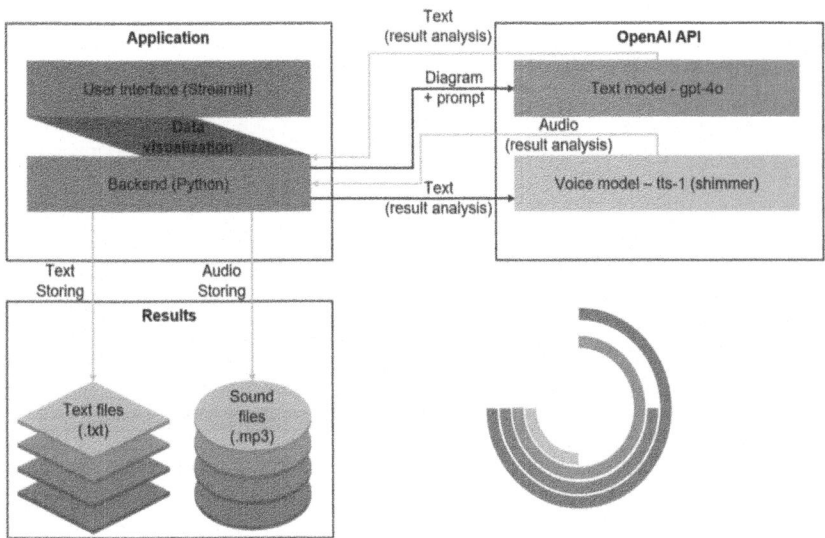

**Fig. 2.** Software architecture

### 3.3   Experiment Setup

The tts-1 (shimmer) audio model is used after the image has been analyzed by the gpt-4o model. The image is recognized, and its parts are defined in text form, then it is narrated to the user to help with improving their understanding, as well as their inclusion in the process itself. The results also highlight possible deficiencies and optimization opportunities in the business process, when comparing it to other good practices in the field of the diagram.

The prompt that was used during the analysis of the diagrams was as follows:

"You are a business expert. I have attached the business process of a company. Analyze it, give me a walkthrough on how everything works. Suggest optimizations, compare it to the good practices in the detected field. Your answer will be voiced, so the response should be in paragraphs that are flowing easily and are not segmented lists."

The prompt follows the good practices of prompt engineering:

- defining the area well – "You are a business expert / business process of a company".
- describing the activity – "Analyze it, give me a walkthrough on how everything works / Suggest optimizations".
- defining the rules well – "response should be in paragraphs that are flowing easily and are not segmented lists".
- giving specific tasks with parameters to follow – "compare it to the good practices in the detected field".
- generating context – "answer will be voiced".

A project and an API key were created and paid for. Models were selected, tested and the ones described on Fig. 2 were used. To ensure data validity and ease of further analysis, rules for the naming of all files and diagrams were created – they all have the same name, with the only difference being their extensions, depending on the file type.

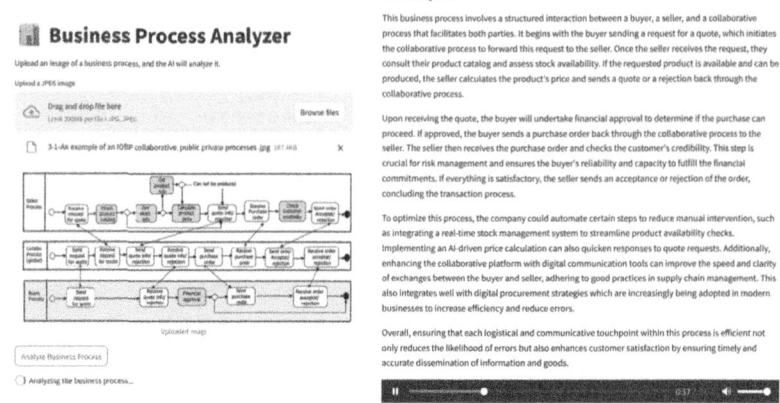

**Fig. 3.** The interface of the created software in possible states of the process

Streamlit [33] was used for generating the interface (Fig. 3) of the application. Every possible state of the application interface is shown. State 1 is the startup before any diagram has been uploaded. State 2 is when a diagram is uploaded (this is also the state after an analysis is made, and the user uploads another diagram). Step 3 is after the analysis of the diagram has been done by the OpenAI API and the resulting text is shown to the user. Step 4 is the end of the process when the audio is generated, and an audio player is available for the user to use and listen to the narration of the text by the tts-1 (shimmer) text-to-audio OpenAI model.

An interesting future application of image generation might be worth researching and testing used applied research - using flux [34] to edit only parts of business process diagrams. It would be useful to test a workflow on a completed process and reuse it. There are many well-described business processes that have had the sources of their diagrams lost, the software that was used for the creation of many of them has been lost over the years, and this method would be a way to revitalize them.

## 4  Results

Evaluating the effectiveness of an AI tool requires a comprehensive assessment of various criteria to determine whether it meets the established standards and performs its intended functions efficiently. Five evaluation criteria were selected to represent the results of the experiment. A fundamental criterion is accuracy, which refers to the extent to which the AI tool provides correct and reliable results. High accuracy ensures that the results can be verified and are trustworthy. Another key factor is efficiency - its ability to generate results in a timely manner. Robustness is also important, as it evaluates whether the prototype performs consistently across different data sets and conditions. In addition, the impact of the AI tool on productivity must be considered, in particular whether it enables time savings or reduces the workload for users. Finally, automation and efficiency gains should be examined, particularly whether the AI tool effectively automates tasks and minimizes human effort [35, 36].

The experiment was conducted with 50 diagrams (Table 1), and their results were analyzed.

Table 2 shows the scores for each of the criteria and the level of satisfaction after the business processes have been processed with the prototype. The first column shows the number of business processes in accordance with Table 1. Some of the processes are grouped together, others are analyzed separately due to their different logic. The other columns show the degree of satisfaction of each evaluation criteria. It is used five-point Likert scale - poor, fair, good, very good and excellent.

**Table 2.** Scores for each of the criteria

| Process/ group of processes | Accuracy | Efficiency | Robustness | Productivity Improvement | Automation |
|---|---|---|---|---|---|
| 1 | Fair | Good | Fair | Fair | Fair |
| 2 | Excellent | Very Good | Very Good | Very Good | Good |
| 3–1 | Good | Very Good | Good | Good | Good |
| 3–2 | Very Good | Very Good | Very Good | Very Good | Very Good |
| 4–1 | Good | Good | Good | Good | Good |
| 4–2 | Very Good | Very Good | Very Good | Very Good | Very Good |
| 5–1 to 5–4 | Excellent | Excellent | Excellent | Excellent | Excellent |
| 5–5 | Very Good | Very Good | Very Good | Very Good | Very Good |
| 5–6 | Excellent | Excellent | Excellent | Excellent | Excellent |
| 5–7 | Fair | Fair | Fair | Good | Fair |
| 6 | Very Good | Very Good | Very Good | Very Good | Very Good |
| 7–1, 7–2 | Good | Good | Good | Good | Good |
| 7–3 | Very Good | Very Good | Very Good | Very Good | Very Good |
| 8 | Excellent | Very Good | Very Good | Very Good | Excellent |
| 9 | Very Good | Very Good | Very Good | Very Good | Very Good |
| 10 | Very Good | Good | Good | Very Good | Good |
| 11 | Very Good | Very Good | Very Good | Very Good | Very Good |
| 12 | Excellent | Excellent | Excellent | Excellent | Excellent |
| 13 | Very Good | Very Good | Very Good | Very Good | Very Good |
| 14 | Very Good | Very Good | Very Good | Very Good | Very Good |
| 15 | Very Good | Excellent | Very Good | Very Good | Excellent |

The summarized scores for each criterion can be seen on Fig. 4. The accuracy of the prototype (Fig. 4) - only 10% of the processes are rated as fair, 14% as good, 52% as very good and 24% as excellent. The efficiency of the prototype - only 9% of the processes are rated as fair, 24% as good, 43% as very good and 24% as excellent. The robustness of the prototype - only 10% of the processes are rated as fair, 19% as good, 57% as very good and 14% as excellent. Productivity improvement of the prototype - only 5% of the processes are rated as fair, 19% as good, 62% as very good and 14% as excellent. The automation criterion is - only 9% of the processes are rated as fair, 24% as good, 43% as very good and 24% as excellent. None of the process improvement suggestions is rated "poor" for any criteria.

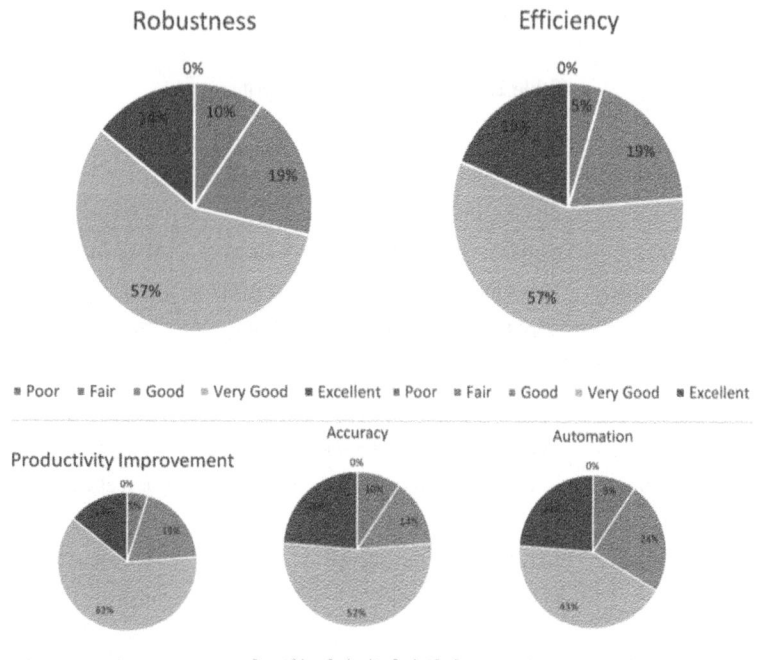

**Fig. 4.** The performance of the AI as rated by an expert for each of the criteria – Robustness, Efficiency, Productivity Improvement, Accuracy and Automation

The results of the study show that the prototype facilitates automation with regard to the generation of synthetic audio information from business processes. The most frequently awarded rating is very good, which shows that this approach offers good possibilities for optimizing processes and accurately describes step by step the necessary actions to make the given process work better.

## 5   Conclusion

Using LLMs and AI to help ease people into understanding complex business processes is possible. Generating text and audio explanations and suggestions for improvements is also deemed beneficial both by the researchers and expert opinion. The analysis of the results shows a good performance of the chosen approach for finding a solution to the defined research problem.

The experience obtained from creating this solution and analysis will be particularly useful when trying to automate similar processes, and discussions must be held in the future about the possible applications in different fields. Of course, both software developers and users of technology should keep in mind the possibility of LLM hallucinations and false data and should always verify the given information. That verification process in the case of the current research will help solidify the results for achieving the actual purpose – people gaining experience and better understanding of business processes through the use of visuals, text and audio.

It can be concluded that the selected approach is a viable solution to generating synthetic text and audio information for fulfilling the goal of teaching and informing people about complex business processes. Future work on this research subject includes requesting more structured data and diagrams that can be later labeled, then training a local model to process the information in a more accurate way, specific to an organization. That would be a great enhancement to most types and sizes of businesses that have already defined and established their business processes.

**Acknowledgement.** This research is supported by the Bulgarian Ministry of Education and Science under the National Program "Young Scientists and Postdoctoral Students-2".

# References

1. Scheruhn, H., Pranta, N.: Concept integration of APQC's process classification framework (PCF)® and enterprise architecture frameworks with Signavio. In: International Conference on Technological Advancement in Embedded and Mobile Systems, pp. 91–103 (2022)
2. Mullins, R., Dettmer, S., Ziemba, E., Eisenbardt, M.: Potential for a process framework to guide the implementation of circular economy activities in enterprises. Adopt. Emerg. Inform. Commun. Technol. Sustainab. 3–26 (2024)
3. Krzywy, J., Hell, M.: Classification of process from the simulation modeling aspect-system dynamics and discrete event simulation. In: International Conference Innovation in Engineering, pp. 86–97 (2022)
4. Corallo, A., Lazoi, M., Marra, M., Quarta, L., Rimini, A., Cesare Liacin, C.: A processes reference framework for the creative and cultural industries. The case of the puglia creativa cluster, business process management cases Vol. 2: Digital Transformation-Strategy, Processes and Execution, pp. 261–276 (2021)
5. Szelągowski, M., et al.: Exploring the diverse nature of business processes in organisations in Industry 4.0/5.0. Future Bus. J. **10**(1) (2024). https://doi.org/10.1186/s43093-024-00395-5
6. Szelągowski, M.: Practical assessment of the nature of business processes. Inform. Syst. e-Bus. Manage. **19**, 541–566 (2021). https://doi.org/10.1007/s10257-021-00501-y
7. Ho, G.T.S., Tang, V., Tong, P.H., Tam, M.M.F.: Demand-driven storage allocation for optimizing order picking processes. Expert Syst. Appl. (2025). https://doi.org/10.1016/j.eswa.2025.126812
8. Becker, J., Fischer, R., Janiesch, C.: Optimizing us health care processes-a case study in business process management. In: AMCIS 2007 Proceedings, p. 504 (2007)
9. Framiñán Torres, J.M., Parra Calderón, C.L., De la Higuera González, J.M., Ruiz Usano, R., Gracia Melero, J.M.: Business process management techniques for health services: experiences and application. In: Second World Conference on Production and Operations Management, Cancún (México) (2004)

10. Bouchbout, K., Alimazighi, Z.: Inter-organizational business processes modelling framework. In: ADBIS (2), pp. 45–54 (2011). https://ceur-ws.org/Vol-789/paper5.pdf
11. van der Aalst, W.M.P., van Hee, K.M.: Workflow management: models, methods and systems (2001)
12. Lanciano, G.: Alignment-Based Conformance Checking of Partially-Ordered Traces and Process Models Using Automated Planning (2018)
13. Weber, B., Reichert, M., Rinderle-Ma, S.: Change patterns and change support features–enhancing flexibility in process-aware information systems. Data Knowl. Eng. **66**(3), 438–466 (2008). https://doi.org/10.1016/j.datak.2008.05.001
14. van der Aalst, W., Rosemann, M., Dumas, M.: Deadline-based escalation in process-aware information systems. Decis. Support. Syst. **43**(2), 492–511 (2007). https://doi.org/10.1016/j.dss.2006.11.005
15. Lenz, R., Reichert, M.: IT support for healthcare processes–premises, challenges, perspectives. Data Knowl. Eng. **61**(1), 39–58 (2007). https://doi.org/10.1016/j.datak.2006.04.007
16. Awad, A., Decker, G., Weske, M.: Efficient compliance checking using BPMN-Q and temporal logic. In International Conference on Business Process Management, pp. 326–341. Springer, Heidelberg (2008)
17. Rozinat, A., Wil van der Aalst, W., ter Hofstede, A., Fidge, C.: Workflow simulation for operational decision support using design, historic and state information, Business Process Management: 6th International Conference, BPM 2008, Milan, Italy, September 2–4, Proceedings 6, pp. 196–211. Springer, Heidelberg (2008)
18. Rozinat, A., Mans, R.S., Song, M., Van der Aalst, W.: Discovering colored Petri nets from event logs. Int. J. Softw. Tools Technol. Transfer **10**, 57–74 (2008)
19. Erasmus, J., Vanderfeesten, I., Traganos, K., Grefen, P.: Using business process models for the specification of manufacturing operations. Comput. Industry 123 (2020). https://doi.org/10.1016/j.compind.2020.103297
20. Martinho, R., Rijo, R., Nunes, A.: Complexity analysis of a business process automation: case study on a healthcare organization. Procedia Comput. Sci. **64**, 1226–1231 (2015). https://doi.org/10.1016/j.procs.2015.08.510
21. Dumas, M., La Rosa, M., Mendling, J., Hajo, A.: Introduction to business process management. Fund. Bus. Process Manage. 1–33 (2018) https://doi.org/10.1007/978-3-662-565 09-4_1
22. Spears, M.: Using a framework to identify and organize your processes — Simplifying Processes. https://www.simplifyingprocesses.com/blog/process-framework. Accessed 25 Mar 2025
23. Jacobson, I., Rumbaugh, J., Booch, G.: The Unified Modeling Language Reference Manual. Addison Wesley Longman (2021)
24. Stefanova, P., Ibryamova, E., Angel Smrikarov, A., Ivanova, G.: Development and integration of audio and visual micro-resources in the learning process through the use of artificial intelligence systems. Strat. Policy Sci. Educ. Strategii na Obrazovatelnata i Nauchnata Politika 32 (2024)
25. Gilakjani, A.P.: Visual, auditory, kinaesthetic learning styles and their impacts on English language teaching. J. Stud. Educ. **2**(1), 104–113 (2012)
26. Brooks, T., et al.: Video generation models as world simulators (2024). https://openai.com/index/video-generation-models-as-world-simulators. Accessed 1 Nov 2024
27. Karaarslan, E., Aydın, O.: Generate impressive videos with Text instructions: a review of openAI Sora, Stable Diffusion, Lumiere and comparable models, Authorea Preprints (2024)
28. Liu Y., et al.: Sora: a review on background, technology, limitations, and opportunities of large vision models (2024)

29. Karaarslan, E., Aydın, O.: OpenAI Sora: generate impressive videos with text instructions. SSRN Electronic J. (2024)

30. Hu, Y., Luo, C., Chen, Z.: Make it move: controllable image-to-video generation with text descriptions. In: Proceedings of the IEEE/CVF Conference on Computer Vision and Pattern Recognition, pp. 18219–18228 (2022)

31. Yu, T., Yang, W., Xu, J., Pan, Y.: Barriers to industry adoption of AI video generation tools: a study based on the perspectives of video production professionals in China. Appl. Sci. **14**, 13 (2024)

32. Viana P., et al.: Photo2Video: semantic-aware deep learning-based video generation from still content. J. Imaging **8**, 3 (2022)

33. Khorasani, M., Abdou, M., Fernández, J.H.: Web application development with streamlit. Softw. Develop. 498–507 (2022). https://doi.org/10.1007/978-1-4842-8111-6

34. Zhou, D., Xie, J., Yang, Z., Yang, Y.: 3DIS-FLUX: simple and efficient multi-instance generation with DiT rendering (2025). https://doi.org/10.48550/arXiv.2501.05131

35. McCormack, L., Bendechache, M.: A comprehensive survey and classification of evaluation criteria for trustworthy artificial intelligence. AI Ethics (2024). https://doi.org/10.1007/s43 681-024-00590-8

36. Purdue University: Evaluating AI tools. Purdue IT (n.d.). Retrieved 27 Mar 2025. https://it. purdue.edu/ai/evaluating-ai-tools

# Collaborating Across Roles: Shaping Strategic Directions for Institutional Implementation of AI Tools in Higher Education

Bistra Vassileva[1]($^{(\boxtimes)}$) (ID), Evgeni Stanimirov[1] (ID), and Plamen Miltenoff[2] (ID)

[1] University of Economics-Varna, Varna, Bulgaria
bistravas@ue-varna.bg
[2] Research Institute at the University of Economics-Varna, Varna, Bulgaria

**Abstract.** Strategic implementation of artificial intelligence (AI) in higher education (HE) is becoming essential as institutions seek to remain relevant and effective in a rapidly evolving digital landscape. The expansion of AI tools presents both transformative opportunities and significant challenges to conventional educational paradigms. This paper investigates how AI can be strategically integrated within HE by using the PDCA cycle as a part of decision support systems (DSS). Beginning with an overview of DSS, the study examines its practical applications in higher education institutions (HEIs) through different models for AI adoption. Using a bibliometric analysis of literature on "artificial intelligence", "strategy", and "university," and grounded in a conceptual framework developed from a systematic review, the research highlights key strategic priorities. These include the necessity of AI adoption to follow phased roadmaps and aligns with institutional mission, often requiring dedicated leadership, planning, and governance structures as well as institutional change management.

**Keywords:** Implementation of AI Tools · Higher Education · Decision Support Systems

## 1 Literature Review

### 1.1 Decision Support Systems (DSS) in Higher Education

Decision Support Systems (DSS) in higher education serve as integral tools for enhancing institutional planning and policy-making through data-driven methodologies. These systems systematically collect and analyze diverse institutional data—including enrollment statistics, financial records, and student performance metrics—to identify trends, develop predictive models, and provide actionable recommendations to administrators.

A study by Gaftandzhieva et al. [1] emphasizes the importance of data-driven decision-making tools in higher education institutions (HEIs) to improve academic performance and support sustainable development. The study highlights the utilization of data analytics tools, including educational data mining, learning analytics, and business intelligence, to extract insights and knowledge from educational data.

© The Author(s), under exclusive license to Springer Nature Switzerland AG 2026
G. De Tré et al. (Eds.): FQAS 2025, LNAI 16119, pp. 88–99, 2026.
https://doi.org/10.1007/978-3-032-05607-8_10

In practice, DSS can simulate various scenarios, such as projecting future enrollment figures or assessing the financial implications of policy changes, thereby enabling institutions to formulate optimal responses. The integration of intelligent DSS, which leverage advanced data analytics and machine learning algorithms, has been shown to enhance decision quality. For instance, by analyzing student trends, these systems facilitate more accurate enrollment management and contribute to improved educational quality, as evidenced by increased student satisfaction.

DSS provide a structured framework that encompasses data integration, analysis, and feedback mechanisms, supporting evidence-based strategic planning within universities. This structured approach ensures that decision-making processes are informed by comprehensive data analysis, thereby enhancing the institution's ability to respond effectively to evolving educational challenges.

A phased, mission-driven approach is vital for adopting AI tools. Experts recommend breaking AI strategy into discrete stages (e.g. AI Strategy → AI Plan → AI Readiness → Govern AI → Manage AI → Secure AI) to cover both technical and governance needs. In this model, institutions first set clear AI goals aligned with their core mission, then build leadership teams and data infrastructure, and finally implement governance and security measures. For instance, a European university might create an AI steering committee to align projects with strategic priorities and ensure compliance with ethical guidelines. Embedding responsible AI principles (privacy, fairness, transparency) at every stage ensures both innovation and accountability [2].

DSS tools directly enhance strategic planning. Research finds that DSS usage is linked to better planning outcomes in universities. Zhang and Goyal [3] report that administrators using DSS saw significant gains in strategic planning, enrollment management, and resource allocation. By translating complex data (e.g. performance metrics, demographics) into clear insights, DSS help leaders set realistic goals and monitor progress. For example, predictive models can forecast student demand across programs, allowing an institution to adjust course offerings or staffing in advance. In this way, DSS reinforce evidence-based decision-making and long-term strategy in higher education.

Rigorous risk assessment is integral to AI strategy. European universities operate under the EU's risk-based framework (as in the AI Act), so they must classify and manage AI risks. Recent frameworks (such as a proposed "Higher Education Act for AI") emphasize formally assessing AI risks to raise awareness and trigger safeguards. In practice, this means categorizing AI tools by risk level and applying stricter validation for high-risk applications (e.g. AI used in grading or admissions). A risk-based approach "ensures that appropriate measures are taken" and alerts stakeholders that potential harms must be addressed. By building these assessments into planning, mid-sized universities can mitigate issues like bias, privacy breaches, or academic integrity violations as they roll out AI tools [4].

DSS also guide resource allocation and operational planning. AI-driven analytics can optimize budgets, scheduling, and infrastructure use. For example, Sposato [5] documents that applying AI-enhanced DSS in universities significantly improved resource allocation and scheduling optimization, reducing administrative burden and enhancing efficiency. Such tools can simulate budget scenarios (e.g. funding new AI labs vs. expanding library resources) and predict outcomes, helping leadership allocate funds more effectively. By revealing hidden patterns (like underused classrooms or staffing bottlenecks), decision models enable universities to re-allocate assets strategically in line with their digital transformation goals.

## 1.2 AI Strategy Adoption Models in Higher Education

Successful AI adoption in higher education requires strategic approach combining both short-term goals with long-term vision. Effective AI adoption usually follows phased roadmaps and aligns with institutional mission, often requiring dedicated leadership, planning, and governance structures [2]. For example, Chan [6] proposes an "AI Ecological Education Policy Framework" with three dimensions: pedagogical, governance, and operational. The pedagogical dimension focuses on using AI to improve teaching/learning outcomes; governance addresses privacy, security, and accountability; and operational covers infrastructure and training. This framework guides universities in planning AI integration across teaching, policy, and technical support.

Every adoption process combined with a change management situation requires a comprehensive taxonomy, in this case, of AI in educational leadership. Sposato [5] suggests organizing AI applications into ten domains (e.g. administrative efficiency, personalized learning, governance, etc.). This taxonomy serves as a structured framework for leaders to understand, evaluate, and implement AI solutions in higher education institutions The model offers a common conceptual structure for planning AI-driven strategies while highlighting areas like ethics and inclusion.

The AAI-HE model (Artificial Intelligence in Higher Education) is introduced by Jantakun, Jantakun and Jantakoon [7]. It comprises seven key components, including AI technologies (user interfaces and systems), roles of AI in education, machine/deep learning modules, decision-support (DSS) modules, AI applications in teaching/learning, and AI-driven campus efficiency enhancements. This model provides a holistic framework for integrating AI across university teaching, learning, and administrative functions.

The UTAUT-based adoption model to AI in higher education links performance expectancy, effort expectancy, social influence, and facilitating conditions to stakeholders' attitudes and intentions toward AI. These constructs are hypothesized to shape behavioral intention to adopt AI tools and systems. In essence, the model predicts that positive beliefs about AI's usefulness, ease-of-use, social support, and available resources will drive AI adoption in universities [8].

Temper, Tjoa and David [4] propose the "Higher Education Act for AI (HEAT-AI)" framework, which adapts the EU's risk-based AI Act to the educational context. This framework categorizes AI use-cases by risk level (prohibited, high-risk, transparency-required, etc.) and provides corresponding guidelines for teaching and learning. As a well-structured governance framework, it helps institutions develop AI policies that foster ethical, responsible AI use and competence-building in faculty and students.

# 2 Methodology

## 2.1 Conceptual Framework

Conceptual models constitute a structured framework for the comprehension, representation, and analysis of complex phenomena [9]. Through the abstraction of critical elements and the delineation of their interrelationships, conceptual models enable a systematic investigation of theoretical constructs and empirical phenomena [10]. This methodological approach is particularly pertinent in disciplines where direct experimentation is impractical or where the synthesis of multiple interacting variables is necessary to construct coherent explanatory frameworks [11, 12]. As a component of conceptual models, conceptual maps function as an effective methodological instrument for the visual organization and representation of knowledge.

This study is to suggest how AI adoption is transforming strategies and decision-making in HEIs. Proposed conceptual framework is based on a systematic literature review on AI in universities conducted by the authors. The review study selected 36 articles from 1234 articles in three academic databases - ProQuest, Web of Science, and Scopus. The methodological framework developed by Chiu [13] and Chiu [14] was used for the screening process of the selected articles. The authors consider this methodology particularly valuable in research requiring the synthesis of diverse ideas, as it helps to uncover underlying patterns, clarify ambiguities, and foster critical thinking.

## 2.2 Bibliometric Analysis

Bibliometric analysis has become an established and methodologically rigorous approach for systematically examining large volumes of scientific literature [15]. Its widespread adoption is facilitated by the increased availability and accessibility of specialized bibliometric software—such as Gephi, Leximancer, and VOSviewer—as well as comprehensive scientific databases including Scopus and Web of Science. Given its inherently interdisciplinary nature, bibliometric methodology is applicable across a wide spectrum of fields, ranging from information science to business research. Visualization techniques are recognized as particularly powerful tools for the analysis of complex bibliometric networks, encompassing citation networks among publications or journals, co-authorship networks among researchers, and co-occurrence networks among keywords [16].

In this study the authors apply VOSviewer to create a bibliometric network which results are used further in their analysis. VOSviewer is a software tool for constructing and visualising bibliometric networks [17]. VOSviewer offers text mining functionality that can be used to construct and visualise co-occurrence networks of important terms extracted from a body of scientific literature. To construct a map, VOSviewer uses the VOS mapping technique, where VOS stands for visualisation of similarities.

Scopus database is used as a source of information. Four searches are performed, starting with a more narrowed focus and sequentially enlarging it. The keywords "strategy", "artificial intelligence", and "university" are extracted from the article title, abstract and keywords of the publications. The publications included in the data collection cover the period from 1960 to present. Altogether 987 documents are included in the analysis.

Using Scopus analyser, it is found that the number of documents containing the three keywords increased significantly in 2024 (Fig. 1).

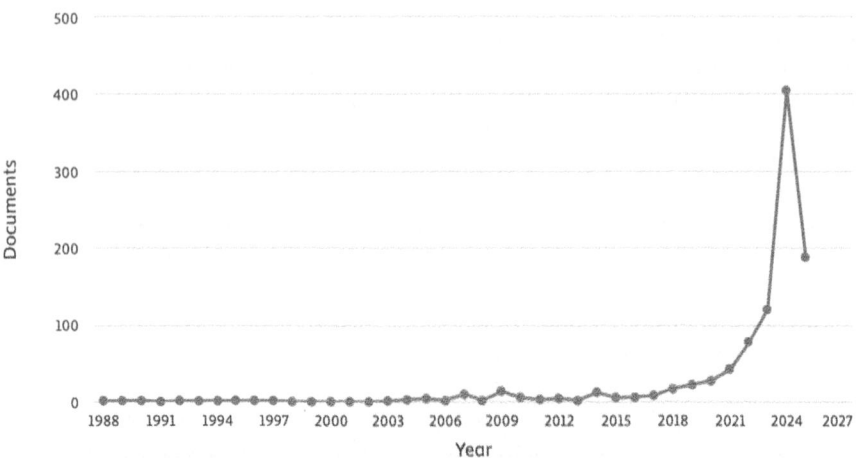

**Fig. 1.** Number of documents with the analysed keywords by year of publication

These keywords are found predominantly in Computer Science subject area (23.3%), Social Sciences (22%), and Engineering (11.7%) (Fig. 2).

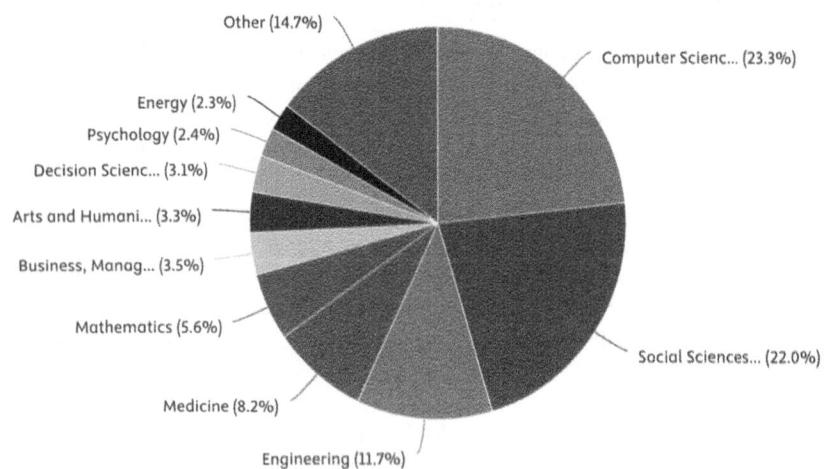

**Fig. 2.** Documents by subject area

The generated file from Scopus search is uploaded as csv file in the VOSviewer software. As a result a co-occurrence bibliometric network of terms is designed (Fig. 3).

VOSviewer software is applied to create a distance-based map. Distance-based maps are maps in which the distance between two items reflects the strength of the relation between the items. A smaller distance typically signifies a stronger relationship. However, in distance-based maps, items are often distributed unevenly. While this uneven

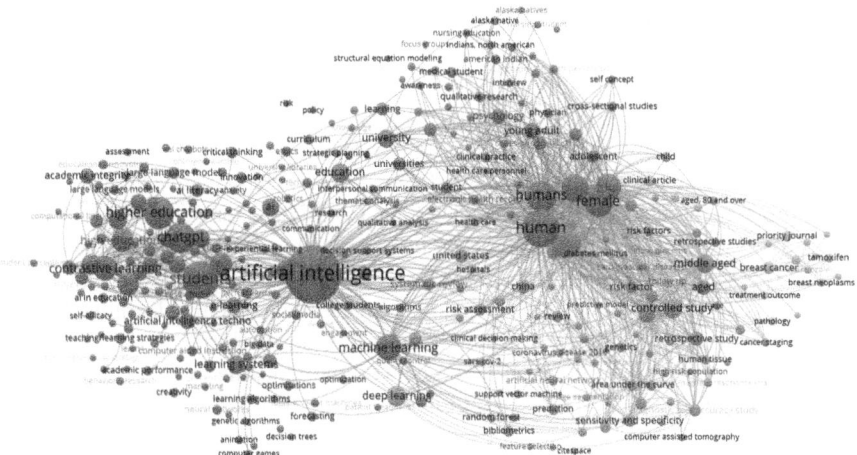

**Fig. 3.** Co-occurrence bibliometric network of terms related to "strategy", "artificial intelligence", and "university"

distribution helps in identifying clusters of related items, it can also pose challenges in labeling all items clearly, as overlapping labels may occur in densely packed areas. In the visualisation presented in Fig. 3, each circle represents a term. The size of a circle indicates the number of publications that have the corresponding term in their title, abstract or keyword. Terms that co-occur a lot tend to be located close to each other in the visualization. The association strength method is used for normalizing the strength of the links between items.

Altogether 334 items are distributed in 4 clusters, as follows: Cluster 1 with 167 items, Cluster 2 with 75 items, Cluster 3 with 66 items, and Cluster 4 with 26 items.

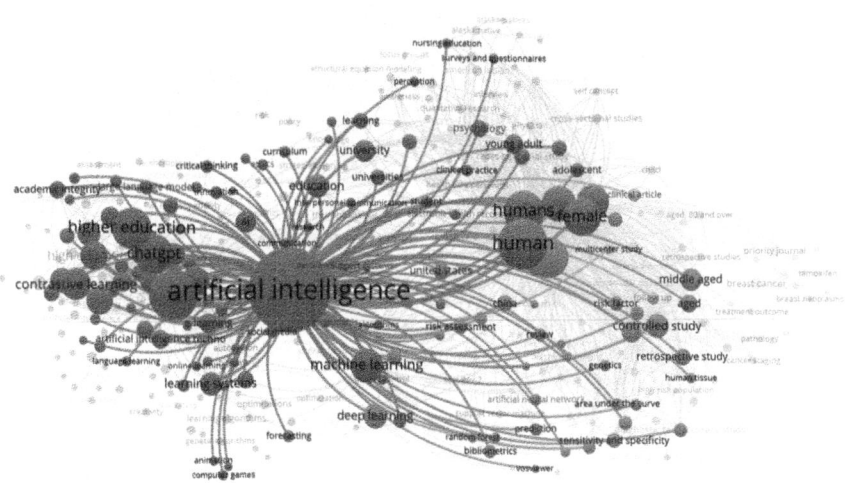

**Fig. 4.** Co-occurrence bibliometric network: focal item "artificial intelligence"

Based on the data provided by the bibliometric analysis the authors reached a set of findings, the most prominent of which are:

AI as an item is closely related with high strength of the links with the following terms: human/humans, machine learning, education, universities, controlled study, and deep learning. The items with the highest total links strength within Cluster 1 include adversarial machine learning, artificial intelligence, chatgpt, contrastive learning, federated learning, higher education, machine learning. Controlled study and risk assessment appear to be the items with the highest total links strength in Cluster 2. Human/humans (Cluster 3) is tightly related not only to the items from the same cluster (e.g. education, university, young adult) but also to artificial intelligence and machine learning (Cluster 1) and controlled study and deep learning (Cluster 2) (Fig. 4).

An interesting situation in bibliometric network presents the item "Artificial Intelligence" (Cluster 1) with 310 links, total links strength 2064, and occurences 358. It is linked with items from Cluster 2 and Cluster 3.

## 3   Strategic Model for AI Adoption in Higher Education Framed on the PDCA Cycle

### 3.1   PDCA Cycle

The PDCA (Plan-Do-Check-Act) cycle is an iterative, four-step methodology primarily applied within quality improvement processes [18]. Nevertheless, it can also serve as a general framework for managing a wide range of processes, including strategic

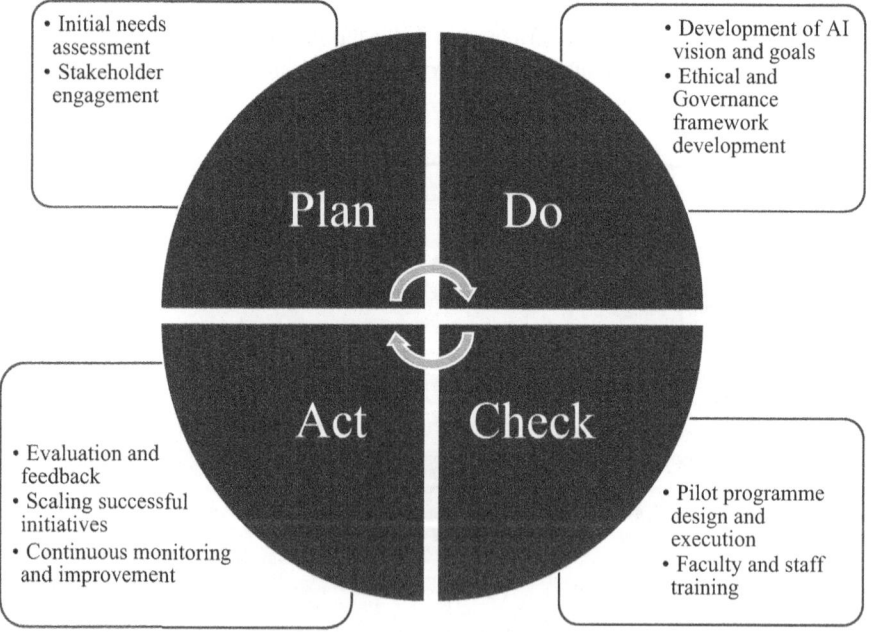

**Fig. 5.** Conceptual model for AI adoption in HE framed on the PDCA cycle - PDCA-AI@HEI

management. An example of its application in strategic management is Hoshin Kanri (Policy Deployment), a Japanese approach that explicitly incorporates the PDCA cycle [19–21]. Furthermore, the principles of the PDCA cycle are also integrated into strategic management frameworks based on the Balanced Scorecard methodology [22].

Based on the literature review and the results from bibliometric analysis, a conceptual model for AI adoption in HE framed on the PDCA cycle is proposed by the authors (Fig. 5).

Detailed description of the PDCA-AI@HEI conceptual model is proveded on Table 1.

**Table 1.** The PDCA-AI@HEI conceptual model activities and tools by stages.

| Stage | Activities | Methodologies and tools |
|---|---|---|
| 1. Plan<br>1.1. Initial needs assessment | Audit and analysis of pedagogical and research workflows, technological infrastructure (including servers, LMS, and data platforms), as well as the competencies of faculty and administrative personnel | Stakeholder surveys (faculty and students challenges)<br>Systematic mapping of AI applications (e.g., intelligent tutoring systems, automated assessment tools, and research analytics) |
| 1. Plan<br>1.2. Stakeholder engagement | Forming an AI steering committee or working group with representatives from various sectors, including faculty, educational technology experts, research offices, students, and administrators, provides a strong foundation for collaboration | Tools such as workshops, town halls, and surveys can be instrumental in gathering stakeholder input<br>Clear and reciprocal communication plays a pivotal role in this process<br>Organizing workshops with academic and administrative leaders |
| 2. Do<br>2.1. Development of AI vision and goals | The vision should define strategic goals, such as enhancing personalized learning experiences, improving research productivity, and increasing operational efficiency within laboratories and classrooms. It is critical to establish both short- and long-term objectives | Establishment of key performance indicators (KPIs) to evaluate progress |
| 2. Do<br>2.2. Ethical and governance framework development | Foundational ethical principles—such as transparency, fairness, accountability, beneficence, and non-maleficence—should underpin ethical policies. Data governance standards must be established to safeguard consent, ensure data security, and maintain anonymization in research contexts | Frameworks like Floridi's five AI principles<br>Dedicated AI policy committees or ethics boards |

*(continued)*

**Table 1.** (*continued*)

| Stage | Activities | Methodologies and tools |
|---|---|---|
| 3. Check<br>3.1. Pilot programme design and execution | - Selection of focused use cases<br>- Adopting an agile "test-and-learn" methodology<br>- Establishing clear success metrics<br>- Iterative refinement and scaling | Implementing adaptive quizzing systems in large lecture courses to personalize learning experience<br>Introducing data-mining tools<br>Setting quantifiable and qualitative success metrics<br>Collecting qualitative feedback from participants |
| 3. Check<br>3.2. Faculty and staff training | Tailored professional development programs are essential, encompassing workshops on AI fundamentals, hands-on sessions with specific tools such as tutoring bots and analytics software, and seminars on ethical AI usage | Promoting a culture of continuous learning through learning communities and informal sessions such as "lunch-and-learns" is vital |
| 4. Act<br>4.1. Evaluation and feedback | It involves systematically assessing the impact of AI initiatives against predefined KPIs, such as enhancements in student academic performance, reductions in administrative workload, and increases in research productivity | Combination of quantitative metrics and qualitative insights gathered through surveys, focus groups, and usage analytics |
| 4. Act<br>4.2. Scaling successful initiatives | The initial pilot programs serve as valuable testbeds, providing insights and evidence to inform broader implementation strategies. By analyzing the outcomes and lessons learned from these initial deployments, institutions can develop comprehensive rollout plans that align with their overarching educational objectives | The Artificial Intelligence Assessment Scale (AIAS)<br>Documenting best practices from pilot programs is crucial |
| 4. Act<br>4.3. Continuous monitoring and improvement | The sustained effectiveness of AI strategies in HE, can be achieved only through a robust, ongoing oversight mechanisms. This involves instituting regular evaluation cycles, such as annual reviews, to assess each AI initiative's performance and its alignment with institutional goals | Maintaining open channels for stakeholder feedback is equally crucial<br>Continuous loop of assessment, feedback, and refinement |

The conceptual model is further developed using the taxonomy of AI in educational leadership proposed by Sposato [5] (Table 2).

**Table 2.** The PDCA-AI@HEI conceptual model adapted to the taxonomy of AI in educational leadership.

| Stage | Domain | Key components |
|---|---|---|
| 1. Plan | 1.1. AI for community engagement and communication | - AI-powered communication tools<br>- Feedback and engagement analytics<br>- Social media monitoring |
| | 1.2. AI for diversity, equity, and inclusion (DEI) initiatives | - AI-driven equity audits<br>- Inclusive curriculum design<br>- Supporting special education needs |
| 2. Do | 2.1. AI in decision-making and policy formulation | - Predictive analytics for policy development<br>- Sentiment analysis for stakeholder feedback<br>- Ethical and equity decision support |
| | 2.2. AI for governance and compliance | - Regulatory compliance monitoring<br>- Fraud detection and data integrity |
| | 2.3. AI in organizational leadership and strategic planning | - Predictive analytics for policy development<br>- Sentiment analysis for stakeholder feedback<br>- Ethical and equity decision support |
| 3. Check | 3.1. AI for personalized learning | - Adaptive learning platforms<br>- Intelligent tutoring systems<br>- Learning analytics |
| | 3.2. AI for enhancing teaching practices | - AI in curriculum design<br>- Teacher professional development<br>- Intelligent classroom management |
| | 3.3. AI for enhancing student support services | - AI-based career counseling<br>- Mental health and behavioral analytics<br>- Virtual assistants for student support |
| 4. Act | 4.1. AI for administrative efficiency | - Automated scheduling systems<br>- Data-driven decision support<br>- HR management<br>- Student enrollment and retention analytics |
| | 4.2. Ethical AI leadership and governance | - Bias mitigation strategies<br>- Privacy and data security management<br>- Transparent AI use policies |

## 4   Conclusions and Implications for Future Research

This study presents a comprehensive framework for AI adoption in higher education institutions (HEIs), integrating findings from a systematic literature review, bibliometric analysis, and a conceptual model grounded in the PDCA cycle. The proposed model highlights the multifaceted role of AI in strategic planning, decision support, pedagogical transformation, and institutional governance. It emphasizes the importance of phased implementation, ethical governance, stakeholder involvement, and continuous evaluation to ensure sustainable and responsible AI integration in academic environments.

The bibliometric analysis, based on data from over 980 scientific publications, confirms a growing academic interest in the convergence of AI, strategy, and higher education, particularly in the areas of machine learning, governance, and student-centered innovation. The clustering of terms reveals both thematic concentrations and interdisciplinary overlaps that validate the complexity of AI implementation in universities. The PDCA-based strategic model synthesizes these insights into an actionable roadmap that educational leaders can adapt to their institutional contexts.

Implications for future research include several promising directions:

Firstly, empirical validation of the proposed PDCA-based AI adoption model in real-world university settings to assess its applicability, impact, and scalability.

Secondly, comparative studies across regions or types of institutions (e.g., public vs. private, research-intensive vs. teaching-focused) to understand contextual factors influencing AI strategy success.

Thirdly, longitudinal studies tracking AI implementation outcomes over time to evaluate improvements in teaching quality, administrative efficiency, student engagement, and research productivity.

Development of evaluation metrics and AI maturity models tailored to educational settings, particularly those that address ethical use, inclusiveness, and human-AI collaboration could provide a solid background for accountable adoption of AI tools in HE.

Overall, this study contributes a theoretically grounded and practically oriented framework for integrating AI into higher education strategy, offering a foundation for future applied research and institutional innovation. By embedding the proposed cyclical conceptual model into their operational frameworks, universities can responsibly integrate AI into teaching, learning, and research.

**Disclosure of Interests.**    The authors have no competing interests to declare that are relevant to the content of this article.

# References

1. Gaftandzhieva, S., Hussain, S., Hilcenko, S., Doneva, R., Boykova, K.: Data-driven decision making in higher education institutions: state-of-play. Int. J. Adv. Comput. Sci. Appl. (IJACSA) **14** (2023)
2. Team, M.E.: Best practices for optimizing AI strategy in higher education. https://www.microsoft.com/en-us/education/blog/2025/04/best-practices-for-optimizing-ai-strategy-in-higher-education/. Accessed 28 Apr 2025
3. Zhang, J., Goyal, S.B.: AI-driven decision support system innovations to empower higher education administration. ResearchGate (2024). https://doi.org/10.57159/gadl.jcmm.3.2.24070
4. Temper, M., Tjoa, S., David, L.: Higher Education Act for AI (HEAT-AI): a framework to regulate the usage of AI in higher education institutions. Front. Educ. **10**, 1505370 (2025)
5. Sposato, M.: Artificial intelligence in educational leadership: a comprehensive taxonomy and future directions. Int. J. Educ. Technol. High. Educ. **22**, 20 (2025)
6. Chan, C.K.Y.: A comprehensive AI policy education framework for university teaching and learning. Int. J. Educ. Technol. High. Educ. **20**, 38 (2023)

7. Jantakun, T., Jantakun, K., Jantakoon, T.: A Common framework for artificial intelligence in higher education (AAI-HE Model). IES **14**, 94 (2021)
8. Mohsin, F.H., Md Isa, N., Ishak, K., Mohamed Salleh, H.: Navigating the adoption of artificial intelligence in higher education. IJBT **14**, 109–120 (2024)
9. Bozlu, B., Demirörs, O.: A conceptual modeling methodology: from conceptual model to design. In: Proceedings of the 2008 Summer Computer Simulation Conference, pp. 1–11. Society for Modeling & Simulation International, Vista, CA (2008)
10. Fettke, P.: How conceptual modeling is used. Commun. Assoc. Inf. Syst. **25** (2009)
11. Grenier, R.S., Dudzinska-Przesmitzki, D.: A conceptual model for eliciting mental models using a composite methodology. Hum. Resour. Dev. Rev. **14**, 163–184 (2015)
12. Heck, R.H., Hallinger, P.: The study of educational leadership and management: where does the field stand today? Educ. Manag. Adm. Leadersh. **33**, 229–244 (2005)
13. Chiu, T.K.F.: Future research recommendations for transforming higher education with generative AI. Comput. Educ. Artif. Intell. **6**, 100197 (2024)
14. Chiu, T.K.F., Xia, Q., Zhou, X.-Y., Chai, C.S., Cheng, M.-T.: Systematic literature review on opportunities, challenges, and future research recommendations of artificial intelligence in education. Comput. Educ. Artif. Intell. 100118 (2023)
15. Donthu, N., Kumar, S., Mukherjee, D., Pandey, N., Lim, W.M.: How to conduct a bibliometric analysis: an overview and guidelines. J. Bus. Res. **133**, 285–296 (2021)
16. van Eck, N.J., Waltman, L.: Visualizing bibliometric networks. In: Ding, Y., Rousseau, R., Wolfram, D. (eds.) Measuring Scholarly Impact: Methods and Practice, pp. 285–320. Springer International Publishing, Cham (2014)
17. Waltman, L., Van Eck, N.J., Noyons, E.C.M.: A unified approach to mapping and clustering of bibliometric networks. J. Informet. **4**(4), 629–635 (2010)
18. Pietrzak, M., Paliszkiewicz, J.: Framework of strategic learning: the PDCA cycle. Management **10**, 149–161 (2015)
19. Cowley, M., Domb, E.: Beyond Strategic Vision. Routledge, London (2012). https://doi.org/10.4324/9780080500058
20. Babich, P.: Hoshin Handbook, 3rd edn. Total Quality Engineering Inc., Poway, CA (2006)
21. Akao, Y., Hoshin, K.: Policy Deployment for Successful TQM. Productivity Press, New York (2020)
22. Kaplan, R.S.: The Balanced Scorecard: Translating Strategy into Action. In: Kaplan, R.S., Norton, D.P. (eds.). Harvard Business School Press, Boston (1996)

# Data-Driven Quality Management and Intelligent Systems for Academic Processes and Flexible Decision-Making

# Academic Profile Management: Benchmarking DeepSeek-R1 for Publication and Citation Data

Boris Bankov$^{(\boxtimes)}$ 🆔, Silvia Parusheva 🆔, Olga Marinova 🆔, Petya Strashimirova 🆔, and Denitsa Petkova 🆔

University of Economics – Varna, Knyaz Boris I, 77, 9002 Varna, Bulgaria
boris.bankov@ue-varna.bg

**Abstract.** The integration of artificial intelligence (AI) models into academic publication management systems presents a promising solution to the difficulties of structuring composite data, manually input by authors and records retrieved from application programing interfaces (API). Current systems face barriers in accurately matching records from diverse scientific databases, such as Scopus or Web of Science, leading to inefficiencies and inaccuracies. In this paper we discuss existing bibliometric solutions at the University of Economics – Varna, Bulgaria and tackle different algorithmic approaches for integrating automated API communication. The research explores the use of AI, specifically the DeepSeek-R1 model based on Qwen or Llama fine-tuning distillations, to enhance automated validation and discoverability of new research for the purpose of institutional accreditation reports. We address two primary challenges: identifying duplicate entries with heterogenous structures and improving bibliometric data management. The proposed solution involves the calculation of similarity scores using metrics like locality-sensitive hashing. The development of AI-powered tools and their integration with academic systems offers a novel approach to overcoming current limitations. This study highlights the potential benefits of using DeepSeek-R1 for enhancing both the accuracy and scalability of publication and citation data management.

**Keywords:** Deepseek-R1 academic integration · bibliometric data · calculating text similarity · automating data management

## 1 Introduction

In the modern education setting, smart data management is critically important for academic success. Machine learning, natural language processing and deep neural networks are being used to develop new state-of-the-art intelligent systems. Artificial intelligence has become the central focus of building the next step in the digitalization process of academic growth. Going forward, breakthroughs in large language models (LLMs) will lead to more precise solutions for textual data management in research institutions and scientific networks. While AI in the classroom focuses on personalized learning – adapting content, automatically assessing essays, or providing intelligent tutoring systems – AI

© The Author(s), under exclusive license to Springer Nature Switzerland AG 2026
G. De Tré et al. (Eds.): FQAS 2025, LNAI 16119, pp. 103–114, 2026.
https://doi.org/10.1007/978-3-032-05607-8_11

for administrative tasks optimizes processes such as student enrollment, financial analysis, and resource management. In the former case, technology directly enhances the learning experience, whereas in the latter, it serves as an "invisible" infrastructure that improves institutional efficiency. However, these two aspects of AI integration in higher education do not paint the full picture.

Automated data management for academic profile tracking has a potential for more advanced research. Bibliometric information about publications, citations, project participation, conference attendance, consulting and practical expertise is fragmented and scattered across multiple online platforms [1]. Global scientific databases like Scopus, Web of Science, ResearchGate and Google Scholar help track publication data but do not provide a unified interface for automatic extraction. Furthermore, systems like ORCID allow both manual and automatic tagging but not all records include proper field syntax matching the actual records. Among the common problems that occur from the heterogeneous data flows are wrong order of co-authors or missing co-authors, incorrect ISSN formats, issues with the publishing date, the type of publication and more. In addition, transliteration of Cyrillic to Latin letters and vice versa in author names and publication titles, can cause unpredicted mistakes. To solve these challenges, we discuss the problem areas of automated author profile management. In this paper, we present a software architecture to streamline data integration from various APIs to process publication and citation data for the academic staff of University of Economics - Varna, Bulgaria.

University of Economics - Varna, Bulgaria is a 105-year-old institution bridging academic traditions into the future. A significant amount of the information business processes at the university are digitized. These range from web-based software for student schedules, e-learning, grading and internship tracking to certified quality control and document management systems. In 2016 we developed an online platform "Register Publications" (publications.ue-varna.bg) to help academic staff track publications, citations, project and editorial board participation, consulting, specializations and scientific event attendance. The project is previously discussed by Bankov [2]. The database and business logic continuously evolve to meet the criteria for academic growth, accreditation and performance assessment at the university. As research and publishing in international databases such as Scopus and Web of Science are becoming crucial for institutional rating and financing, the need for automated academic profile management arises. Currently all data is being manually submitted by our academic members for the purpose of extracting reports and statistics that are required by different procedures. Due to an ever-increasing demand for balanced workload the authors of this paper are working on an automated profile management system that employs access to scientific database APIs with the goal of collecting publication and citation data.

In this paper we present the challenges of such a software solution and discuss how an LLM like DeepSeek-R1 can be integrated into our existing system architecture. The model, introduced by Guo et al. [3] was publicly released at the start of 2025. DeepSeek-R1 is a reasoning model, trained via large-scale unsupervised reinforcement learning. The authors [3] have presented the model weights as well as the training method. The implementation of the training itself is not open, however the model is announced as open-source.

## 2   Related Work

A significant step into the adoption of AI in the digital environment is the release of ChatGPT at the end of 2022. One of the most cited meta-analysis of the Pre-GPT era AI tools in education is conducted by Zawacki-Richter et al. [4]. A systematic review of 2 656 publications, identified between 2007 and 2018, yielded 146 articles that demonstrate potential and offer valuable insights into the pedagogical benefits of using AI applications. After aggregating the results, the authors [4] formulate four areas in which AI services are being applied. These areas include: *profiling and prediction, assessment and evaluation, adaptive systems and personalization* and finally *intelligent tutoring systems*. Institutional administrative software is not discussed; however it is our firm belief that such tools are interconnected with the rest of the mentioned groups and can benefit from intelligent integrations. Academic profile management is an important factor in drawing attention to research and funding and active presence in platforms like ResearchGate and Academia.edu generates networking opportunities [5].

Researchers often cite AI as the driving force for the evolution in Education 4.0 and 5.0. Authors like Kamalov, Santandreu and Gurrib [6] discuss the potential effects of applying AI in personalized training, intelligent tutoring systems, teacher-student collaboration and assessment automation from a theoretical point of view. Their analysis shows that modern technological solutions like ChatGPT are suitable for certain tasks in the academic field, but there needs to be precise control and ethical consideration about trusting these systems to lower the workload responsibilities of tutors in the classroom. Rane, Choudhary and Rane [7] also bring up the use of AI in automation of administrative tasks and gamification in education. According to them, AI integration is limited to basic data analytics and rudimentary adaptive learning platforms. Their publication also stimulates the discussion about the ethical dimensions of relying on AI to streamline the supporting function of educational software. In addition, Rane, Choudhary and Rane [7] conclude that digital inequality is a major problem as people with disabilities use intelligent systems in a specific capacity. Hearing-impaired students benefit greatly from AI-powered solutions that can produce speech-to-text notes [8–10]. Emerging research on the topic of accessibility suggests that intelligent tutoring systems will be able to autonomously adapt in real-time to performance feedback and behavioral cues. Research done by Nacheva [11], Hearing [12], Pierrès, Darvishy and Christen [13] presents software solutions in education in the context of e-learning and mobile accessibility for students. The most commonly generated texts from ChatGPT, Microsoft Copilot and Jasper are used as a template for benchmarking readability, which include content complexity and clarity. AI tools help visually impaired users in a myriad of ways, such as lecture narration, text summary, question comprehension, grammatical feedback and more.

A significant number of published research focuses on the ethical side of AI-assisted writing, both in the academic environment and in student's works [14–16]. Students perceive AI as more than text-generating tool, but rather as a virtual tutor or a digital peer. Science workers are aware of AI misconceptions and urge institutions to promote clear guidelines for "AI-giarism". Various instruments have emerged to help evaluate potential AI-generated papers and academic dishonesty [17]. Platforms such as TurnItIn and Compilation score very well against writing misconduct according to Weber-Wulff et al. [18]. Others like Perkins, Roe, Postma, McGaughran and Hickerson [19] suggest changing assessment types to avoid provoking AI use in academic works. However, a comprehensive study of AI's impact on the academic ecosystem shows that these tools do not necessarily impose additional responsibilities or workload.

Recent papers on the application of AI in bibliometric analysis on Web of Science data have shown strong potential for discovering insights into co-authorship and collaborative dynamics in research [20]. Researcher profiles are under close observation with different machine learning approaches being presented in order to evaluate performance based on data in global scientific portals as stated by Abramo and D'Angelo [21] and Rehs [22]. Saeidnia, Hosseini, Abdoli and Ausloos [23] conduct an extensive overview of AI application in scientometrics, webometrics and bibliometrics is presented. Their findings show that AI is crucial for the enhancement of accuracy and efficiency of data collection, recognition of citation patterns and impact evaluation, keyword extraction and more.

In summary, AI tools are seen as pivotal for the improvement of data management and analytics. The potential to bring cutting-edge software solutions into the classroom and the academic environment will continue to inspire revolutionary projects, provided institutions keep pace with technological adoption.

As one of the recent competitive breakthroughs in LLMs, DeepSeek has gained attention from researchers and investors. Comparative analyses suggest that while Chat-GPT excels in linguistic variation, referring to its ability to generate diverse text, while DeepSeek distinguishes itself through superior grammatical structure according to AlAfnan [24]. The work of several researchers such as Wang and Kantarcioglu [25] praise several areas of innovation that DeepSeek improves on, such as reinforcement learning and high sample efficiency. Our paper demonstrates an approach to utilizing DeepSeek to compare publication and citation bibliometric records retrieved from global scientific databases and records stored in the University of Economics - Varna's own archival system for academic profile tracking. The focus on this model stems from its advertised ability to semantically understand the context beyond surface-level record matching that can be achieved with regular algorithms. Classical similarity metrics typically operate on synthetic or statistical similarity, potentially disregarding or struggling with variations in language, grammatical or spelling issues, structure, missing fields and more. While LLMs are sometimes seen as black boxes, prompt-based interfaces with DeepSeek allow injecting reasoning steps or structured instructions. This adds interpretability and flexibility, especially in iterative data cleaning or matching workflows. Key considerations are:

- **Validation and quality control**: Ensuring the accuracy of comparisons, particularly in publication and citation titles, will involve rigorous validation processes and quality checks.
- **Structured data integration**: Developing a system that combines textual information with structured academic data will be essential for comprehensive profile tracking.

## 3   System Design and Architecture

"Register Publications" is a PHP Laravel-based web platform that helps track publication and citation data. Information is structured on an individual researcher level, department and faculty. Academic members, PhD students and regular employees from the university can submit bibliometric descriptions of their published documents. Laravel utilizes the MVC architecture, which ensures better organization by dividing the application into three main components: Model, View, and Controller. Each of these components has its specific role, which facilitates maintenance, scalability, and code readability [26].

The extraction, validation and standardization of bibliometric data from various academic databases such as Scopus, Web of Science, ORCID and Google Scholar is a key stage in the process of building efficient and reliable scientific systems. These databases provide extremely valuable resources for research, citations, metadata and author information, but processing the data requires attention to their accuracy, validity and consistency with each other. In this context, the application of semi-automated approaches for extracting, validating and standardizing bibliometric data is crucial to ensure quality and accurate results.

Initially, the data is retrieved using the respective APIs provided by each source: Scopus via Elsevier's API (in XML or JSON), WoS via Clarivate's XML schema, ORCID via JSON or XML, and Google Scholar via SerpApi.com (since the platform does not have a public API to retrieve this data) in JSON format. Each of these systems maintains its own data model, requiring transformation to achieve interoperability.

The initial extraction of bibliometric data from the Scopus, WoS, ORCID and Google Scholar platforms is done using validated structured formats such as ORCID identifiers, DOI (Digital Object Identifier), BibTeX and other metadata formats. Each of these formats offers different options for accessing and structuring data, with ORCID and DOI identifiers used to specify authors and publications, while BibTeX provides a structured list of bibliographic data for cited documents. Sasmoko, Manalu and Danaristo [27] state that existing algorithms and APIs offer possibilities to extract this data, allowing its automated processing in the context of various scientific tasks, such as publication matching, citation analysis and the creation of bibliometric profiles.

Therefore, it is important to note that for data extracted from bibliometric databases to be usable, it should meet certain requirements to ensure reliability, reusability, and integrability into various scientific analysis systems. Foremost among these are the so-called FAIR principles (Findable, Accessible, Interoperable, Reusable), which provide a framework for the management and sharing of academic data as discussed by Wilkinson et al. [28]. They require that data be easily discoverable through unique and persistent identifiers (such as DOI or ORCID ID), accessible through standardized protocols, compatible with existing web systems using common formats and metadata standards and reusable under clearly defined structuring and citation conditions.

In this regard, the extracted bibliographic records should undergo a series of validation checks to confirm their completeness and structural correctness. First, the mandatory fields of each publication should be checked - author(s), title, year of publication, source (for example scientific journal or conference), identifiers such as DOI or ISBN, as well as publication language. Missing or incorrectly filled fields may compromise subsequent analyses and statistical inferences related to research productivity, co-authorship patterns and citation impact.

The goal of the current project is to aggregate data from public APIs and match the new records with existing information in "Register Publications". To achieve this there are two features that need to be implemented and an LLM can help create a more reliable comparison algorithm. Initially we need to standardize the input format and then we need to process and compare the records. A simplified version of the communication infrastructure is shown on Fig. 1.

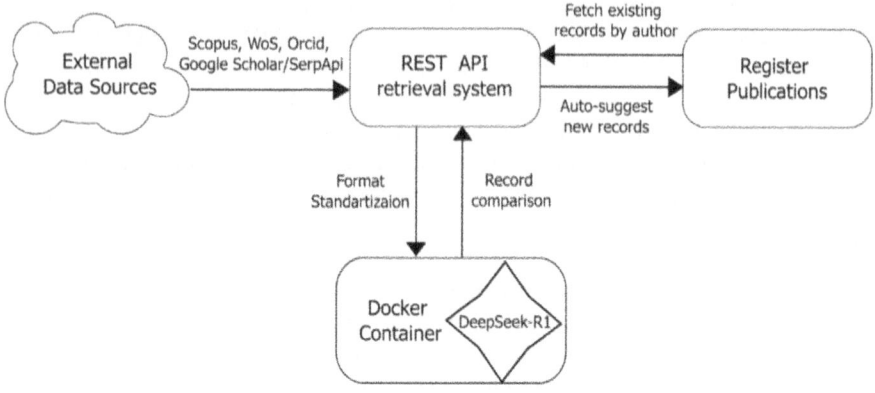

**Fig. 1.** API infrastructure

Integrating Large Language Models into the academic data system enhances its intelligence, particularly for tasks like comparing records, matching similar meanings, and standardizing metadata. Given the significant computing power LLMs require, they often need high-performance graphics units (GPUs) or powerful cloud services. To enable secure and stable run across different environments, Docker containerization can help in packaging the service and all its dependencies making sure compatibility issues are avoided. In the case of high demand due to multiple LLM requests, Kubernetes is considered to manage or "orchestrate" the containers, based on usage. Huang, Cai, Zong and Mao [29] evaluate this approach stating this will make the system portable and reliable.

The LLM service is exposed through RESTful endpoints, which are set up using simple Python tools like Flask. These endpoints allow other applications to send prompt inputs via API using HTTP POST requests. Our main system is built with PHP Laravel, but thanks to RESTful APIs, different services created in various programming languages can work well together. This setup lets us add advanced features, such as record similarity scoring and citation matching, to our current system without needing a complete redesign. The server takes care of model requests and sends back structured outputs like JSON, which can then be processed further in our PHP application.

Getting access to scientific APIs requires a developer account, verification and key authorization. After completing this step, we collect author unique author identifiers for researchers from each scientific database. These include Scopus ID, Web of Science ID, ORCID ID and Google Scholar ID and are needed to retrieve information about published and indexed works in those platforms. Here we encounter the first problem area: we need to be able to compare archived records in "Register Publications" and the downloaded new data. The reason for this is to tag each publication with its unique key given by each of the above-mentioned databases. As a result, we can periodically update our system since we know which articles, papers, book chapters, etc., are already accounted for and which ones are newly published works. After we discover data that is missing from our system, we can begin transferring it to researchers' profiles and streamline the process of validating publications. We apply the same logic with citations.

While the publishing process is something authors are actively monitoring, automating citation extraction is more difficult. In addition, the number of citations can be significantly higher. In our current system, publication records include twenty-one distinct fields such as paper type, title, conference or journal name, issue, volume, pages, indexing, ISSN, ISBN, author(s), DOI and hyperlink to the publication. Some of these fields are mandatory, while others are optional. Authors are encouraged to provide as much detail as possible to ensure comprehensive and detailed reports. For citations we require only three columns: year of publishing, journal index (e.g. Scopus or Web of Science Q1), and full bibliometric description in a single field. This was done to alleviate inputting meta labels for each citation which can be an extensive process and as a result now it is difficult to properly structure citation data and compare it with existing records in the global scientific databases. When "Register Publications" was initially developed we imported 5000 publications, which were being archived by our Library department. They include a similar issue as the title, name of publisher or conference name, book volume, edition and page range are all concatenated into a single field. In addition, some records in the database are missing DOI or have incorrectly submitted DOI, which in general is one of the easiest ways to compare existing data and new additions. As a traditional coding problem, most programming languages have similarity calculation functions like Hamming distance, Levenshtein distance, Soundex, etc., that can be applied but each record needs to be broken down into separate columns. Since there can be incomplete data about a publication, trying to automate this process presents a significant challenge. To solve these negative traits of our business logic we perform a practical study on the use of the DeepSeek-R1 model.

As of April 2025, there are several fine-tuned variants of the model. Part of them are based on Qwen, while the others are Llama distillations. The goal of fine-tuning on one hand is to create a smaller in size model, while on the other it has better performance as usually training data is task-specific and domain-oriented. To complete our research, there are two options: fine-tune for text matching in publication records or perform similarity calculations. For the first a large dataset of correctly labeled matching pairs with both outcomes is required, e.g. similar/dissimilar or confidence rating between 0 and 1, however we do not yet have such a resource available. The second poses different challenges: the process of recognizing matching records needs to be compared against template outcomes. Within the context of our paper the algorithm options for this approach are:

- **Brute force with nested loops** - iterate each object from the smaller dataset against the larger collection (respectively the API records and our system's database), quadratic time complexity $O(n^2)$.
- **Hashing** - $O(n + m)$, where **n** and **m** represent the lengths of the two datasets. Objects are converted to strings and hashed to be used as keys, with the option to use locality-sensitive hashing (LSH). We use this method for publications as a

benchmark for expected similarity grade against the results produced by the two models as publication titles should have very little difference in syntax.

- **Pairwise similarity with embeddings** - for each object produce an embedding and calculate cosine similarity with a minimum threshold and a time complexity $O(n*d)$ where n is the number of objects in the combined datasets and d is the dimensionality of the embedding model. We apply this method for citations since bibliometric data is stored in a single column and it is difficult to correctly extract each label individually.

## 4   Experimental Design

Considering technical limitations, we create an experiment using two DeepSeek-R1 distillations: Llama-8b and Qwen-14b (where **b** stands for billions of parameters). The experiment is conducted on a Windows 11 platform, Intel Core i5-12400F (12 CPUs), ~ 2.5 GHz, 32 GB Ram, NVIDIA GeForce RTX 3060, 12 GB, VENTUS 2X OC and the following settings for the two models: Context Length: 18384; Max Tokens: 8192; Threads: 10; GPU layers: 150.

To assess the abilities of the Qwen and Llama DeepSeek-R1 models we construct three test cases. We choose an author from our existing system that has 10 or more publications discoverable via public APIs. Two datasets are created in JSON format with 10 and 50 works (respectively external records and existing ones). We then send both to DeepSeek-R1 using a Docker OpenWebUI container for the model to run on the local machine. The DeekSeek-R1 local API returns a similarity grade for each pair without previous instructions on how to perform the grading. Three trial passes are constructed: all publications from the first array exist in the second; half of the publications from the first exist in the second; some publications have altered wording in the title in the first array.

The prompt for setting up the comparison is as follows:

*You are given two arrays, the first has N records, the second has N + M, find if one, some or all of the N objects from the first array exist in the second array, compare based on string matching. The goal is to know which objects from the first array exist and which do not in the second. Pretend you are API that returns a JSON response from the comparison and how certain you are that the objects match for each of the N records in the first array, so that the expected response shows the confidence grade.*

DeepSeek-R1's key advantage is the thought process. The model agent tries to understand the prompt, more specifically what does "string matching" means, which the model deduces it could be both exact and partial matching with the expectation of providing confidence levels from 0 to 1. Then the agent creates a plan of specific actions to fulfill the task and produces the output. The results of the three tests for publication similarity matching are presented in Table 1. As stated above, in the second test half of the records are new and they do not appear in the existing (larger) dataset, thus the expected similarity grade is 0.00. This means the models correctly did not find a publication that matches publications in our current system.

We apply the same method to discover existing citations in our system when compared to those retrieved by access to public APIs. We take 10 citations on a single

**Table 1.** Comparison of similarity grading between Llama/Qwen distillations for publications

| № | DeepSeek-R1-Llama-8B similarity grade | | | DeepSeek-R1-Qwen-14B similarity grade | | | Expected similarity grade | | |
|---|---------|---------|---------|---------|---------|---------|------------|------------|------------|
|   | Pass #1 | Pass #2 | Pass #3 | Pass #1 | Pass #2 | Pass #3 | Pass #1 | Pass #2 | Pass #3 |
| 1 | 0.90 | 0.00 | 0.65 | 1.00 | 0.00 | 0.70 | 0.98 | 0.00 | 0.62 |
| 2 | 1.00 | 1.00 | 1.0 | 1.00 | 1.00 | 0.90 | 1.00 | 1.00 | 0.85 |
| 3 | 0.95 | 0.00 | 0.95 | 1.00 | 0.00 | 1.00 | 0.98 | 0.00 | 0.98 |
| 4 | 1.00 | 1.00 | 1.0 | 1.00 | 1.00 | 1.00 | 1.00 | 1.00 | 1.00 |
| 5 | 1.00 | 1.00 | 0.81 | 0.95 | 0.95 | 0.82 | 0.95 | 0.95 | 0.82 |
| 6 | 0.85 | 0.00 | 0.85 | 0.95 | 0.00 | 0.98 | 0.98 | 0.00 | 0.98 |
| 7 | 1.00 | 1.00 | 1.00 | 0.95 | 0.95 | 0.98 | 0.98 | 0.98 | 0.98 |
| 8 | 1.00 | 1.00 | 0.44 | 0.95 | 1.00 | 0.82 | 0.98 | 0.98 | 0.76 |
| 9 | 0.95 | 0.00 | 0.95 | 0.95 | 0.00 | 0.95 | 0.95 | 0.00 | 0.95 |
| 10 | 0.65 | 0.00 | 0.30 | 0.95 | 0.00 | 0.80 | 0.98 | 0.00 | 0.71 |

publication and compare them against 45 manually submitted citations. We alter the prompt by adding an additional rule:

*The problem is the title in the first array appears as a standalone label, while in the second it is part of a larger bibliometric description.* Table 2 shows the citation similarity scores. Again, in the second trial half of the "discovered" citations are not present in our system's dataset, thus the expected similarity grade is 0.00, since there are no matches for them.

The results in both cases demonstrate an interesting outcome. The DeepSeek-R1 models produce slightly higher grades in some cases, while others are less favored. The observed variations are based on string length: Qwen and Llama give lower confidence to longer titles in the bibliometric description. Extraction of citing titles is less reliable in the smaller Llama-8b model. Resulting grades show stronger fluctuations. Increasing the size of the input labels causes confidence decrease. Both Llama and Qwen distillations favor partial matches in similarity more strongly than in the cases of applying traditional algorithmic approaches. Larger models, conceived from fine-tuning, take more time and resources but can be used to further improve the precision of the comparison. The expansion of our systems will enable us to generate high-quality training datasets, which can be used to fine-tune open-source models like DeepSeek-R1.

One limitation of the study is that in our existing system, a considerable amount of records are written in Cyrillic. While publishing in English is encouraged, some conferences and journals in Bulgaria offer the opportunity to supply titles, abstracts and keywords both in Bulgarian and in English. Although rare, we have document cases in which the Cyrillic title and metadata is provided for a publication from a journal in Web of Science, which for obvious reasons is indexed with its English title. Manual submission of data requires verification and similar issues exist, which are not covered

**Table 2.** Comparison of similarity grading between Llama/Qwen distillations for citations

| № | DeepSeek-R1-Llama-8B similarity grade | | | DeepSeek-R1-Qwen-14B similarity grade | | | Expected similarity grade | | |
|---|---------|---------|---------|---------|---------|---------|---------|---------|---------|
|   | Pass #1 | Pass #2 | Pass #3 | Pass #1 | Pass #2 | Pass #3 | Pass #1 | Pass #2 | Pass #3 |
| 1 | 0.87 | 0.00 | 0.60 | 1.00 | 0.00 | 0.71 | 0.97 | 0.00 | 0.65 |
| 2 | 0.83 | 0.83 | 0.75 | 0.98 | 0.98 | 0.86 | 0.96 | 0.96 | 0.81 |
| 3 | 1.00 | 0.00 | 1.00 | 0.99 | 0.00 | 0.99 | 0.98 | 0.00 | 0.98 |
| 4 | 1.00 | 1.00 | 1.00 | 1.00 | 1.00 | 1.00 | 1.00 | 1.00 | 1.00 |
| 5 | 0.94 | 0.94 | 0.75 | 1.00 | 1.00 | 0.86 | 1.00 | 1.00 | 0.79 |
| 6 | 0.83 | 0.00 | 0.80 | 0.98 | 0.00 | 0.98 | 0.95 | 0.00 | 0.95 |
| 7 | 0.95 | 0.95 | 0.95 | 0.99 | 0.99 | 0.99 | 0.99 | 0.99 | 0.99 |
| 8 | 0.94 | 0.94 | 0.78 | 0.97 | 0.97 | 0.81 | 0.97 | 0.97 | 0.75 |
| 9 | 1.00 | 1.00 | 1.00 | 1.00 | 0.00 | 1.00 | 0.98 | 0.00 | 0.98 |
| 10 | 1.00 | 0.00 | 0.68 | 1.00 | 0.00 | 0.78 | 1.00 | 0.00 | 0.70 |

in this paper. Further opportunity to build upon this study is to consider localization and author name transliteration when discovering matching records from public APIs and our current systems.

## 5  Conclusion

In this paper we discussed the complex infrastructure of existing software at the University of Economics – Varna, aimed at collecting bibliometric data and the opportunities for automatic profile management via public API access. Global scientific databases like Scopus, Web of Science, ORCID and Google Scholar have various data schemas and consolidating those records in a single system is a considerable task. We presented the core challenges in processing diverse information and propose the use of DeepSeek-R1 to match existing and discover new entries in published works for the purpose of validating reports for institutional accreditation and academic assessment procedures. The results show a promising basis for large-scale adoption of open-source projects. AI is essential to bringing the traditional academic environment into the next age of digital education and scientific research. Classroom AI solutions often utilize natural language processing and computer vision, improve equality for students with special needs with speech-to-text or text-to-speech transformation, while administrative AI relies on predictive analytics and workflow automation. Further research into heterogenous data streams for bibliometric management as well as sufficient training data for fine-tuning is needed. As LLMs continue to develop their reasoning capabilities, they are proving to be a powerful foundation for optimizing text-based tasks and shaping the future of software business logic.

**Disclosure of Interests.**  The authors have no competing interests to declare.

# References

1. Martín-Martín, A., Orduña-Malea, E., López-Cózar, E.: Author-level metrics in the new academic profile platforms: the online behaviour of the bibliometrics community. J. Informet. **12**(2), 494–509 (2018). https://doi.org/10.1016/j.joi.2018.04.001
2. Bankov, B.: Software evaluation of PHP MVC web applications. In: International Multidisciplinary Scientific Geo Conference: SGEM, vol. 19, no. (2.1), pp. 603–610 (2019). https://doi.org/10.5593/sgem2019/2.1/S07.079
3. Guo, D., et al.: Deepseek-r1: incentivizing reasoning capability in LLMs via reinforcement learning (2025). https://doi.org/10.48550/arXiv.2501.12948
4. Zawacki-Richter, O., Marín, V., Bond, M., Gouverneur, F.: Systematic review of research on artificial intelligence applications in higher education–where are the educators? Int. J. Educ. Technol. High. Educ. **16**(1), 1–27 (2019). https://doi.org/10.1186/s41239-019-0171-0
5. Campos, F., Valencia, A.: Managing academic profiles on scientific social networks. In: New Contributions in Information Systems and Technologies. Springer International Publishing Volume 1, pp. 265–273 (2015)https://doi.org/10.1007/978-3-319-16486-1_27
6. Kamalov, F., Santandreu, D., Gurrib, I.: New era of artificial intelligence in education: towards a sustainable multifaceted revolution. Sustainability **15**(16), 12451 (2023). https://doi.org/10.3390/su151612451
7. Rane, N., Choudhary, S., Rane, J.: Education 4.0 and 5.0: integrating artificial intelligence (AI) for personalized and adaptive learning. J. Artif. Intell. Robot **1**(1), 29–43 (2023). https://doi.org/10.61577/jaiar.2024.100006
8. Nacheva, R.: Conversational AI for students with hearing disabilities: approach to the text quality evaluation. In: 2024 International Conference Automatics and Informatics (ICAI), pp. 130–135 (2024). https://doi.org/10.1109/ICAI63388.2024.10851526
9. Alkahtani, N.: The impact of artificial intelligence on quality of life for deaf and hard of hearing students. Am. Ann. Deaf **169**(4), 329–347 (2024). https://doi.org/10.1353/aad.2024.a946587
10. Pierrès, O., Darvishy, A., Christen, M.: Exploring the role of generative AI in higher education: semi-structured interviews with students with disabilities. Educ. Inform. Technol. 1–30 (2024). https://doi.org/10.1007/s10639-024-13134-8
11. Bogdanova, G., Todorov, T., Noev, N., Tomov, Z., Chehlarova, N.: Model of computer game at education of visually impaired people. In: 2024 21st International Conference on Information Technology Based Higher Education and Training, pp. 1–7 (2024). https://doi.org/10.1109/ITHET61869.2024.10837626
12. Nacheva, R. Analysis of AI mobile applications for ensuring digital accessibility in higher education for people with disabilities. Acta Educationis Generalis **15**(1) (2025). 0.2478/atd-2025–0009
13. Sulova, S.: Application of natural language processing technologies to improve accessibility of e-learning resources. In: Proceedings of the International Conference on Computer Systems and Technologies 2024, pp. 180–184 (2024)https://doi.org/10.1145/3674912.367491
14. Chan, C.: Students' perceptions of 'AI-giarism': investigating changes in under-standings of academic misconduct. Educ. Inform. Technol. 1–22 (2024). https://doi.org/10.1007/s10639-024-13151-7
15. Gulumbe, B., Audu, S., Hashim, A.: Balancing AI and academic integrity: what are the positions of academic publishers and universities? AI & Soc. 1–10 (2024). https://doi.org/10.1007/s00146-024-01946-8
16. Kim, J., Yu, S., Detrick, R., Li, N.: Exploring students' perspectives on generative AI-assisted academic writing. Educ. Inf. Technol. **30**(1), 1265–1300 (2025). https://doi.org/10.1007/s10639-024-12878-7

17. Pudasaini, S., Miralles-Pechuán, L., Lillis, D., Llorens Salvador, M.: Survey on AI-generated plagiarism detection: the impact of large language models on academic integrity. J. Acad. Ethics 1–34 (2024) https://doi.org/10.1007/s10805-024-09576-x

18. Weber-Wulff, D., et al.: Testing of detection tools for AI-generated text. Int. J. Educ. Integr. **19**, 26 (2023). https://doi.org/10.1007/s40979-023-00146-z

19. Perkins, M., Roe, J., Postma, D., McGaughran, J., Hickerson, D.: Detection of GPT-4 generated text in higher education: combining academic judgement and software to identify generative AI tool misuse. J. Acad. Ethics **22**(1), 89–113 (2024). https://doi.org/10.1007/s10805-023-09492-6

20. Maghsoudi, M., Shokouhyar, S., Ataei, A., Ahmadi, S., Shokoohyar, S.: Co-authorship network analysis of AI applications in sustainable supply chains: key players and themes. J. Clean. Prod. **422**, 138472 (2023). https://doi.org/10.1016/j.jclepro.2023.138472

21. Abramo, G., D'Angelo, C.: How reliable are unsupervised author disambiguation algorithms in the assessment of research organization performance? Quant. Sci. Stud. **4**(1), 144–166 (2023). https://doi.org/10.1162/qss_a_00236

22. Rehs, A.: A supervised machine learning approach to author disambiguation in the web of science. J. Informet. **15**(3), 101166 (2021). https://doi.org/10.1016/j.joi.2021.101166

23. Saeidnia, H., Hosseini, E., Abdoli, S., Ausloos, M.: Unleashing the power of AI: a systematic review of cutting-edge techniques in AI-enhanced scientometrics, webometrics and bibliometrics. Library Hi Tech. (2024). https://doi.org/10.1108/LHT-10-2023-0514

24. AlAfnan, M.: DeepSeek vs. ChatGPT: a comparative evaluation of AI tools in composition, business writing, and communication tasks. J. Artif. Intell. Technol. (2025). https://doi.org/10.37965/jait.2025.0740

25. Wang, C., Kantarcioglu, M.: A review of DeepSeek models' key innovative techniques. arXiv preprint arXiv:2503.11486 (2025). https://doi.org/10.48550/arXiv.2503.11486

26. Andri, S.: MVC architecture: a comparative study between Laravel framework and slim framework in freelancer project monitoring system web based. Procedia Comput. Sci. **157**, 134–141 (2019). https://doi.org/10.1016/j.procs.2019.08.150

27. Sasmoko, Y., Manalu, S., Danaristo, J.: Analyzing database optimization strategies in Laravel for an enhanced learning management. Procedia Comput. Sci. **245**, 799–804 (2024). https://doi.org/10.1016/j.procs.2024.10.306

28. Wilkinson, M., et al.: Evaluating FAIR maturity through a scalable, automated, community-governed framework. Sci. data **6**(1), 174 (2019). https://doi.org/10.1038/s41597-019-0184-5

29. Huang, Y., Cai, K., Zong, R., Mao, Y. Design and implementation of an edge computing platform architecture using Docker and Kubernetes for machine learning. In: Proceedings of the 3rd International Conference on High Performance Compilation, Computing and Communications, pp. 29–32 (2019). https://doi.org/10.1145/3318265.3318288

# A Query-Based Customizable LSP Recommender System for Nonprofessional Users

Jozo Dujmović[(✉)] [ID] and Malavya Raval [ID]

Department of Computer Science, San Francisco State University, 1600 Holloway Avenue, San Francisco, CA 94132, USA
{jozo,mraval}@sfsu.edu

**Abstract.** In this paper we present the structure and implementation of a general customizable recommender system designed specifically for nonprofessional users. The recommender system (LSPrec) is based on the Logic Scoring of Preference (LSP) decision method. Our goal is to develop LSPrec as a decision-making aid that can be used without any user preparation. LSPrec users can systematically develop sophisticated decision criteria using only the natural verbal communication and a commonsense logic. The mathematical infrastructure of LSPrec is a graded propositional logic. To develop decision criteria, LSPrec exploits human capability to verbally specify the intensity of four fundamental percepts: truth, importance, simultaneity, and substitutability. LSPrec acts as a guide in a dialog with users, asking them to provide answers to questions about alternatives or objects that they want to evaluate and compare. That includes the necessary suitability attributes, their importance, and logic conditions that must be satisfied. The collected answers are then combined to build the LSP criterion function that is used for evaluation and comparison of multiple objects or alternatives. In a special case, LSPrec can be used for evaluation of a single object. The resulting decision models are saved so that users can visit them multiple times for updating, refining, and multiple evaluations. The results of decision making are recommendations presented to users in both verbal and numeric forms.

**Keywords:** LSP method · Graded Logic · Decision-support systems · Evaluation · Recommender systems · Query tables

## 1 Introduction

Decision making is a fundamental human mental activity. Most frequently, we have several competitive alternatives, and the decision problem is to select the best alternative. Sometimes, we have a single alternative (e.g., a single job offer) which we must evaluate and then decide to accept or reject. If a recommender (decision aid) system can evaluate a single object, then the comparison of $m > 1$ alternatives is reduced to $m$ evaluations of a single alternative. This approach is the core feature of the LSP decision method [1] and the LSPrec recommender system. For each alternative, LSPrec creates a degree of overall suitability, which is the degree of satisfaction of specific user (stakeholder) requirements.

© The Author(s), under exclusive license to Springer Nature Switzerland AG 2026
G. De Tré et al. (Eds.): FQAS 2025, LNAI 16119, pp. 115–130, 2026.
https://doi.org/10.1007/978-3-032-05607-8_12

The overall suitability degree is a value in the range from no satisfaction (usually coded 0) to complete satisfaction (coded 1). Each value of the overall satisfaction degree in the range [0,1] can be interpreted as a continuum-valued degree of truth of the statement "evaluated object completely satisfies all requirements." It can also be interpreted as a degree of membership of the evaluated object in a fuzzy set of objects that completely satisfy all user's requirements. These interpretations are equivalent, and in this paper, we use the logic interpretation and create decision models based on Graded Logic [2, 3].

Decision making is an area that naturally attracts attention in many disciplines and application areas, resulting in rich literature in the areas of soft computing [4–6], fuzzy systems [7, 8], operations research [9, 10], business decision analysis [11–13] and utility theory [14–17]. It is surprising that existing decision-making literature is not primarily human-centered: it is not focused on modeling observable and measurable natural decision activities of human decision-makers and the study of decision-making as a commonsense logic activity. We believe that decision methods must be fully consistent with human commonsense reasoning and logical decision making. That approach results in the LSP method [1] which is based on Graded Logic [3] and the theory of logic aggregators [18]. Unsurprisingly, the use of LSP methodology and supporting software tools [19] require mathematical prerequisites and are not accessible to nonprofessional users.

The first attempt to use LSP criteria by nonprofessional users [20] is restricted to a fixed application area (hotel recommender systems) and a fixed LSP criterion (fixed decision attributes and a fixed structure of the decision model). In this paper, our goal is to develop a general decision aid tool (LSPrec) that offers the development and use of LSP decision models to nonprofessional users. We propose an LSP-based guided decision process based on a sequence of queries specifically designed for users who are not familiar with mathematical logic and can only communicate using a dialog based on natural language.

Our methodology is following the standard model of commonsense evaluation reasoning and the LSP method [1] resulting in the following basic steps: (1) the development of suitability attributes, (2) the specification of attribute criteria, and (3) logic aggregation of attribute suitability degrees (computing the overall suitability degree, which is used for selecting the best alternative).

The paper is organized as a presentation of the LSP evaluation process (Sect. 2), the queries that specify the LSP evaluation process (Sect. 3), the LSPrec software tool (Sect. 4), and conclusions (Sect. 5).

## 2   LSP Evaluation Process

To identify all activities that nonprofessional users must perform, it is convenient to present the LSP evaluation process using a simplified example of a stakeholder who evaluates job offers. The assumption of this example is that the primary motivations for the new job search are a better salary, and improved job characteristics.

The first step in the LSP method is to identify suitability attributes (these are attributes that affect the overall suitability of the job offer). A simple suitability attribute tree structure and the corresponding suitability attribute list are shown in Fig. 1. For each suitability attribute the stakeholder creates the attribute criterion shown in Table 1.

**1 JOB OFFER**
  **11 Monetary compensations**
    111 Offered starting salary [%]
    112 Anticipated 3-year salary [%]
  **12 Main characteristics of the job**
    121 Total time at work
      1211 Average work week [h]
      1212 Daily commute time [min]
    122 Attractiveness of job [0..8]

**List of input attributes**

1. Offered starting salary [%]
2. Anticipated 3-year salary [%]
3. Average work week [h]
4. Daily commute time [min]
5. Attractiveness of job [0..8]

**Fig. 1.** A sample attribute tree and the list of five suitability attributes for evaluation and comparison of job offers

The attribute criteria are defined as tables where for each selected value we assign a suitability score and linearly interpolate between the adjacent value-score points. For example, in the attribute criterion 111, the offered starting salary $S_{new}$ is compared to the existing salary $S_{old}$. $S_{old}$ is denoted as 100% and satisfies only 20% of user requirements. The ideal job offer that fully satisfies user expectation (satisfaction degree 100%) would be one that increases the existing salary by 50%. The reduction of the existing salary to 90% of its current value, regardless of the possible improvements of other conditions, is considered unacceptable and yields the satisfaction degree 0. So, such criterion can be denoted in compact vertex notation as follows: Crit (Salary) = {(90, 0), (100, 20), (150, 100)} (e.g., if the offered salary is 125%, then the corresponding suitability degree of this attribute would be 60%).

All attribute suitability degrees are interpreted as degrees of truth and logically aggregated to compute the overall suitability degree. The basic logic aggregator is the Graded Conjunction/Disjunction $GCD(X; W, \alpha) : [0,1]^n \to [0,1]$, where $X$ denotes $n$ input attribute suitability degrees, $W$ denotes their importance degrees, and the andness $\alpha$ denotes the conjunction degree, as follows:

$$X = (x_1, \ldots, x_n), \quad W = (w_1, \ldots, w_n), \quad 0 \le x_i \le 1, \ i = 1, \ldots, n,$$

$$0 < w_i < 1, i = 1, \ldots, n, \quad n > 1, w_1 + \ldots + w_n = 1, \quad 0 \le \alpha \le 1.$$

The properties of GCD aggregator are summarized in Fig. 2. According to [1], the andness $\alpha$ is defined as the logic parameter that satisfies the condition.

$$\alpha = \frac{n}{n-1} - \frac{n+1}{n-1} \int_0^1 \ldots \int_0^1 GCD(X; \overline{W}, \alpha) dx_1 \ldots dx_n, \ \overline{W} = \left(\frac{1}{n}, \ldots, \frac{1}{n}\right).$$

**Table 1.** Suitability attribute criteria

| 111 | | Offered starting salary [%] |
|---|---|---|
| Value | % | Evaluation is based on the following relative salary: |
| 90 | 0 | Srel = 100*Snew/Sold |
| 100 | 20 | where:    Snew  = offered new starting salary |
| 150 | 100 | Sold   = the current job salary |

| 112 | | Anticipated 3-year salary [%] |
|---|---|---|
| Value | % | Evaluated as the following relative anticipated salary: |
| 100 | 0 | RAS = 100*A/Snew |
| 130 | 100 | where:  A    = anticipated 3-year salary |
| | | Snew = the offered starting salary |

| 1211 | | Average work week [h] |
|---|---|---|
| Value | % | Average work week time, measured in hours: |
| 40 | 100 | Time <= 40 : standard workload |
| 50 | 75 | 50 h = high load: 5 days * 10 hours |
| 72 | 0 | 72 h = startup mode: 6 days * 12 hours |

| 1212 | | Daily commute time [min] |
|---|---|---|
| Value | % | Total average daily commute time measured in minutes: |
| 0 | 100 | 0 = working online from home |
| 30 | 80 | 30 min = 2 * 15 min (working close to home) |
| 90 | 0 | 90 min = 2 * 45 min (not acceptable) |

| 122 | | Attractiveness of job [0..8] |
|---|---|---|
| Value | % | Evaluated using the following rating scale:  0 = lowest, |
| 0 | 0 | 1 = very low,   2 = low,   3 = medium-low, 4 = average, |
| 8 | 100 | 5 = medium-high, 6 = high, 7 = very high,   8 = highest |

If $GCD(X; W, \alpha) = x_1 \wedge \cdots \wedge x_n$, then $\alpha = 1$ and if $GCD(X; W, \alpha) = x_1 \vee \cdots \vee x_n$, then $\alpha = 0$. Therefore, by selecting a desired andness, $GCD(X; W, \alpha)$ enables the continuous andness-directed transition from the pure conjunction to the pure disjunction. The transition can be organized in 15 steps shown in Fig. 2. The difference between adjacent aggregator steps is 1/14. There are four conjunctive hard aggregators that support annihilator 0 (HC−, HC, HC+, C) and four disjunctive hard aggregators (HD−, HD, HD+, D) that support the annihilator 1. All other conjunctive and disjunctive aggregators are soft, i.e., they don't support annihilators. Both conjunctive and disjunctive aggregators are dual, i.e., $GCD(X; \overline{W}, \alpha) = 1 - GCD(1 - X; \overline{W}, 1 - \alpha)$. E.g., if $\alpha = 0$, then we have the classic De Morgan duality: $x_1 \vee \cdots \vee x_n = \overline{x}_1 \wedge \cdots \wedge \overline{x}_n$. Graded logic aggregators have simple verbalized interpretation shown in Fig. 2. The GCD aggregator is symmetric in the sense that all inputs $x_1, \ldots, x_n$ are symmetric: either mandatory (in the case or hard conjunctive aggregators) or optional (in the case of soft aggregators).

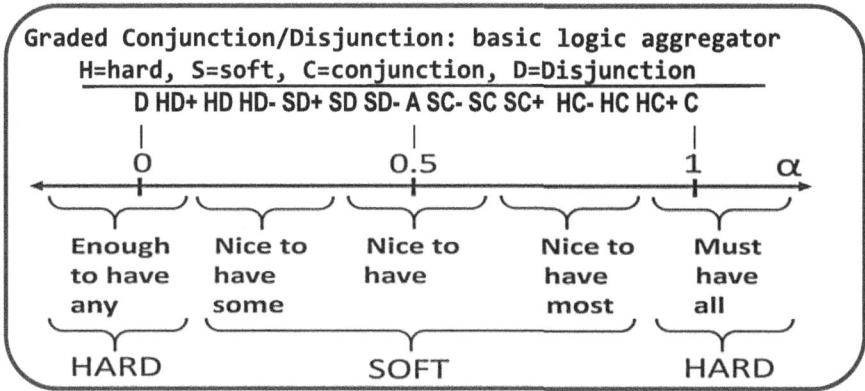

**Fig. 2.** Fifteen basic logic aggregators as special cases of the GCD logic function

Hard conjunctive aggregators have andness $\alpha_h \geq 0.75$ and soft aggregators have andness $0.25 < \alpha_s < 0.75$. In the case of two mandatory inputs $x_1$ *and* $x_2$ the GCD aggregator is $GCD(x_1, x_2; w_h, 1 - w_h; \alpha_h)$. In the case of two optional inputs $y_1$ *and* $y_2$ the GCD aggregator is $GCD(y_1, y_2; w_s, 1 - w_s; \alpha_s)$. These aggregators can be combined to get compound aggregators with various desirable properties. The most frequent compound aggregators is the conjunctive partial absorption, defined as follows:

$$CPA(x_1, y_2; w_h, w_s; \alpha_h, \alpha_s) = GCD(x_1, GCD(x_1, y_2; w_s, 1 - w_s; \alpha_s); w_h, 1 - w_h; \alpha_h).$$

This aggregator combines the mandatory input $x_1$ and the optional input $y_2$ and has the following easily provable properties:

- $CPA(0, y_2; w_h, w_s; \alpha_h, \alpha_s) = 0$, ($x_1$ is a mandatory input which must be satisfied; its nonsatisfaction cannot be compensated by the optional input $y_2 > 0$)
- $CPA(x_1, 0; w_h, w_s; \alpha_h, \alpha_s) = x_1 - p$, ($p$ is a penalty for not satisfied optional input)

**Table 2.** Complete LSP criterion table for evaluation of job offers

| ID | Suitability attributes | Aggregation structure | | | | | |
|----|------------------------|---|---|---|---|---|---|
| 111 | Starting salary [%]: {(90,0), (100, 20), (150, 100)} | M | 11 Monetary compensations | | | 58 | 1 |
| 112 | Anticipated 3-year salary [%]: (100, 0), (130, 100)} | O | CPA:  P=20%, R=10% | | | | Job of-fer |
| 1211 | Average work week [h]: {(40, 100), (50, 75), (72, 0)} | 73 | 121 To-tal time at work HC- | M | 12 Main charac-teristics of the job | 42 | HC |
| 1212 | Daily commute time [min] {(0, 100), (30, 80), (90, 0)} | 27 | | | | | |
| 122 | Attractiveness of job [0..8]: {(0, 0), (8, 100)} | O | | | CPA: P=30%, R=15% | | |

- $CPA(x_1, 1; w_h, w_s; \alpha_h, \alpha_s) = x_1 + r$, ($r$ is a reward for perfectly satisfied optional input)

The size of penalty and reward can be adjusted by selecting the parameters $w_h, w_s, \alpha_h, \alpha_s$. . To simplify this problem, we usually specify the desired mean penalty $P$ and the mean reward $R$, and from these values compute the parameters $w_h, w_s, \alpha_h, \alpha_s$ using tables or software tools. This process is illustrated in Table 2, where we show the logic aggregation structure. The starting salary is considered the mandatory requirement (denoted M), while anticipated future salary is considered an optional requirement (denoted O). The mean penalty and reward are selected to be 20% and 10%, respectively. Similarly, the total time at work is a mandatory requirement while the job attractiveness is optional. The hard aggregators HC- and HC show that in this LSP criterion the attributes 111, 1211, 1212 are mandatory (must be satisfied and in the case of non-satisfaction of any of them the overall suitability automatically becomes zero). The attributes 112 and 122 are optional (their nonsatisfaction does not yield the zero overall suitability). The values of 73%, 27% as well as 58% and 42% are importance weights.

**Table 3.** Results of evaluation and comparison of the old job and two new job offers

| Id | Attribute | NewJob1 | NewJob2 | OldJob |
|----|-----------|---------|---------|--------|
| 111 | Offered starting salary [%] | 125 | 140 | 100 |
| 112 | Anticipated 3-year salary [%] | 120 | 115 | 100 |
| 1211 | Average work week [h] | 45 | 50 | 40 |
| 1212 | Daily commute time [min] | 0 | 40 | 30 |
| 122 | Attractiveness of job [0..8] | 7 | 6 | 4 |

| Id | Attribute | NewJob1 | NewJob2 | OldJob |
|----|-----------|---------|---------|--------|
| 1 | JOB OFFER | 68.54 | 75.85 | 19.38 |
| 11 | Monetary compensations | 61.04 | 78.10 | 16.01 |
| 12 | Main characteristics of the job | 89.80 | 73.11 | 82.16 |
| 121 | Total time at work | 90.53 | 72.53 | 93.58 |
| 122 | Attractiveness of job [0..8] | 87.50 | 75.00 | 50.00 |
| 1212 | Daily commute time [min] | 100.00 | 66.67 | 80.00 |
| 1211 | Average work week [h] | 87.50 | 75.00 | 100.00 |
| 112 | Anticipated 3-year salary [%] | 66.67 | 50.00 | 0.00 |
| 111 | Offered starting salary [%] | 60.00 | 84.00 | 20.00 |

The LSP criterion defined in Tables 1 and 2 is sufficient for evaluation and comparison of job offers. An example of a comparison of the old (current) job and two new job offers is shown in Table 3. The winner is NewJob2 which satisfies 75.85% of user requirements, while the NewJob1 satisfies 68.54%. The low-paid old job satisfies only 19.38% of requirements. The question is now how to implement this evaluation process and get the same results without any knowledge of the LSP method and using only verbal communication. Below we propose a solution to this problem.

## 3  The LSP Evaluation Process Specified as a Sequence of Queries

The LSP method can be structured as a sequence of verbalized queries. The level of logic detail and the precision of LSP criterion is adjusted for general users. Each query is identified by its reference number and structured as a table that contains questions specified by the LSPrec and answers collected from the user. A survey of 16 LSP queries is shown in Table 4 and the details of individual queries are presented in Table 5.

**Table 4.** A survey of queries that implement the LSP decision method

| Query | Topic |
|---|---|
| 1 | Welcome and optional user registration |
| 2 | Specification of the object(s) that will be evaluated |
| 3 | Specification of the suitability attribute tree |
| 4 | Selection of the type of attribute criterion |
| 5 | Specification of the attribute criterion that prefers the high values |
| 6 | Specification of the attribute criterion that prefers the low values |
| 7 | Specification of the attribute criterion that prefers the range of values |
| 8 | Selection of logic aggregator as GCD or partial absorption |
| 9 | Selection of intensity of the hard graded conjunction or disjunction |
| 10 | Selection of intensity of the soft graded conjunction or disjunction |
| 11 | Specification of the relative importance of attributes |
| 12 | Selection among 9 degrees of relative importance |
| 13 | Selection among 9 degrees of suitability |
| 14 | Specification of mandatory and optional components of conjunctive partial absorption and the impact of optional components |
| 15 | Selection of relative importance in groups of mandatory and optional components of the conjunctive partial absorption |
| 16 | Specification of alternatives: name, cost, and attribute values |

**Table 5.** The LSP evaluation method specified as a sequence of 16 queries

| | | |
|---|---|---|
| Welcome! I am LSPrec, your decision-making assistant and recommender. I use the LSP method to help you find the best among several alternatives or objects. We can determine the overall suitability of each object/alternative, including the case of a single alternative. I use a verbal query; so, you can use me without any preparation. | | |

| QUERY 1 | QUESTION |
|---|---|
| | Do you want to register, so that you can save your work and come later to reuse it? (You can use me without registration) |
| ANSWER | Yes / No |

| QUERY 2 | QUESTION |
|---|---|
| | Please enter the type of object you want to evaluate (examples of object: car, home, laptop, job offer, school, hotel, etc.) |
| ANSWER | <object> |

| QUERY 3 | QUESTIONS | |
|---|---|---|
| Defining components of the following compound item | Enter up to 5 components of the analyzed item | Do you want to further decompose this component? |
| <analyzed item> | | Y/N  [Q3] |
| To preserve the accuracy, the maximum number of components is limited to 5 | | Y/N  [Q3] |
| | | Y/N  [Q3] |
| | | Y/N  [Q3] |
| | | Y/N  [Q3] |

| QUERY 4 | QUESTIONS | ANSWER | |
|---|---|---|---|
| Specification of requirements that should be satisfied by the following item: | We offer three major evaluation options. Please select the most appropriate option | Help | Your choice |
| <analyzed item> | I prefer high values of this item | ? | Q5 |
| | I prefer low values of this item | ? | Q6 |
| | I prefer a specific range of values | ? | Q7 |

| QUERY 5 | QUESTIONS | ANSWER |
|---|---|---|
| Preferred high values of this item: | Please answer the following questions. The first value must be less than the second value. | Your choice |
| <analyzed item> | It is unacceptable if the analyzed item is less than or equal to the following value: | |
| | I am fully satisfied if the analyzed item is greater than or equal to the following value: | |
| Optional condition to increase precision | If the analyzed item has the following value: | |
| | then my satisfaction degree is the following: | [%] |

*Note*: Query 3 is a loop that repeats until the end of the decomposition process and all suitability attributes have been developed

| QUERY 6 | Q U E S T I O N S | ANSWER |
|---|---|---|
| Preferred low values of this item: | Please answer the following questions. The first value must be less than the second value. | Your choice |
| <analyzed item> | I am fully satisfied if the analyzed item is less than or equal to the following value: | |
| | It is unacceptable if the analyzed item is greater than or equal to the following value: | |
| Optional condition to increase precision | If the analyzed item has the following value: | |
| | then my satisfaction degree is the following: | [%] |

| QUERY 7 | Q U E S T I O N S | ANSWER |
|---|---|---|
| Preferred range of values of this item: | Please answer the following questions. Your values must create a strictly increasing sequence. | Your choice |
| <analyzed item> | It is unacceptable if the offered value is less than | |
| | I am fully satisfied if the offered value is between the following two values (smaller value first) | |
| | It is unacceptable if the value is greater than | |

| QUERY 8 | Q U E S T I O N S | ANSWER |
|---|---|---|
| Components of <analyzed item> | Select the most appropriate logic requirement that should be satisfied by the listed components. | Your choice |
| <component 1> <component 2> ... | All components are mandatory and must be simultaneously highly satisfied. It is not acceptable to have a single component requirement not satisfied. | Q9 + Q11 |
| ... ... | Simultaneously high satisfaction of all components is desirable but not mandatory. We can tolerate the cases where some input requirements are not satisfied. | Q10 + Q11 |
| | Nice to have a good satisfaction of most component requirements. The negative impact of small input values is balanced by the positive impact of large input values. | Q11 |
| | These components can effectively substitute each other. The positive impact of large input values is stronger than the negative impact of small input values. | Q10 + Q11 |
| | It is enough to have any input highly satisfied. A single fully satisfied component requirement is sufficient to fully satisfy the compound requirement. | Q9 + Q11 |
| Some component requirements in this group are mandatory and must be satisfied. The remaining components are optional: their satisfaction is desirable but not necessary. Each group has at least one component. | | Q14 |

| QUERY 9 | QUESTION |
|---|---|
| | Select the most appropriate intensity of selected relationship |
| ANSWERS | Highest |
| | High |
| | Medium |
| | Low |

| QUERY 10 | QUESTION |
|---|---|
| | Select the most appropriate intensity of selected relationship |
| ANSWERS | High |
| | Medium |
| | Low |

| QUERY 11 | QUESTIONS | ANSWER |
|---|---|---|
| Specification of the relative importance of components of the following item: | These components can have different degrees of relative importance. Please select the most appropriate option. | Your choice |
| <analyzed item> | <component 1> | Q12 |
| | <component 2> | Q12 |
| | … | Q12 |
| | … | Q12 |
| | … | Q12 |

| | QUERRY 12 | | QUERRY 13 | |
|---|---|---|---|---|
| | QUESTION | VALUE | QUESTION | VALUE |
| | Select the most appropriate degree of importance of selected input using the following options | | Select the most appropriate degree of suitability (or satisfaction or truth) using the following options | |
| ANSWERS | Highest | 9 | Excellent | 100% |
| | Very high | 8 | Very good | 87.5% |
| | High | 7 | Good | 75% |
| | Medium-high | 6 | Above average | 62.5% |
| | Medium | 5 | Average | 50% |
| | Medium-low | 4 | Below average | 37.5% |
| | Low | 3 | Poor | 25% |
| | Very low | 2 | Very poor | 12.5% |
| | Lowest | 1 | Unacceptable | 0 |

| QUERY 14 | QUESTIONS | ANSWER |
|---|---|---|
| Specification of mandatory and optional components of the following item: | For these components, please select those that are mandatory (must be satisfied) and those that are optional (can be not satisfied with a desired impact) | Your choice |
| | <component 1> | M/O |
| | <component 2> | M/O |
| <analyzed item> | ... | M/O |
| | ... | M/O |
| | ... | M/O |
| Select the impact of optional components  (low or medium or high) | | L/M/H |

| QUERY 15 | QUESTIONS | ANSWER |
|---|---|---|
| Specification of the relative importance of components. This query is conditional: it is applied separately for mandatory and separately for optional components, assuming that each group has 2 or more components. | These components can have different degrees of relative importance. Please select the most appropriate values. | Your choice |
| | <component 1> | Q12 |
| | <component 2> | Q12 |
| | ... | Q12 |
| | ... | Q12 |
| | ... | Q12 |

| QUERY 16 | QUESTIONS   AND   ANSWERS | |
|---|---|---|
| Complete specification of an evaluated object / alternative (values of attributes) | Please enter the name, total cost, and the values of all input components that characterize the evaluated object/alternative | |
| | Object/alternative name | Total cost (it can be 0) |
| This table contains all input components (suitability attributes) that are defined in previous queries | Component | Value |
| | <component 1> | <numeric value or Q13> |
| | <component 2> | <numeric value or Q13> |
| | ... | ... |
| | ... | ... |
| | ... | ... |

To illustrate the user's effort in evaluating specific alternatives, we present the job offer dialog between the *LSPrec* and a *User*. User input is denoted as bold and underlined.

1. *LSPrec* Q2: Please enter the name of object you want to evaluate
   *User:* **Job offer**
2. *LSPrec* Q3: Enter all components of the Job offer
   *User:* **Monetary compensations** - more components
   **Main characteristics of the job** – more components
3. *LSPrec* Q3: Enter all components of the Monetary compensations
   *User:* **Starting salary [%]** - no components
   **Anticipated 3-year salary [%]** - no components

4. *LSPrec* Q3: Enter all components of the Main characteristics of the job
   *User:* **Total time at work** – more components
   **Attractiveness of job** – no components
5. *LSPrec* Q3: Enter all components of the Total time at work
   *User:* **Average work week [h]** – no components
   **Daily Commute time [min]** – no components
6. *LSPrec* Q4: Specify requirements for the Starting salary [%]
   *User:* I prefer **high** values of the Starting salary [%]
   Q5: It is unacceptable if the starting salary [%] is less than or equal to **90**
   I am fully satisfied if the starting salary [%] is greater than or equal to **150**
   If the starting salary is **100**% my satisfaction is **20**%.
7. *LSPrec* Q4: Specify requirements for the Anticipated 3-year salary [%]
   *User:* I prefer **high** values of the Anticipated 3-year salary [%]
   Q5: It is unacceptable if the anticipated 3-year salary [%] is less than or equal to **100**
   I am fully satisfied if the Anticipated 3-year salary[%] is greater than or equal to **130**
8. *LSPrec* Q4: Specify requirements for the Average work week [h]
   *User:* I prefer **low** values of the Average work week [h]
   Q6: I am fully satisfied if the Average work week [h] is less than or equal to **40**
   It is unacceptable if the Average work week [h] is greater than or equal to **72**
   If the Average work week is **50** h my satisfaction is **75**%.
9. *LSPrec* Q4: Specify requirements for the Daily commute time [min]
   *User:* I prefer **low** values of the Daily commute time [min]
   Q6: I am fully satisfied if the Daily commute time is less than or equal to **0**
   It is unacceptable if the Daily commute time [min] is greater than or equal to **90**
   If the Daily commute time [min] is **30** my satisfaction is **80**%.
10. *LSPrec* Q4: Specify requirements for the Attractiveness of job
    *User:* I prefer **high** values of the Attractiveness of job
    Q5: It is unacceptable if the Attractiveness of job is less than or equal to **0**
    I am fully satisfied if the Attractiveness of job is greater than or equal to **8**
11. *LSPrec* Q8: Select the most appropriate logic requirement to be satisfied by the Job offer
    *User:* **simultaneously high** satisfaction. Q9: Intensity **Medium** (HC).
    Q11/W12: Importance of the Monetary compensations: **High**
    Importance of the Main characteristics of the job: **Medium**
12. *LSPrec* Q8: Select the most appropriate logic requirement to be satisfied by the Monetary compensations
    *User:* **mandatory/optional** satisfaction.
    Q14: Starting salary: **Mandatory** ;  Anticipated 3-year salary: **Optional**
    Impact [low (P=10%, R=5%), medium (P=20%, R=10%), high (P=30%, R=15%)]: **Medium**
13. *LSPrec* Q8: Select the most appropriate logic requirement to be satisfied by the Main characteristics of the job

*User:* **mandatory/optional** satisfaction.

    Q14: Total time at work: **Mandatory** ;  Attractiveness of job: **Optional**

    Impact [low (P=10%, R=5%), medium (P=20%, R=10%), high (P=30%, R=15%)]: **High**

14. *LSPrec* Q8: Select the most appropriate logic requirement to be satisfied by the Total time at work

    *User:*  **simultaneously high** satisfaction. Q9: Intensity **Low** (HC-).

    Q11/Q12: Importance of the Average work week: **Very high**

    Importance of the Daily commute time: **Low**

15: *LSPrec* Q16:  Please select the name, total cost, and the values of all input components

| *User:* | | **NewJob1** | **NewJob2** | **OldJob** |
|---|---|---|---|---|
| | Name: | **NewJob1** | **NewJob2** | **OldJob** |
| | Cost: | - | - | - |
| | Offered starting salary [%]: | **125** | **140** | **100** |
| | Anticipated 3-year salary [%]: | **120** | **115** | **100** |
| | Average work week [h]: | **45** | **50** | **40** |
| | Daily commute time [min]: | **0** | **40** | **30** |
| | Attractiveness of job: | **7** | **6** | **4** |

Therefore, the job offer selection problem reduces to the above fifteen query interactions, where each of them can be completed in less than one minute and the total user's effort (bold and underlined values) is very modest, below 15 min. The interactions 1–5 specify the suitability attribute tree, the interactions 6–10 specify attribute criteria, and the interactions 11–14 specify the logic aggregation structure, creating a complete LSP logic criterion. The last interaction (15) specifies competitive objects/alternatives and initializes the evaluation and comparison, creating results shown in Table 3.

## 4   LSPrec Software Tool

The presented query-based LSP criterion development process is used as a specification for the development of the LSPrec software tool. The LSPrec tool is created using development tools and services provided by vercel.com. It is posted on https://lsprec. vercel.app. Sample components of the LSPrec are shown in Figs. 3, 4 and 5. Figure 3 is developed according to query 3. It shows the first step of development of the suitability attribute tree where the user defines two components of the job offer which should be further decomposed. Figure 4 is based on query 7. It shows the development of attribute criterion Crit (Salary) = {(90, 0), (100, 20), (150,100)}. Figure 5 is based on query 16 and shows the specification of input attributes for NewJob1. The user can append more alternatives (job offers) or request the evaluation. Results of evaluation are shown in Table 3.

Each query is implemented as a separate JavaScript program module, and their sequencing depends on user inputs. For example, the attribute tree is expanded as long as the user provides inputs that can be decomposed. Attribute criteria are defined for each of suitability attributes and the aggregation functions are defined for each node in the suitability attribute tree. The number of competitive objects/alternatives is not limited.

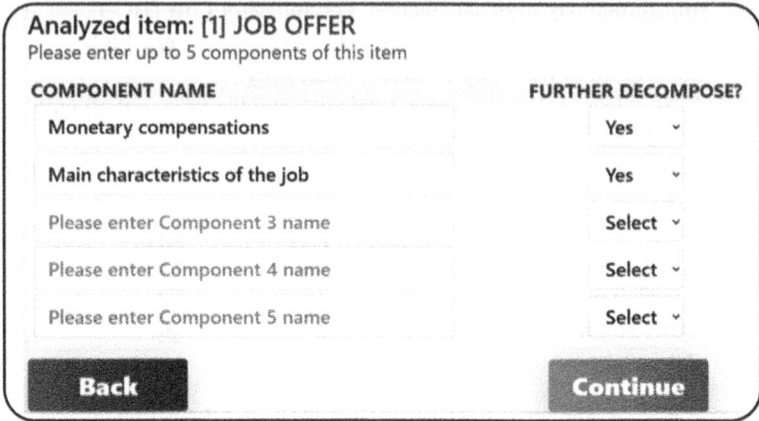

**Fig. 3.** Sample definition of an attribute decomposition structure

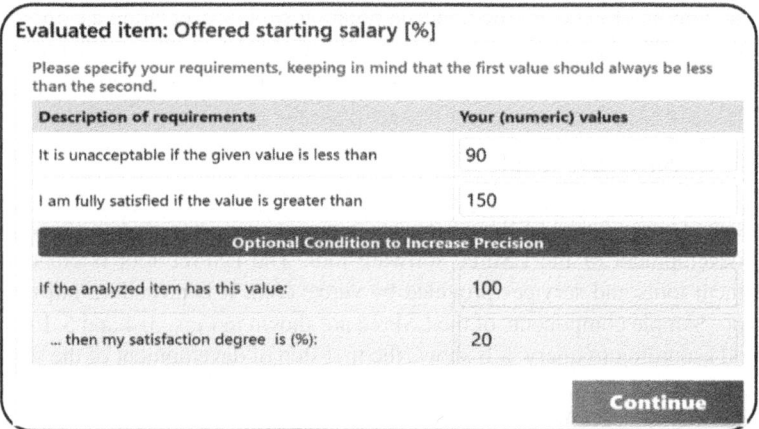

**Fig. 4.** Sample definition of an attribute criterion

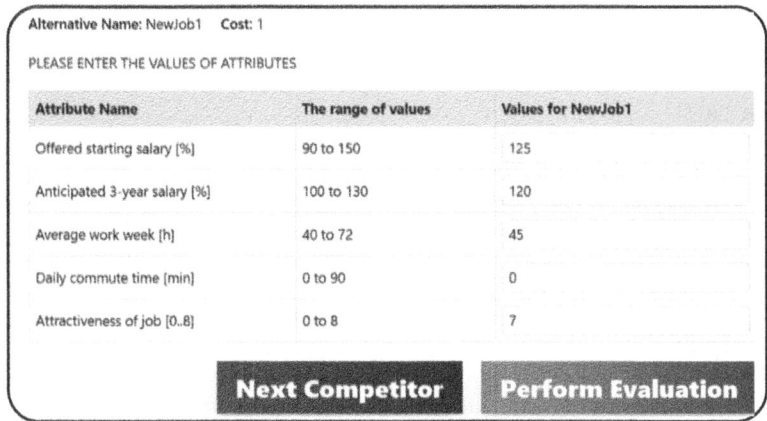

**Fig. 5.** Sample definition of a job offer attributes

## 5 Conclusions

The LSP method is primarily used for professional decision making where it is necessary to combine a high domain expertise and a detailed knowledge of graded logic. Such prerequisites are not acceptable for nonprofessional users. This paper proposes a method for creating the decision support tool LSPrec based on simple verbalized queries. That enables nonprofessional users to benefit from the expressive power of the LSP method and make justifiable complex decisions with minimum effort.

In addition to evaluation and comparison of competitive objects the LSP method also offers the explainability of results, as well as the analysis of confidence and credibility of proposed decisions. Presenting explainability and confidence results in a form suitable for nonprofessional users are topics for the future development of LSPrec.

## References

1. Dujmović, J.: Soft Computing Evaluation Logic. Wiley and IEEE Press, Hoboken (2018)
2. Dujmović, J.: Graded logic for decision support systems. Int. J. Intell. Syst. **34**, 2900–2919 (2019). https://doi.org/10.1002/int.22177
3. Dujmović, J.: Graded logic. Intelligent Systems Reference Library, vol. 273, Springer, Heidelberg (2025)
4. Torra, V., Narukawa, Y.: Modeling Decisions. Springer, Heidelberg (2007)
5. Figueira, J., Greco, S., Ehrgott, M. (eds.): Multiple Criteria Decision Analysis. Springer, Heidelberg (2005)
6. Ray, K.S.: Soft Computing and Its Applications. Apple Academic Press, Waretown (2015)
7. Klir, G.J., Yuan, B.: Fuzzy Sets and Fuzzy Logic. Prentice-Hall (1995)
8. Zimmermann, H.-J.: Fuzzy Set Theory and Its Applications, 4th edn. Springer, Heidelberg (2015)
9. Ishizaka, A., Nemery, P.: Multi-Criteria Decision Analysis. Wiley, Hoboken (2013)
10. Olson, D.L.: Decision Aids for Selection Problems. Springer (1996)
11. Belton, V., Stewart, T.J.: Multiple Criteria Decision Analysis. Kluwer Academic Publishers

12. Saaty, T.L.: The Analytic Hierarchy Process. McGraw-Hill (1980)
13. Saaty, T.L.: Principia Mathematica Decerendi. RWS Publications, Pittsburgh (2010)
14. Hensher, D.A., Rose, J.M., Greene, W.H.: Applied Choice Analysis. Cambridge University Press (2015)
15. Fishburn, P.C.: Decision and Value Theory. J. Wiley (1964)
16. Fishburn, P.C.: Utility Theory for Decision-making. J. Wiley (1970)
17. Keeney R.L., Raiffa, H.: Decisions with Multiple Objectives/ Preferences and Value Tradeoffs. J. Wiley, Hoboken (1976)
18. Dujmović, J., Torra, V.: Logic aggregators and their implementations. In: Torra, V., Narukawa, Y. (eds.) MDAI 2023, LNAI 13890, pp. 3–42. Springer (2023)
19. SEAS Co.: LSP.NT – LSP method for evaluation over the Internet. LSP.NT User Manual, SEAS (2017)
20. Solano-Barliza, A., et al.: Personalized hotel recommender system based on graded logic with asymmetric criteria, KES2024 conference. Procedia Comput. Sci. **246**, 2864–2873 (2024)

# Software System for Monitoring of Student Academic Performance in School Using Intuitionistic Fuzzy Evaluations

Petar Petrov[iD] and Veselina Bureva[(✉)][iD]

Laboratory of Intelligent Systems, Burgas State University,
"Prof. Dr. Assen Zlatarov", "Prof. Yakimov" Blvd., Burgas 8010, Bulgaria
vbureva@btu.bg

**Abstract.** In the Bulgarian school education system, the use of electronic grade-books has become widespread, yet the full analytical potential of the data they collect remains largely untapped. Despite significant technological advancements, educational institutions still underutilize automated tools and artificial intelligence (AI) for educational diagnostics and administrative decision-making. This paper presents an approach based on Intuitionistic Fuzzy Evaluations (IFE) to assess student academic performance and detect early signs of learning difficulties.

**Keywords:** Big Data · Data Mining · Intuitionistic Fuzzy Sets · Intuitionistic Fuzzy Evaluations · Student Performance · Educational Data Analysis · Artificial Intelligence in Education · Education decision making · Data Science

## 1 Introduction

The proposed methodology applies the principles of Intuitionistic Fuzzy Sets (IFS) to assess academic performance on three levels: individual students, class groups, and schools using Intuitionistic Fuzzy Evaluations (IFE). Similar investigations are published in [5–10]. The proposed investigations of Sotirova et al. [6–9] are targeted at university students' e-learning platforms. In the presented approaches, Inutitionistic fuzzy evaluations (IFE) are calculated based on right/wrong answers in e-learning tests. Approaches using distance measurements are suggested by Çitil [5]. The aim of Çitil's research is to determine proper highschools for students based on their results on a test. Other approaches incorporate IFEs to measure quality of education and school ranking using intuitionistic fuzzy logic and PROMETHEE algorithm [10].

The suggested approach in this research work is based on the construction of Intuitionistic Fuzzy Evaluations (IFE) for each entity, derived from academic performance data, typically obtained from electronic gradebooks with the aim to calculate personal IFE for each student and use this in further analysis for detecting students at risk. Beyond this the approach also aims at calculating aggregate IFEs for classes and schools. The novelty of this approach is in the area of personalized education and the potential to apply clustering algorithms on the obtained intuitionistic fuzzy evaluations data. Another

G. De Tré et al. (Eds.): FQAS 2025, LNAI 16119, pp. 131–138, 2026.
https://doi.org/10.1007/978-3-032-05607-8_13

strong side of the suggested methodology is the developed software web-based solution for analysing and visualizing data.

The paper has the following structure - Sect. 1 Introduction and comparison with similar research works. Section 2 - Brief introduction on IFS and theoretical remarks. Section 3 - the suggested methodology for calculation of IFEs. Section 4 demonstrates the web-based system. Section 5 shows some conclusions and discussion remarks.

## 2   Brief Introduction on Intuitionistic Fuzzy Sets (IFS)

Intuitionistic Fuzzy Sets (IFS) theory introduced by Krassimir Atanassov is thoroughly presented in [1–4]. Let $E$ denote the universe and the subset $A$ will be given. Thereafter, the intuitionistic fuzzy set has the following form:

$$A^* = \{\langle x, \mu_A(x), \nu_A(x) | x \in E \rangle\}$$

where $0 \leq \mu_A(x) + \nu_A(x) \leq 1$; $\mu_A: E \to [0,1]$ and $\nu_A: E \to [0,1]$ are called degree of membership and degree of non-membership of element $x \in E$. The degree of uncertainty is defined as:

$$\pi(x) = 1 - \mu_A(x) - \nu_A(x).$$

In the current investigation, the intuitionistic fuzzy evaluations are constructed to estimate the academic performance of students, classes or schools. A software web-based system is implemented using Python. The system allows for data to be imported in it and an analysis is done by calculating the intuitionistic fuzzy evaluations and displaying the results in a user-friendly interface. Based on the results, teachers and school administration can proceed with educational decision-making based on data and recommendations from the system.

## 3   Methodology of Calculating Intuitionistic Fuzzy Evaluations for Students, Classes And Schools

The methodology on obtaining IFEs is based on multiple levels - subjects, students, classes and schools. Each student has grades for multiple subjects. For each subject we calculate the intuitionistic fuzzy evaluation for each subject and then aggregate the intuitionistic fuzzy evaluations to obtain the student's overall intuitionistic fuzzy evaluation. Let us define the following:

- Let $S_i$ be the $i$-th subject studied by the student;
- Let $G_{S_i} = \{g_1, g_2, ..., g_k\}$ be the set of $k$ grades obtained by student in subject $S_i$, where $g_i \in \{2, 3, 4, 5, 6\}$ and the maximum possible grade is $g_{max} = 6$;
- Let $g_{max} = 6$ be the maximum possible grade;
- Define the average grade in subject $S_i$ as follows: $\overline{g}_{S_i} = \frac{1}{k} \sum_{i=1}^{k} g_i$.

The normalized degree of success (membership) is given by:

$$\mu_{S_i} = \frac{\overline{g}_{S_i}}{g_{max}}$$

The degree of difficulty (non-membership) is defined using a buffer parameter $\delta \in [0, 0.2]$, typically $\delta = 0.1$ as follows:

$$v_{S_i} = \max(0, 1 - \mu_S - \delta)$$

The hesitation degree (uncertainty) is calculated as:

$$\pi_{S_i} = 1 - \mu_{S_i} - v_{S_i}$$

The final intuitionistic fuzzy evaluation for subject $S_i$ is:

$$IFE_{S_i} = \langle \mu_{S_i}, v_{S_i} \rangle$$

Let a student $A_i$ be enrolled in $n$ subjects $S_1, S_2, ..., S_n$, each with an associated intuitionistic fuzzy evaluation:

$$IFE_{S_j}^{(A_i)} = \langle \mu_{S_j}^{(A_i)}, v_{S_j}^{(A_i)} \rangle$$

for $j = 1, 2, ..., n$.

The overall intuitionistic fuzzy evaluation for student $A_i$ is denoted as:

$$IFE_{A_i} = \langle \mu_{A_i}, v_{A_i} \rangle$$

It is computed by averaging the respective components over all subjects. Thereafter the degree of membership has the following form:

$$\mu_{A_i} = \frac{1}{n} \sum_{j=1}^{n} \mu_{S_i}^{(A_i)}$$

The degree of non-membership has the following form:

$$v_{A_i} = \frac{1}{n} \sum_{j=1}^{n} v_{S_i}^{(A_i)}$$

The degree of uncertainty has the following form:

$$\pi_{A_i} = \frac{1}{n} \sum_{j=1}^{n} \pi_{S_i}^{(A_i)}$$

This evaluation provides a comprehensive intuitionistic fuzzy profile of student $A_i$ based on performance across all enrolled subjects.

Let class $C_j$ consist of $m$ students $A_1^{(C_j)}, A_2^{(C_j)}, ..., A_m^{(C_j)}$, each with an individual intuitionistic fuzzy evaluation:

$$IFE_{A_i}^{(C_j)} = \langle \mu_{A_i}^{(C_j)}, v_{A_i}^{(C_j)} \rangle,$$

for $i = 1, 2, ..., m$.

The overall intuitionistic fuzzy evaluation for class $C_j$ is defined as:

$$IFE_{C_j} = \langle \mu_{C_j}, \nu_{C_j} \rangle$$

with components having the form: the degree of membership

$$\mu_{C_j} = \frac{1}{m} \sum_{i=1}^{m} \mu_{A_i}^{(C_j)}$$

the degree of non-membership,

$$\nu_{C_j} = \frac{1}{m} \sum_{i=1}^{m} \nu_{A_i}^{(C_j)}$$

and the degree of uncertainty

$$\pi_{C_j} = \frac{1}{m} \sum_{i=1}^{m} \pi_{A_i}^{(C_j)}$$

This evaluation provides a class-level intuitionistic fuzzy profile, reflecting the general academic status, difficulty levels, and performance uncertainty within class $C_j$.

Let school $S_r$ consist of $l$ classes $C_1^{(S_r)}, C_2^{(S_r)}, ..., C_l^{(S_r)}$, each with a class-level intuitionistic fuzzy evaluation:

$$IFE_{C_j}^{(S_r)} = \langle \mu_{C_j}^{(S_r)}, \nu_{C_j}^{(S_r)} \rangle$$

for $j = 1, 2, ..., l$.

The overall intuitionistic fuzzy evaluation for school $S_r$ is defined as:

$$IFE_{S_r} = \langle \mu_{S_r}, \nu_{S_r} \rangle$$

with components having the form: the degree of membership

$$\mu_{S_r} = \frac{1}{l} \sum_{j=1}^{l} \mu_{C_j}^{(S_r)}$$

the degree of non-membership,

$$\nu_{S_r} = \frac{1}{l} \sum_{j=1}^{l} \nu_{C_j}^{(S_r)}$$

and the degree of uncertainty

$$\pi_{S_r} = \frac{1}{l} \sum_{j=1}^{l} \pi_{C_j}^{(S_r)}$$

This evaluation provides a high-level overview of the academic performance, learning difficulties, and uncertainty patterns across the entire school $S_r$, based on class-level aggregation.

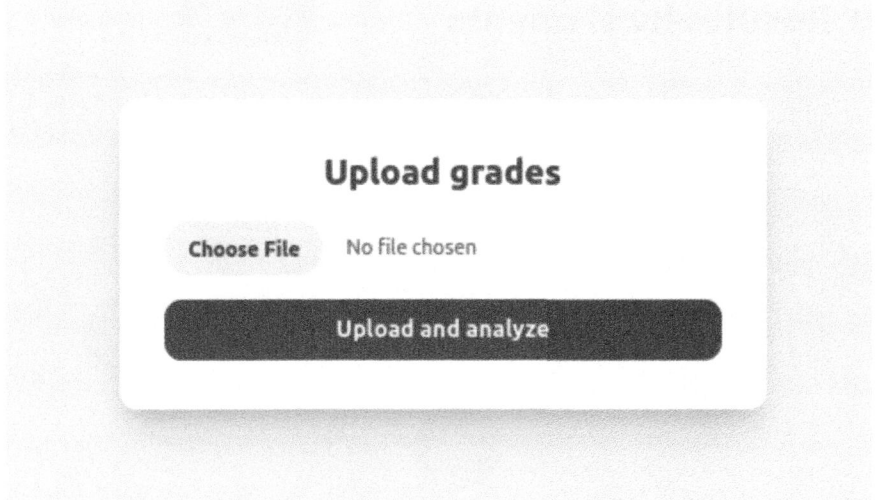

**Fig. 1.** The interface for importing grades dataset

## 4   Software Implementation

An implementation of the proposed methodology is done using Python. The system works as follows: It imports a CSV file with data for student grades (Fig. 1).

The *pandas* library and Flask framework are used for the web-based system. Once the dataset with grades is imported, the intuitionistic fuzzy evaluations are calculated. The results are displayed (Fig. 2). The results for each student are calculated as per described in Sect. 3. If the obtained non-membership value for a student is below 0.3, the student is considered a good student and is assigned to green color. If the non-membership value is between 0.3 and 0.6, the student is considered average and is assigned to yellow color. If the non-membership value is above 0.6, the student is considered at risk and is assigned to red color. The threshold values are selected empirically based on simulated data and can be further tweaked in consideration with different analytical strategies. The threshold constants can be modified using a configuration file in the software.

Data for each student is presented by subjects with their respective IFEs (Fig. 3). The IFEs are calculated respectively for each subject and listed in the table. These results are aggregated so that the student's IFE is obtained.

The frontend uses the *ChartJS* library to visualize data for whole classes/schools (Fig. 4). The data is visualized with the membership degree (good academic results) on the horizontal axis and non-membership degree (poor academic results) on the vertical axis. The students at top left are with poor results, the students in the middle are with average results and the students at bottom right are with good academic results. The proposed algorithm is chosen due to its efficiency and easy application over data. The analysis potential of the suggested algorithm can be extended further if combined with clustering machine learning algorithms like k-means or DBSCAN.

# Results by students

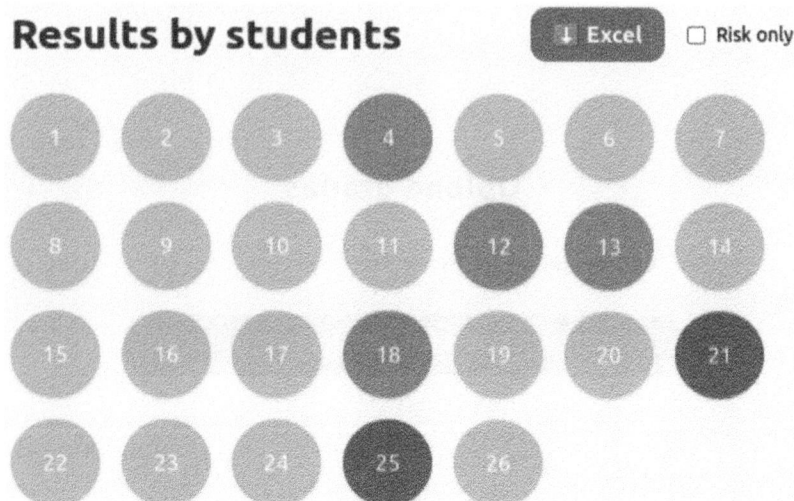

**Fig. 2.** Results by students

## Details for student № 3

Good academic results (membership, μ): **0.621**
Bad academic results (non-membership, ν): **0.304**,
Uncertainty π: **0.076**

| Subject | μ | ν | π |
|---|---|---|---|
| English | 0.42 | 0.48 | 0.1 |
| Biology and health education | 0.44 | 0.46 | 0.1 |
| Bulgarian | 0.5 | 0.4 | 0.1 |
| Geography and economics | 0.75 | 0.2 | 0.05 |
| History and civilizations | 0.94 | 0.04 | 0.03 |
| Mathematics | 0.5 | 0.4 | 0.1 |
| Physics and astronomy | 0.44 | 0.46 | 0.1 |
| Physical education | 0.92 | 0.05 | 0.03 |
| Philosophy | 0.88 | 0.07 | 0.05 |
| Chemistry and environment protection | 0.42 | 0.48 | 0.1 |

**Fig. 3.** Details for student

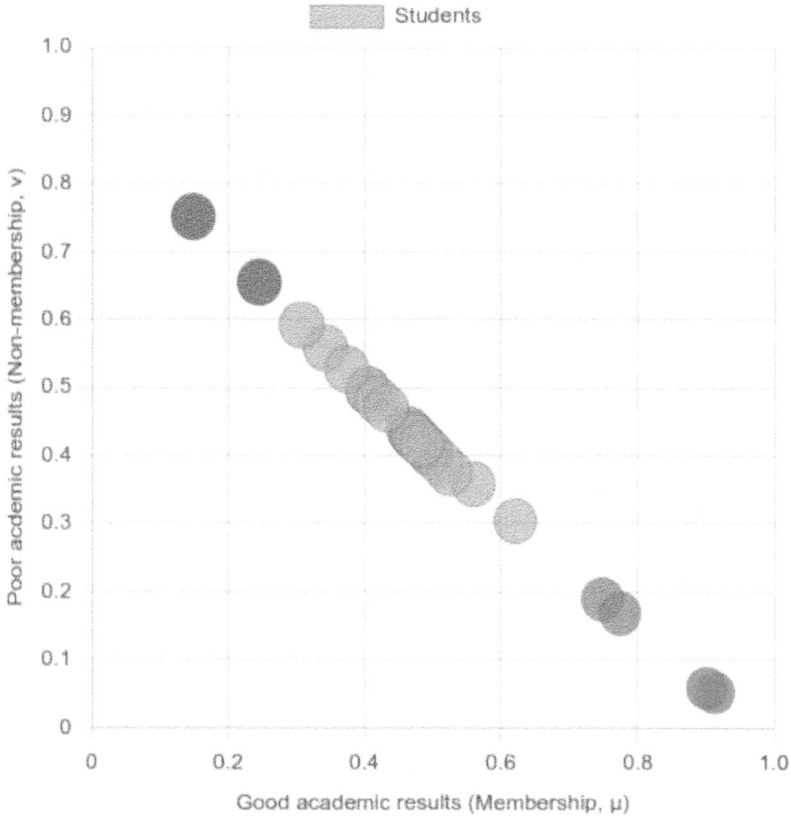

**Fig. 4.** Chart with data for a whole class

## 5  Conclusion

In the current paper a methodology for monitoring of student academic performance in school using intuitionistic fuzzy evaluations is proposed. A web-based system for analyzing and visualizing the data is developed. The presented methodology and system can be used to help school administration and teachers to make decisions for the education process based on data. The methodology also focuses on personalized education by helping school staff to identify potential learning difficulties and recommend actions on time.

**Acknowledgments.** This research was funded by Burgas State University Prof. Dr. Asen Zlatarov, Project: UNITe, BG16RFPR002-1.014-0004.

## References

1. Atanassov, K.: Generalized Nets and Intuitionistic Fuzziness in Data Mining, Professor Marin Drinov Academic Publishing House (2020)

2. Atanassov, K.: Intuitionistic Fuzzy Sets. Springer, Heidelberg (1999)
3. Atanassov, K.: On Intuitionistic Fuzzy Sets Theory. Springer, Berlin (2012)
4. Atanassov, K., Szmidt, E., Kacprzyk, J.: On intuitionistic fuzzy pairs. Notes Intuitionistic Fuzzy Sets **19**(3), 1–13 (2013)
5. Çitil, M.: Application of the intuitionistic fuzzy logic in education. Commun. Math. Appl. **10**(1), 131–143 (2019)
6. Kim, T., Sotirova, E., Shannon, A., Atanassova, V., Atanassov, K., Jang, L.: Interval valued intuitionistic fuzzy evaluations for analysis of a student's knowledge in university e-learning courses. Int. J. Fuzzy Logic Intell. Syst. **18**(3), 190–195 (2018)
7. Sotirova, E., Shannon, A., Kim, T., Krawczak, M., Melo-Pinto, P., Riečan, B.: Intuitionistic fuzzy evaluations for the analysis of a student's knowledge in university e-learning courses, intuitionistic fuzziness and other intelligent theories and their applications, studies in computational. Intelligence **757**, 95–100 (2018)
8. Sotirova, E., Petkov, T., Krawczak, M.: Generalized net modelling of the intuitionistic fuzzy evaluation of the quality assurance in universities, Advances in fuzzy logic and technology 2017. Adv. Intell. Syst. Comput. **643**, 341–347 (2017)
9. Sotirova, E., et al.: Intuitionistic fuzzy evaluations for analysis of a student's knowledge of mathematics in university e-learning courses. In: 2016 IEEE 8th International Conference on Intelligent Systems (IS), Sofia, Bulgaria, pp. 535–537 (2016), https://doi.org/10.1109/IS.2016.7737474
10. Tuğrul, F., Çitil, M.: A new perspective on evaluation system in education with intuitionistic fuzzy logic and promethee algorithm. JUM **4**(1), 13–24 (2021). https://doi.org/10.33773/jum.796173

# Automated Data Collection and Intelligent Analysis in Support of Academic and Research Management

Stanimir Kabaivanov$^{(\boxtimes)}$ (iD) and Veneta Markovska (iD)

Plovdiv University Paisii Hilendarski, Plovdiv, Bulgaria
stanimir.kabaivanov@uni-plovdiv.bg

**Abstract.** In this paper we suggest a flexible model for software support system that is able to automate data collection and analysis of academic and research management information. We follow on the experimental implementation, tested at the Plovdiv University to assess the strengths and challenges that face introduction of intelligent data processing and application of LLMs in support for higher education. Usability and quality of various support tools is also assessed, based on feedback and use statistics collected over the complete experiment period.

**Keywords:** automated data collection · local LLMs · open domain question answering · data vectorization

## 1  Introduction

### 1.1  The Need for Automated Collection and Intelligent Analysis

It is hardly needed to highlight the benefits of automated data collection to support business and administrative processes, considering the advance in technology and computer systems in the last decades. However, the abundance of information does not necessarily lead to better decisions, as discussed in details in (Boczkowski, 2021), (van Knippenberg, Dahlander, Haas, & Gerard, 2015) and (Kashada, Isnoun, & Aldali, 2020). This is particularly true, when it comes to public finance, subsidies and funding of public and common goods. Public institutions that are responsible for offering services and producing intangible goods need a dedicated approach in assessing their efficiency in a way that is able to justify the allocation of always scarce funds. Studies that address the efficiency in public spending often focus on the impact of organization, as for example in (Omar, Qasim, Kawad, & Kalenychenko, 2024), accounting and reporting methods (Reynilda & Renal, 2025) and general application of software to improve various processes (Ikwuanusi, Onunka, Owoade, & Uzoka, 2024), to name a few.

Yet, regardless of the main focus, a common assumption of different studies is that credible and justified management decisions should be based on equally credible and up to date information. Financial and accounting details are often obtained through established and tested software systems, that rely on common standards and legally specified

G. De Tré et al. (Eds.): FQAS 2025, LNAI 16119, pp. 139–144, 2026.
https://doi.org/10.1007/978-3-032-05607-8_14

obligations to report on regular basis. Assessment of quality of services however requires less structured inputs that are of various nature, precision and often come from different sources. In addition to complicating the quality assessment, these peculiarities often end up with creating additional information-collecting tasks imposed on assessed organizations and their employees. Some studies question the use of performance measurement, as for example in (Greiling, 2006) and others argue that striving for more transparency is not always improving public services (Bauhr & Carlitz, 2021) but in any case the overhead created by data collecting and reporting has a negative impact on the efficiency of public agencies and funded institutions.

In this paper we suggest a flexible model for software support system that is able to automate data collection and analysis of information required to track down the performance of higher education institutions and facilitate assessment of quality of offered service and public goods. Like any other process-oriented solution, it is better to address a specified area and problem set, therefore we focus on quality assessment in higher education in Bulgaria, and in particular on data needed for accreditation procedures.

### 1.2 The Challenges with Data Collection

Theoretically, data collection for the purpose of quality assessment in university education should be straightforward and trivial task. Thus, automating it, would require basic understanding of necessary indicators and use of publicly available databases and registration utilities. To some extent, it is indeed possible to stick to these statements and prepare a set of criteria that have to be met and observed by educational institutions. The not-so-trivial part comes when the problem is to make sure that the selected indicators are really capable to act as a proxy for the quality of the education, while at the same time provide impartial and unbiased comparison between various institutions.

We assume that coming up with a reasonable and justified assessment of the quality of education, should be based on inputs, that are:

– Both qualitative and quantitative in nature, as its not possible to address various professional areas with only one of these groups.
– Verifiable and fully transparent, as this is particularly important for institutions that are funded by taxpayer money and have strong impact on future development of economy and society.
– Logically and empirically related to the quality of education and fulfillment of long-term and current policies as imposed by the respective governing and funding bodies.
– Adaptive and focused on small step improvements, thus capable of providing continuous feedback on development and progress of the respective educational institutions.

The last two requirements deserve special attention, as they slightly deviate from the traditional view of following an established standard and a "recipe book" of good practices. Even conservative sector as academia is subject to strong influence from changes in the economic conditions and social changes, so quality assessment should take these in consideration as well. Furthermore, educational systems where some institutions are strongly dependent on governmental funding have to consider that financing goes along with the respective long-, mid- and short-term policies. It is therefore essential to assess quality in the aspect of educational institutions being able to facilitate and carry out the execution of these policies.

Adaptive systems, focused on small-step improvements on the other hand can provide flexibility needed to respond to rapid changes in economic and social processes that educational institutions have to cope with – following the notion of "accelerated society" discussed in (Rosa, 2013).

Table 1 summarizes the most important challenges related to data acquisition and subsequent processing in order assess quality of university education.

**Table 1.** Important challenges with data collection for university accreditation.

| Challenge | Remarks |
|---|---|
| Necessity of qualitative inputs | Qualitative inputs impose specific challenges in gathering the necessary information in a comparable way, as well as with extracting important notations without extensive review and manual processing of all the details |
| Periodic retrieval | Traditional accreditation and inspection times range from few months to few years, which is hard to match increased dynamics of economic and social processes. To counter this challenge, information needs to be retrieved with higher frequency, which in turn increases the overhead |
| Overhead and manual processing | Manual processing results in limiting the frequency of data acquisition and prevents retrieving information that is comparable (refers to the same point in time) and usable to detect problems on time |
| Relevance of indicators to quality | Concise and clear relevance prevents acting in a way that is solely meant to improve a specific indicator, regardless of the impact on the final goal of improving quality of education |
| Transparency and backward compatibility | Very important as it allows the monitored institutions to compare and adapt their behavior in order to improve, thus turning them into proactive participants |

## 2  Automated System for Data Acquisition and Analysis

To overcome the challenges described in Table 1, we suggest an approach that combines automatic retrieval from structured data sources with natural language processing for qualitative indicators. This approach has been implemented at Plovdiv University as a set of accreditations and reporting support tools for several years. Figure 1 provides an overview of the fundamental components included in the automatic data acquisition procedures:

- A central registrar database that contains unique identifiers about scholars and students alike, thus serving as independent source that assigns each individual to particular institution.
- Research databases with respective public APIs that allow to retrieve information about each scholar and/or student publication activity, including citations and confirmed reviews.
- Data sources that are internal to institutions and provide anonymized statistical indicators on student activities and success (like for example attendance to classes, average score and failure/success rate).

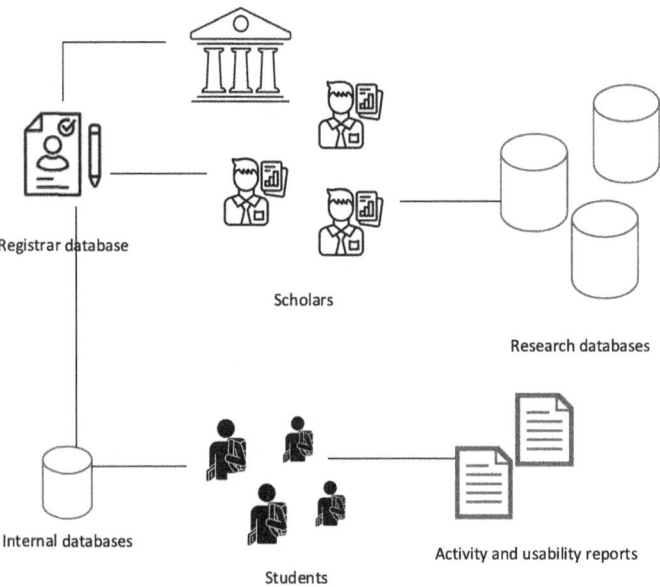

Registrar database

Scholars

Research databases

Internal databases

Students

Activity and usability reports

**Fig. 1.** Overview of the core information sources and links between them, that allow automated data acquisition.

An important advantage of the approach described above is that unique identification used for scholars (and that include Scopus ID, Web of Knowledge ResearcherID and ORCID identifier) allows for swift detection of new information, like published research or citations, while at the same time prevents double counting and error prone manual processing. With the experimental implementation, it is allowed to add additional filters for research papers, notably such related to affiliation. This allows to fine tune the inputs, though strictly speaking the affiliation is important for institutional prestige and ranking and the quality of education is correlated to the scholar/teacher research output and not his/her current affiliation.

The same applies for student information, where unique identifiers can be either the national registrar number or the internal student number, as long as both map in a unique way. This also helps in eliminating records that are of invalid or non-active status.

## 2.1   Analysis of Non-Structured Inputs and AI Supported Systems

In order to account for all aspects of the quality of education, it is also necessary to consider inputs that are non-structured and may be expressed in various forms. For analyzing them, we suggest to apply a locally-run large language model, that embeds the respective contexts (in terms of documents, internal regulations and other specific output). Figure 2 provides an overview of the whole process, which is based on regular updates of the knowledge contained in the internal documents and data sources.

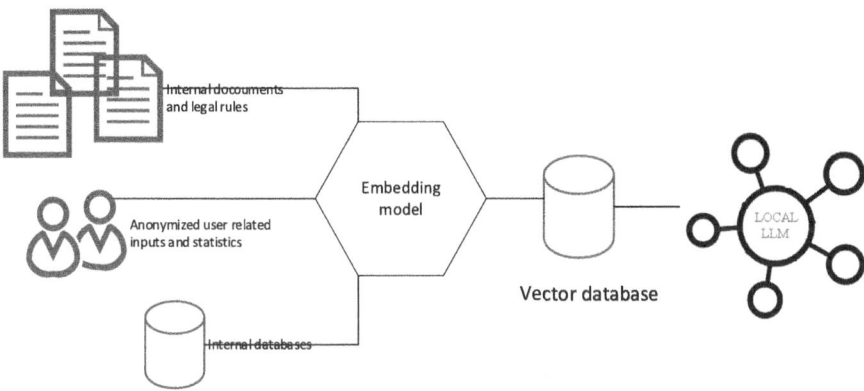

**Fig. 2.** Overview of the locally-run large language model applications in the automated data acquisition

The first step in the process is the integration of non-structured inputs, which may be free-text answers or specific quality reports, to name a few. Typically, these documents are reviewed by human experts and this is a time-consuming process that requires great care in reading and highlighting the important details. When large language models are used, the respective documents can be preprocessed and used as a specific context to generate summaries and answer specific queries.

Embedding the contents of the available documents to later serve as a context is done by the following steps:

- Separating textual inputs into separate parts, using a standard sentence and paragraph-based separation, making sure that each chunk is no more than 7500 characters long. While this is a standard approach, as discussed in the numerical results, it offers an opportunity to improve the output by adjusting the separation depending on the type of document inputs.
- Information from the previous step is vectorized using Nomic Embed (Nussbaum, Morris, Duderstadt, & Mulyar, 2024). The output of this step is cached on a persistent storage and stored in Chroma[1] database.
- Vectorized inputs are then used along with Gemma 2 LLM - BgGPT-Gemma-2–2.6B-IT-v1.0 (INSAIT, 2024) to generate responses on queries based on the provided context.

---

[1] https://github.com/chroma-core/chroma.

## 3. Numerical Results
## 4. Conclusion

**Acknowledgments.** This paper has been supported by the European Union-NextGenerationEU initiative, through the National Recovery and Resilience Plan of the Republic of Bulgaria, project DUECOS BG-RRP-2.004-0001-C01.

# References

Bauhr, M., Carlitz, R.: When does transparency improve public services? Street-level discretion, information, and targeting. Public administration **99**(3), 500–516 (2021). https://doi.org/10.1111/padm.12693

Boczkowski, P.J.: Abundance: On the Experience of Living in a World of Information Plenty. Oxford University Press (2021)

Greiling, D.: Performance measurement: a remedy for increasing the efficiency of public services? Int. J. Prod. Perform. Manag. 1741–0401 (2006)

Ikwuanusi, U.F., Onunka, O., Owoade, S.J., Uzoka, A.: Digital transformation in public sector services: enhancing productivity and accountability through scalable software solutions. Int. J. Appl. Res. Soc. Sci. **6**(11), 2744–2774 (2024). https://doi.org/10.51594/ijarss.v6i11.1724

INSAIT. (2024). BgGPT-Gemma-2–2.6B-IT-v1.0, a state-of-the-art Bulgarian language model based on google/gemma-2–2b and google/gemma-2–2b-it. INSAIT. Retrieved from https://huggingface.co/INSAIT-Institute/BgGPT-Gemma-2-2.6B-IT-v1.0

Kashada, A., Isnoun, A., Aldali, N.: Effect of information overload on decision's quality, efficiency and time. Int. J. Latest Eng. Res. Appl. **5**(1), 53–58 (2020)

Nussbaum, Z., Morris, J.X., Duderstadt, B., Mulyar, A.: Nomic embed: training a reproducible long context text embedder. Nomic-AI (2024)

Omar, N.J., Qasim, N.H., Kawad, R.T., Kalenychenko, R.: The role of digitalization in improving accountability and efficiency in public services. Revista Invest. Operacional **45**(2), 203–224 (2024)

Reynilda, R., Renal, M.: Evaluation of public sector financial management and costing system in improving performance effectiveness. Econ. Digit. Bus. Rev. **6**(1), 1015–1033 (2025)

Rosa, H.: Acceleration and growth: external drivers of social acceleration. In: Rosa, H. (ed.) Social Acceleration: A New Theory of Modernity, pp. 160–194. West Sussex: Columbia University Press (2013). https://doi.org/10.7312/rosa14834-011

van Knippenberg, D., Dahlander, L., Haas, M.R., Gerard, G.: Information, attention, and decision making. Acad. Manag. J. **53**(3), 649–657 (2015). https://doi.org/10.5465/amj.2015.4003

# Enhancing the Quality of Education Through the Implementation of an Intelligent Tutoring System

Snezhana Sulova$^{(\boxtimes)}$ ⓘ and Iviana Hristova ⓘ

University of Economics – Varna, Varna, Bulgaria
{ssulova,ivianahristova}@ue-varna.bg

**Abstract.** Improving the quality of education is a key priority for higher education institutions, with technological innovations playing a crucial role in this process. In the era of digitalization, universities are increasingly integrating modern technological solutions that facilitate communication between students, faculty, and administration. This study focuses on the automation of tutoring systems and the support of students in their interactions with academic mentors. A model of an intelligent tutoring system is proposed, which can be implemented in higher education institutions. The goal is not to replace academic mentors but to assist them in their work, making them more effective, informed, and engaged in supporting students. The system can be viewed as a virtual assistant that reduces the mentor's workload. The system is flexible and can be upgraded with new functionalities to meet the specific needs of different educational institutions and adapt to evolving educational requirements.

**Keywords:** Intelligent Tutoring System · Education · Virtual Assistant

## 1 Introduction

The educational process is complex and various strategies and innovations can be applied to improve its quality [1]. One of them is the integration of technological solutions that support the learning process [2], also known as digitalization [3]. Information and communication technologies are used in teaching, grading and in the administrative services provided to students. Modern higher education institutions constantly strive to enhance the quality of education by implementing innovative technological solutions in the learning process. With the advancement of digital technology and automation, the need for more effective tools of communication and student support arises.

One of the key aspects of this transformation is the role of academic mentors and tutoring systems that facilitate interaction between students and teachers. The active involvement of teachers and students in the feedback process improves student retention and increases their achievements [4]. In this context, the current study proposes a model of an intelligent tutoring system that aims to support the work of academic mentors without replacing them. This system functions as a virtual assistant that provides timely

© The Author(s), under exclusive license to Springer Nature Switzerland AG 2026
G. De Tré et al. (Eds.): FQAS 2025, LNAI 16119, pp. 145–154, 2026.
https://doi.org/10.1007/978-3-032-05607-8_15

and relevant information, reducing the workload of tutors and increasing the effectiveness of academic support.

The proposed model is characterized by flexibility and enhancement options, which allows adaptation to different educational institutions and their specific requirements. With appropriate training of language models, the intelligent tutoring system can serve as a valuable tool for students' academic progress and personal growth. The adoption and implementation of such technologies can significantly improve the educational process and create a more effective and engaging academic environment.

## 2 Integrating Smart Technologies into the Learning Process

Computer-assisted learning (CAL) is a well-known concept. Information technologies, and especially AI tools, are increasingly entering the learning process [5]. Modern electronic and distance learning platforms use Artificial intelligence (AI) to adapt the learning process according to the individual needs of learners, offering analysis of their performance and recommendations for improvement. Several studies have investigated the potential and impact of AI in education [6–8]. In this regard, innovative game mechanisms are being implemented to engage students [9] such as virtual classrooms, AI-based tutors [10], and training systems using intelligent chatbots [11].

One of the manifestations of the implementation of AI technologies in the educational process is the Intelligent Tutoring System (ITS). They are of many different types. Most of them are designed to help students better master the material in a specific discipline such as mathematics, computer science, foreign language, etc. [12]. The so-called collaborative ITS also exist. They help learners interact with each other. Based on a thorough analysis, Mousavinasab et al. define the main areas of application of ITS, among which they indicate: adaptive feedback, hint or recommendation generation; defining classification or updating the learner's characteristics; learner's evaluation; presenting adaptive learning material or content; adaptive learning path navigation; presenting adaptive test and exercises [13]. This gives us reason to summarize that the functions of ITS vary widely, depending on their purpose. In the present study, we focus on systems for aiding feedback and generating recommendations.

The proposed model aims to improve the work of the tutoring systems introduced in Bulgarian higher education institutions. Personal support through tutoring is provided by academic tutors according to previously developed rules. The authors of this study argue that an automated tutoring system cannot replace the role and place of the tutor, but can significantly facilitate the parties involved in the learning process through additional opportunities for interactivity and convenient work in real time. Figure 1 shows the conceptual model for ITS proposed by us.

The intelligent tutoring system is inherently hybrid in nature. It includes both physical meetings and software modules to facilitate the communication process. An essential element of the automated processes are AI-based tools. The main processes covered are:

- Initial in-person meeting with the students and introduction to the tutoring system.
- Meetings with students in various formats: in-person group and individual meetings, and virtual ones through a specially developed virtual assistant. Regardless of

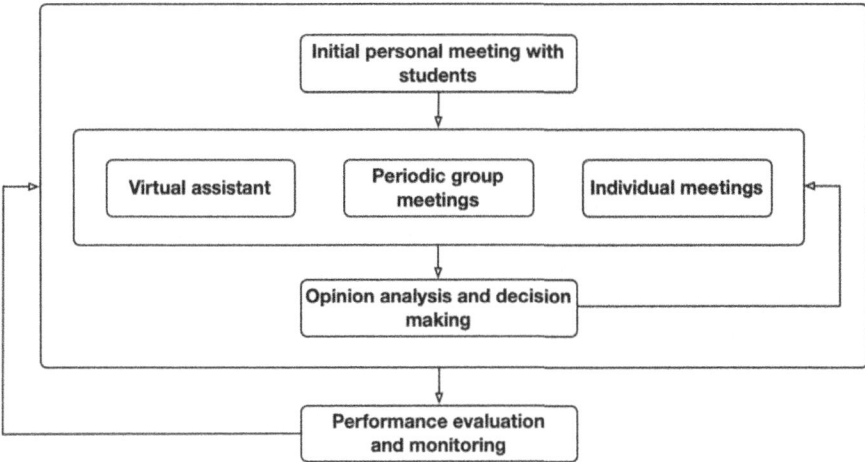

**Fig. 1.** A conceptual model for an intelligent tutoring system.

the format of the meeting, their purpose is to discuss academic progress, personal development and administrative services provided to students.

• Analysis of the expressed opinions and decision-making for improvement. For convenience, we suggest that, in addition to the analysis of the reports, tools for natural language processing (NLP) [14] be used for summarizing the opinions and identifying the issues.

• Evaluation and monitoring the effectiveness of the system – based on internal audits, collecting feedback from students and tutors, evaluation and monitoring of the system's effectiveness – based on internal audits, gathering feedback from students and tutors, suggestions for improvements to the system and its information support are made.

## 3   Testing of Modules from the Proposed ITS

In this development, we will demonstrate a sample implementation of two of the intelligent modules – the virtual assistant and the processing of reports using Natural language processing tools.

### 3.1   Virtual Chatbot Assistant for a Tutoring System

As part of the present work, we have developed a working prototype of a virtual assistant integrated within the concept of an Intelligent Tutor System focused on administrative, organizational, and mentoring support for students in a university environment. After testing and evaluating different tools, we have concluded that the assistant will be built and implemented using **Google Dialogflow ES** (Essentials). Dialogflow ES is a natural language understanding platform that makes it easy to design and integrate a conversational user interface into your mobile apps, web applications, devices, bots, interactive

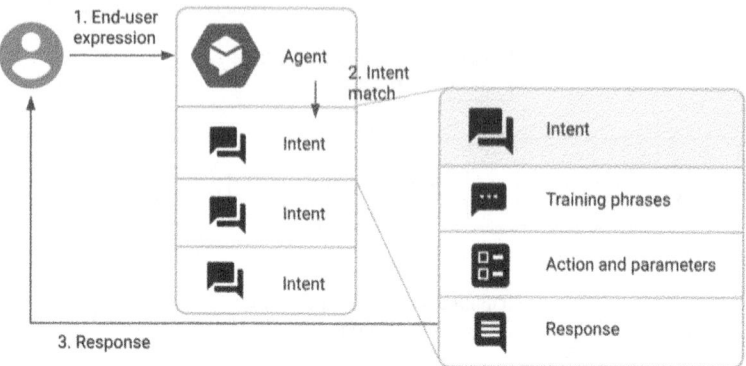

**Fig. 2.** Overview of flow

voice response systems, and more. The diagram presented in Fig. 2. – Overview of flow shows the basic flow for intent matching and responding to the end user.

The design of our system reflects the hybrid nature of the tutor model, which includes both in-person mentoring and digital support. The assistant acts as an intelligent, always-available intermediary between students and the broader tutor system.

The virtual assistant was designed to:

- support communication with tutors (e.g., scheduling or rescheduling meetings).
- provide organizational help (deadlines, reminders, contact info).
- collect feedback and suggestions for system improvement.
- serve as a structured tool to help students navigate their tutoring process independently [15].

The structure of the assistant was based on a realistic set of expected interactions within the tutor system and modeled through a series of defined intents in Dialogflow. A total of over 10 intents were developed to cover key administrative and support scenarios such as scheduling and rescheduling meetings, requesting meeting details, providing feedback, suggesting improvement and others. The **intent** represents the purpose or goal behind a user's message [16]. It is a predefined structure that helps the system recognize what the user wants to achieve. Each intent includes example phrases (called training phrases) that the system uses to match similar user input and respond appropriately. By organizing dialogue into intents, the assistant can interpret natural language and trigger meaningful actions or responses that align with the user's needs.

Figure 3 represents the typical structure of the intent named "Provide feedback" and its training phrases. Training phrases are the terms which are given by the user when interacting with the assistant. Dialogflow uses machine learning (ML) and NLP to analyze these examples and automatically detect similar user inputs, even if they do not exactly match the original phrases. This enables the assistant to understand variations in language, intent, and phrasing, and to provide appropriate responses based on the user's underlying goal rather than exact keywords.

As mentioned above, chatbot responses also need to be defined when creating intents. It's important to make sure they are logical, match the user's input, and can lead naturally

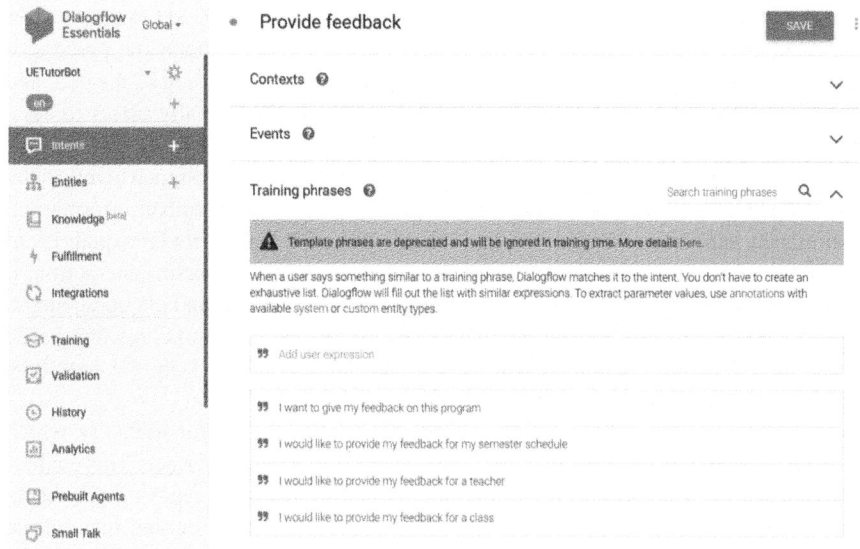

**Fig. 3.** Intents: training phrases

to another step in the conversation if needed. Responses should feel supportive and helpful, guiding the user without breaking the flow. Typical responses for the intent "Provide feedback" are shown in Fig. 4, where the assistant invites the user to share their thoughts and acknowledges the feedback they give.

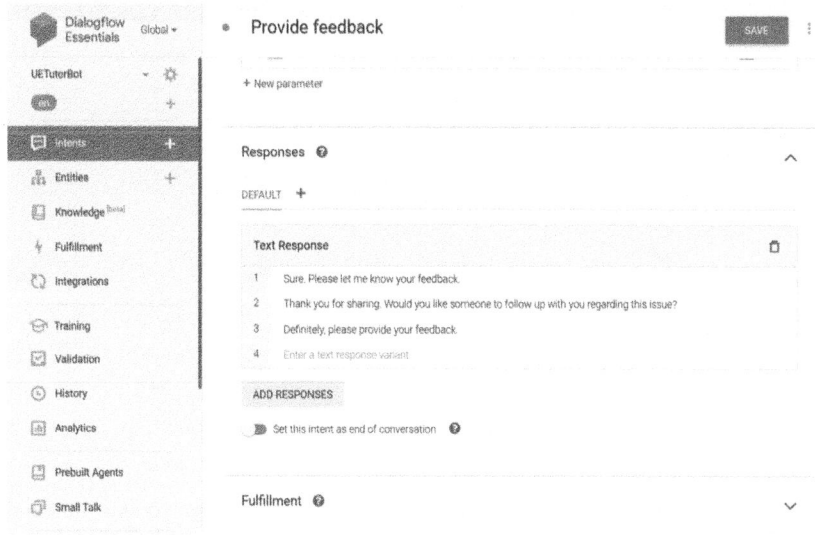

**Fig. 4.** Intents: responses

Dialogflow contexts are used to guide multi-turn conversations and maintain state when required by the interaction. For example, after a student initiates the process of scheduling a meeting, a context is activated to await further input, such as the date and time, after which the assistant confirms the scheduling and optionally offers to set a reminder.

The tone and behavior of the virtual assistant were intentionally designed to reflect the values of the tutor model. The assistant is designed also to not only deliver information, but simulate a supportive, responsive, and reliable presence that mirrors the qualities of a real mentor. Although the system is not intended to replace in-person interaction, it ensures that students can always access basic guidance, structure, and encouragement, even outside scheduled tutor meetings. The assistant currently supports only text-based interaction and was implemented without external integrations to keep the prototype lightweight and focused.

Deployment was accomplished using Dialogflow's Web Demo functionality, which allowed for immediate testing and public access via a hosted chat interface. This enables the assistant to be shared easily for validation, demonstration, and real-time feedback. Furthermore, the structure of the assistant supports future expansion and integration, including embedding into e-learning platforms such as Moodle, connecting to institutional student systems, or enhancing the assistant with additional natural language processing capabilities such as sentiment analysis or personalized follow-ups.

Interface of the assistant through a web page and basic conversation can be observed on Fig. 5 and implementation in mobile device is displayed on Fig. 6. The conversations represent the intents which were initialized in the assistant earlier.

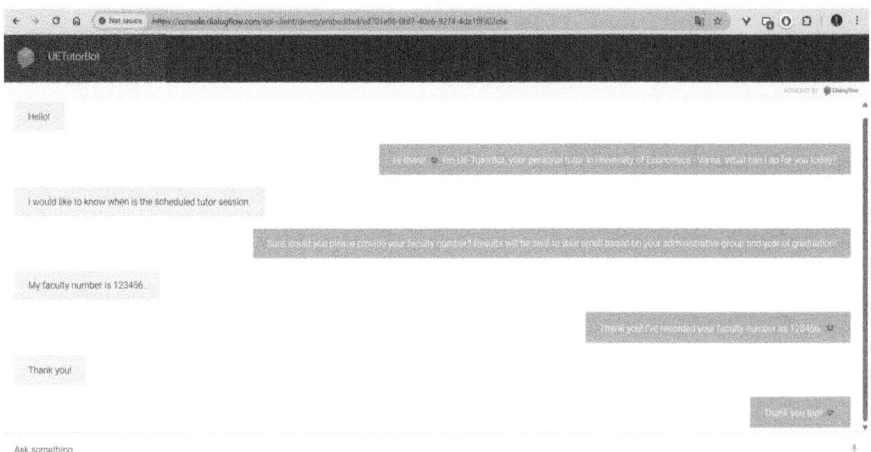

**Fig. 5.** Conversation with the assistant in web version

In future implementations, the virtual assistant can be integrated into university platforms such as student portals or e-learning systems like Moodle, making it more accessible and useful in everyday academic communication. A practical addition would

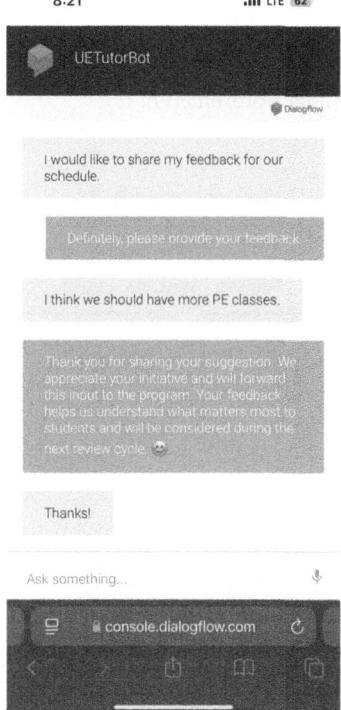

**Fig. 6.** Conversation with the assistant in mobile version

be connecting the assistant to a backend database where feedback and inquiries submitted by students can be stored and reviewed by tutors or administrative staff. This would allow the system not only to collect input but also to provide follow-up support based on previous interactions. For example, the assistant could recognize repeat issues, summarize feedback trends, or notify staff when certain types of suggestions appear frequently. This kind of integration would enhance the assistant's role from a basic helper to an active part of the tutoring workflow, supporting continuous improvement and better communication between students and the institution.

### 3.2 Application of Natural Language Processing in a Tutoring System

The feedback collected through the virtual assistant, as well as the reports from individual and group tutoring sessions, can be further processed using NLP techniques. It is known that NLP finds applications in machine translation, speech recognition, text data analysis, search engines, automated document processing, and many other fields. NLP can be considered as a synthesis between disciplines such as philosophy in ontological models of human language, psychology, behavior, computational linguistics, and mathematical models [17].

The proposed processing can be implemented using Large Language Models (LLMs), such as GPT, BERT, T5, Gemini, etc., or by developing models through Python and libraries for extracting text from various document types, as well as libraries like NLTK (Natural Language Toolkit) and spaCy for natural language processing. Although the process has quite a few differences depending on the chosen implementation tools, it can be summarized in the stages presented in Fig. 7.

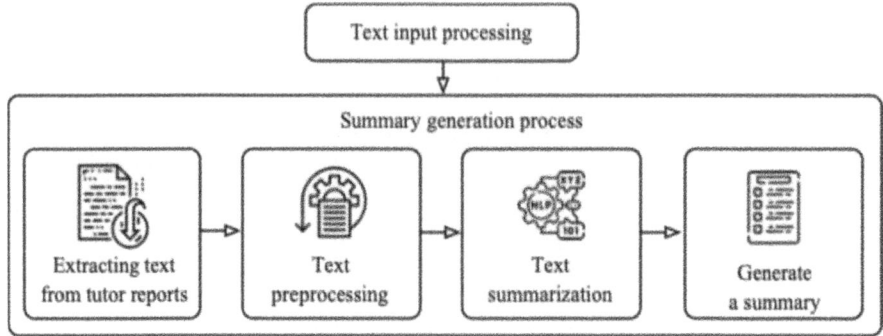

**Fig. 7.** Process of Automatic Text Processing.

Summarization, also known as text summarizing, is based on three main techniques: extractive (the source document is constructed from the most important sentences of the input document), abstractive (new sentences are generated based on the document), and hybrid methods (a combination of the previous two approaches, where carefully selected sentences are included along with generated ones) [18].

It should be noted that LLMs have the advantage of being pre-trained on large datasets and possess a self-attention mechanism [19], which helps the models better identify relationships between words and pay attention to different parts of the text in order to correctly interpret its meaning. There are studies that present computational methods specifically designed for a given language, or those adapted for preprocessing, normalization, and analyzing similar languages, language varieties, and dialects [20]. A suitable development for use with the Bulgarian language is presented in [21], which is based on the Python library spaCy. The authors present an implementation of an open-source pipeline for processing the Bulgarian language.

The choice of approach for implementing natural language processing is crucial for the accuracy of analyses based on text data. However, this process is also associated with a number of challenges. Working with texts in different languages, using informal speech, foreign words, and jargon creates various difficulties. The complexity of grammar and language structures in many languages also poses problems for automatic processing. The authors recommend the use of LLMs with additional fine-tuning settings by adding specialized data from educational dialogues related to university learning environments.

It should be noted that, at present, NLP has a very broad application in education. Currently, in the proposed system, the use of NLP is limited to summarizing student feedback and identifying issues related to a given subject in order to support the learning process. However, its scope can be expanded with functionalities such as summarizing each student's progress and providing personalized recommendations, as well as supporting the learning process through, for example, automatic generation of summaries from large texts and highlighting key content, definitions, and more.

## 4 Conclusion

The present study presents a conceptual model of an intelligent tutoring system designed to support academic mentors in the consultation process, without replacing their role. The developed approach aims to create a virtual assistant that not only facilitates communication between students and mentors but also provides relevant information, collects feedback, and supports decision-making based on data analysis.

A key focus of the development is the integration of modules based on modern natural language processing (NLP) methods, which enable effective interpretation and synthesis of textual information related to the educational process. The virtual chatbot, as a key component of the system, demonstrates the potential of artificial intelligence as a useful tool in supporting academic engagement and student success.

The results achieved reveal opportunities for enhancing the system through integration with e-learning platforms (e.g., Moodle), adding functionalities such as personalized recommendations, emotional and behavioral analysis, as well as automated report and recommendation generation for mentors. Additionally, the adaptation of language models to specific terminology and communication practices in the academic environment would further enhance the system's efficiency and relevance.

In conclusion, the proposed intelligent tutoring system is a step towards modernizing and digitalizing academic mentoring through the use of artificial intelligence technologies.

**Acknowledgments.** This research was conducted as part of the project PNI-CS24-04-DCAAITM "Development of Competencies for Applying AI Tools and Methods".

## References

1. Peicheva, M.: A Model for implementing innovations in training. J. Choveshki resursi & Tehnologii = HR & Technol. Creative Space Assoc. **1**, 5–17 (2023)
2. Parusheva, S., Bobek, S., Zabukovsek, S.: Sternad sustainable higher education: from e-learning to smart education. Multidisc. Digit. Publishing Inst. **10378**, 1–2 (2023)
3. Shishmanov, K.: Advantages and disadvantages of digitization of education. Natl. Sci. Pract. Conf. Digit. Transf. Educ. Prob. Solutions Assess. Accred. 138–142 (2023)
4. Williams, A.: Delivering effective student feedback in higher education: an evaluation of the challenges and best practice. Int. J. Res. Educ. Sci. **10**(2), 473–501 (2024)
5. Wang, S., Wang, F., Zhu, Z., Wang, J., Tran, T., Du, Z.: Artificial intelligence in education: a systematic literature review. Expert Syst. Appl. **252**(124167), 124167–124167 (2024). https://doi.org/10.1016/j.eswa.2024.124167
6. Crompton, H., Burke, D.: Artificial intelligence in higher education: the state of the field. Int. J. Educ. Technol. High. Educ. **20**(1), 1–22 (2023). https://doi.org/10.1186/s41239-023-00392-8

7. Chu, H., Tu, Y., Yang, K.: Roles and research trends of artificial intelligence in higher education: a systematic review of the top 50 most-cited articles. Australas. J. Educ. Technol. **38**(3), 22–42. (2022). https://doi.org/10.14742/ajet.7526

8. Vassileva, B., Daneva, T.: The role of GenAI in transforming educational process in HEIs. Bus. Manag. Compass. **69**(1), 43–57. (2025). https://doi.org/10.56065/4kznvd77Received:6. 1.2025Revised:20.1.2025

9. Hare, R., Ferguson, S., Tang, Y.: Enhancing student experience and learning with iterative design in an intelligent educational game. Br. J. Edu. Technol. **56**(2), 551–568 (2024). https://doi.org/10.1111/bjet.13526

10. Banik, B.G., Gullapelly, A.: AI-powered gamification and interactive learning tools for enhancing student engagement. In: Murugan, T., Karthikeyan, P., Abirami, A. (eds.) Driving Quality Education Through AI and Data Science, pp. 283–310. IGI Global Scientific Publishing (2025). https://doi.org/10.4018/979-8-3693-8292-9.ch013

11. Ilieva, G., Yankova, T., Klisarova-Belcheva, S., Dimitrov, A., Bratkov, M., Angelov, D.: Effects of generative Chatbots in higher education. Information **14**(9), 492 (2023). https://doi.org/10.3390/info14090492

12. Arnau-González, P., Solera-Monforte, S., Wu, Y., Arevalillo-Herráez, M.: A framework for adapting conversational intelligent tutoring systems to enable collaborative learning. Expert Syst. Appl. **271**, 126663 (2025)

13. Mousavinasab, E., Zarifsanaiey, N., R. Niakan Kalhori, S., Rakhshan, M., Keikha, L., Ghazi Saeedi, M.: Intelligent tutoring systems: a systematic review of characteristics, applications, and evaluation methods. Interact. Learn. Environ. **29**(1), 142–163 (2018). https://doi.org/10. 1080/10494820.2018.1558257

14. Lee, R.: Natural language processing. A Textbook with Python Implementation. Springer Nature Singapore Pte Ltd. (2024)

15. Google Cloud Team. Dialogflow ES documentation. https://cloud.google.com/dialogflow/es/docs. Accessed 3 Apr 2025

16. Rahman, S.: Build an AI tutor Chatbot: a step-by-step guide. https://www.linkedin.com/pulse/build-ai-tutor-chatbot-step-by-step-guide-sohanur-rahman-z81bc/. Accessed 4 Apr 2025

17. Li, S., Huang, X., Wang, T., et al.: Using text mining and machine learning to predict reasoning activities from think-aloud transcripts in computer assisted learning. J. Comput. High. Educ. **37**, 477–496 (2025). https://doi.org/10.1007/s12528-024-09404-6

18. Vaswani, A. et al.: Attention is all you need. In: Proceedings of the 31st International Conference on Neural Information Processing Systems (NIPS 2017). Curran Associates Inc., Red Hook, NY, USA, 6000–6010 (2017)

19. Zamperi, M., Nakov, P., Scherrer, Y.: Natural language processing for similar languages, varieties, and dialects: a survey. Nat. Lang. Eng. **26**(6), 595–612 (2020)

20. Cajueiro, D.O., et al.: A comprehensive review of automatic text summarization techniques: method, data, evaluation and coding. arXiv (Cornell University) (2023). https://doi.org/10. 48550/arxiv.2301.03403

21. Berbatova, M., Ivanov, F.: An improved Bulgarian natural language processing pipeline. Ann. Sofia Univ. Fac. Math. Anf. Inf. **110** (2023). https://doi.org/10.60063/gsu.fmi.110.37-50

# Using Old Lessons for New AI – A Trainer for Project Risk Management

Ioannis Patias(✉) ⓘ, Dafinka Miteva ⓘ, and Elitsa Peltekova ⓘ

Faculty of Mathematics and Informatics, Sofia University "St. Kliment Ohridski",
5 James Bourchier Blvd., 1164 Sofia, Bulgaria
{patias,dafinca,epeltekova}@fmi.uni-sofia.bg

**Abstract.** The secondary use of training materials as fine-tuning data for Intelligent Tutoring Systems (ITS) and Adaptive Learning Platforms (ALP) represents a transformative approach in educational technology. This method enhances the effectiveness of ITS by re-using existing educational resources to improve personalized learning experiences. As demand for adaptive learning solutions increases, the integration of fine-tuning and in-context learning methodologies underscores the potential to create robust systems that respond to diverse learner needs, supporting better academic outcomes in various educational settings. This strategy provides tailored transfer learning, instruction-tuning, and alignment-tuning that can accommodate individual learning styles, allowing for greater engagement and longer retention of the training materials. However, the application of fine-tuning techniques also presents challenges, such as ensuring the quality and relevance of training data, which is crucial for mitigating issues like overfitting. Additionally, educators must consider the architectural designs of ITS to ensure alignment with pedagogical goals, as not all systems support every instructional strategy effectively. Addressing these concerns is essential for maximizing the potential of ITS in providing equitable and effective learning experiences. To demonstrate the strategy a simplified triples-based methodology is proposed for the use of existing training materials as fine-tuning data in ITS. A case study of the use of existing training materials helps evaluate the methodology. The step-by-step case study of the project risk management trainer highlights both the opportunities and challenges in the effort for optimized learning experiences.

**Keywords:** Large Language Models (LLMs) · Intelligent Tutoring Systems (ITS) · adaptive learning platforms (ALP) · Project Risk Management (PRM)

## 1 Introduction

The integration of technology into education has paved the way for innovative approaches to enhance learning experiences. Intelligent Tutoring Systems (ITS) and Adaptive Learning Platforms (ALP) represent key advancements in this domain, offering personalized and adaptive educational environments [1]. These systems aim to answer to diverse learner needs and improve academic outcomes across various educational settings. A transformative strategy to further enhance the effectiveness of ITS and ALP

© The Author(s), under exclusive license to Springer Nature Switzerland AG 2026
G. De Tré et al. (Eds.): FQAS 2025, LNAI 16119, pp. 155–167, 2026.
https://doi.org/10.1007/978-3-032-05607-8_16

involves the secondary use of existing training materials as fine-tuning data. This method focuses on re-using educational resources to refine personalized learning experiences, acknowledging the increasing demand for adaptive learning solutions.

Fine-tuning, a machine learning (ML) technique, involves taking a pre-trained model and adapting it to a specific task by training it on a smaller, task-specific dataset. In the context of ITS and ALP, fine-tuning can be employed to tailor transfer learning, instruction-tuning, and alignment-tuning. This customization allows the systems to better accommodate individual learning styles, potentially leading to greater engagement and improved retention of training materials. Transfer learning, a related concept, leverages knowledge gained from one task to improve learning in another, which is inherently achieved by re-using training materials. Instruction-tuning refines the model's ability to follow instructions, while alignment-tuning ensures the system's output aligns with specific learning objectives [2].

The potential benefits of fine-tuning in this context are substantial. By adapting ITS and ALP to better align with the specific content and approaches embedded within existing training materials, these systems can provide more relevant and effective personalized learning experiences. This approach can lead to improved learner engagement, as the system becomes more attuned to individual learning preferences and needs. Furthermore, it can contribute to enhanced retention of the training materials, as the adaptive nature of the system allows for reinforcement and personalized review.

However, the application of fine-tuning techniques also presents challenges. A critical concern is ensuring the quality and relevance of the training data. The effectiveness of fine-tuning is heavily dependent on the data used to train the model; if the data is of poor quality or not relevant to the learning objectives, it can lead to issues such as overfitting. Overfitting occurs when the model learns the training data too well, including its noise and idiosyncrasies, resulting in poor generalization to new, unseen data. This can undermine the system's ability to provide effective and adaptive learning experiences [3].

Moreover, educators must carefully consider the architectural designs of ITS to ensure alignment with specific goals. Different ITS architectures may support various instructional strategies with varying degrees of effectiveness. It is crucial to select or design systems that can effectively implement the desired approaches to maximize their potential in providing equitable and effective learning experiences [4–7].

To address these challenges and demonstrate the strategy's viability, a simplified triples-based methodology is proposed for utilizing existing training materials as fine-tuning data in ITS. The effectiveness of this methodology is evaluated through a case study involving the use of the Project Risk Management (PRM) course training materials. This step-by-step case study aims to highlight both the opportunities and challenges inherent in the effort to optimize learning experiences through the secondary use of training materials in ITS and ALP.

## 2   Intelligent Tutoring Systems and Adaptive Learning

Traditionally, ITSs have operated primarily as autonomous tutors, providing students with personalized guidance. However, they can also adopt the role of tutees in learning-by-teaching exercises. This dual role is supported by evidence indicating that learning by teaching is a powerful strategy for enhancing self-explanation, boosting self-efficacy, and improving educational retention. Such an approach not only encourages active participation from learners but also helps in building a collaborative learning environment.

The integration of fine-tuning data into ITSs enables a more tailored approach to instruction, enhancing student engagement and fostering improved learning outcomes. By analyzing past training materials, educators can identify effective teaching methods and adapt them for use in ITSs. This not only enhances the system's instructional capabilities but also supports educators in refining their assessment strategies.

Adaptive education approaches that leverage this data also contribute to developing better writing, analytic, and self-regulation skills among students. With the use of learning analytics, teachers can gain insights into student performance and customize their teaching methodologies, making education more responsive to individual learner needs.

The integration of advanced learning techniques such as fine-tuning and in-context learning has become increasingly important in the development of ITS and ALP. Fine-tuning enhances the model's performance by providing task-specific robustness, which is particularly beneficial in educational applications that require high accuracy and control over the learning experience. This approach, however, demands significant computational resources and a level of expertise in machine learning, making it less accessible for all educational contexts [8].

As educational technology evolves, the need for personalized learning experiences has grown. The shift from traditional, rigid teaching methods towards more adaptive learning solutions reflects a broader demand for personalization in education. This transition is underpinned by advances in Artificial Intelligence (AI) and Machine Learning (ML), which enable the development of systems that can adjust to individual learning styles and preferences. The traditional educational model, often based on fixed content delivery and usage metrics, is increasingly seen as inadequate for modern learners. Thus, the application of fine-tuning and in-context learning in ITS and ALP represents a critical advancement in creating effective, personalized educational experiences.

The recent developments in artificial intelligence (AI) and the introduction of Large Language Models (LLMs) come to contribute in this direction. LLMs, are sophisticated neural networks trained on extensive textual corpora. They have demonstrated remarkable capabilities in natural language processing (NLP), understanding and generation. Their pre-training allows them to work with a broad semantic and syntactic comprehension. But, their direct applicability to specific downstream tasks often necessitates a process of refinement known as fine-tuning. This paper will define and describe the fine-tuning process, ant its significance in tailoring general-purpose LLMs to achieve optimal performance in targeted domains and applications related to the development of ITS and ALP.

At its direction we use fine-tuning, as it represents a supervised transfer learning technique, instruction-tuning, or alignment-tuning that involves taking a pre-trained LLM, the foundational weights of which encapsulate a vast reservoir of linguistic knowledge, and subjecting it to further training on a smaller, task-specific dataset. This secondary training phase aims to adapt the model's existing parameters, enabling it to effectively capture the intricate patterns and nuances inherent in the target domain or task. Unlike training a model from initial random weights, fine-tuning leverages the rich feature representations learned during pre-training, thereby often requiring significantly less task-specific data and computational resources to achieve comparable or superior performance [9].

## 3  Methodology

The fine-tuning process typically unfolds through several key stages. Initially, a relevant and high-quality dataset, curated specifically for the intended application, is assembled. This dataset comprises input-output pairs that exemplify the desired behavior of the fine-tuned model [9].

Subsequently, the pre-trained LLM is initialized with its learned weights. Depending on the nature of the downstream task, minor architectural modifications, such as the addition of task-specific output layers, may be implemented. The model is then exposed to the training subset of the task-specific data. During this supervised training phase, a loss function, appropriate to the task at hand (e.g., cross-entropy for classification, mean squared error for regression), quantifies the discrepancy between the model's predictions and the ground truth labels.

A crucial aspect of the fine-tuning process is the careful selection of parameters, and data. The learning rate, in particular, often requires adjustment to a smaller value compared to the pre-training phase to prevent catastrophic forgetting – the loss of previously acquired knowledge. The validation dataset plays a pivotal role in parameter tuning and in monitoring the model's generalization performance, allowing for the implementation of early stopping to mitigate overfitting, a phenomenon where the model learns the training data too well and performs poorly on unseen data [10, 11].

The fine-tuning of LLMs is a critical process in adapting these powerful general-purpose models for effective deployment in a diverse range of specialized applications. By leveraging the knowledge acquired during extensive pre-training and focusing subsequent training on task-specific data, fine-tuning enables LLMs to achieve state-of-the-art performance with enhanced data efficiency. In this paper a use case of the transfer learning technique for fine-tuning with prompts will be implemented step-by-step, using existing training data.

### 3.1  Steps in Fine-Tuning with Prompts

In standard fine-tuning, the focus is primarily on learning the input-output mapping for a specific task. When fine-tuning with prompts, you are explicitly teaching the model to understand and follow instructions provided in the prompts to perform the task. The prompts become an integral part of the learning process and the model's expected behavior.

The concept of "prompt-input-output" triples is a structured way to organize data for training and evaluating Large Language Models (LLMs), particularly when fine-tuning or using prompt engineering. It emphasizes the importance of context and instruction in guiding the model's behavior [12].

In traditional machine learning, data is often structured as input-output pairs. The model learns to map a given input to a specific output. However, LLMs are unique in their ability to understand and generate human language, making it possible to guide their behavior not just with input examples but also with explicit instructions. The "prompt-input-output" triple leverages this capability.

The "prompt" acts as an instruction or a cue that sets the context for the LLM. It tells the model what to do with the "input." The "input" is the data that the model needs to process according to the prompt. The "output" is the desired response or action from the LLM.

This structure is particularly useful for the key tasks we need to implement in the use case of the secondary use of training data, namely:

- Fine-tuning: Training an LLM to perform specific tasks by providing examples of how it should respond to different prompts and inputs.
- Prompt Engineering: Designing effective prompts to elicit desired behavior from a pre-trained LLM.
- Evaluation: Assessing an LLM's ability to follow instructions and process information correctly.

A more detailed definition of the so provided components prompt, input, and output may provide with more insight on their use.

The prompt is as known and, in this case, i.e. a text-based instruction, question, or cue given to the LLM. It defines the task, sets the tone, and provides context.

The input is the data that the LLM needs to process according to the prompt. It can be text, but it could also represent other forms of data that have been textualized. Having the concrete set up of development of an ITS and ALP the input is the user's feedback that provides the platform with the information to help it adapt.

The output is the desired response or action from the LLM. It's the target that the model should generate. Provides more details on the format of the output.

The "triples-based" methodology centers around structuring data as "prompt-input-output" sets. The prompt provides instructions or context, the input is the data to be processed, and the output is the desired response.

This contrasts with input-output pairs, which form the foundation of supervised learning, where data is structured as (input, output), and the model learns to map inputs to outputs. While the input-output component is present in triples, triples add the prompt to provide explicit instructions, going beyond a simple mapping.

Contextual learning emphasizes the importance of surrounding information (context) for processing data. The prompt in the triples-based methodology provides context to the LLM, guiding its interpretation of the input. Triples are a way to implement contextual learning in LLMs, making the context explicit in the form of a prompt.

Instruction tuning is a fine-tuning technique where LLMs are trained on datasets containing instructions and desired outputs. Triples are a prime example of instruction tuning, as the prompt is the instruction. Fine-tuning with triples is essentially a form of instruction tuning [12].

Few-shot learning is a technique where a model learns from very few examples. Prompts within the triples can incorporate few-shot examples to guide the LLM. The prompt itself provides the few-shot learning examples [12].

Task-oriented learning focuses on training models for specific tasks. The prompt in the triple defines the task, making the data inherently task-oriented. Triples are well-suited for task-oriented learning. In essence, the triples-based methodology is distinctive in its systematic combination of instruction, context, and data. It formalizes the use of prompts to guide LLM behavior, going beyond simple input-output mapping. While related to the other concepts, it provides a structured approach for training, evaluating, and controlling LLMs, especially in tasks that require nuanced understanding and instruction following.

Having those, here follows the simplified triples-based three-steps methodology for fine-tuning LLMs specifically incorporating prompts into the learning process:

### Step 1: Prepare Clean, Labeled and Representative Prompted Dataset

- **Prompt-Input-Output Examples:** Gather or create data where each instance includes a prompt, the relevant input for the task, and the correct output.
- **Design Effective Prompts for Training:** Craft prompts that clearly instruct the LLM on what to do with the input to generate the desired output. These prompts should be representative of how you intend to use the model after fine-tuning.
- **Split Prompted Data:** Divide dataset into training, validation, and test sets, ensuring a good distribution of different prompt styles and task variations across the sets.
- **Choose a Base Model:** Select an LLM architecture suitable for your task and resources. Consider models known for their ability to follow instructions well.

### Step 2: Initiate the Fine-Tuning Process (Prompt-Driven Case Shown)

- **Train with Prompted Data:** Feed the training data (prompt + input as input, output as target) to the LLM. The model learns to associate specific prompts with the desired ways of processing the input and generating the output.
- **Monitor Prompt-Based Performance:** Track performance on the validation set using metrics relevant to your task. Pay attention to how well the model follows the instructions in the prompts.

### Step 3: Evaluate and Iterate (Prompt Effectiveness)

- **Evaluate on the Validation Set with Diverse Prompts:** Assess the model's ability to generalize to new examples and to understand variations in prompts for the same task.
- **Evaluate on the Test Set with Target Prompts:** Perform a final evaluation using prompts that closely resemble how you intend to use the model.

- **Analyze Prompt Following:** Examine instances where the model struggled to follow instructions or produced incorrect outputs. Refine your training data with more diverse and clearer prompt examples, or adjust your fine-tuning hyperparameters. You might also need to revisit your prompt design strategy.

## 3.2  Implementation and Results

In this section prompt examples to implement the provided triples-based methodology for fine-tuning an LLM in the field of PRM will be crafted. The overall target task is to improve the PRM ability to provide accurate, and helpful responses to user queries related to specific related issues.

### Step 1: Prepare Clean, Labeled and Representative Prompted Dataset
To develop examples of Prompt-Input-Output triplets we went through the training materials as developed in an existing course for Project Risk Management. Data was cleared and where necessary labeled before included in your dataset. All data considered as representative as prepared accordingly.

We used the platform Vercel.AI [13, 14]. It provides tools and cloud infrastructure to build, scale, and secure a faster, more personalized web applicable in numerus application areas [15]. Various models were tested by providing prompts as:

- **prompt:** how to mitigate a major risk in my project?

  o **Input:** Software development for the Municipality Register.
  o **Output:** ...

- **prompt:** how to mitigate a major risk in my project?

  o **Input:** use PMI standard for your answer.
  o **Output:** ...

From the results we see that various models perform differently, based on their initial pre-training dataset, and parametrization. Additional parametrization for the output improves with more personalized responses.

### Step 2: Initiate the Fine-Tuning Process (Triples-Based)
Concrete prompt-input-output examples were given to LLM. The model thus learns to associate the specific prompts with the desired, detailed, and informative responses. These following examples demonstrate how the prompt-input-output triple structure can be applied to a PRM course for various purposes including: define key concepts, explain processes, provide examples, test understanding, and others.

Topic: Identifying Project Risks.
Triple 1: Prompt: "List common categories of project risks."

- **Input:** (None)
- **Output:** "Common categories of project risks include: scope creep, budget overruns, schedule delays, resource constraints, communication breakdowns, technological issues, and external factors."

**Triple 2: Prompt:** "For each risk category, give an example of a specific risk."

- **Input:** "Risk categories: scope creep, budget overruns, schedule delays"
- **Output:** "Scope creep: Adding new features not in the original plan. Budget overruns: Unexpected increases in material costs. Schedule delays: Key tasks taking longer than estimated."

**Topic:** Risk Assessment.
**Triple 3: Prompt:** "Describe the steps involved in a qualitative risk assessment."

- **Input:** (None)
- **Output:** "Qualitative risk assessment involves identifying risks, assessing their likelihood and potential impact, and prioritizing them based on a risk matrix."

**Topic:** Risk Response Strategies.
**Triple 4: Prompt:** "Give an example of when you would use the 'Mitigation' risk response strategy."

- **Input:** "Mitigation"
- **Output:** "You would use mitigation when you cannot avoid a risk entirely, but you can take actions to reduce its probability or its impact. For example, implementing testing protocols to reduce the risk of software bugs."

### Step 3: Evaluate and Iterate (Prompt Effectiveness)

For testing the fine-tuned model new triples were used, to get a better sense of how effectively it has learned the nuances of anxiety and how well it can use that knowledge in a more open-ended context.

### Sub-Step 3.1. Evaluate on the Validation Set with Diverse Prompts

The fine-tuned model was tested with new, unseen prompts related to project risk management:

**Triple 5 – Conceptual Understanding:** This dimension assesses the trainer's comprehension of the theoretical foundations of project risk management. It goes beyond simple definitions to evaluate the model's ability to articulate relationships between core concepts and principles.

- **Prompt:** "Explain the relationship between risk likelihood, risk impact, and risk priority."
- **Input:** (None)
- **Output:** "Risk likelihood is the probability of a risk event occurring. Risk impact is the potential effect on project objectives. Risk priority is the ranking of risks based on their likelihood and impact, often using a risk matrix, to determine which risks need the most attention."

**Triple 6 – Scenario Analysis:** This evaluates the capacity to apply risk management knowledge to hypothetical project situations by the trainer. Tests the ability to identify potential risks, analyze their implications, and propose appropriate responses within a given context.

- **Prompt:** "A project is developing a new software application. Identify potential risks related to team communication and suggest mitigation strategies."
- **Input:** "New software application development"
- **Output:** "Potential risks include: unclear requirements, lack of regular meetings, conflicting priorities, and lack of documentation. Mitigation strategies: establish clear communication channels, hold regular status meetings, define roles and responsibilities, and use collaborative tools."

**Triple 7 – Quantitative Reasoning:** Focuses on the ability to handle numerical aspects of risk management. Assesses skills like performing calculations, interpreting quantitative data, and applying quantitative techniques to risk assessment and analysis.

- **Prompt:** "Describe how you would estimate the potential financial impact of a risk that has a 20% probability of occurring and an estimated cost overrun of $50,000."
- **Input:** "20% probability, $50,000 cost overrun"
- **Output:** "To estimate the potential financial impact, you would multiply the probability of the risk (20% or 0.20) by the estimated cost overrun ($50,000). This results in an expected monetary value of $10,000."

**Triple 8 – Process Application:** Evaluates the knowledge of the structured processes and methodologies used in project risk management. Examines the understanding of the steps involved in risk identification, assessment, response planning, and monitoring and control.

- **Prompt:** "Outline the key steps in the risk monitoring and control process."
- **Input:** (None)
- **Output:** "The key steps in risk monitoring and control are: identifying and tracking identified risks, implementing risk response plans, monitoring risk triggers, re-assessing risks, and communicating risk status to stakeholders."

**Triple 9 – Ethical Considerations:** Assesses the awareness of the ethical responsibilities and professional conduct expected of project managers in relation to risk management. Evaluates the understanding of issues such as transparency, disclosure, and stakeholder communication.

- **Prompt:** "Discuss the ethical responsibilities of a project manager in disclosing project risks to stakeholders."
- **Input:** (None)
- **Output:** "Ethically, a project manager is responsible for honest and transparent disclosure of project risks to stakeholders. This includes providing accurate information, avoiding concealment of potential problems, and communicating both the potential positive and negative impacts of risks."

### Sub-Step 3.2. Evaluate on the Test Set with Target Prompts
To effectively evaluate the fine-tuned LLM using the generated "prompt-input-output" triples on a test set, a structured approach that assesses how well the model generalizes and adheres to prompt instructions was followed.

The evaluation process centered on presenting the fine-tuned LLM with the "prompt-input" pairs from the test triples and then critically analyzing the generated "output" against the expected "output." This is not just about accuracy, but it's about assessing the model's ability to understand and respond appropriately to nuanced prompts.

**Sub-Step 3.3. Analyze Prompt Following**
If the model provided inaccurate, insensitive, or unhelpful responses, additional analysis of the prompts that led to these errors was conducted. Then:

- more examples to your training data that specifically address the nuances of those prompts or topics were advised to be added; or
- the prompts in the training data were advised to be clearer and less ambiguous.

In conclusion the proposed step-by-step example demonstrates how the fine-tuning can contribute to a multi-dimensional personalization. The trainer can be further fine-tuned with examples focusing concrete project-wise (for example Triples 6 and 7 to diversify according to concrete project specifics), or standard-wise (for example Triples 3 and 8 to diversify without input, or with input some methodology as PMI or PRINCE).

# 4 Discussion

This paper has explored the integration of Large Language Models (LLMs) in education, within the frame of re-use of existing training materials for their fine-tuning. The key findings include the overall assessment of the triples-based fine-tuning methodology, as applied to LLMs and as illustrated with the project risk management examples. The methodology presents a focused and potentially effective approach to adapting these models for specific domains. This method centers around creating a dataset of "prompt-input-output" triples, using these to fine-tune an LLM, and then evaluating the results with a focus on prompt adherence.

The proposed triples-based fine-tuning methodology brings with it a set of compelling advantages. Its key strengths, including targeted learning, improved instruction following, and contextual understanding, contribute to its effectiveness.

**Targeted Learning:** By explicitly including prompts in the fine-tuning data, the LLM learns to associate specific instructions with desired outputs.

**Improved Instruction Following:** LLMs are known to sometimes struggle with following complex or nuanced instructions. Fine-tuning with prompt-input-output triples directly addresses this by providing numerous examples of how to interpret and act on different prompts.

**Contextual Understanding:** The inclusion of input within the triples allows the model to learn how to process information within the context of a specific prompt.

**Data Efficiency:** While a substantial amount of data is still beneficial, this method can potentially be more data-efficient than standard fine-tuning for certain tasks.

**Enhanced Evaluation:** The evaluation phase, which emphasizes prompt effectiveness, ensures that the fine-tuned model is not only generating accurate outputs but also doing so in a way that aligns with the intended use case.

To ensure the effective application of the triples-based fine-tuning methodology, it's important to be aware of certain practical considerations and potential challenges. These include the complexity of prompt engineering, the data preparation overhead, and the risk of overfitting, all of which can impact the efficiency and success of the process.

**Prompt Engineering Complexity:** Designing effective and diverse prompts for the training data requires careful consideration. Prompts need to be clear, unambiguous, and representative of the prompts that will be used in the final application.

**Data Preparation Overhead:** Preparing a high-quality dataset of prompt-input-output triples can be time-consuming and resource-intensive.

**Overfitting to Specific Prompts:** There's a risk that the model might overfit to the specific prompts used in the training data and fail to generalize to novel or slightly different prompts.

**Evaluation Metrics:** Evaluating the effectiveness of prompt-driven fine-tuning requires more nuanced metrics than simple accuracy.

**Generalization vs. Memorization:** It's important to ensure that the model is truly learning to follow instructions and apply knowledge, rather than simply memorizing the training data.

The triples-based fine-tuning methodology offers a promising approach for adapting LLMs to specific tasks and improving their ability to follow instructions. By incorporating prompts directly into the fine-tuning process, this method can lead to more controlled, effective, and reliable LLM behavior. However, it also requires careful attention to prompt design, data creation, and evaluation to ensure optimal results.

# 5 Conclusions

This paper has explored the integration of existing training materials, into the process of fine-tuning Large Language Models (LLMs) to implement a downstream task related to project risk management. The secondary use of training materials for fine-tuning Intelligent Tutoring Systems (ITS) and Adaptive Learning Platforms (ALP) presents a promising avenue for enhancing personalized learning experiences. By repurposing existing educational resources, this approach aims to create robust systems capable of adapting to diverse learner needs and fostering improved academic outcomes. The integration of fine-tuning and in-context learning methodologies underscores the potential to deliver tailored transfer learning, instruction-tuning, and alignment-tuning, thereby accommodating individual learning styles and promoting greater engagement and retention.

However, the application of fine-tuning techniques is not without its challenges. Ensuring the quality and relevance of training data is paramount to mitigating issues such as overfitting, which can compromise the system's effectiveness. Additionally, educators must carefully consider the architectural designs of ITS to guarantee alignment with pedagogical goals, recognizing that not all systems inherently support every instructional strategy.

The simplified triples-based methodology proposed in this context offers a structured approach to utilizing existing training materials as fine-tuning data in ITS. The evaluation of this methodology, as demonstrated by the project risk management training materials, highlights both the opportunities and challenges associated with optimizing learning experiences. Addressing these challenges and leveraging the identified opportunities will be crucial for maximizing the potential of ITS to provide equitable and effective learning experiences in diverse educational settings.

**Acknowledgments.** This study is financed by the European Union-NextGenerationEU, through the National Recovery and Resilience Plan of the Republic of Bulgaria, project № BG-RRP-2.004-0008-C01.

# References

1. Frank, L., Herth, F., Stuwe, P., Klaiber, M., Gerschner, F., Theissler, A.: Leveraging GenAI for an intelligent tutoring system for R: a quantitative evaluation of large language models. In: 2024 IEEE Global Engineering Education Conference (EDUCON), Kos Island, Greece, pp. 1–9 (2024). https://doi.org/10.1109/EDUCON60312.2024.10578933, https://ieeexplore.ieee.org/abstract/document/10578933
2. Balne, C.C.S., Bhaduri, S., Roy, T., Jain, V., Chadha, A.: Parameter efficient fine tuning: a comprehensive analysis across applications. https://arxiv.org/abs/2404.13506 (2024)
3. Han, Z., Gao, C., Liu, J., Zhang, J., Zhang, S.Q.: Parameter-efficient fine-tuning for large models: a comprehensive survey. https://arxiv.org/abs/2403.14608 (2024)
4. Gao, L., et al.: Fine-tuned large language model for visualization system: a study on self-regulated learning in education. IEEE Trans. Vis. Comput. Graph. **31**(1), 514–524 (2025). https://doi.org/10.1109/TVCG.2024.3456145, https://ieeexplore.ieee.org/abstract/document/10670435
5. Adeshola, I., Adepoju, A.P.: The opportunities and challenges of ChatGPT in education. Interact. Learn. Environ. **32**(10), 6159–6172 (2023). https://doi.org/10.1080/10494820.2023.2253858, https://www.tandfonline.com/doi/abs/10.1080/10494820.2023.2253858
6. Vodenitcharova, A., Leventi N., Popova, K.: Innovative information technologies in medicine the ethical aspects - medical students' opinion published in the proceedings of the "ISGT2022 conference". In: CEUR Workshop Proceedings, vol. 3191, pp. 89–97 (2022). http://ceur-ws.org/Vol-3191/paper08.pdf
7. Leventi, N., Vodenitcharova A., Popova, K.: Guidelines for trustworthy AI application in clinical trials. In: 16th World Congress on Public Health 2020 European Journal of Public Health, vol. 30, no. Supplement_5 (2020). https://doi.org/10.1093/eurpub/ckaa165.806
8. Edwards, A., Camacho-Collados, J.: Language models for text classification: is in-context learning enough? https://arxiv.org/abs/2403.17661 (2024)
9. Weng, B.: Navigating the landscape of large language models: a comprehensive review and analysis of paradigms and fine-tuning strategies. https://arxiv.org/abs/2404.09022 (2024)
10. Huang, X., Ruan, W., Huang, W., et al.: A survey of safety and trustworthiness of large language models through the lens of verification and validation. Artif. Intell. Rev. **57**, 175 (2024) (2024). https://doi.org/10.1007/s10462-024-10824-0
11. Dong, Y., et al.: Safeguarding large language models: a survey. https://arxiv.org/abs/2406.02622 (2024)
12. Liu, P., Yuan, W., Fu, J., Jiang, Z., Hayashi, H., Neubig, G.: Pre-train, prompt, and predict: a systematic survey of prompting methods in natural language processing. https://arxiv.org/abs/2107.13586 (2021)
13. Vercel Inc.: The AI Toolkit for TypeScript (2025). https://sdk.vercel.ai/docs/introduction. Accessed Mar 2025

14. Stein, B., Beck, N., Becker, D., Wegener, D.: Building a generative AI showroom for foundation models with different modalities. In: 2024 IEEE 7th International Conference on Multimedia Information Processing and Retrieval (MIPR), San Jose, CA, USA, pp. 630–633 (2024). https://doi.org/10.1109/MIPR62202.2024.00108
15. Gozalo-Brizuela, R., Garrido-Merchán, E.C.: A survey of generative AI Applications, https://arxiv.org/abs/2306.02781 (2023)

# Challenges for Assessing the Programme Accreditation Metrics: An Approach

Dimitar Christozov[1] , Valeriya Simeonova[3]([✉]) , Nadia Zlateva[3] ,
Ridvan Isufov[2,3], and Eliza Stefanova[2,3] 

[1] American University in Bulgaria, 1 Georgi Izmirliev Sq., 2700 Blagoevgrad, Bulgaria
dgc@aubg.bg
[2] National Evaluation and Accreditation Agency, 125 Tsarigradsko Shose Blvd., Bl. 5, 1113
Sofia, Bulgaria
[3] Sofia University "St. Kliment Ohridski", 5 James Bourchier Blvd., 1164 Sofia, Bulgaria
simeonova@fmi.uni-sofia.bg

**Abstract.** The paper summarizes the work done so far in analyzing effectiveness
of metrics used in evaluating quality of education as applied by National Agency
for Evaluation and Accreditation for professional fields. The analytical methodology for assessing relevance of quantified indicators is presented as well as metrics to identify problematic indicators to address in revision of the accreditation
procedure.

**Keywords:** University Accreditation · Evaluation Metrics · Quantified
Indicators

## 1 Introduction

Quality of education and relevance to the diverse needs of professionals is an essential issue for societies. University education, in general, is a conservative industry with
effects of changes usually delayed in years. This raises a difficult decision for candidates
to choose a professional field of study and the most adequate institution to offer reasonable training, corresponding to the background, abilities, and objectives for the professional career of candidates. Accreditation of university education is a tool established
by society to objectively inform the candidates and their parents regarding educational
institutions. In that role accreditation procedure serves as the "trusted-third-party". The
other role assigned to University Accreditation is to provide information to the Government regarding the quality of education of the given University in a way to help with the
adequate support provided by the State, corresponding to the value the Higher Education
Institution (HEI) offers to the Society.

The European Higher Education Area (EHEA) sets up a framework - standards and
criteria - for evaluating quality of education. Each country uses own specific methodology within the framework. Bulgarian National Evaluation and Accreditation Agency
(NEAA) develop a methodology to evaluate the performance in each criterium at the
basis of a set of quantitative and qualitative indicators. The objective of the paper is

© The Author(s), under exclusive license to Springer Nature Switzerland AG 2026
G. De Tré et al. (Eds.): FQAS 2025, LNAI 16119, pp. 168–179, 2026.
https://doi.org/10.1007/978-3-032-05607-8_17

to estimate the relevance of the quantitative indicators. The NEAA, based on feedback and assessment by external experts, has identified the need to update the methodology of the criteria system, which should include optimizing the number and refining the formulation of the quantitative indicators. The aim is to facilitate the decision of NEAA in providing a meaningful analysis of data collected so far within the conducted accreditation procedures.

### 1.1  Standards for Quality Assurance in the European Higher Education Area (ESG)

University Accreditation follows the established 1980s practices associated with quality of products and services, as in the series of ISO 9000 standards. The major tool is an independent accreditation agency, which reviews the adopted policies, procedures and practices, in a way to ensure that the HEI systematically addresses issues that influence quality. Because of the diversity of educational institutions, the job of the Agency is difficult and challenging.

The work of the European accreditation agencies is in compliance with the Standards and Guidelines for Quality Assurance in the European Higher Education Area (ESG) [1]. These provide the framework for internal and external quality assurance for the EHEA and were adopted at the EHEA Ministerial Conference in 2015 as part of the Bologna Process.

On one side the Agency must provide a uniform set of metrics to assess quality across the HEI, and on the other side to emphasize the specifics of any institution and any professional field. The third aspect challenged by the Agencies in establishing the set of evaluation indicators is the globalization of education and necessity to allow transfer and acceptance of students results in international exchange. The European Union attempts to establish a common mobility environment in education, preserving the national perspectives. The role of National Accreditation Agencies has become inevitable to ensure mobility and transfer.

University evaluation and accreditation in Bulgaria is based on a self-assessment report made by the university in a way to provide the necessary information to the NEAA, presented by an expert team, to verify the information in the self-study, and an Agency Standing Committee to summarize the collected data and expert opinions, in applying across the board standards. The final decision is made by the governing body of NEAA - the Accreditation Council. For some data, the HEI, expert team, and standing committee may use data provided by reliable and trustful external sources.

### 1.2  Quality of Education

Evaluation of quality of education requires addressing all aspects influencing the performance of HEI. This holistic approach resulted in setting 12 criteria within the 10 ESG standards – addressing different areas of evaluation, and indicators to measure performance of HEI for any criteria. Indicators are quantified (N) or qualified (Q).

Accreditation in Bulgaria as an EU country, follows the established after the Bologna process standards. The novel set of indicators employed to assess the extent of compliance with the standards was established by the NEAA in June 2023.

### 1.3 Objectives of the Study

The objective of this study is to assess the current systems of indicators regarding their informativeness toward quality of education and their verifiability, especially regarding the quantitative indicators used for program accreditation [6]. The scope of this analysis is limited to quantitative indicators regarding problems observed in data collected so far. This includes identifying the indicators that need to be altered in a way to improve the feasibility of the accreditation process, as well as reliability of obtained results.

Altering may include redefining the indicator in a way to avoid misinterpretation, transform of quantitative indicators to qualitative when it is not feasible to verify data or collected data demonstrate instability, or to remove the indicator when it is not informative – not providing metrics allowing to assess quality of education.

The study examines the data collected in a standard evaluation form. The forms are collected for the professional fields scheduled for the first three terms after adopting the system in 2023. The objectives of the study are to identify indicators that show anomalies in the data, to subsequently analyze their utility and informativeness for the evaluation process. We set the following research questions: 1) find out indicators with outliers; 2) determine correlated indicators; 3) discover other anomalies in the values of a given indicator.

## 2  Background

Higher Education in Bulgaria is classified in nine academic areas – from Natural Sciences to Arts. Within any of those areas professional fields are separated. Each HEI may offer education in more than one academic area and in several professional fields.

Two types of accreditations are defined in the Higher Education Act – institutional and program. Institutional accreditation investigates the policies, procedures and practices adopted by the institution to guarantee quality of education across the entire portfolio of professional fields offered. The classifier of higher education areas and professional fields can be found in [4]. Program accreditation is oriented to given professional field by assessing the quality of provided bachelor and master programs by applying common criteria and indicators. More detailed information about the procedures and criteria concerning program accreditation of a professional field can be found at the official web page of NEAA [5].

Performing systematic approach to evaluation of the methodology is a pioneering work. This study is the first one based on unified data collection as well. The aim is to explore statistical data driven decision making in context of updating the methodology for application the European Evaluation System in Bulgarian context.

### 2.1  Standards, Criteria, Indicators

Evaluation and accreditation criteria system requires an institution to demonstrate quality oriented performance in ten standards, assessed by 12 criteria, see [1]. Within these NEAA formulate multiple indicators - over a hundred in total. The set of indicators is with great diversity in a way to measure the complexity of the performance of the HEI in a given professional field.

## 2.2 Historical Perspective – Inheritance

The NEAA was established in 1995. The latest updates of the methodology used, criteria, indicators and procedures have been developed in 2023. The simple tools for their implementation are developed in the beginning of 2024. Then they began to be implemented. The accumulated experience and data collected from accreditation procedures scheduled for January and September 2024 and April 2025 allows us to start to analyze the effectiveness of the accreditation process of a professional field.

Over the almost 30 years of applying for accreditation in higher education resulted in accumulated experience, both in NEAA and in higher education institutions. Changes need to be made by careful analysis in a way to reduce turmoil and resistance.

# 3    Data Analysis Framework

The study applies a quantitative data analysis approach. It reveals the properties of numerical data such as distribution, observed outliers, correlations, etc. It is trying to identify problems in collected numerical data that may result in removing or altering the definitions and/or the way of measuring indicators.

## 3.1    Informativeness of Data of an Indicator as a Measure of Its Relevance for "Quality of Education"

The informativeness of a given indicator is considered as its ability to distinguish one professional field as offered by one institution in comparison with the rest.

## 3.2    Identify Problems Observed in Data Related to Indicators

Metrics that allow visualizing the anomalies across the professional fields were developed. Such metrics allow distinguishing indicators from the point of view of its power in characterizing the given professional field.

## 3.3    Impact of Lack of Data Domains Homogeneity

It is natural to observe noise, outliers, lack of symmetry and other anomalies. The acceptable level of any of the anomalies to distinguish the indicators definitely is a matter that need to be addressed. In such a diversity of domains it is natural to expect some anomalies. The problem of defining what value of the metric is an acceptable level of anomaly and what represents a significant problem that needs to be considered was an issue that was addressed in this study.

At least one of the Universities in Bulgaria is accredited also in the USA by New England Commission of Higher Education (NECHE). The standards of NECHE are quite different and mostly qualitative to allow more flexibility in addressing diverse styles in training [2]. One way to address lack of homogeneity in evaluating the quality of education is to redefine problematic quantitative indicators as qualitative. At the same time the idea of the introduction of currently applied methodology with use of predominant quantitative indicators to be kept in order to isolate as much as possible subjectivity component in the process of evaluation.

### 3.4 Data Used in the Analysis

Assessment of the quality of higher education and accreditation in Bulgaria has been carried out for 30 years. Following 2023 update of the evaluation methodology data are collected within unified Excel forms and from trusted external sources as Bulgarian University Ranking System [7] and the registers of the National Centre for Information and Documentation (NACID) [8], not solely by the self-study of HEI. The values of the quantitative indicators are calculated based on the collected data using protected formulas.

The sources of the data and the way of calculating the value of indicators are described in Methodological guidelines for preparing a self-assessment report for program accreditation of Professional Field [9]. Data used in analysis is representative. It includes records from program accreditation in every academic area and more than a quarter of professional fields - 16 of 52 professional fields in total. Data collection is on-going, subject to the schedule of reviewing institutions. Data analysis will follow the inclusion of new data sets and will allow an update of results presented here.

| Professional Field | 1.1. | 1.2. | 2.2. | 2.3. | 3.5. | 3.9. | 4.1. | 4.5. | 5.1. | 5.11. | 5.12. | 6.2. | 7.3. | 7.6. | 8.3. | 9.1. |
|---|---|---|---|---|---|---|---|---|---|---|---|---|---|---|---|---|
| Primary Data Files | 5 | 11 | 8 | 5 | 8 | 13 | 4 | 8 | 11 | 7 | 5 | 3 | 7 | 2 | 7 | 13 |

**Fig. 1.** Data set description

Figure 1 shows data sets used in the current stage of the research. In professional fields 7.6 and 8.3 there are a few specific indicators which are excluded from current study to ensure uniformity. All 56 indicators for all studied professional fields are analyzed.

## 4 Methodology

The methodology applied in analysis follows typical data mining procedures [3], with one significant exception. Data cleansing, a typical preprocessing procedure, is not applied. It is not allowed to alter data, even in cases where pollution is obvious. Data processing includes two stages. Firstly, processing data for every quantitative (N) indicator separately across the set of professional fields to highlight the anomalies related to data collected according to its current definition and requirements. As part of this first step, metrics to measure anomalies were defined and thresholds for distinguishing the "interesting" anomalies was set on. Second stage includes assessing the cross-indicators relationship.

## 5 Findings

### 5.1 Stage 1

The analysis of data allows to highlight two groups of measures that allow to identify problematic indicators: 1) Coefficient of Variation, Z-score and a heuristic metric based on field experience named as NZ; 2) IQR and an alternative metric named as VNS.

Variation provided the most visible results and IQR offered additional details. Figure 2 includes statistical metrics applied to highlight the problematic indicators. Each metric is calculated for the tuple "Professional field - Indicator". The following statistics are calculated across the professional fields:

- Descriptive statistics: Minimum, Maximum, Mean, Median, Standard deviation
- Classical methods to discover outliers and other anomalies in data: Coefficient of Variation (CV), MAD, Z-Score, IQR defined as follow:
- CV definition by empirical observations:

  - Low variation in [0; 0.5]: those indicators don't have informative value to allow distinguishing the quality of education.
  - Middle variation in (0.5;1]: those indicators are meaningful, but do not possess a high impact on evaluation of quality of education.
  - High variation (lower level) in (1;2]: those indicators possess a high potential to evaluate quality of education and to distinguish performance.
  - High variation (middle level) in (2;6]: those indicators possess a high potential to evaluate quality of education and to distinguish performance.
  - High variation (upper level) in $(6; +\infty)$: not observed in the processed data set.

- MAD with coefficient = 2.5
- Z-Score with coefficient = 3
- IQR with coefficient = 1.5
- Variations of classical methods: NZ and VNS, as follows
- NZ

  - NZ_lower_outlier = (median-min)/(max-min) < 0.1
  - NZ_upper_outlier = (max-median)/(max-min) < 0.1
  - NZ = OR (NZ_lower_outlier; NZ_upper_outlier)

- VNS

  - VNS_upper_outlier = AND((max-median)/median > 1; (median-min)/median < 0.1)
  - VNS_mass_at_max = (max-median)/max < 0.1 – the median is near the max value
  - VNS_mass_at_min = (median-min)/min < 0.1 – the median is near the min value
  - VNS = OR (VNS_upper_outlier, VNS_mass_at_max, VNS_mass_at_min)

The number of professional fields in which outliers are detected is presented for each indicator and for each method.

The objective of this data analysis is to identify problematic indicators that need to be addressed in updating the criteria system. Outliers is the natural candidate for identifying the indicators that need revision. In the next histograms are shown different ways to measure outliers.

If in a given professional field the median of an indicator equals zero this means that for one half of the Universities providing education in the field the value of this indicator

| Indicators | Zero Median | Z-Score Outliers | IQR Outliers | MAD Outliers | VNS_mass_at_max | VNS_upper_outlier | VNS_mass_at_min | NZ_lower_outlier | NZ_upper_outlier | High variation (lower level) | High variation (middle level) |
|---|---|---|---|---|---|---|---|---|---|---|---|
| N1.1.1. | | | 2 | 9 | 1 | | 1 | | | 1 | |
| N1.1.2. | | | 4 | 10 | | | | 1 | | 4 | |
| N1.2.1. | | | 9 | 14 | | | | 4 | | 8 | |
| N2.1.1. | | | 6 | 9 | 1 | | 1 | 2 | | 5 | |
| N2.1.2. | | | 5 | 10 | 3 | | | | 3 | 2 | |
| N2.1.3. | 11 | 1 | 9 | 14 | 1 | | | 10 | 1 | 7 | 5 |
| N2.1.4. | 13 | | 9 | 12 | | | | 11 | | 7 | 5 |
| N2.1.5. | 15 | 1 | 8 | 10 | | | | 10 | | 4 | 7 |
| N2.1.6. | | | 12 | 15 | 9 | | 3 | 1 | 7 | | |
| N3.1.1. | | | 9 | 14 | 8 | | 3 | | 6 | 1 | |

**Fig. 2.** Part of table with descriptive statistics by indicators

is zero. A total of 44 indicators demonstrates consistent non-zero median values across all professional fields, suggesting their applicability and relevance across the full spectrum.

In contrast, 7 indicators exhibit a zero median in at least one and up to five professional fields, indicating limited applicability or potential data sparsity in specific fields. Furthermore, 5 indicators display a zero median in at least 11 and up to all 16 examined professional fields, which raises concerns about their overall usefulness. Such a pattern may reflect misinterpretation, limited applicability, or policy-driven interventions promoting actions considered as beneficial to the evolution of Higher Education Services which are not performed yet in sufficient volume (Fig. 3).

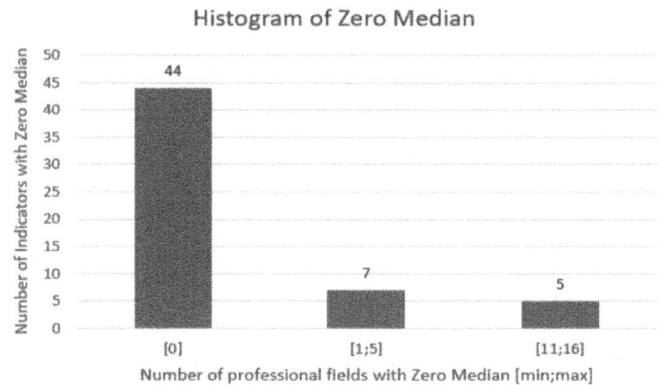

**Fig. 3.** Histogram of distribution of number of indicators with Zero Median.

These findings underscore the importance of assessing not only the variation within indicators, but also their coverage and representativeness across fields, as indicators with systematically zero medians may fail to capture meaningful distinctions and thus require reconsideration for inclusion in comparative analysis (Fig. 4).

This CV Histogram illustrates the distribution of indicators based on their coefficient of variation. It is evident that 33 of the indicators exhibit outliers in multiple professional fields— more precisely, in at least five professional fields simultaneously.

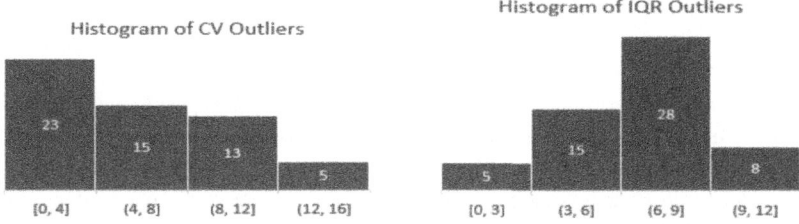

**Fig. 4.** Histograms of CV and IQR Outliers

This IQR Histogram illustrates the distribution of indicators based on their IQR. It shows that 36 of the indicators exhibit outliers in at least seven professional fields simultaneously.

## 5.2 Stage 2

Regarding the results shown on the next Fig. 5, we found two groups of statistics that describe the row data in a different way.

The first group of metrics in Fig. 5 includes MAD, Zero Median, Z-Score, NZ, and the Coefficient of Variation (CV), with the latter having different most clearly defined spikes. The second group comprises the IQR and VNS measures, which describe indicators similarly.

**Fig. 5.** Stacked chart of Outliers trends

Among these metrics, as representatives of each group CV and IQR were selected for further analysis as classical and particularly effective descriptors of raw data. When visualized together in a dot plot, they reveal four distinct quadrants.

In Fig. 6 one can see four clearly formed clusters. The separate lines cross the point (6.5;6.5). This means that the indicators appearing in I and IV quadrants (red and yellow dots) need more attention.

The indicators appearing in I quadrant (red dots) are the most problematic. **The combination of high IQR and high CV** implies that the variation in the data is not confined to isolated outliers but is more broadly distributed. It reflects a complex structure in which both the core of the distribution and its tails contribute to the overall inconsistency. Such patterns may point to heterogeneity within the observed data, or inherent instability in the indicator itself. As a result, interpreting central tendency measures becomes more challenging, and further analysis will be performed in order to determine the source and nature of the variation.

The indicators appearing in II quadrant (blue dots) are the most undetermined. **The combination of low IQR and high CV** suggests that the data are concentrated around the median (indicated by a low IQR), but the presence of isolated extreme values (outliers) substantially increases the standard deviation, resulting in a high coefficient of variation (CV). Since there are more than one possible interpretation of this fact, detailed examination of these indicators (N5.2.1 and N.6.1.1) will be performed in the next working flow.

Only 18 of the 56 indicators fall into the quadrant representing "expected behavior", see III quadrant (green dots) in Fig. 6. There one observes **the combination of low IQR and low CV** which indicates a high degree of consistency within the dataset.

This combination points to a **uniform and stable distribution**, with little deviation from central values and an absence of significant outliers. It suggests that the indicator behaves in a consistent manner across different observations or groups, such as professional fields or institutions. While such stability may indicate reliable measurement, it may also reduce the **discriminatory power** of the indicator. However, we consider only high-level variation of CV, hence we can exclude this possibility in our case.

Observed in IV quadrant (yellow dots) combination of a high IQR and a low CV represents an interesting distributional pattern. A high IQR indicates substantial variability within the central 50% of the data, suggesting that values between the first and third quartiles are widely dispersed. In contrast, a low CV reflects low overall variation relative to the mean, typically implying that extreme values (i.e., those in the tails of the distribution) do not deviate substantially from the average.

This pattern suggests that **the variability is concentrated within the middle range of the distribution**, while the overall spread of the data remains proportionally modest in relation to the mean.

From an analytical perspective, this configuration implies a **balanced yet internally diverse distribution**. Such indicators may be considered **informative and robust**, offering meaningful differentiation across observations while maintaining statistical stability. It will be performed further analysis of this group of indicators, moreover - in our case *low variation* actually means *high variation (lower level).*

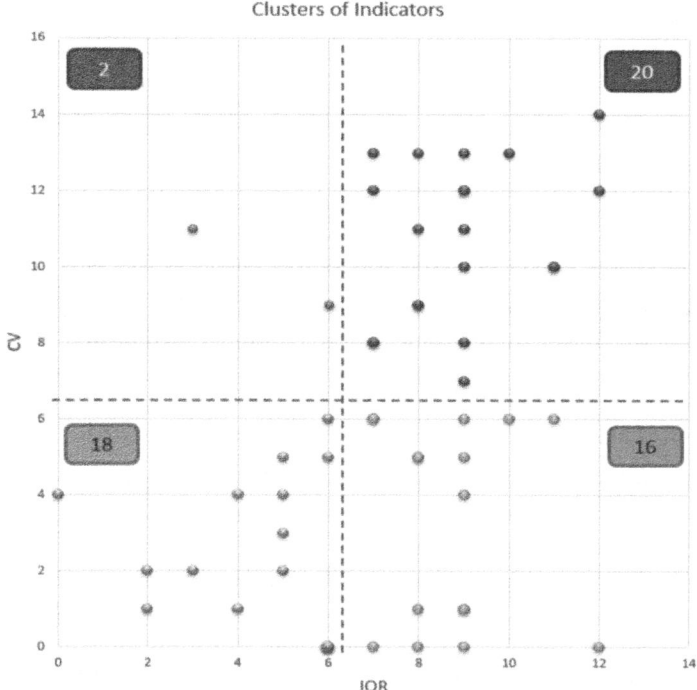

**Fig. 6.** Clusters of Indicators

## 6  Conclusion

The analytical approach presented in the paper identifies issues such as low informativeness, inconsistent variation, and zero-median behavior of certain indicators. These challenges closely align with the scope of Flexible Query Answering Systems (FQAS), which are designed to support reasoning under uncertainty, incompleteness, and heterogeneity of data. The analysis conducted is a prerequisite for both optimizing the existing system of indicators and creating specific approaches for its monitoring, as well as for building an automated information system for data collection and evaluation, which would include opportunities for monitoring the system itself over the time and making timely management decisions for the quality of higher education in Bulgaria. Integrating FQAS principles in this system would enhance the process of interacting with complex accreditation datasets, enabling semantic search over indicator behavior, flexible exploration of evaluation outcomes, and adaptive classification of problematic metrics. Thus, FQAS represents a promising direction for building intelligent, user-friendly interfaces for navigating evolving accreditation frameworks.

This study is still on-going. It is based on already registered data. The methodology of analysis is developed and tested on a representative sample of so far completed evaluation procedures. Metrics to allow measuring the informativeness of quantify indicators were proposed and their practical effectiveness demonstrated. The boundaries of applicability of metrics to identify indicators needed altering were established. Potential anomalies are identified. The results of the study are relevant to assessing the effectiveness of indicators included in various criteria systems - not only those related to assessing the quality of higher education, and have a wide field of applicability.

## 7  Future Works

The next phase of the analysis will focus on identifying and excluding indicators that do not carry meaningful information. This will involve complementary approaches:

**Significance-Based Filtering.** Indicators with low CV will be examined, as low variation may indicate limited discriminatory power. In parallel, an **information gain analysis** will be conducted to assess the relevance of each indicator. The overlap between these two methods will allow for a more robust selection process and will support the classification of indicators into four distinct groups through clustering.

**Correlation and Expert Evaluation.** A **correlation analysis** will be carried out to identify similarities between indicators and reduce redundancy. To support this, expert input will be gathered through a structured questionnaire. Respondents will evaluate the **quality and origin of raw data**, using a predefined scale. The survey will be conducted in two stages, targeting two key stakeholder groups: representatives of **universities** and **representatives from the NEAA**. The results will guide the refinement of the methodology for the next cycle of the accreditation of professional fields.

**Establishing Ongoing Data Monitoring.** As part of the long-term evaluation framework, we anticipate the regular inflow of data. Evaluation procedures are going on and new data sets are regularly added to the scope of this research that may update the findings reported above. The research will be completed when all scheduled accreditation procedures of professional fields will be completed and registered data analyzed. The latter will enable periodic re-evaluation of indicator behavior, and will support the intended improvement of the evaluation process.

**Disclosure of Interests.** The authors have no competing interests to declare that are relevant to the content of this article.

## References

1. Standards and guidelines for quality assurance in the European Higher Education Area (ESG). https://www.enqa.eu/wp-content/uploads/2015/11/ESG_2015.pdf
2. Standards of New England Commission for Higher Education (NECHE). https://www.neche.org/wp-content/uploads/2020/12/Standards-for-Accreditation-2021.pdf
3. Han, J., Kamber, M., Pei, J.: Data Mining: Concepts and Techniques. 3th edn. Morgan Kaufmann Publisher (2012). ISBN 978-0-12-381479-1
4. DECREE No. 125 of the Council of Ministers of 24 June,2002 for approval of a Classifier of higher education and professional fields. https://neaa.government.bg/images/Legislation/Decrees/DECREE-No_125-of-the-Council-of-inisters-of-24-June-2002.pdf
5. Programme accreditation of professional fields. https://neaa.government.bg/en/evaluation-and-accreditation/programme-accreditation/professional-fields

6. Criteria for programme accreditation of professional field/specialty from the regulated professions. https://www.neaa.government.bg/images/Criteria_EN/ENG_Kriterii_za_progra mna_akreditacija_na_PN-SRP.pdf
7. Bulgarian University Ranking System. https://rsvu.mon.bg/#/?locale=en
8. National Centre for Information and Documentation (NACID). https://nacid.bg/en/
9. Methodological guidelines for preparing a self-assessment report for programme accreditation of Professional field/Specialty from the regulated professions. https://neaa.government.bg/ima ges/Criteria_EN/PA_na_PN-SRP_Metodicheski_nasoki_2023_en.pdf

# Application of Artificial Intelligence
# in the Management of the Educational Process:
# Practical Experience and Effectiveness

Dean Vasilev[✉]

University of Economics, Varna 9000, Bulgaria
dean.vasilev@ue-varna.bg

**Abstract.** The rapid advancements in artificial intelligence (AI) are driving significant transformations in education, among other sectors of society. AI offers new opportunities for personalized learning, automation of administrative tasks, and improvement of teaching methods. Despite its potential advantages, however, questions arise regarding the effectiveness of AI in the learning process, its impact on students' critical thinking, and the need for ethical standards. This article explores the impact of AI on the management of the educational process, analyzing the performance of three classes in Bulgaria studying the discipline "Digital Technologies in Business". The study compares a class that uses AI tools such as ChatGPT and Canva with two classes that rely on traditional technologies and teaching methods. The results show that students who use AI demonstrate higher engagement, increased efficiency in completing assignments, and better academic results. AI-based tools facilitate the preparation of projects in schools, automate the evaluation of assignments, and stimulate students' creativity by helping them generate innovative ideas and develop critical thinking. The study highlights the key challenges associated with the ethical use of AI in education, including the need for a balanced approach that combines traditional pedagogical methods with technological innovations. The importance of training for teachers and students is emphasized in order to effectively and responsibly implement AI in the learning process. In conclusion, the study offers recommendations for future strategies and policies that would support the sustainable and ethical application of artificial intelligence in education.

**Keywords:** artificial intelligence (AI) · educational process management · digital technologies

## 1 Introduction

Over the years, traditional teaching methods – based on classical approaches such as lectures, textbooks, and standardized assignments – have proven their value as a solid foundation for the development of education. However, these methods are often limited in their ability to address the individual needs of students and to adapt to the dynamic changes in society and technology [1]. With the introduction of digital technologies into

© The Author(s), under exclusive license to Springer Nature Switzerland AG 2026
G. De Tré et al. (Eds.): FQAS 2025, LNAI 16119, pp. 180–190, 2026.
https://doi.org/10.1007/978-3-032-05607-8_18

the educational process, new opportunities arise for personalized learning, more efficient time and resource management, as well as increased student engagement. Tools such as cloud-based platforms (Google Classroom, Microsoft Teams) and specialized software for visualization and design greatly facilitate the work of both teachers and students [2, 3].

With the latest innovations in the field of AI, education is entering a new era, in which the planning, implementation, and evaluation of the learning process acquire a completely different dimension. Tools like ChatGPT allow teachers to create detailed lesson units within minutes by generating content, structuring curricula, and offering interactive tasks [4]. For example, a teacher can define the basic parameters of a course, and AI will suggest a logically structured and age-appropriate set of topics. This saves time and allows a stronger focus on the quality of instruction.

AI tools offer dynamic solutions for assignment creation – from generating quiz questions to designing scenarios for practical exercises [5]. In subjects such as "Digital Technologies in Business," AI can suggest sample tasks, structure team projects, or even simulate business cases for students to solve. From an assessment perspective, AI systems can automatically analyze and evaluate both multiple-choice and complex open-ended answers. This not only reduces the administrative burden on teachers but also provides faster feedback for students.

For learners, AI tools mean better access to educational materials, more flexible learning formats, and more opportunities for self-expression. Image generators, such as those available in Canva or other specialized platforms, allow students to create visual content aligned with their ideas, even if they lack technical skills.

Artificial intelligence has become a core technology that is transforming many sectors—including education [6]. With the emergence of generative AI tools such as Chat-GPT, Copilot, Gemini, and various web-based applications with built-in intelligent features, both educators and learners now have access to tools that accelerate the learning process, enable the creation of innovative solutions, and improve academic outcomes [7]. In today's educational systems, digital technologies play a central role in increasing student motivation and making knowledge acquisition more accessible [8]. However, a key question remains – can AI tools not only complement traditional technologies but also deliver substantial advantages in educational effectiveness?

This study explores the application of AI-based tools in managing the learning process and assessing the subject "Digital Technologies in Business," which is taught in the 10th grade of a vocational high school in Bulgaria. Through a comparative analysis of three classes – two using traditional technologies and one integrating AI tools – the study evaluates the influence of AI on the quality of education, student performance, and learning efficiency. The goal of the research is not only to measure the impact of AI on education but also to provide recommendations for its optimal implementation in future teaching practices.

In the context of Flexible Query Answering Systems (FQAS), this study also highlights how AI tools such as ChatGPT and Perplexity AI enable students and teachers to access, retrieve, and apply relevant knowledge dynamically. These tools support personalized learning by allowing users to pose natural-language queries and receive contextualized, task-specific responses. As such, the integration of AI into the educational process aligns with the broader objectives of FQAS—namely, improving accessibility, adaptability, and efficiency in information retrieval for decision-making and learning.

## 2   Theoretical Background and Research Design

The subject "Digital Technologies in Business" is taught in some vocational high schools in Bulgaria. It aims to build upon and expand students' knowledge in the fields of marketing, management, and digital technologies. Through a well-structured curriculum, it develops practical skills that are directly applicable in the modern business world. Instruction is carried out through project-based learning, placing students at the center of the process, which, according to various researchers, contributes to increased student motivation [9]. Throughout the academic year, students work in teams of four, formed at the beginning of the year and remaining unchanged until all assignments are completed. This structure promotes collaboration, role distribution, and shared responsibility, which contribute to the successful completion and presentation of projects. The curriculum is designed to ensure a balance between new knowledge and practical tasks. Over the course of 36 academic hours, students go through the following main modules: Introduction to Marketing, Business Management, Digital Technologies and Internet Platforms, Digital Marketing, and Digital Entrepreneurship. Each module includes exercises that allow students to apply their knowledge to real-world cases and situations.

The syllabus includes a combination of theoretical and practical modules. Key theoretical topics such as "Introduction to Marketing," "Marketing Policies," and "Introduction to Business Management" provide a stable foundation on which practical tasks are built. The theoretical part explains core concepts such as the marketing mix, enterprise structure, and corporate identity development. The program enables students to go through all stages of digital business development, including:

- Company creation: Choosing a name, legal structure, and business focus, as well as developing a logo and corporate identity.
- Online market analysis: Students research competitors and define their target audience.
- Digital identity creation: Developing a website and planning an online presence using platforms like Wix or other web development tools.
- Digital marketing: Designing marketing strategies, managing social media, and conducting online advertising using specialized SEO and web analytics tools.
- Advertising campaign development: Students plan, implement, and evaluate the effectiveness of digital campaigns.
- Through these assignments, students acquire skills such as:
- Teamwork: Completing projects in groups requires effective communication and role distribution.
- Creative thinking: Designing logos, websites, and marketing strategies fosters creativity.
- Analytical thinking: Market research and web analytics require in-depth analysis and data evaluation.
- Technical skills: Students work with modern software tools widely used in the business world.

The ultimate goal of the subject is to prepare students for active participation in economic life by providing them with real knowledge and practical skills related to e-commerce and digital marketing. As a result, they can pursue careers in existing companies or become entrepreneurs capable of developing their own business ideas.

The purpose of this study is to analyze how the use of AI affects the quality of the learning process and student outcomes in the subject "Digital Technologies in Business." It compares three classes, two of which use traditional digital technologies, while the third integrates AI tools such as ChatGPT, Canva, and AI-based image generators. By analyzing the assignments, teamwork, and final results, the study seeks to answer whether AI increases efficiency and facilitates the learning process.

**Object of the Study:** Three 10th-grade classes – aged 15–16, with a total of 79 students. Two classes (A and B) used only traditional digital tools, while class 10E used both traditional and AI tools.

**Subject of the Study:** The impact of artificial intelligence on the quality of the learning process, student performance, and assignment effectiveness in the subject "Digital Technologies in Business."

**Description of the Focus Groups:** Class 10A is enrolled in the "Finance" track, and 10B in "Office Management," using the following digital tools: Google Workspace tools, Wix for website creation, and Photoshop/GIMP for image editing.

Class 10E is enrolled in the "Design" track and uses Google tools, Wix, Photoshop/CorelDraw, and additionally Perplexity AI (for data retrieval and analysis), ChatGPT, Canva with AI, and image generators for visual content.

**Study period:** 15.09.2023 – 30.06.2024.

**Methods for data collection and analysis:**

- Quantitative data: Average assignment grades and final grades;
- Qualitative data: Observations of teamwork, creativity, and project quality;
- Analysis tools: Tables and charts for visualizing results.

## 3   Results

The results of the completed assignments in the subject "Digital Technologies in Business" provide valuable insights into the impact of different technologies on the quality and effectiveness of the learning process. The comparison between the outcomes of the studied groups allows for the identification of both the advantages and limitations of AI tools in the educational context. For the purpose of the analysis, student performance was assessed across six key assignments: company creation, online market analysis, digital identity, social media, advertising campaign, and final project presentation. Each task covered a variety of aspects—from creativity and analysis to technical execution. The table below (Table 1) presents the average grades for each assignment, which will be analyzed in the following sections. The analysis focuses on performance differences and evaluates how AI tools influenced the results.

The results demonstrate clearly defined differences in performance between the classes using traditional technologies and the class that utilized AI-based tools. Class 10E, which integrated AI technologies, significantly outperformed the other two classes in every assignment. This highlights the potential of AI to improve both the quality and

**Table 1.** Class performance results across assignments.

| № | Task Name | Discription | 10A | 10B | 10E (AI) |
|---|-----------|-------------|-----|-----|----------|
| 1 | Company creation | Choosing name, legal form, logo, and business activity | 4,84 | 4,48 | 4,62 |
| 2 | Online market analysis | Researching competitors and defining target audience | 4,16 | 4,30 | 5,20 |
| 3 | Digital identity | Creating a website, logo, and slogan | 4,00 | 3,89 | 5,27 |
| 4 | Social media | Planning and creating profiles and content for social media | 4,36 | 4,03 | 5,58 |
| 5 | Advertising campaign | Creating promotional materials and media plans | 3,36 | 3,22 | 5,81 |
| 6 | Project presentation | Final public presentation of the project | 4,56 | 4,73 | 5,88 |

**Table 2.** Midterm and Final Evaluations in "Digital Technologies in Business."

| Evaluation Type | 10A AI Teacher | 10B AI Teacher | 10 E AI Teacher |
|-----------------|----------------|----------------|-----------------|
| First term | 4,34 4,44 | 4,34 4,42 | 5,05 5,31 |
| Second term | 4,12 4,36 | 3,96 4,15 | 5,68 5,77 |
| Final grade | 4,21 4,56 | 4,11 4,50 | 5,39 5,88 |

efficiency of learning tasks. The student scores across tasks allow for both quantitative and qualitative analysis of each class's performance. The following conclusions can be drawn:

- Company creation – Minor differences are observed. All groups performed well, as the task mainly required basic creative skills and organizational planning knowledge.

  - 10E:4.62
  - 10A and 10B: 4.84 and 4.48, respectively.

- Online market analysis – A substantial performance gap is observed. Students in 10E used tools like Perplexity AI and ChatGPT to generate structured analysis, improving the overall quality.

  - 10E:5.20
  - 10A and 10B: 4.16 and 4.30, respectively.

- Digital identity – The greatest performance differences were observed here. Students in 10E used Canva and image generators to produce more professional visual elements.

- 10E:5.27
- 10A and 10B: 4.00 and 3.89, respectively.

- Social media – Again, 10E outperformed the others, using AI tools to create more attractive and innovative content.

    - 10E: 5.58
    - 10A and 10B: 4.36 and 4.03, respectively.

- Advertising campaign – This task proved to be the most challenging for classes without AI. 10E benefited from automated idea generation tools.

    - 10E: 5.81
    - 10A and 10B: 3.36 and 3.22, respectively.

- Project presentation – This final task reflected accumulated experience and the impact of tools used. Class 10E delivered well-structured and visually appealing presentations.

    - 10E: 5.88
    - 10A and 10B: 4.56 and 4.73, respectively.

The findings confirm that AI tools significantly improve task performance and educational outcomes. Class 10E achieved notably better results in tasks requiring creativity, visualization, and analysis. Although students using traditional tools also performed well, their progress was limited by the lack of automated and advanced technologies.

In addition to assignment scores, an essential part of the analysis includes a comparison of term and final grades across the three classes. These grades provide deeper insight into overall student performance and the long-term effectiveness of the tools used. The following table (Table 2) presents both traditional grades and those generated using AI.

The comparison of AI-generated and teacher-assigned grades reveals interesting trends. Across all classes, AI grades were slightly lower than those given by teachers, possibly due to a stricter and more objective evaluation process. Nevertheless, both evaluation methods highlight the substantial advantage of class 10E, which used AI tools extensively.

Detailed observations for each group include:

- Class 10A (traditional technologies):

    - AI scores for the first and second terms (4.34, 4.12) are slightly lower than those of the teacher (4.44, 4.36).
    - The final teacher grade (4.56) exceeds the AI grade (4.21), suggesting a more supportive and motivational teacher approach.

- Class 10B (traditional technologies):

– Similar trends to 10A, with the teacher's final grade (4.50) exceeding the AI grade (4.11).
– Overall performance is steady but not as pronounced, matching the use of traditional tools.

- Class 10E (with AI tools):

    – AI grades for the first and second terms (5.05, 5.68) are notably higher than those of 10A and 10B.
    – The teacher's final grade (5.88) is close to the AI result (5.39), indicating stronger agreement between the two approaches.

    The performance gap confirms the advantage of AI-assisted learning.
    **Key insights from grade analysis:**

- **Objectivity of AI:** AI offers consistent and impartial evaluation of student work.
- **Improved results with AI:** Class 10E's superior performance confirms the effectiveness of AI in enhancing the learning process.
- **Role of the teacher:** Despite AI's objectivity, teacher evaluation reflects human factors that can motivate students – especially in traditionally equipped classrooms.

## 4  Discussion

The study of the application of AI technologies in educational management reveals its significant potential to improve the efficiency, quality, and engagement of students in the learning process. Although the results highlight the numerous benefits of AI, they also emphasize the importance of a balanced approach and the need for careful implementation. Therefore, it is necessary to provide recommendations for optimizing the use of AI and to outline the main trends shaping the future of AI-driven education.

Based on the presented data and analysis, several key conclusions can be drawn regarding the impact of artificial intelligence on learning effectiveness and its role in assignment management and assessment, such as:

Increased efficiency: The use of AI tools significantly improves the quality of the learning process, as seen in the results of class 10E.

Objectivity and automation: AI-supported assessment provides a more consistent and objective approach to measuring performance, reducing the administrative burden on teachers.

Improved engagement: Students working with AI tools are more motivated and engaged due to easy access to innovative technologies.

The findings emphasize the need for specific actions and guidelines to optimize the integration of AI in education. Based on the analysis, the following recommendations are proposed for better implementation and management of AI in the learning process:

Balance between AI and the human approach. Despite the advantages of AI, teachers must retain their role as mentors who encourage creative thinking and individualization.

Training for teachers and students. Providing training is essential to ensure proper and effective use of AI tools.

Ethical standards. Establishing clear rules for the ethical use of AI in education is crucial to avoid overdependence on technology. As AI tools increasingly integrate into educational practices, ethical considerations become crucial for maintaining a responsible and fair learning environment. Two foundational pillars of AI ethics in schools are data privacy and the avoidance of algorithmic bias. Students and educators must understand concepts such as justice, discrimination, and transparency when working with AI systems, especially those using opaque "black-box" algorithms like large language models [10].

In educational contexts, ensuring that AI-generated outputs can be ethically justified is essential—not only in terms of how algorithms operate, but more importantly, in whether the outcomes are fair, respect student autonomy, and promote well-beings [10]. This is particularly relevant when AI systems are used for assessment or personalized instruction. Misuse or misunderstanding of such tools could lead to unintended inequalities in learning opportunities.

Moreover, data governance is a central concern. Schools must comply with regulations such as the GDPR, ensuring that data collection is limited, clearly explained, and based on verifiable consent—especially when minors are involved [11]. AI in education must not become a channel for unchecked surveillance or commercial exploitation of students' data.

The implementation of ethical AI also involves the role of teachers. They need to be trained not only to use these technologies but to understand their limitations and societal implications. Teachers serve as mediators between students and AI, and their critical awareness helps prevent blind reliance on automated suggestions or evaluations.

For these reasons, introducing AI ethics education early—just as students are taught about scientific integrity or social responsibility—is vital. AI literacy must go hand-in-hand with ethical reasoning, enabling students to question AI outcomes and reflect on their broader societal impacts.

In addition to the conclusions and recommendations, it is important to consider the future trends that will shape the role of artificial intelligence in education. These trends will play a crucial role in adapting educational systems to new technological capabilities [12, 13]:

Personalized learning. AI tools allow for adaptation of learning programs to individual student needs.

Automation of administrative tasks. Increasingly, schools may use AI to automate tasks such as lesson planning, assessment, and progress analysis.

Progress data analysis. Using AI to collect and analyze student performance data will help educators identify weaknesses and offer tailored solutions.

Virtual assistants. AI-based chatbots can support students and parents in real-time by providing information and assistance.

At a higher level, AI can be used to optimize the entire educational process. AI-powered data analytics systems can identify gaps in learning, monitor student progress, and provide personalized recommendations. This enables teachers to gain a comprehensive view of student performance and make informed decisions [14].

The shift from traditional methods to the integration of digital technologies and AI is not merely a novelty but a necessity in modern education. Currently, schools have the prerequisites for introducing AI, thanks to well-developed infrastructure, growing use of digital educational platforms, and increasing teacher readiness to adopt new technologies. Platforms such as Google Classroom, Microsoft Teams, and Moodle already offer smart features for organizing the learning process, and with the integration of AI algorithms, they can analyze student progress, provide customized feedback, and enhance communication between teachers and students.

Another key condition for successful AI implementation is the availability of modern technological resources in schools. Interactive whiteboards, laptops, and tablets are already common in classrooms, and their role can be greatly expanded through AI-based learning platforms. Adaptive learning systems, which adjust content and difficulty based on individual progress, also contribute to a more effective learning environment.

However, to ensure a successful digital transformation, schools must invest not only in infrastructure but also in teacher training. The implementation of AI will be more successful if teachers have the necessary knowledge to use it and understand its potential. To support the professional development of teachers, the Bulgarian Ministry of Education and Science has issued guidelines for using AI in the educational system (Ministry of Education and Science, 2024) [15]. The document serves as a practical guide for working with generative AI. The available tools and support measures for teachers facilitate the planning and execution of the learning process and contribute to a better future for both students and educators. Combining innovation with established practices is key to building an effective and engaging educational system.

In this context, STEM disciplines (Science, Technology, Engineering, and Mathematics) play a crucial role in developing the knowledge and skills necessary for working with emerging technologies. Expanding STEM education and integrating AI and programming into school curricula will enable students to develop analytical thinking and practical skills related to algorithms and databases [16].

For example, more schools are offering programming and robotics courses that lay the foundation for understanding algorithmic thinking and automated processes. Students who work with AI-based tools not only gain technical competencies but also develop the ability for critical analysis and problem-solving [17].

In addition to programming, AI can also be integrated into subjects like mathematics and physics, where adaptive educational technologies can analyze student strengths and weaknesses and offer personalized exercises and explanations. Using AI-based simulation tools, students can experiment with scientific concepts in a safe and interactive environment.

Another important aspect is the creation of innovation and robotics labs in schools, which can provide opportunities for practical projects involving AI programming, big data processing, and model analysis. This will contribute to preparing students for future professions where AI will play a key role.

Expanding AI education within STEM disciplines will help build a generation that is not only a user of new technologies but also actively involved in their development and optimization. With well-structured training, students will be able to use AI as a tool for solving real-world problems, developing innovations, and improving the efficiency of the educational process.

Artificial intelligence offers significant potential to transform education, but its implementation must be carefully balanced with traditional approaches. Successful AI integration in educational management requires thoughtful planning, ethical standards, and continuous development of both teacher and student competencies.

Although the results clearly demonstrate trends in improved student outcomes when using AI tools, the study is limited in terms of statistical generalization. No formal significance testing was applied, and the findings are based on descriptive analysis of average performance and qualitative observations. In future research, the use of statistical methods such as t-tests or ANOVA could provide a more rigorous basis for comparing student groups and validating the impact of AI-enhanced learning. Additionally, estimating effect sizes could help better quantify the observed benefits.

## 5   Conclusions

The study clearly demonstrates that integrating artificial intelligence into the management of the educational process offers significant advantages for both students and teachers. AI tools enhance assignment efficiency, improve project quality, and facilitate assessment, while also stimulating students' creativity and engagement. However, the implementation of AI in education must be accompanied by training for both teachers and students, clear ethical standards, and a balance between traditional and innovative technologies. The teacher remains an irreplaceable part of the educational process, with their role as mentor and motivator not fully replaceable by AI.

Trends indicate that artificial intelligence will play an increasingly important role in education, offering personalized learning, automated administrative processes, and data analysis for tracking student progress. With the right approach, these technologies can become a powerful tool for enhancing the quality and accessibility of education in the future.

**Acknowledgments.** This research was conducted as part of the project DNP-KC24-08-IISDTSM24 "Integrated information system for digital transformation of school management".

## References

1. Hwa, Y.-Y., Leaver, C.: Management in education systems. Oxf. Rev. Econ. Policy **37**(2), 367–391 (2021). https://doi.org/10.1093/oxrep/grab004
2. Nacheva, R., Jansone, A.: Multi-layered higher education E-learning framework. Baltic J. Modern Comput. **9**(3), 345–362, (2021). https://doi.org/10.22364/bjmc.2021.9.3.08
3. Hussaini, I., et al.: Effectiveness of Google classroom as a digital tool in teaching and learning: students' perceptions. Int. J. Res. Innov. Soc. Sci. (IJRISS) **4**(4), 51–54 (2020)
4. Fitria, T.N.: Artificial Intelligence (AI) in education: using AI tools for teaching and learning process. Prosiding Seminar Nasional & Call for Paper STIE AAS, Surakarta, pp. 134–147 (2021)
5. Mittal, U., Sai, S., Chamola, V., Sangwan, D.: A comprehensive review on generative AI for education. IEEE Access **12**, 142733–142759 (2024). https://doi.org/10.1109/ACCESS.2024.3468368

6. Babu, K.E.K.: Artificial intelligence, its applications in different sectors and challenges: Bangladesh context. In: Montasari, R., Jahankhani, H. (eds.) Artificial Intelligence in Cyber Security: Impact and Implications. Advanced Sciences and Technologies for Security Applications, pp. 103–119. Springer, Cham (2021). https://doi.org/10.1007/978-3-030-88040-8_4

7. Nikolic, S., et al.: ChatGPT, Copilot, Gemini, SciSpace and Wolfram versus higher education assessments: an updated multi-institutional study. Australas. J. Eng. Educ. **29**(2), 126–153 (2024). https://doi.org/10.1080/22054952.2024.2372154

8. Nikolov, N.: Design and implementation of a prototype web platform to enhance student motivation through specific functionalities. In: 32nd National Conference with International Participation (TELECOM), Sofia, pp. 1–5 (2024). https://doi.org/10.1109/TELECOM63374.2024.10812326

9. Simatupang, S., Hz, B.I.R.: Analysis of the effectiveness of project-based learning in improving high school students motivation in speaking. IDEAS: J. English Lang. Teach. Learn. Linguist. Lit. **12**(1), 663–675 (2024)

10. Dabbagh, H., et al.: AI ethics should be mandatory for schoolchildren. AI and Ethics **5**(1), 87–92 (2025)

11. Kousa, P., Hannele, N.: Artificial intelligence ethics from the perspective of educational technology companies and schools. Learn. Des. Future **283** (2023). https://doi.org/10.1007/978-3-031-09687-7_17

12. Harry, A.: Role of AI in education. Interdiscip. J. Humanity (INJURITY) **2**(3), 260–268 (2023)

13. Karakose, T., Tülübas, T.: School Leadership and management in the age of Artificial Intelligence (AI): recent developments and future prospects. Educ. Process Int. J. **13**(1), 7–14 (2024)

14. Igbokwe, I.C.: Application of artificial intelligence (AI) in educational management. Int. J. Sci. Res. Publ. **13**(3), 300–307 (2023). https://doi.org/10.29322/IJSRP.13.03.2023.p13536

15. Ministry of education and science. Accessed 22 Apr 2025. https://www.mon.bg/nfs/2024/02/nasoki-izpolzvane-ii_190224.pdf

16. Tytler, R.: STEM education for the twenty-first century. In: Anderson, J., Li, Y. (eds.) Integrated Approaches to STEM Education. Advances in STEM Education. Springer, Cham (2020). https://doi.org/10.1007/978-3-030-52229-2_3

17. Hacıoğlu, Y., Gülhan, F.: The effects of STEM education on the students' critical thinking skills and STEM perceptions. J. Educ. Sci. Environ. Health **7**(2), 139–155 (2021). https://doi.org/10.21891/jeseh.771331

# Language Models in Advanced Information Retrieval

# Hybrid Ontology Matching for Company Name Alignment: Combining Text Matching, String Similarity, SBERT, and Siamese Networks in Italian and German Job Market Data

Sophie Gvasalia[1], Mauro Pelucchi[1,2(✉)], and Simone Perego[1]

[1] Global Data Science, Lightcast, Italy
{sophie.gvasalia,mauro.pelucchi,simone.perego}@lightcast.io
[2] University of Bergamo, Bergamo, Italy

**Abstract.** Ontology matching, particularly when applied to large and noisy web-based datasets, presents significant challenges related to both volume and veracity. In this paper, we introduce a novel hybrid methodology designed to address these complexities effectively. Our approach integrates traditional text matching techniques, string similarity metrics (Levenshtein distance and TF-IDF cosine similarity), Sentence-BERT embeddings, and a Siamese neural network based on LSTM architectures. We focus on the practical task of matching company names extracted from online job postings to formal company registries in Italy and Germany.

To assess our methodology, we conducted extensive empirical experiments matching distinct company names from Lightcast job postings with entries from the Orbis dataset. After initial normalization procedures, we combined exact matching and similarity-based approaches, enhancing robustness through deep learning-driven embeddings from our Siamese network. Our evaluation shows that while traditional methods (particularly TF-IDF-based matching) performed reliably, the integration of deep learning provided additional discriminative power, especially beneficial in handling noisy, inconsistent naming conventions. Our proposed hybrid methodology significantly improves ontology matching accuracy, thus offering an effective solution to large-scale, real-world entity resolution tasks.

**Keywords:** Named Entity Disambiguation · Natural Language Processing · Language Models

## 1 Introduction

In many real-world contexts, especially in labour market analytics, there is a growing need to reconcile entity information, such as company names, across

G. De Tré et al. (Eds.): FQAS 2025, LNAI 16119, pp. 193–205, 2026.
https://doi.org/10.1007/978-3-032-05607-8_19

noisy and heterogeneous datasets. These tasks are challenged by large volumes of unstructured data, typographical errors, inconsistent formats, and missing metadata, which hinder traditional ontology matching methods. Named Entity Disambiguation (NED) is crucial in aligning textual references to real-world entities. A particularly difficult case involves matching company names from online job postings with those in formal business registries. Due to inconsistent naming practices and high data variability, robust, scalable methodologies are needed to ensure accurate cross-source integration.

In this paper, we address this problem by introducing a novel approach for *Hybrid Ontology Matching*. Our methodology combines multiple techniques to improve matching accuracy and robustness. Specifically, we integrate traditional text matching strategies, string similarity measures (Levenshtein distance and TF-IDF cosine similarity), dense vector representations using Sentence-BERT (SBERT) [13], and a custom-trained Siamese neural network leveraging LSTM-based character-level embeddings. We evaluate our approach on a real-world task involving over 5M company names extracted from Lightcast[1] global job postings and matched against 300k unique entities in the Orbis[2] company registry for Italy and Germany. Following an initial normalization process–including lowercasing, punctuation removal, and legal suffix filtering, we applied exact matching, fuzzy string similarity, and neural embedding-based matching. We find that a classifica metric, like the TF-IDF, offers high precision and recall in the presence of moderate name variation, while the Siamese network demonstrates strong potential for handling highly noisy and ambiguous cases.

Our results confirm that the proposed hybrid framework significantly improves ontology matching in noisy environments, offering a scalable solution for real-world entity resolution tasks. Key contributions include: (i) a hybrid method combining text matching, transformer embeddings, and deep learning; (ii) application to a large labour market dataset; (iii) a robust normalization pipeline; (iv) comparative evaluation against baseline methods; and (v) demonstrated scalability for broader applications.

The paper is structured as follows: Sect. 2 reviews relevant work on entity matching and NED. Section 3 outlines the datasets. Section 4 describes our hybrid approach. Section 5 reports evaluation outcomes, and Sect. 6 summarizes key findings and future directions.

## 2   Related Works

Classical approaches to Named Entity Disambiguation and ontology matching often rely on deterministic string similarity techniques such as Levenshtein distance, Jaccard similarity, and TF-IDF-based cosine similarity ([3,4]). These methods, while efficient, struggle with variations due to typos, abbreviations, or

---

[1] https://lightcast.io/euro.

[2] https://www.moodys.com/web/en/us/capabilities/company-reference-data/orbis.html.

inconsistent naming conventions. Recent studies have introduced machine learning and deep learning techniques to improve robustness. For example, [2] proposed a Siamese LSTM architecture for company name disambiguation, showing improved performance over traditional methods when sufficient labeled data are available. Their use of active learning further optimized labeling efficiency, a strategy we also acknowledge in our pipeline.

BERTMap [6] shows how fine-tuned transformers improve ontology alignment by capturing semantic relationships beyond string similarity. DeepOnto [8] offers a framework that combines ontology structure with deep learning for tasks like alignment and completion. Agent-OM [12] leverages LLM agents for few-shot matching using planning, memory, and retrieval, though it requires significant resources and struggles in noisy environments. Marrara et al. [11] propose blind querying over JSON document stores using lexical and semantic similarity to address structural variability at scale via Hadoop. OntoJob [15] explores unsupervised ontology learning from labour market data, extracting structured relations from job postings.

Zhan et al. [16] provide a comprehensive overview of Deep Active Learning (DAL), highlighting how uncertainty- and diversity-based sampling strategies reduce annotation costs while maintaining performance. Their findings support the integration of DAL in NED pipelines to optimize training efficiency in noisy environments. Hybrid approaches like that of Jiménez-Ruiz et al. [9] demonstrate how lexical indices and neural embeddings scale large ontology alignments–a principle we apply by layering TF-IDF and embeddings. Recent work by He et al. [7] investigates the use of LLMs like Flan-T5 and GPT-3.5 for zero- and few-shot ontology alignment, showing that prompt design and structural cues can outperform traditional models like BERTMap in complex semantic tasks.

## 3  Data

In this section, we describe the datasets used in our study. Section 3.1 introduces the Lightcast job postings data; Sect. 3.2 presents the Orbis business registry used; and Sect. 3.3 discusses the main challenges in matching company names across sources.

### 3.1  Job Postings Dataset

The Lightcast global database contains over 3 billion online job postings, of which more than 1 billion have been validated through rigorous cleaning and de-duplication. These postings, often semi-structured or unstructured, require advanced processing to extract structured, analyzable information. Covering national and subnational labour markets, the dataset supports detailed analysis of occupations, sectors, regions, and skills [15].

Job postings follow a multi-step pipeline: (i) **Data ingestion** via APIs, scraping, and bulk imports; (ii) **Data treatment**, where entries are cleaned and standardized; (iii) **Text processing**, including parsing job titles, descriptions, and company names; and (iv) **Classification** through machine learning models to identify occupations and extract skills.

While online postings may exhibit selection bias, they provide timely insights into labour demand. Studies by [10,14], and [5] validate their usefulness, comparing Lightcast data with national statistics and confirming its value for trend monitoring despite some discrepancies.

## 3.2 Orbis Company Dataset

Orbis is one of the most comprehensive cross-country firm-level databases available for economic and financial research, maintained by Bureau van Dijk[3]. It provides standardized data on over 200 million firms globally, including financials, industry codes, ownership, and employment figures. However, its coverage varies by country, time, sector, and firm size, with a tendency to overrepresent larger and more productive firms, particularly in manufacturing [1].

For this study, we extracted a stratified sample of approximately 300,000 firms from Italy and Germany, balancing for firm size and sector diversity:

- **Firm size:** Micro (26.7%), Small (32.4%), Medium (24.6%), and Large (16.3%).
- **Sectors:** Manufacturing (27.8%), Professional Services (14.3%), Construction (12.5%), ICT (11.1%), and Retail Trade (10.9%).

The sample includes 150,324 firms from Italy and 149,982 from Germany. Matching was based on company names, the only attribute consistently available in both Orbis and job posting datasets. Table 1 presents illustrative examples.

**Table 1.** Sample company names from the Orbis dataset.

| Country | Sector | Company name (Orbis) |
|---------|--------|----------------------|
| Italy | Electricity, gas, steam and air conditioning supply | Eni S.p.A. |
| Italy | Information and Communication | Telecom Italia S.p.A. |
| Italy | Manufacturing | Luxottica Group S.p.A. |
| Germany | Manufacturing | Bosch GmbH |
| Germany | Manufacturing | Bayerische Motoren Werke AG |

Bajgar et al. [1] provides a comprehensive analysis of Orbis's strengths and limitations, emphasizing its representative and suitability for top-performing firm analysis while highlighting coverage gaps for smaller or underperforming firms.

---

[3] https://www.moodys.com/web/en/us/capabilities/company-reference-data/orbis.html.

### 3.3   Company Names and Matching Challenges

Company names in online job postings are often noisy and inconsistently formatted. Unlike formal registries with strict naming conventions, job ads may use informal terms, brand names, or partial identifiers.

Key challenges include:

- **Brand vs legal name:** Names like "QC Terme Chamonix" reflect brand identities rather than legal entities.
- **Abbreviations and suffixes:** Variants such as "Delfin s.r.l." vs. "DELFIN SRL" create matching inconsistencies.
- **Fragmented or misspelled entries:** Names like "Vedi srl" deviate from the official "VE.DI. SRL".
- **Special characters:** Examples like "$.VENDITASERVICE S.r.l." or "@NORD..." disrupt standard comparisons.
- **Duplicate variants:** Identical entities may appear under multiple slightly altered names.

These inconsistencies demand a robust hybrid matching strategy. Traditional methods often fail, while embedding-based and neural approaches better capture semantic and structural variations.

## 4   Methodology

In this section we will present our *Hybrid Ontology Matching* methodology to address the complex task of reconciling company names extracted from online job postings with formal business. Our methodology comprises the following components, as depicted in Fig. 1:

- **Fuzzy String Matching:** All company names were pre-processed to ensure consistency. This step included transforming all characters to lowercase, removing punctuation and special symbols, and eliminating jurisdiction-specific legal suffixes (e.g., *S.p.A.*, *GmbH*, *S.r.l.*). Then, a fuzzy text matching approach was applied over a Hadoop Cluster.
- **String Similarity-Based Matching:** Company names were encoded into character-level TF-IDF vectors. Cosine similarity was then used to compute the closeness between job posting names and Orbis entries, selecting the top-ranked candidate for each. We also applied a string comparison using the Levenshtein distance metric, ranking candidate matches by the normalized edit distance.
- **SBERT:** A SBERT model was fine-tuned to use the web language to match company names and brands over the two datasets.
- **Siamese Neural Network:** A deep learning architecture was introduced based on a Siamese network with LSTM character-level encoders. The model was trained to learn a semantic similarity score between name pairs, using both real and synthetically generated training samples.

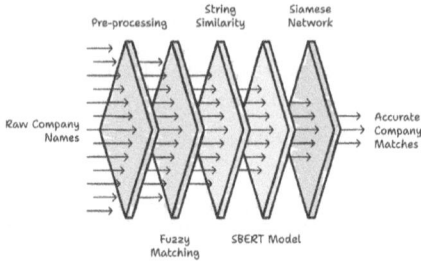

**Fig. 1.** Overview of the different steps of our Hybrid Matching Methodology

## 4.1   Step 1: Fuzzy String Matching

The first step in our matching pipeline focuses on cleaning and fuzzy matching raw company names from job postings. We refer to this as fuzzy matching because it does not rely on exact string equality; instead, it tolerates small variations such as typographical errors, inconsistent punctuation, and non-standard formatting. Matching is performed by computing string similarity scores (e.g., Jaccard distance) between normalized name variants, rather than requiring exact matches. This approach allows us to align names like "RANDSTADITALIA" with "RANDSTAD ITALIA S.P.A.", even though they differ significantly in format. Implemented using a distributed PySpark framework[4] on a 30-node AWS EMR cluster (r5.8xlarge), this process handles large-scale, noisy datasets efficiently. It aims to remove irrelevant elements and normalize names into a clean format (`company clean`) for reliable comparison with Orbis legal entities. The best match is selected using a Jaccard score between cleaned names and registry entries.

The pipeline transforms the original `company raw` field using preprocessing activities composed by the following actions:

- **Normalization:** Lowercasing, removal of punctuation and non-ASCII characters.
- **Suffix removal:** Filtering legal suffixes like *S.p.A.*, *S.r.l.*, or *GmbH*.
- **Keyword filtering:** Removing terms like *filiale*, *franchising*, or *affiliato*.
- **Length/blacklist filters:** Excluding too short/long names, stopwords, generic or location-based terms.
- **Canonicalization:** Selecting the most frequent normalized variant as the reference form.

To scale matching, we compute a Cartesian product between job posting and Orbis names, evaluating candidate pairs with a series of scoring flags. The top match is selected for each entry. This process improves precision significantly by resolving noisy variants such as AC D TECHNOLOGIES vs. AC&D TECHNOLOGIES SRL, or RANDSTADITALIA vs. RANDSTAD ITALIA S.P.A.

---

[4] https://spark.apache.org/docs/latest/api/python/index.html.

A structured set of control flags supports data filtering: **Match black-listed, Match location, Too short/Too long, Match stopword, Match too generic, Error suffix,** and **Match common names**.

This stage alone resolves 35% of company names and provides a high-precision foundation for downstream semantic matching.

## 4.2   Step 2: String Similarity-Based Matching

Following the first cleaning and text based fuzzy matching of company names, the second phase of the matching pipeline applies a series of string similarity techniques to link job posting entities to their corresponding legal names in the Orbis database. This step captures minor variations and typographical inconsistencies that prevent exact matches. We implemented multiple complementary algorithms, each offering distinct advantages in comparing textual data. The techniques used are summarized below:

- **TF-IDF with cosine similarity:** Each cleaned company name was encoded as a sparse vector using Term FrequencyInverse Document Frequency over character n-grams (ranging from 3 to 5 characters). The similarity between job posting names and Orbis records was computed using cosine distance, selecting the most similar entry as a potential match.
- **Levenshtein distance:** This approach calculates the minimum number of single-character edits (insertions, deletions, or substitutions) required to transform one string into another. We normalized this distance and used it to rank candidate matches.
- **Jaro-Winkler similarity:** Designed for short strings like names, this metric accounts for transpositions and character proximity. It places more weight on prefix matches, making it well-suited for typographic distortions common in job posting data.

Each method independently generates a similarity score between each job posting name and all entries in the Orbis database. The top-ranked result from each method is stored alongside its confidence score. A match decision is made based on the highest-confidence score across all methods.

These similarity-based techniques are to detect close matches in cases where company names differ only slightly. For instance, GRUPPO ABETE SRL *vs.* GRUPPO ABETE S.R.L., UNIEURO SPA *vs.* UNIEURO S.P.A., INTESASANPAOLO *vs.* INTESA SANPAOLO S.P.A..

These methods improved recall by 3% and offered robust performance in the presence of formatting irregularities. At the end of the second stage we were able to arrive to the 38% of the dataset matched.

## 4.3   Step 3: Fine-Tuned SBERT Embeddings for Semantic Similarity

To complement the lexical and character-level approaches, we employed Sentence-BERT to model semantic similarity between company names. SBERT has proven effective in capturing contextual and semantic relationships across short text strings, making it suitable for recognizing conceptual similarities where literal overlap is weak.

**Training Data Preparation.** We used the positive and negative company name pairs curated for the Siamese network (see Step 4), adapting them for SBERT training. Positive pairs consisted of name variants that were known or manually verified to refer to the same company, while negative pairs were generated by combining unrelated names or introducing realistic textual noise. Each pair was formatted for contrastive learning with a binary label (1 for match, 0 for no match). The dataset was balanced to prevent bias, and stratified into training and validation sets.

**Fine-Tuning Procedure.** Starting from the `all-MiniLM-L6-v2`[5] SBERT model, we fine-tuned the sentence encoder using the contrastive loss. This approach assures the model to minimize embedding distance for similar names and maximize it for dissimilar ones. The SBERT model was fine-tuned on an AWS `g5.2xlarge` instance, equipped with a single NVIDIA A10G GPU, 8 vCPUs, and 32 GB of memory. Fine-tuning was conducted with early stopping based on validation loss to prevent overfitting. We trained for 4 epochs with a batch size of 16, learning rate of 2e-5, and warmup steps for stable convergence.

**Application and Inference.** After training, the SBERT model was used to encode all cleaned names from both the job posting and Orbis datasets into fixed-size dense vectors. Matching was then performed via cosine similarity in embedding space, selecting the top-ranking Orbis entry for each job posting company name.

**Results and Evaluation.** SBERT produced semantically rich embeddings, outperforming traditional string similarity methods on complex cases involving abbreviations, language variation, or reordering. Manual validation highlighted the model's capacity to identify nuanced equivalences such as: UNIVERSITÀ DI BOLOGNA vs. ALMA MATER STUDIORUM, PRADA S.P.A. vs. GRUPPO PRADA, OSPEDALE MAGGIORE MILANO vs. FONDAZIONE IRCCS CA' GRANDA.

While the SBERT model was not the top-performing method in isolation, it provided important disambiguation power in cases where other models disagreed or returned low-confidence scores. As such, it played a key role in the final ensemble approach enhacing the recall by 9%.

### 4.4   Step 4: Siamese Neural Network

To finally enhance matching robustness and overcome the limitations of traditional techniques, we implemented a deep learning approach using a Siamese

---

[5] https://huggingface.co/sentence-transformers/all-MiniLM-L6-v2.

neural network. This model is designed to learn a similarity function over pairs of company names, enabling it to identify matches even when names share limited lexical overlap.

**Training Data Generation.** To train the model, we constructed a labeled dataset comprising both positive and negative examples:

- *Positive pairs* were created from known company name variants either derived from internal frequency-based canonicalization (e.g., "ENI", "ENI SPA", "ENI S.P.A.") or matched against confirmed Orbis entries.
- *Negative pairs* were synthetically generated by pairing unrelated names and by applying controlled noise to positive examples (e.g., random character swaps, deletions, and insertions).

This training set was then split into training and validation partitions. Extensive data augmentation ensured the model's robustness to real-world noise and misspellings.

**Model Architecture.** The network follows a Siamese design with shared weights. Each input name is tokenized at the character level and passed through an embedding layer followed by a bi-directional LSTM. The resulting vector representations are compared using a combination of element-wise operations (cosine similarity, L1, L2, and max absolute difference), and the result is passed through fully connected layers to yield a final match probability.

- Input: Company name pairs (e.g., "UNIEURO S.P.A." vs. "UNIEURO").
- Embedding: Character-level embeddings.
- Encoder: BiLSTM (Bidirectional Long Short-Term Memory).
- Merge: Concatenation of similarity features (cosine, L1, L2, max).
- Output: Sigmoid activation for match probability.

The model was trained using binary cross-entropy loss and optimized with the Adam optimizer. Regularization was applied via dropout layers and early stopping to avoid overfitting. The Siamese model achieved perfect recall on the evaluation set but showed a tendency to overpredict matches. While it contributed only 1.4% of final selected matches in production (due to conservative selection thresholds), its ROC AUC reached 0.967, indicating strong discriminative ability when properly tuned.

Manual review of high-confidence Siamese matches revealed that it was particularly effective in capturing non-trivial equivalences missed by conventional methods, such as: UNIVERSITA' DEGLI STUDI DI MILANO vs. UNIMI, AUTOGRILL ITALIA SPA vs. AUTOGRILL, INTESA SANPAOLO SPA vs. INTESA SANPAOLO.

The Siamese network proved to be a valuable complement to the other approaches, contributing to improved recall for difficult cases, and reinforcing the robustness of the hybrid matching framework.

# 5    Results

The combination of the four matching strategies allowed us to achieve a final match rate of 48% across the 308,346 distinct company names extracted from job postings. This integrated, multi-method pipeline allowed for incremental coverage increases at each stage:

- **Step 1 (Fuzzy String Matching):** Covered 35% of the dataset through deterministic string matching after cleaning and canonicalization.
- **Step 2 (String Similarity):** Added an additional 3% of matches via fuzzy methods including TF-IDF cosine similarity and Levenshtein distance.
- **Step 3 (Fine-Tuned SBERT):** Provided the final 9% of successful matches through semantic embedding comparison.
- **Step 4 (Siamese Network):** Contributed a further 1.4%, capturing semantically similar but lexically distant name variants.

Despite this considerable success, 52% of names remained unmatched. A qualitative review of the residual set revealed that most unmatched entries fall into one of the following categories: (i) **Small enterprises** such as restaurants, bars, and small local shops, which often lack formal online presence or use highly variable naming conventions; (ii) **Generic company names** such as STUDIO DI ARCHITETTURA or STUDIO LEGALE, which are inherently ambiguous and occur frequently across unrelated entities; (iii) **Non-registered employers** including temporary work agencies, intermediaries, or postings where the name reflects a brand or store branch that cannot be mapped to a legal entity in Orbis. On the other side, several companies are not posts job ads online.

This breakdown highlights both the achievements and limitations of the current pipeline, and it informs directions for future enhancement, including the integration of metadata, geographic disambiguation, and external knowledge bases.

## 5.1    Comparative Evaluation of Matching Approaches

To assess the qualitative performance of individual components within the hybrid pipeline, we conducted a manual evaluation based on a stratified random sample of 120 matched results. Each record was labeled as *correct, incorrect, or partially matched (N/A)*. From this labeled dataset, standard classification metrics were computed for three principal methods: TF-IDF, Levenshtein distance, SBERT (not fine tuned) and the *Hybrid Ontology Matching*. The results are reported in 2.

The higher performance in Table 2 compared to the overall match rates in Sect. 5 reflects different evaluation scopes. Table 2 is based on 120 manually labeled samples with identified matches, focusing on method quality. In contrast, Sect. 5 reports coverage over the entire dataset, including unmatched and ambiguous cases. The two evaluations are therefore complementary. The results clearly demonstrate the superiority of the hybrid approach, which outperformed

**Table 2.** Performance comparison across matching methods (based on 120 manually labeled samples)

| Method | Accuracy | Precision | Recall |
|---|---|---|---|
| TF-IDF Matching | 83.5% | 80.9% | 100.0% |
| Levenshtein Distance | 35.3% | 35.3% | 100.0% |
| SBERT (not fine tuned) | 75.2% | 67.8% | 81.8% |
| *Hybrid Ontology Matching* | 91.2% | 95.4% | 100.0% |

all individual methods in terms of accuracy and precision while maintaining perfect recall. TF-IDF emerged as the most effective standalone method, handling moderate name variation with strong overall reliability. Levenshtein distance, while capable of identifying similar strings, frequently returned false positives, especially for short or common terms. The non-fine-tuned SBERT model showed promising performance, suggesting that transformer-based embeddings effectively capture deeper semantic relations even without task-specific tuning.

The hybrid approach, which integrates lexical, fuzzy, and semantic similarity techniques - including a fine-tuned SBERT model and rule-based disambiguation - proved most effective in real-world conditions. Its high precision and accuracy make it suitable for deployment in production systems where both matching quality and interpretability are essential.

# 6    Conclusions

This study has addressed the complex task of company name disambiguation across heterogeneous data sources, specifically matching entities extracted from Lightcast job postings to those registered in the Orbis business database. Our methodology combined rule-based preprocessing, string similarity metrics, and advanced neural approaches into a scalable hybrid pipeline.

We found that TF-IDF performed robustly as a standalone method, striking an effective balance between precision and recall, while Levenshtein distance, despite its theoretical simplicity, was more susceptible to false positives in practice. The use of SBERT embeddings, even without fine-tuning, delivered promising results and highlighted the semantic richness that contextualized transformer models can bring to short-text entity matching.

Although the Siamese neural network displayed excellent theoretical discriminative power (as indicated by its perfect ROC AUC), its practical effectiveness was hindered by limitations in training data and overfitting to synthetic samples. Nevertheless, it proved valuable in capturing highly non-trivial matches and contributed to the overall accuracy of the hybrid framework.

The *Hybrid Ontology Matching* pipeline, which intelligently combines deterministic, probabilistic, and deep learning components, ultimately delivered a match accuracy of 91.2%, with 95.4% precision and 100% recall on manually validated samples. Importantly, this layered design enables scalability and modularity, making it adaptable for use in other domains where entity disambiguation is critical.

While our current hybrid pipeline combines classical and neural architectures for effective company name matching, we recognize the transformative potential of LLMs in ontology alignment. Fine-tuning Sentence-BERT represented a first step toward leveraging transformer-based models. Building on this, we plan to experiment with LLM-driven approaches–including few-shot matching, prompt-based inference, and synthetic data generation–to further enhance performance in low-resource or ambiguous scenarios. Future work will focus on expanding the matching signal beyond name-based features, integrating additional metadata such as company location, industry sector, and ownership structure. Furthermore, we aim to investigate the use of active learning strategies and creation of synthetic dataset using LLMs to reduce manual labeling efforts.

**Acknowledgments.** Simone Perego handled data preprocessing and preparation for online job posting datasets. Sophie Gvasalia performed models training and testing over the German dataset and curated the results. Mauro Pelucchi implemented data mining and model selection and curated the overall approach.

# References

1. Bajgar, M., Berlingieri, G., Calligaris, S., Criscuolo, C., Timmis, J.: Coverage and representativeness of Orbis data (2020)
2. Basile, A., et al.: Disambiguation of company names via deep recurrent networks. Expert Syst. Appl. **238**, 122035 (2024)
3. Christen, P.: A comparison of personal name matching: techniques and practical issues. In: Sixth IEEE International Conference on Data Mining-Workshops (ICDMW'06), pp. 290–294. IEEE (2006)
4. Cohen, W.W., Ravikumar, P., Fienberg, S.E., et al.: A comparison of string distance metrics for name-matching tasks. In: IIWeb. vol. 3, pp. 73–78 (2003)
5. Enrique, F.M., Matteo, S.: Skewed signals? Confronting biases in online job ads data. Tech. rep, Joint Research Centre (2024)
6. He, Y., Chen, J., Antonyrajah, D., Horrocks, I.: BERTMap: a BERT-based ontology alignment system. In: Proceedings of the AAAI Conference on Artificial Intelligence. vol. 36, pp. 5684–5691 (2022)
7. He, Y., Chen, J., Dong, H., Horrocks, I.: Exploring large language models for ontology alignment. arXiv preprint arXiv:2309.07172 (2023)
8. He, Y., et al.: DeepOnto: a python package for ontology engineering with deep learning. Semantic Web **15**(5), 1991–2004 (2024)
9. Jiménez-Ruiz, E., Agibetov, A., Samwald, M., Cross, V.: Breaking-down the ontology alignment task with a lexical index and neural embeddings. corr abs/1805.12402 (2018) (2018)
10. Lovaglio, P.G.: Do job vacancies variations anticipate employment variations by sector? some preliminary evidence from Italy. Labour **36**(1), 71–93 (2022)
11. Marrara, S., Pelucchi, M., Psaila, G.: Blind queries applied to JSON document stores. Information **10**(10), 291 (2019)

12. Qiang, Z., Wang, W., Taylor, K.: Agent-OM: Leveraging LLM agents for ontology matching. arXiv preprint arXiv:2312.00326 (2023)

13. Reimers, N., Gurevych, I.: Sentence-BERT: Sentence embeddings using Siamese BERT-networks. arXiv preprint arXiv:1908.10084 (2019)

14. Vermeulen, W., Amaros, F.G.: How well do online job postings match national sources in European countries?: Benchmarking lightcast data against statistical and labour agency sources across regions, sectors and occupation (2024)

15. Vrolijk, J., Mol, S.T., Weber, C., Tavakoli, M., Kismihók, G., Pelucchi, M.: Onto-Job: automated ontology learning from labor market data. In: 2022 IEEE 16th International Conference on Semantic Computing (ICSC), pp. 195–200. IEEE (2022)

16. Zhan, X., Wang, Q., Huang, K.h., Xiong, H., Dou, D., Chan, A.B.: A comparative survey of deep active learning. arXiv preprint arXiv:2203.13450 (2022)

# A Semantic Schema-Based Catalog for Identifying Joinable Columns via LLMs

Emanuele Cavalleri[ID], Matteo Castagna[ID], and Marco Mesiti[(✉)][ID]

Department of Computer Science, University of Milan, Milan, Italy
{emanuele.cavalleri,matteo.castagna1,marco.mesiti}@unimi.it

**Abstract.** Joinable table discovery consists of the identification of tabular datasets that can be joined with a given query dataset. The use of contextual information associated with the datasets and columns (tailored to the kinds of analyses the user intends to carry out) is seldom considered in the approaches proposed so far. In this paper, the generation of semantic task-oriented schema-based catalogs that facilitate the identification of joinable columns is proposed. By identifying a schema diagram that outlines the classes and relationship types for a certain kind of analysis, datasets are semantically annotated, and annotations are used to generate the catalog. The catalog, represented as a property graph, can then be leveraged for visual exploration, query formulation, and identification of joinable datasets useful for a specific analysis. The approach leverages the availability of metadata about datasets and their columns, combined with general-purpose large language models (LLMs). Initial experiments suggest that our approach is both practical and efficient, yielding promising results in terms of both accuracy and usability.

**Keywords:** data lake · joinable table discovery · semantic catalog

## 1 Introduction

Data lakes [12] have recently emerged as critical infrastructures for storing vast collections of data. Unlike traditional data warehouses, data lakes allow storage of data in native format without requiring schema definition. In this scenario, identifying "joinable" columns is a challenging task due to the inherent heterogeneity of the tabular datasets and the lack of standardized schemas or ontologies [15]. Traditional join operations based on exact matches are insufficient in data lake scenarios, where semantically equivalent columns may have entirely different names, formats, or value representations. For this reason, innovative approaches (e.g., pexeso [9], DeepJoin [10]) that rely on the use of pre-trained language models (PLM) have been proposed that leverage a vectorial representation of dataset columns. Dataset columns whose vectorial representations are close in the latent space share similar semantics and can be joined together.

© The Author(s), under exclusive license to Springer Nature Switzerland AG 2026
G. De Tré et al. (Eds.): FQAS 2025, LNAI 16119, pp. 206–218, 2026.
https://doi.org/10.1007/978-3-032-05607-8_20

Even if these approaches are very effective [7], they still present drawbacks due to the lack of contextual information in which the datasets have been generated. Suppose, for example, the existence of a dataset containing information about the production of cereals in the Lombardy provinces and another one reporting the amount of rainfall in the same provinces. At first glance, the two datasets appear to be joinable for correlating the production of cereals with the weather conditions. However, if the first dataset refers to cereal production at the beginning of the 19th century and the other to the weather conditions of the last year, putting together these datasets might not make sense. This highlights the need of incorporating contextual information (e.g., column headers, data types, constraints, and textual descriptions) through metadata to ensure that joinable columns are meaningfully and appropriately identified.

To better characterize the context of the datasets that can be exploited for downstream analyses, in this paper, LinkML schemas [19] are adopted. LinkML is a yaml-based language used to describe the characteristics and constraints of classes and their relationships. Moreover, it allows the specification of instances for classes and relationships, references to ontological concepts, and the textual description of each class attribute. In our approach, LinkML schemas do not enforce constraints on the data lake itself but serve as blueprints for constructing task-specific semantic catalogs of the datasets enriched with schema-relevant information. A semantic catalog is organized as a *property graph*. Its nodes correspond to the datasets that can be exploited for conducting certain kinds of analyses, and their properties represent metadata associated with the datasets. The graph edges identify the joinability conditions. The edge properties report the dataset columns that can be used for joining and the similarity level identified between them.

Although the specification of a schema might appear cumbersome at first glance, especially given the schema-less paradigm of data lakes, we argue that it can help in narrowing down the datasets to those most relevant for specific kinds of analyses. Moreover, its development can be simplified by using Schema-Link [4], a recent AI-based tool for designing LinkML schemas. By exploiting diagrams already developed on the same data lake, the system suggests to the user the organization of a diagram useful for downstream analyses. The combination of GUI facilities and AI tools accelerates the generation of meaningful schemas. Another obstacle to adopting schemas in the data lake context is usually the cost of semantic annotations. However, a recent approach [11] showed that this procedure can be executed quite efficiently and, combined with indexing structures, can reduce the datasets that should be considered for a given analysis.

The proposed approach relies on the use of general-purpose LLMs at different stages. First, by exploiting a LinkML schema and the ArcheType system [11], semantic annotations of the dataset columns are generated. Then, LLMs are used for embedding dataset columns in a latent space by considering a prompt that encodes the main characteristics of each column (including semantic annotations and metadata). By clustering similar columns in the latent space, joinable pairs of columns that are highly similar and belong to different datasets can be easily identified. This information is then used to generate the semantic catalog. In the paper, experiments on the usefulness of the proposed approach are presented.

The paper is organized as follows. Section 2 discusses related work in joinable table discovery and semantic annotation. Section 3 introduces the use of LinkML schema for the specification of task-oriented semantic catalogs. Section 4 discusses our LLM pipeline to generate semantic catalogs. Section 5 presents our preliminary experimental results. Concluding remarks are in Sect. 6.

## 2   Related Work

**Joinable Table Discovery.** Joinable table discovery has become a relevant operation in data lake management [6] and is usually conceived as the problem of identifying the datasets in a collection $DL$ that can be joined to a query dataset [22]. The approaches proposed so far can be classified as *EQUI-JOIN* approaches (e.g., Arda [6]) that apply the exact-match operator among column values, and *semantic-JOIN* approaches. These last ones are further classified into set-oriented approaches (e.g., JOSIE [24] e LSH [25]) that find joinable tables via set similarity search, and LLM-based approaches (e.g., pexeso [9] and Deep-Join [10]) which join columns with similar semantics via word/text embedding. This has the advantage of dealing with misspellings and discrepancies in formats/terminologies. DeepJoin uses a PLM (e.g., BERT) to represent columns in a fixed-length vector space, where columns that are joinable are located close to each other. Join discovery is then reduced to the application of an efficient approximate K-nearest neighbor search algorithm (ANNS) [17]. LLM-based join approaches have shown superior accuracy compared to traditional ones [10].

In our approach, the same path of DeepJoin is followed, except for the use of a general-pourpose LLM (OpenAI's text-embedding-3-small [20]). In this way, the identification of specific datasets for training the model and the overhead due to the training phase can be avoided. Moreover, the approach can be applied in different contexts and takes advantage of metadata associated with the datasets, descriptions of annotated columns, samples contained within a LinkML schema, and samples of the column values. Note that, the use of samples makes our approach applicable also to tables that present many more tuples than WebTables.

**Column Type Annotation (CTA).** The relevance of schema-matching techniques for data discovery has been highlighted in [15]. Indeed, the majority of the proposed approaches rely on the use of schema-matching techniques for capturing relationships between the columns of two datasets and determining whether they are *unionable* (i.e., they share the same attributes), *view-unionable* (i.e., they share a common subset of attributes), or *joinable* (i.e., they store complementary data and present few joinable columns). Traditional schema-matching approaches can be classified in: *i*) *schema-based* [8,18] that consider only source column headers to capture potential relationships; *ii*) *instance-based* that rely on data instances (e.g., [23]); and, *iii*) *hybrid methods* that combine both schema and value information [2,3]. Newer approaches use ontologies to annotate the schemas of datasets. In this research line, many ML approaches have been proposed (like ColNet [5], Sherlock [14]) that require a large volume of training data and their performances, when applied to test sets extracted from different domains, degrade substantially even when their column types match closely.

A hybrid CTA method based on LLMs and prompt engineering has been explored in [13], where a LLM-based framework is proposed for few-shot classification of tabular data that produces better results with respect to fine-tuned approaches based on neural networks both in the zero- and few-shot settings. Moreover, in [11], the ArcheType approach achieves high accuracy in semantic column type annotation without prior exposure to the target schema. By dynamically recognizing new semantic types, an LLM can infer relationships between attributes that are not explicitly labeled in a dataset.

In our approach, ArcheType is used in a "schema-driven prompt engineering" fashion that relies on a LinkML schema [19] for the semantic annotation of dataset columns. The advantage of this procedure is twofold. From one side, the columns of datasets are annotated with class properties available in the identified diagram. On the other hand, irrelevant datasets and columns not required for conducting the analyses can be pruned. Moreover, LLMs are used for improving the metadata representation associated with datasets. This is quite relevant in real applications where metadata are often missing or not-well organized.

## 3 Conceptual Schemas and Semantic Catalogs

A collection of tabular data $DL = \{T_1, \ldots, T_n\}$ is coupled with conceptual schemas $\{S_1, \ldots, S_h\}$ representing different kinds of analyses. Each schema is associated with a task-oriented semantic catalog $PG_S$ representing the datasets in $DL$ containing the concepts and relationships provided by $S$. Their role is to identify useful datasets in $DL$ for conducting certain analyses.

**Tabular Dataset.** A tabular dataset $T \in DL$ is a 3-tuple $\langle Col, Rows, Meta \rangle$, where $Col = [col_1, \ldots, col_j, \ldots, col_m]$ denotes the list of column names (when available, otherwise the symbol ? is used to denote the lack of the column name), and $Rows = \{row_1, \ldots, row_r\}$ is the set of rows. $Meta$ is optional and, when available, contains metadata about the table $T$. $Meta$ can be a simple textual description about the table content or a more structured representation in which specific fields can be represented (like the period of time/spatial coverage the dataset content refers to, or a description of the meaning of columns).

**Conceptual Schema.** Each schema $S \in \mathcal{S}$ is represented by using LinkML [19]. Classes and relationships are expressed in a textual format along with constraints existing in the domain, samples of values of the considered classes/relationships, and annotations grounded in well-established ontologies. The textual representation of LinkML facilitates the translation of classes and attributes into LLM prompts. The schema specification process is supported by the adoption of SchemaLink [4] that exploits a RAG technique for suggesting the structure of a new schema by exploiting diagrams already developed on the same data lake. A schema $S$ in SchemaLink is a triple $\langle \mathcal{C}, \mathcal{R}, \mathcal{M} \rangle$, where $\mathcal{C}$ and $\mathcal{R}$ are the set of classes and relationships with the description of their attributes and $\mathcal{M}$ is a set of metadata and constraints associated with the schema (details in [4]).

*Example 1.* Suppose the user is interested in analyzing cereal production across countries and years. Figure 1 shows an excerpt of LinkML schema realized with SchemaLink representing the key classes and relationships involved in cereal cultivation. The `Cereal` class models the crop name and its water requirements per kilogram of harvest; the `Country` class is defined analogously. The `CerealToCountry` (C2C for short) relationship models the annual production of each crop in a specific country and year. Descriptions and instance samples are provided for schema classes and their attributes.

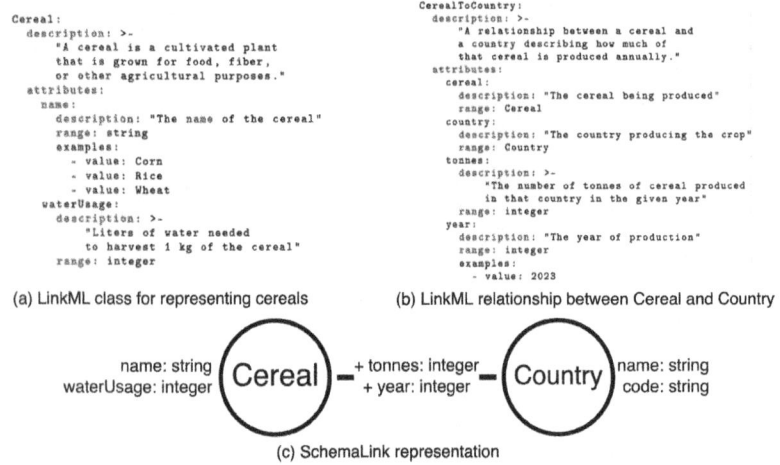

(a) LinkML class for representing cereals

(b) LinkML relationship between Cereal and Country

(c) SchemaLink representation

**Fig. 1.** Excerpt of LinkML for representing cereal production across countries.

**Semantic Catalog.** The semantic catalog according to a schema $S$ is a property graph $PG_S = (V_S, E_S)$, where $V_S$ represents the tabular datasets that are relevant according to $S$, and $E_S$ represent the join-relationships among datasets. Nodes are typed according to the classes and relationships available in $S$ and contain different kinds of properties extracted from the corresponding datasets in $DL$. An edge $(T_s, T_t)$ between a source node $T_s$ and a target $T_t$ is annotated with list of triples $(a_s, a_t, \theta)$, where: $a_s$ is the name of an attribute of $T_s$, $a_t$ is the name of an attribute of $T_t$, and $\theta$ is the level of similarity between the corresponding columns (only if this value is greater than a threshold $\theta_{min}$).

The semantic catalog can be exploited for different activities. First, it can be used for exploring the subsets of datasets that can be used for conducting certain kinds of analyses. Once a specific dataset is identified, the other datasets with which the join operation should be applied can be easily determined. Overall, the catalog can be used as an indexing structure for evaluating the joinability of datasets but can be also exploited for developing Cypher queries starting from user requests expressed in natural language on the data lake [21].

## 4   Pipeline for the Construction of a Semantic Catalog

A three-step pipeline is used for the construction of the semantic catalog: *i) pre-processing and semantic tagging*; *ii) LLM-based embedding*; and *iii) semantic similarity and clustering*. In the first step, metadata (when available) are first pre-processed through the summarization capabilities of LLMs (i.e., a prompt for summarizing each metadata according to a given template is issued to a LLM). Moreover, by exploiting a schema $S$, dataset columns are semantically annotated according to classes and relationship properties of $S$. In the second step, prompts are generated to embed the columns in a latent space by considering the metadata associated with the datasets and their columns. In the third phase, by applying a classical clustering approach, similar columns (i.e., columns in the same cluster and belonging to different datasets) are identified and they can be considered joinable when the similarity of their embeddings is greater than a given threshold. Finally, the semantic catalog is generated.

### 4.1   Pre-processing and Semantic CTA

Whenever a new tabular dataset $T_{new}$ is included in $DL$, it passes through a data cleaning process devoted to eliminating blank columns and providing a uniform data representation (e.g., columns of type `date` should be represented according to the same format). Moreover, whenever metadata are associated with $T_{new}$, a prompt for enhancing their representation is created. Specifically, the LLM is asked to organize the metadata according to three perspectives:

- *thematic perspective.* A summary of the content of the dataset should be provided. In this perspective, the following information is maintained: the author of the dataset, the creation date, the organization that developed it, and the ontologies that can be used to characterize the dataset content.
- *temporal perspective.* Whenever a column $col_i \in T_{new}$ contains temporal data, the period covered by $value(col_i)$ and the temporal granularity (e.g., daily, weekly, monthly) are identified.
- *spatial perspective.* Whenever a column $col_i \in T_{new}$ contains spatial data, the spatial coverage of $value(col_i)$ (e.g., Italy, EU, global) is identified.

The developed prompt asks the LLM to extract these perspectives from $T_{new}$ along with its metadata, and to organize them in a structured way.

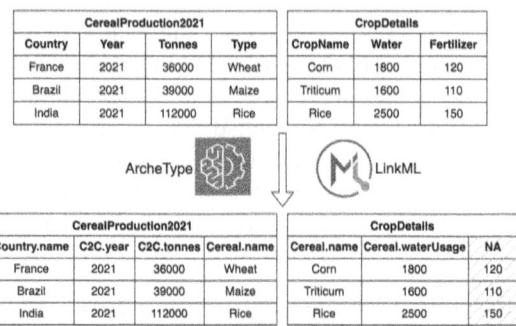

**Fig. 2.** Semantic CTA process using ArcheType and a LinkML schema.

Moreover, the four-stage ArcheType pipeline (Context Sampling, Prompt Serialization, Model Querying, and Label Remapping) [11] is applied to $T_{new}$ by relying on the schemas contained in $S$. Each stage is customized to ensure that the semantic annotations align with and enhance the schema structure. The Context Sampling stage selects a small set of representative values (less than 100) from each column to provide the LLM with sufficient information for accurate type inference and keep the prompt size manageable to avoid exceeding token limits. The Prompt Serialization stage constructs a concise and focused prompt that asks for the classification of a column into schema classes. For example, a real prompt for classifying a column containing country names might look like:

```
SYSTEM: Please select the class from Country.name, Country.code,
... which best describes the context. A Country is described as:
'A country is a nation with its own government, occupying a
particular territory'. Please report only the class name.
CONTEXT: ['Austria', 'Belgium', 'France', 'Italy', 'USA', ...]
If the context is not informative enough to select a class, return
'NA'.
```

The Model Querying stage sends the constructed prompt to the LLM and processes the response. To enhance reliability, a zero temperature is used to encourage more deterministic responses and outputs are generated in JSON format to facilitate parsing and processing. Last stage ensures that the LLM responses align perfectly with the standardized semantic types defined in $S$.

*Example 2.* Suppose table $T_1$=`CerealProduction` and $T_2$=`CropDetails` in top part of Fig. 2 are acquired in $DL$ and are processed for the schema $S$ in Fig. 1. $T_1$ reports the total production of cereals for selected countries and years. $T_2$ provides agronomic characteristics of crops, such as average water and fertilizer usage per cultivation cycle. The bottom part of Fig. 2 illustrates the tables after the CTA process obtained through ArcheType. Each column is annotated with a class attribute of $S$ (whenever a match is found by ArcheType). Note that the column related to fertilizer usage in `CropDetails` is discarded , as it does not have a direct correspondence in the proposed schema.

Even if this activity can be considered time-consuming, it is applied only once when the tabular dataset is included in the data lake and allows us to improve the quality of the metadata associated with $T_{new}$ (and consequently improve the quality of the inferred joins). This activity can be considered part of the usual data cleaning activity that is carried out during the data acquisition process.

## 4.2   Embedding Generation Process

After semantic column annotation, the pipeline proceeds with the embedding of columns. These embeddings capture the semantic meaning of columns in a high-dimensional space, leveraging the rich contextual information accumulated in previous steps (i.e., enhanced metadata, LinkML schema, and semantic annotations) and enabling similarity calculations that identify potential joins between columns across different datasets. This comprehensive approach produces embeddings that reflect the syntactic properties of columns but also their semantic meaning and relationships within the broader data context.

For the generation of the column embeddings, the information reported in Fig. 3.b) are extracted for each column and used for generating prompts. Figure 3.c) shows an example of a prompt for a column containing the acronym of the Italian regions. We remark that, in our approach, a sample with at most 100 different values for each column is considered. The embedding generation process utilizes OpenAI's text-embedding-3-small model [20], which provides a good balance between embedding quality and computational efficiency. This model generates 1536-dimensional vector representations that effectively capture semantic relationships between textual descriptions.

The embeddings of the columns and the metadata associated with a dataset (whose structure is shown in Fig. 3.a) are then combined to obtain the vectorial representation of the dataset. This operation is crucial for determining datasets that deal with similar types of information. The embedding of a table $T$ (presenting $m$ annotated columns) is computed through the following formula:

$$\mathbf{Emb}(T) = \mathbf{Emb}(T.Meta) + \frac{1}{m} \sum_{col \in T} \mathbf{Emb}(col)$$

## 4.3   Semantic Catalog Generation

For the computation of similarity between two vectors, cosine similarity measure and ANNS algorithm [17] can be used. Cosine similarity measures the angle between two vectors, providing a metric that is independent of vector magnitude and focuses on the orientation of the vectors. By contrast, ANNS constructs specialized data structures to quickly identify the most similar vectors with high probability (instead of exact distances between pairs of vectors).

Starting from the embeddings of the dataset columns, the HDBSCAN algorithm is used to cluster similar columns. Columns in the same cluster with a

| Name |
| --- |
| Description |
| [{col$_1$, desc$_1$},....,{col$_N$, desc$_N$}] |
| Spatial coverage |
| Temporal interval |
| Themes |
| Author, organization, last update |

(a) Metadata associated with a dataset

| Header |
| --- |
| Semantic annotation |
| Column length |
| Sample ([val$_1$..., val$_N$]) |
| (min,max,average) |

(b) Metadata associated with a column

The column with header **'Country'** and semantic annotation **'name'** belongs to instances of type **'Country'** and is described as: **'The name of a country.'** The class **'Country'** can be described as: **'A country is a nation with its own government, occupying a particular territory.'** Examples of values for this attribute include: **'Austria'**, **'Belgium'**, **'France'**, **'Italy'**, **'USA'**, ...
The column contains **128 entries**. Key statistics: Maximum value length: **7 characters**; Minimum value length: **4 characters**; Average value length: **5.5 characters**. Top 20 most frequent values in the column: **'Austria'**, **'Belgium'**, **'Bulgaria'**, **'Cyprus'**, **'Germany'**, **'Denmark'**, ...

(c) Example of prompt generated for a column

**Fig. 3.** Metadata and prompt structure.

similarity above a given threshold and belonging to different datasets are considered joinable. This information is then exploited for the construction of the semantic catalog. Indeed, the nodes of the catalog correspond to the datasets, and the information reported in Fig. 3.a) are used for defining the node properties. An edge is generated between two datasets only if they present at least a pair of columns that are joinable according to the previous definition. The edge is labeled with the list $[(c_{s_1}, c_{t_1}, \theta_1), \ldots, (c_{s_q}, c_{t_q}, \theta_q)]$ of joinable triples between the two datasets. The semantic catalog has been implemented and stored in a Neo4j property graph database.

*Example 3.* Figure 4.a) shows the two tables introduced in our example with the possible join between their columns. Figure 4.b) illustrates a data catalog generated for these tables. Each table is modeled as a node in a property graph, with metadata attached as node properties. Join relationships between tables are represented as edges. Distances between columns are reported as edge properties.

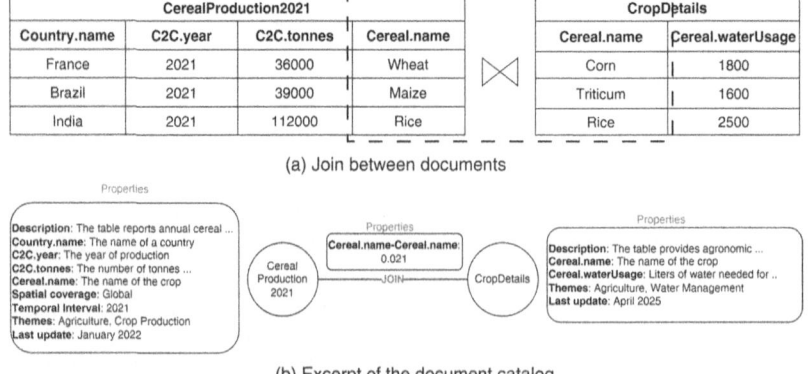

| CerealProduction2021 | | | | | CropDetails | |
| --- | --- | --- | --- | --- | --- | --- |
| Country.name | C2C.year | C2C.tonnes | Cereal.name | | Cereal.name | Cereal.waterUsage |
| France | 2021 | 36000 | Wheat | | Corn | 1800 |
| Brazil | 2021 | 39000 | Maize | | Triticum | 1600 |
| India | 2021 | 112000 | Rice | | Rice | 2500 |

(a) Join between documents

Properties

**Description:** The table reports annual cereal ...
**Country.name:** The name of a country
**C2C.year:** The year of production
**C2C.tonnes:** The number of tonnes ...
**Cereal.name:** The name of the crop
**Spatial coverage:** Global
**Temporal Interval:** 2021
**Themes:** Agriculture, Crop Production
**Last update:** January 2022

Cereal Production 2021 —JOIN— CropDetails

Properties
**Cereal.name-Cereal.name:** 0.021

Properties

**Description:** The table provides agronomic ...
**Cereal.name:** The name of the crop
**Cereal.waterUsage:** Liters of water needed for ..
**Themes:** Agriculture, Water Management
**Last update:** April 2025

(b) Excerpt of the document catalog

**Fig. 4.** Join identified between tables and its representation in the catalog.

# 5    Experimental Results

The effectiveness of the proposed approach was validated across three datasets: (*i*) PKT [1], that consists of 18 tabular files with a total of 87 columns related to biomedical entities (e.g., genes, diseases, and chemicals) and their relationships (e.g., chemical-disease interactions); (*ii*) Valentine [15], a benchmark for evaluating joinable table discovery approaches that involves 18 tables (182 columns) from the Wikidata and Magellan subsets; (*iii*) Eurostat Agricultural (EA) Dataset, that includes 100 Eurostat tables (975 columns) covering agricultural data from EU countries enriched with metadata (like dataset descriptions, update frequencies, data providers, and column-level documentation), developed in the context of the AMELIA platform (`https://ameliadp.grins.it/`). PKT and Valentine are coupled with ground truth for semantic column annotations and valid join pairs. Moreover, LinkML schemas were developed for each dataset.

In the remainder, the main experimental results are reported.

**Evaluation of the Accuracy of ArcheType Module.** The aim of the first experiment is to evaluate the semantic CTA relying on a LinkML schema. This experiment was done on the Valentine and PKT datasets that provide the ground truth. 73.56% of the columns in PKT and 85.16% in Valentine are correctly annotated. These results are consistent with those obtained by ArcheType [11].

**Evaluation of the Quality of Detected Joins and Impact of the Semantic Annotations on Join Discovery.** An ablation study was conducted to compare the performance of our pipeline with and without the semantic annotations and related schema-level attribute descriptions in the embedding prompts. Results are summarized in Table 1. For both setups, the threshold for the ANNS algorithm is fixed at 0.2 because it balances the trade-off between precision and recall. For the Valentine benchmark, incorporating semantic annotations improved recall with a drop in precision reflecting an increase in false positives. In the PKT dataset, semantic annotations improved both precision and recall. Results suggest that semantic annotations enhance the quality of vector representations, i.e., they provide additional contextual information that helps the model in generating more accurate and discriminative embeddings.

**Impact of Schemas in Pruning Irrelevant Datasets for Certain Analyses.** For checking the impact of schema in creating semantic catalogs, a schema with chemical, disease, and phenotype entities and their relationships was used. Among the 87 columns in PKT, 31 of them pertain to the targeted entity types, and 11 out of the 18 files are relevant to this task. When applying ArcheType with its default prompt, 56 of the 87 target columns (64%) were correctly annotated, and only 2 documents were discarded. To assess whether performance could be improved through prompt engineering,  a task-specific

**Table 1.** Join performance with and without semantic annotations.

| Metric | Valentine | | PKT | |
|---|---|---|---|---|
| | No Ann. | Ann. | No Ann. | Ann. |
| True positives | 53 | 64 | 67 | 110 |
| False positives | 0 | 12 | 40 | 4 |
| False negatives | 18 | 7 | 80 | 34 |
| Precision (%) | **100** | 85.00 | 62.61 | **96.49** |
| Recall (%) | 76.05 | **90.85** | 45.47 | **76.38** |
| F1 Score (%) | 85.95 | **87.85** | 52.68 | **85.26** |

prompt was specified and ArcheType correctly annotated 71 columns (82%), and the 7 documents irrelevant for this analysis were discarded. An improvement of detected joins can be observed when the custom prompt for CTA is used, reaching a 80% precision (~45% more compared to the standard ArcheType prompt).

**Impact of Metadata on the Obtained Embeddings.** The EA collection is equipped with metadata extracted from the original source. Since this collection does not provide the truths for joinable columns and column annotations, a qualitative analysis was performed to assess the embedding quality through t-SNE. The column embeddings were obtained from the original metadata and enhanced through our approach. Figure 5 shows their t-SNE representation in the two-dimensional plane in which nodes are colored according to the semantic annotation. The comparison shows that the use of structured metadata significantly improves the clustering of semantically related columns that can be joined.

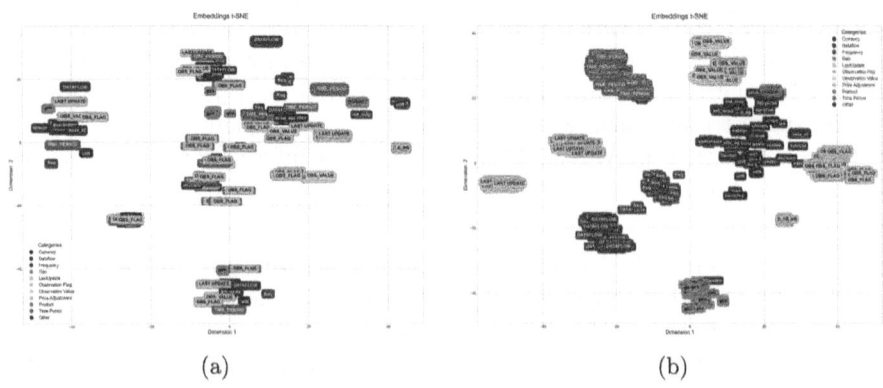

(a)                                        (b)

**Fig. 5.** t-SNE projection of column embeddings for the Eurostat dataset. Embeddings computed on: (a) uncleaned Eurostat metadata; (b) structured metadata.

Prompts were issued to OpenAI models using their API. Thus, our approach avoids CPU, GPU, or memory constraints. For the Valentine benchmark, full pipeline execution (to detect joins for a CSV pair) took ~3 min. and cost \$0.60.

# 6  Conclusion and Future Work

In this paper, a pipeline for the construction of semantic catalogs representing datasets in a data lake is proposed that can be exploited to perform certain kinds of analyses. A catalog is task and schema oriented, includes the metadata of the datasets that can be involved in the task, and reports the possibility of semantic joins. The approach exploits LLMs, and semantic column annotations that are obtained through ArcheType and datasets metadata. Initial experiments indicate that our approach is practical and efficient, with promising results in terms of both accuracy and usability. However, further experiments should be conducted with collections of larger size to validate scalability and robustness. For this purpose, datasets made available in the AMELIA platform will be considered. Moreover, the approach should be extended to take in deeper consideration the spatial and temporal dimensions for the identification of joinable columns. The code for reproducing experiments is available at: https:// github.com/matteochestnut/SemLink.

# References

1. Callahan, T.J., et al.: An open source knowledge graph ecosystem for the life sciences. Sci. Data **11**, 363 (2024)
2. Cappuzzo, R., et al.: Creating embeddings of heterogeneous relational datasets for data integration tasks. In: SIGMOD, pp. 1335–1349 (2020)
3. Castro Fernandez, R., et al.: Seeping semantics: linking datasets using word embeddings for data discovery. In: ICDE, pp. 989–1000 (2018)
4. Cavalleri, E., et al.: SchemaLink: An intelligent web-based editor for LinkML schema curation. Tech. rep., University of Milan (2025)
5. Chen, J., et al.: ColNet: embedding the semantics of web tables for column type prediction. In: Proceedings of AAAI Conference on AI. vol. 33, pp. 29–36 (2019)
6. Chepurko, N., et al.: ARDA: automatic relational data augmentation for machine learning. Proc. VLDB Endow. **13**(9), 1373–1387 (2020)
7. Deng, Y., et al.: A benchmark for discovering joinable and unionable tables in data lakes. Proc. VLDB Endow. **17**(8), 1925–1938 (2024)
8. Do, H.H., Rahm, E.: A system for flexible combination of schema matching approaches. In: VLDB, pp. 610–621 (2002)
9. Dong, Y., et al.: Efficient joinable table discovery in data lakes: a high-dimensional similarity-based approach. In ICDE, pp. 456–467 (2020)
10. Dong, Y., et al.: Deepjoin: joinable table discovery with pre-trained language models. Proc. VLDB Endow. **16**(10), 2458–2470 (2023)
11. Feuer, B., et al.: ArcheType: a novel framework for open-source column type annotation using large language models. In: Proceedings of VLDB Endow. **17**(9) (2024)
12. Hai, R., et al.: A survey of functions and systems. IEEE TKDE **35**(12), 12571–12590 (2023)

13. Hegselmann, S., et al.: TabLLM: few-shot classification of tabular data with large language models. In: International Conference on AI and Statistics, pp. 5549–5581. PMLR (2023)
14. Hulsebos, M., et al.: Sherlock: a deep learning approach to semantic data type detection. In: ACM SIGKDD, pp. 1500–1508 (2019)
15. Koutras, C., et al.: Valentine: evaluating matching techniques for dataset discovery. In: ICDE, pp. 468–479 (2021)
16. Madhavan, J., Bernstein, P.A., Rahm, E.: Generic schema matching with cupid. In: VLDB, pp. 49–58 (2001)
17. Malkov, Y.A., Yashunin, D.A.: Efficient and robust approximate nearest neighbor search using hierarchical navigable small world graphs. IEEE Trans. Pattern Anal. Mach. Intell. **42**(4), 824–836 (2020)
18. Melnik, S., et al.: Similarity flooding: a versatile graph matching algorithm and its application to schema matching. In: ICDE, pp. 117–128 (2002)
19. Moxon, S., et al.: The linked data modeling language (LinkML): a general-purpose data modeling framework grounded in machine-readable semantics. In: International Conference on Biomedical Ontologies (2021)
20. OpenAI: GPT-4 tech. report (2023)
21. Ozsoy, M.G.: Text2Cypher: Bridging natural language and graph databases (2024)
22. Paton, N.W., Chen, J., Wu, Z.: Dataset discovery and exploration: a survey. ACM Comput. Surv. **56**(4) (2023)
23. Zhang, M., et al.: Automatic discovery of attributes in relational databases. In: SIGMOD, pp. 109–120 (2011)
24. Zhu, E., et al.: JOSIE: overlap set similarity search for finding joinable tables in data lakes. In: SIGMOD, pp. 847–864 (2019)
25. Zhu, E., Nargesian, F., Pu, K.Q., Miller, R.J.: LSH ensemble: internet-scale domain search. Proc. VLDB Endow. **9**(12), 1185–1196 (2016)

# Detecting Semantic Relationships Among Datasets

Paolo Fosci[1], Vincenzo Carbone[2], Matteo Leo[2], Andrea Marmorato[2],
Giuseppe Psaila[1(✉)], Giampiero Rosa[2], and Mohammadsadegh Torabi[2]

[1] University of Bergamo, Viale Marconi 5, 24044 Dalmine (BG), Italy
{paolo.fosci,giuseppe.psaila}@unibg.it
[2] Exprivia SpA, Via Olivetti, 11/A, 76059 Molfetta (BA), Italy
{matteo.leo,giampiero.rosa}@exprivia.com
http://www.unibg.it, https://www.exprivia.it/

**Abstract.** The novel context of Big Data has demonstrated that classical relational databases are not suitable: novel platforms for managing an incredible variety of datasets have become necessary, as demonstrated by the popularity of "data lakes" and "data lakehouses".

One common issue of modern data platforms is to detect pairs of datasets that concern the same topic. However, a matching that is purely syntactic is not effective: the exploitation of modern AI techniques for Natural-Language Processing, such as word embedding and sentence embedding, promise to address the issue in a (more or less) semantic way.

The contribution of the paper is a novel methodology (called "TopicRank") for flexible querying data platforms, so as to find out pairs of datasets that concern the same topic, on the basis of the textual description that accompany datasets as meta-data. The paper presents the results of a preliminary experiment that was conducted on a real pool of datasets.

**Keywords:** Big Data Platforms · Flexible Query on Datasets · Methodology for Topic Detection · Language Models for Information Retrieval · Semantic Topic Detection

## 1 Introduction

The volumes of data produced every day have increased exponentially in the last decades (see [10]). With the expansion of the so-called "Big Data" [1,12], traditional data management systems (such as relational databases) have shown to be inadequate, due to volumes and variety of datasets to collect and integrate.

Novel data management solutions have been devised, and concepts such as "data lake" and "data lakehouse" have emerged and become popular solutions for managing Big Data [4,15–17,22,27,30]. In this context, a set of integrated and orchestrated "Big-Data tools", is generally referred to as "Data Platform".

A data platform can follow the entire journey of data, in particular taking care of aspects such as (for a survey on Big Data platforms, see [24]):

© The Author(s), under exclusive license to Springer Nature Switzerland AG 2026
G. De Tré et al. (Eds.): FQAS 2025, LNAI 16119, pp. 219–231, 2026.
https://doi.org/10.1007/978-3-032-05607-8_21

– data ingestion from different and heterogeneous sources, where datasets can enter the platform in a variety of flavors: structured (table-like), semi-structured and unstructured (documents, images, videos, audios) format;
– data quality and integration, where the ingested datasets are checked with the aim of removing unwanted information and standardizing their values to be able to "talk with" other datasets in the platform;
– data querying, processing and analysis, where data are interrogated, transformed and aggregated to extract domain-specific patterns;
– data governance, security and access management, that deals with secure data access, masking policies and data accessibility;
– data visualization, reporting and dashboarding, where results from elaboration are presented in a clear and simple way.

In the context of the EU initiative known as "Recovery Fund", the GRINS project[1] is working on the development of an innovative data platform, named *AMELIA* (dAta platforM for the transfEr of knowLedge and statistIcal Analysis) *Data Platform* (in the following, just AMELIA for short).

Among all the requirements, some of the key aspects are: (i) ingesting large amounts of datasets, coming from heterogeneous sources and in different formats[2]; (ii) collecting and harmonizing them in a single integrated system that will act as a single and reliable source for data; (iii) handling advanced statistical and ML analysis; (iv) summarizing results coming from a variety of different scientific domains (e.g., in the field of environment, finance, social-economics and healthcare) in visualizations and dashboards; (v) ensuring high data security, privacy and managing user-access control based on GDPR regulation[3].

A common issue in a data platform is providing users the capability to retrieve pairs of datasets that possibly concern the same topic. This is indeed a flexible-querying capability, which can be realized by exploiting textual descriptions that usually accompany datasets as meta-data, by exploiting techniques for Natural-Language Processing (NLP). In this respect, the advent of Artificial Intelligence (AI) in NLP has completely changed the perspective in the last decade and is promising to solve the above-mentioned issue.

While working on AMELIA, the authors developed a methodology, called *TopicRank*, which has been implemented as a prototype service enabling flexible querying within AMELIA; the solution exploits a "keyword extraction" technique along with vector representations from a pre-trained word/sentence embedding model, aiming to identify semantic similarities among keywords extracted from textual descriptions that accompany datasets. The paper presents the *TopicRank* methodology and its implementation within AMELIA, as well as the first (encouraging) results that were obtained by performing a preliminary experimental campaign on real data sets stored within AMELIA.

---

[1] See GRINS website for more info https://grins.it/, accessed on 28/04/2025.
[2] Tabular (e.g., CSV), semi-structured (e.g., JSON) data or datasets with geographical structure are just some examples of data typologies that can enter AMELIA.
[3] GDPR regulation: https://gdpr-info.eu/, accessed on 28/04/2025.

In the following, Sect. 2 presents the related work. Section 3 presents some preliminary concepts on NLP. Section 4 introduces the approach, by means of a practical example. Section 5 discusses the results of the preliminary experimental campaign. Finally, Sect. 6 draws conclusions and possible future work.

## 2   Related Work

The concept of "data lake" is not uniquely defined, as shown by [8], someone imagines a data lake as a simple schema-less and cheap storage system; someone else thinks that a data lake should provide tools for generating value from datasets that are stored within it. Specifically, the authors of [8] identified a set of functionalities for dataset management that a data lake should provide. Among all, they mention "Semantic enrichment", "meta-data processing" and "similarity links": to avoid the risk of "data swamp" (the data lake becomes useless because it is impossible to correlate datasets) meta-data should enrich datasets, so that the system can tell users which datasets concern the same topics.

The work [16] provides detailed descriptions of tiers that should compose a data lake and the functionalities that each tier should provide. As far as the present paper is concerned, [16] identifies the "Maintenance Tier", which should provide the functionality named "Related dataset discovery".

Generally, data-lake systems exploit syntactic or lexicographic matching, such as schema matching, attribute name matching, instance matching. Only a few (among the ones censed by [16]) consider textual description and NLP. The closest approach to the present paper is the "Relational Natural Language Inference Model" [23, 26]: having the goal of joining two tabular datasets through semantically-related attributes/fields, it exploits a pre-trained language model for representing values of textual attributes; and train a classification model. In contrast, this paper works on textual meta-data, not on attribute values.

An idea, that is somehow close to the present paper, was presented in [9]: in order to discover topics that characterize documents in a data lake, a data mining technique based on a statistical analysis of texts in documents, supported by "Latent Dirichlet Allocation" (LDA), was proposed. A topic is represented as a probability distribution of words, obtained by a preliminary pre-training of the probabilistic model. It is designed to work with large textual documents.

Specifically, [9] comes out from the variety of techniques for detecting topics in social media. An extensive survey on the topic is [18]. In general, techniques for topic detection are designed to extract topics from a mass of messages/documents, so as to detect trends of public speech. For this reason, usually they are clustering techniques as well as pattern-based techniques; classification (supervised-learning) techniques can be used too [2].

However, the problem that is addressed in this paper is different: detecting pairs of datasets that are semantically related on the basis of their (usually short) textual descriptions in meta-data; in such a context, it can happen that only two datasets are related each other (because they are the only two ones that concern a given topic), so any pre-trained approach is not effective.

## 3  Preliminaries

This section provides the preliminary notions about the techniques for Natural-Language Processing (NLP) that are exploited in the methodology that is presented in Sect. 4, i.e., "Keyword Extraction" and "Word Embedding".

**Keyword Extraction.** The term "Keyword Extraction" denotes a pool of techniques devoted to process a textual document so as to extract, from it, a small set of keywords that synthesize the main content of the document.

The current trend is to develop unsupervised techniques that are "language independent". A few techniques, among all, are "KP-Miner" [11], "RSKE" [28], and "PositionRank" [13]. The proposal that appears to be one of the most effective is *YAKE!* [6,7]. Very shortly, *YAKE!* works as follows: (1) it scans the text to build $n$-grams (typically, $1 \leq n \leq 3$) of words; (2) balancing several metrics that are based on $n$-gram frequencies, it builds a pool of keywords that possibly contain stop-words; (3) a short pool of representative keywords is selected and returned as a result. The interested reader can refer to [6] for an extensive presentation of *YAKE!*.

**Word Embedding.** The technique that probably has provided an incredible impulse to NLP in the last decade is named "Word Embedding". The questions behind it are the following ones: (1) given a sequence of words, what is the most likely subsequent word? (2) Is it possible to trim a model that can be used to answer Question 1?

Word Embedding is a dense representation of statistical parameters, such that words are represented as vectors in a multi-dimensional space (typically, no less than 300 dimensions). This model is trained in such a way that vectors that represent words with similar semantics (typically, based on co-occurrences in texts) are close to each other. The consequence is that it is possible to detect semantic similarity between two words by evaluating the "cosine similarity" between the vectors representing those words. "Word2Vec" is the first modern technique for word embedding ever proposed [20], but other famous proposals are "Glove" [25], "FastText" [5], and "BERT" [19]. The interested reader can refer to [29] for a review. However, some of these projects are evolving towards *short-sentence embedding*, i.e., not only single words are encoded, but also short sentences or parts of sentences (i.e., 3 words), such as in *BERT*.

An interesting practical tool for NLP tasks is *spaCy*[4]. It is a Python module that supports many NLP tasks, Among all capabilities, such as tokenization, lemmatization and language parsing, it provides a large pool of pre-trained word-embedding/sentence-embedding models; specifically, for each language, three pre-trained models are available, i.e., small, medium and large, based on the size of the model. The large model may be too big for most standard computational architectures, while the medium model is a proper compromise between

---

[4] *spaCy*: https://spacy.io/models/en accessed on 28/04/2025.

accuracy and computational performance; the small model may provide insufficient accuracy (refer to [3] for a detailed presentation).

**Natural-Language Translation.** An interesting application of deep neural networks and language models (obtained by training deep neural networks) is the task of "natural-language translation", i.e., translating a sentence in a given natural language into a different one. The effectiveness of the modern solutions for natural-language translation is under the eyes of everyone and, again, shows the power of deep neural networks. The interested reader can refer to [33] for a comprehensive introduction.

A notable project is *OPUS-MT*[5], an open-source project that makes libraries and trained models available to developers, which implements the *Helsinki-NLP* methodology [31,32].

## 4   Approach

The goal of this section is to present the *TopicRank* methodology that has been developed for topic matching within the AMELIA platform. The *TopicRank* methodology is presented in Sect. 4.1; an example is illustrated in Sect. 4.2.

### 4.1   TopicRank Methodology

First of all, it is worth defining the actual problem to address.

**Problem 1.** *Consider a pool $\mathcal{D} = \{ds_1, ds_2, \ldots, ds_n\}$ of datasets $ds_i$ (with $1 \leq i \leq n$). Given a dataset $ds \notin \mathcal{D}$, provide the set $\mathcal{S} \subseteq \mathcal{D}$ of datasets that most likely concern the same topic as $ds$, based on their textual meta-description.*

Clearly, solving Problem 1 asks for a "pairwise comparison" of $ds$ with every $ds_i \in \mathcal{D}$, in such a way that an eponym function called $TopicRank(ds_1, ds_2) \in [0, 1]$ is evaluated. To do so, it is assumed that both $ds_1$ and $ds_2$ are provided with a textual description, denoted as $ds_1.text$ and $ds_2.text$.

The *TopicRank* function performs the following tasks.

**Language Detection and Translation,** The input datasets might be accompanied by textual descriptions in different languages; however, to be effective, it is necessary to have descriptions in the same language. Specifically, English was used as the reference language, to exploit the incredible variety of language models that are currently available. Consequently, the next steps of the *TopicRank* methodology will work on $t_1$ and $t_2$: if $ds_1.text$ (resp., $ds_2.text$) is written in English, $t_1 = ds_1.text$ (resp., $t_2 = ds_2.text$); otherwise, $t_1$ (resp., $t_2$) is the automatic translation of $ds_1.text$ (resp., $ds_2.text$) into English.

In the implementation of the *TopicRank* methodology, language detection is performed using the Python library **langdetect**[6]. This library is a Python implementation of the Google Language-Detection Library [21] (written in Java).

---

[5] OPUS-MT: https://github.com/Helsinki-NLP/Opus-MT, accessed on 28/04/2025.
[6] langdetect: https://pypi.org/project/langdetect/ accessed on 28/04/2025.

Currently, only the translation from Italian to English is considered in the implementation, since many datasets that are collected within AMELIA are in Italian. The translation was implemented by using *Helsinki-NLP/opus-mt-it-en* from the *OPUS-MT* project[7]. (see Sect. 3).

**Keyword Extraction.** Relevant keywords that characterize both $t_1$ and $t_2$ are extracted. These sets of keywords are denoted as $KW_1$ (extracted from within $t_1$) and $KW_2$ (extracted from within $t_2$). The tool named *YAKE!*[8]. (see Sect. 3) is used in the implementation of the *TopicRank* methodology.

Clearly, different words that are actually synonyms could be used in different descriptions, so it can happen that the same topic is denoted by different keywords in $KW_1$ and $KW_2$; this is normal, and explains why a technique for keyword extraction does not suffice.

**Detecting Word Vectors.** To solve the issue of synonym keywords in $KW_1$ and $KW_2$ that denote the same topic, a language model is exploited. Given a model for word embedding $WE$, the sets of vectors $V_1$ and $V_2$ are built, in such a way $V_1$ (resp., $V_2$) contains the vectors in $WE$ representing each of the keywords in $KW_1$ (resp., in $KW_2$). In the implementation, *spaCy* (see Sect. 3), with the medium-size embedding for English, is used[9]; for each keyword, even when it is composed of multiple words, *spaCy* returns a single vector.

**Cosine-Similarity Ranking.** Based on the assumption that the word embedding $WE$ encodes words in such a way possibly semantically-similar words are encoded by vectors that are located nearby in the same region of multidimensional space, given two vectors $w_1$ and $w_2$ representing words that are semantically similar, their cosine similarity ($sim(w_1, w_2) \in [-1, 1]$) should give a value (very) close to 1. By aggregating the cosine similarities of pairs ($w_{1,i}, w_{2,j}$), it is possible to compute the value returned by the *TopicRank* function.

For calculating the similarity between two groups of keywords, the following strategy was devised. Given $V_1$ and $V_2$, for each vector $v_{1,i} \in V_1$, the most similar vector $v_{2,j} \in V_2$ is looked for; specifically, the best similarity degree is looked for, as in Eq. 1.

$$m(v_{1,i}, V_2) = \max_{v_{2,j} \in V_2} \cos(v_{1,i}, v_{2,j}) \qquad (1)$$

---

[7] Model version taken from commit https://huggingface.co/Helsinki-NLP/opus-mt-it-en/commit/42556a0848fc726f4d27399f20b19ff6f01afe11, accessed on 28/04/2025.

[8] *YAKE!* Python library with version 0.4.8

[9] *spaCy* Python library with version 3.8.3 and its English embedding model *en_core_web_md* with version 3.8.0.

**Table 1.** Description of the Eurostat datasets.

| Dataset id | Dataset name | Dataset description | Keywords |
|---|---|---|---|
| ds1 | estat_teimf200 | The Euro-national currency exchange rate represents the equivalent of one euro expressed in national currency. For example, the euro-dollar exchange rate is the equivalent of one euro expressed in United States dollars. Monthly data are the average of the observed business day rates. Data are presented in raw form. | Euro-national currency exchange<br>Euro-national currency<br>currency exchange rate |
| ds2 | estat_tec00033 | Exchange rates are the price or value of one country's currency in relation to another. Here the exchange rates are those for the euro published by the European Central Bank. Before 1999 the exchange rates are those of the ECU, as published by the European Commission. | European Central Bank<br>Exchange rates<br>country's currency |
| ds3 | estat_ttr00005 | Data displayed in this table cover the carriage of good by road by means of goods road transport vehicles registered in the reporting countries. | transport vehicles registered<br>road transport vehicles<br>goods road transport |

At this point, it is possible to compute the *TopicRank* function as the final "topic-similarity score", by averaging the previously computed similarity measures $m(v_{1,i}, V_2)$, as in Eq. 2.

$$TopicRank(ds_1, ds_2) = \frac{1}{|V_1|} \sum_{i=1}^{|V_1|} m(v_{1,i}, V_2) \qquad (2)$$

The average is a simple concept, easy to compute; nevertheless, the authors plan to evaluate the effectiveness of alternative aggregations for pair ranking.

Once the *TopicRank* function is computed for a pair of datasets, a threshold $\alpha = 0.7$ determines which dataset pairs to select, because they pertain to the same topics (or subject matters).

### 4.2   Example

Hereafter, an example of how the *TopicRank* methodology works is reported.

To show in practice all the relevant steps of the *TopicRank* methodology, the focus is on three specific datasets acquired from the Eurostat database[10], identified as *ds1*, *ds2*, and *ds3*, respectively, and described in Table 1. For each dataset: column `Dataset id` reports the identifier of the dataset; column `Dataset name` reports the name of the dataset on the Eurostat database; column `Dataset description` reports the textual description of the dataset; finally, column `Keywords` reports the list of the three most relevant keywords identified by *YAKE!* from within the dataset description (Table 1).

---

[10] Eurostat database: https://ec.europa.eu/eurostat/data/database, accessed on 28/04/2025.

**Table 2.** Results of the *TopicRank* function applied to all possible pairs formed from the datasets *ds1*, *ds2*, and *ds3*.

| Dataset 1 | Dataset 2 | TopicRank |
|-----------|-----------|-----------|
| ds1 | ds2 | 0.735 |
| ds2 | ds3 | 0.527 |
| ds1 | ds3 | 0.507 |

To apply the *TopicRank* methodology, for each dataset the keywords are converted into multi-dimensional vectors (embedding). Then, the *TopicRank* function (see Eq. 2) is calculated for each possible pair of datasets. The result of this step is shown in Table 2.

For the dataset pair *(ds1, ds2)*, the *TopicRank* function returns a similarity score of 0.735, which is greater than threshold $\alpha$. This indicates that, although the descriptions of the two datasets are not entirely identical, they do exhibit a noticeable degree of shared content. This observation is further supported by a manual comparison of their textual descriptions, which reveals overlapping themes or terms.

In contrast, for the other two pairs, *(ds2, ds3)* and *(ds1, ds3)*, the *TopicRank* function yields lower similarity scores of 0.527 and 0.507, respectively. Both values fall below the threshold $\alpha$, suggesting that the textual descriptions of these dataset pairs do not contain significant commonalities.

Therefore, based on the output of the *TopicRank* function, we can conclude that only the pair *(ds1, ds2)* demonstrates a meaningful level of semantic similarity. This is also expected because *ds3* is a dataset that contains information on transport of goods by roads in Europe, while the other two datasets treat the European currency exchange rates.

## 5   Preliminary Results

To assess the effectiveness of the *TopicRank* methodology for detecting semantic similarity among datasets, a structured evaluation was conducted.

From the whole pool of datasets that were stored at the time of writing in AMELIA, many datasets were acquired from the open data portals of *Eurostat*[11] and *ISTAT*[12] (the Italian body for official statistical analysis), or from freely available machine learning datasets repository such as the popular Iris dataset[13].

These datasets encompass a variety of thematic areas, such as economics, transportation, health, environment, and demographics. The heterogeneous nature of this initial dataset collection ensures that the evaluation reflects a broad range of use cases and textual description styles.

---

[11] Eurostat: https://ec.europa.eu/eurostat/data/database, accessed on 28/04/2025.
[12] ISTAT: https://esploradati.istat.it/databrowser/, accessed on 28/04/2025.
[13] Iris: https://archive.ics.uci.edu/dataset/53/iris, accessed on 28/04/2025.

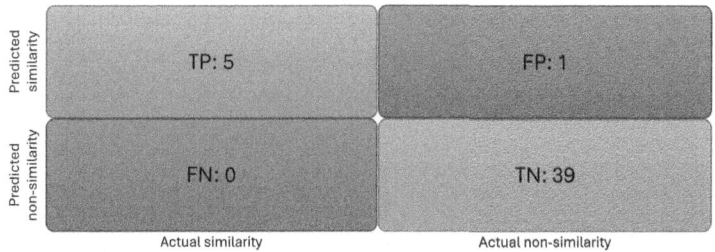

**Fig. 1.** Confusion matrix for dataset similarities.

From this set, a subset of 10 datasets was selected by a panel of domain experts. The selection process was designed to ensure thematic diversity, coverage of multiple domains, and clear textual documentation. All possible pairs between the selected datasets were considered, resulting in 45 unique dataset pairs. Each pair was manually evaluated by the experts, who labeled them as either "similar" or "non-similar" based on their qualitative analysis of the dataset meta-data and descriptions.

This expert-labeling yields 5 pairs considered to be similar and 40 pairs considered to be non-similar. These annotations are treated as the ground truth for the subsequent evaluation of the *TopicRank* methodology. The criteria used by the experts include shared topical content, consistent keyword usage, and alignment in the intended purpose or informational domain of the datasets.

The *TopicRank* methodology described in Sect. 4.1 was applied to the same subset. The *TopicRank* function was computed for each of the 45 dataset pairs, and the resulting similarity score was compared to a fixed threshold $\alpha = 0.7$.

Pairs with a score greater than or equal to $\alpha$ were classified as similar; otherwise, they were classified as non-similar. The classification outcomes were then compared with the expert labels.

The results of this comparison are shown in Fig. 1, which reports the corresponding confusion matrix. The matrix summarizes the classification results as follows:

- **True Positives (TP):** 5 pairs are correctly classified as similar;
- **True Negatives (TN):** 39 pairs are correctly classified as non-similar;
- **False Positives (FP):** 1 pair is incorrectly classified as similar when it is actually non-similar;
- **False Negatives (FN):** 0 pair is incorrectly classified as non-similar despite being labeled as similar by the experts.

Based on this matrix, standard classification metrics (i.e., *Precision*, *Recall*, *F1-Score*, and *Accuracy*) are computed to quantitatively assess the performance of the *TopicRank* methodology.

*Precision* (i.e., the proportion of pairs classified as similar that are truly similar) is calculated as:

$$Precision = \frac{TP}{TP + FP} = \frac{5}{5 + 1} = 0.833 \tag{3}$$

*Recall* (i.e., the proportion of all truly similar pairs that are correctly classified) is calculated as:

$$Recall = \frac{TP}{TP + FN} = \frac{5}{5 + 0} = 1.000 \tag{4}$$

*F1-Score*, which is the harmonic mean of *Precision* and *Recall* and in practice is a measure of predictive performance, is given by:

$$F1\text{-}score = 2 \times \frac{Precision \times Recall}{Precision + Recall} = 2 \times \frac{0.833 \times 1.000}{0.833 + 1.000} \approx 0.909 \tag{5}$$

*Accuracy* (i.e., the proportion of correctly retrieved pairs —both similar and non-similar—out of all similar and non-similar pairs) is calculated as:

$$Accuracy = \frac{TP + TN}{TP + FP + TN + FN} = \frac{5 + 39}{5 + 1 + 39 + 0} \approx 0.978 \tag{6}$$

These metrics demonstrate the high reliability of the proposed approach. Indeed, the *TopicRank* methodology promises to closely replicate expert-level judgment, achieving a *Precision* score of 83% and a *Recall* score of 100% in the preliminary experiment, making it a reliable tool for supporting automated topic (thematic) discovery in AMELIA.

## 6    Conclusions

The paper presented a methodology, called *TopicRank*, for solving the problem of flexible querying in data platforms for Big Data, i.e., discovering pairs of datasets that semantically concern the same topic, on the basis of the textual description in their meta-data. The problem is relevant in current data platforms for managing Big Data, since the variety of datasets that could be gathered in them is impressive and an automatic way to detect datasets that are semantically related each other has become fundamental.

The novelty of the *TopicRank* methodology is to exploit a classical technique for keyword extraction together with modern AI technique for NLP, i.e., word embedding and sentence embedding. Through a preliminary experimental campaign on a limited number of datasets, taken from official portals: results show that the *TopicRank* methodology promises to be quite effective.

As a future work, the authors will continue developing the technique: the idea is to consider column/field names and their accompanying textual description, so that once two datasets are claimed to concern the same topic, it is possible to detect those columns/fields that actually denote that topic; this task could be powered by novel tools for flexible querying with fuzzy logic [14]. Furthermore, the computational power that is necessary to apply the methodology on a very large number of datasets (such as tens of thousands of datasets) will be evaluated: indeed, AI techniques for NLP usually heavily consume computational power; consequently, it is necessary to evaluate if the current choices for implementation are able to scale for a large number of datasets.

**Acknowledgments.** This study was funded by the European Union - *NextGenerationEU, in the framework of the GRINS - Growing Resilient, INclusive and Sustainable project (GRINS PE00000018  CUP F83C22001720001)*. The views and opinions expressed are solely those of the authors and do not necessarily reflect those of the European Union, nor can the European Union be held responsible for them.

The authors thank Prof. Marco Mesiti (University of Milan, Italy) for his high-valuable comments on the manuscript.

# References

1. Agrahari, A., Rao, D.: A review paper on big data: technologies, tools and trends. Int. Res. J. Eng. Technol. **4**(10), 10 (2017)
2. Ali, M., Baqir, A., Psaila, G., Malik, S.: Towards the discovery of influencers to follow in micro-blogs (twitter) by detecting topics in posted messages (tweets). Appl. Sci. **10**(16), 5715 (2020)
3. Altinok, D.: Mastering spaCy: An end-to-end practical guide to implementing NLP applications using the Python ecosystem. Packt Publishing Ltd (2021)
4. Armbrust, M., Ghodsi, A., Xin, R., Zaharia, M.: Lakehouse: a new generation of open platforms that unify data warehousing and advanced analytics. In: Proceedings of CIDR. vol. 8, p. 28 (2021)
5. Athiwaratkun, B., Wilson, A.G., Anandkumar, A.: Probabilistic fasttext for multi-sense word embeddings. arXiv preprint arXiv:1806.02901 (2018)
6. Campos, R., Mangaravite, V., Pasquali, A., Jorge, A., Nunes, C., Jatowt, A.: YAKE! Keyword extraction from single documents using multiple local features. Inf. Sci. **509**, 257–289 (2020)
7. Campos, R., Mangaravite, V., Pasquali, A., Jorge, A.M., Nunes, C., Jatowt, A.: YAKE! Collection-independent automatic keyword extractor. In: European Conference on Information Retrieval, pp. 806–810. Springer (2018)
8. Cherradi, M., EL Haddadi, A.: Data lakes: a survey paper. In: The Proceedings of the International Conference on Smart City Applications, pp. 823–835. Springer (2021)
9. Cherradi, M., El Haddadi, A.: Enhancing data lake management systems with LDA approach. J. Data Sci. Intell. Syst. **3**(1), 58–66 (2025)
10. Clissa, L., Lassnig, M., Rinaldi, L.: How big is big data? A comprehensive survey of data production, storage, and streaming in science and industry. Front. Big Data **6**, 1271639 (2023)
11. El-Beltagy, S.R., Rafea, A.: KP-Miner: a keyphrase extraction system for English and Arabic documents. Inf. Syst. **34**(1), 132–144 (2009)
12. Fan, J., Han, F., Liu, H.: Challenges of big data analysis. Natl. Sci. Rev. **1**(2), 293–314 (2014)

13. Florescu, C., Caragea, C.: PositionRank: an unsupervised approach to keyphrase extraction from scholarly documents. In: Proceedings of the 55th Annual Meeting of the Association for Computational Linguistics (volume 1: long papers), pp. 1105–1115 (2017)
14. Fosci, P., Psaila, G.: J-co, a framework for fuzzy querying collections of JSON documents. In: Flexible Query Answering Systems: 14th International Conference, FQAS 2021, Bratislava, Slovakia, September 19–24, 2021, Proceedings 14, pp. 142–153. Springer International Publishing (2021)
15. Gardner, S.R.: Building the data warehouse. Commun. ACM **41**(9), 52–60 (1998)
16. Hai, R., Koutras, C., Quix, C., Jarke, M.: Data lakes: a survey of functions and systems. IEEE TKDE **35**(12), 12571–12590 (2023)
17. Hlupić, T., Oreščanin, D., Ružak, D., Baranović, M.: An overview of current data lake architecture models. In: 2022 45th Jubilee International Convention on Information, Communication and Electronic Technology (MIPRO), pp. 1082–1087. IEEE (2022)
18. Ibrahim, R., Elbagoury, A., Kamel, M.S., Karray, F.: Tools and approaches for topic detection from twitter streams: survey. Knowl. Inf. Syst. **54**, 511–539 (2018)
19. Kaliyar, R.K.: A multi-layer bidirectional transformer encoder for pre-trained word embedding: a survey of BERT. In: 2020 10th International Conference on Cloud Computing, Data Science & Engineering (confluence), pp. 336–340. IEEE (2020)
20. Kombrink, S., Mikolov, T., Karafiát, M., Burget, L.: Recurrent neural network based language modeling in meeting recognition. In: Interspeech. vol. 11, pp. 2877–2880 (2011)
21. Nakatani, S.: Language detection library for JAVA (2010). https://github.com/shuyo/language-detection (2010)
22. Oreščanin, D., Hlupić, T.: Data lakehouse-a novel step in analytics architecture. In: 2021 44th International Convention on Information, Communication and Electronic Technology (MIPRO), pp. 1242–1246. IEEE (2021)
23. Orihuela, M.A.R., Bogatu, A., Paton, N., Freitas, A.: Natural language inference over tables: Enabling explainable data exploration on data lakes. In: Eighteenth Extended Semantic Web Conference-Research Track (2021)
24. Oussous, A., Benjelloun, F.Z., Lahcen, A.A., Belfkih, S.: Big data technologies: a survey. J. King Saud Univ. Comput. Inf. Sci. **30**(4), 431–448 (2018)
25. Pennington, J., Socher, R., Manning, C.D.: GloVe: global vectors for word representation. In: Proceedings of the 2014 Conference on Empirical Methods in Natural Language Processing (EMNLP), pp. 1532–1543 (2014)
26. Ramirez, M., Bogatu, A., Paton, N.W., Freitas, A.: Natural language inference over tables: enabling explainable data exploration on data lakes. In: Verborgh, R., et al. (eds.) ESWC 2021. LNCS, vol. 12731, pp. 304–320. Springer, Cham (2021). https://doi.org/10.1007/978-3-030-77385-4_18
27. Rifaie, M., Kianmehr, K., Alhajj, R., Ridley, M.J.: Data warehouse architecture and design. In: 2008 IEEE International Conference on Information Reuse and Integration, pp. 58–63. IEEE (2008)
28. Rose, S., Engel, D., Cramer, N., Cowley, W.: Automatic keyword extraction from individual documents. Text Mining: Applications and Theory, pp. 1–20 (2010)
29. Selva Birunda, S., Kanniga Devi, R.: A review on word embedding techniques for text classification. Innovative Data Commun. Technol. Appl. Proc. ICIDCA **2020**, 267–281 (2021)
30. Shiyal, B.: Modern data warehouses and data lakehouses. In: Beginning Azure Synapse Analytics: Transition from Data Warehouse to Data Lakehouse, pp. 21–48. Springer (2021)

31. Tiedemann, J., et al.: Democratizing neural machine translation with OPUS-MT. Lang. Resour. Eval. **58**, 713–755 (2023). https://doi.org/10.1007/s10579-023-09704-w

32. Tiedemann, J., Thottingal, S.: OPUS-MT – Building open translation services for the World. In: Proceedings of the 22nd Annual Conference of the European Association for Machine Translation (EAMT). Lisbon, Portugal (2020)

33. Zhang, J., Zong, C., et al.: Deep neural networks in machine translation: an overview. IEEE Intell. Syst. **30**(5), 16–25 (2015)

# Dialogue Style Transfer
# with Reinforcement Learning
# and Parameter Efficient Fine-Tuning

Ruslan Pravosud[1]([⊠]) [iD], Oleksii Adamov[1] [iD], and Oleksandr Marchenko[1,2] [iD]

[1] Taras Shevchenko National University of Kyiv, Kyiv, Ukraine
{pronod9999,oleksii.v.adamov}@gmail.com, omarchenko@univ.kiev.ua
[2] Institute of Information Technologies and Systems of the National Academy of
Sciences of Ukraine, Kyiv, Ukraine

**Abstract.** This paper focuses on applying reinforcement learning and parameter efficient fine-tuning methods to train NLP model to generate dialogue utters in a style of a specific character. The goal is to fine-tune relatively small model that will not consume a lot of computing resources and can be deployed and used on a single machine. As a result, this resource efficient method can be used for implementation of character-specific chat bots playing role of a specific character, generating fiction stories or new data sets. We propose using PPO algorithm together with LoRA to fine-tune GPT2 model to generate a character style utterances. For the reward function, BERT model was trained to distinguish between the desired style texts and regular ones, BERTScore and Self-BLUE were used to improve the dialogue flow quality. Dataset for training was generated with GPT4-mini.

**Keywords:** NLP · RL · PEFT · LoRA · PPO

## 1 Introduction

In recent years, large language models (LLMs) have demonstrated remarkable abilities in generating natural language text across a variety of applications, including dialogue systems, story generation, and personalized content creation. However, fine-tuning such models for specific tasks or stylistic outputs often demands substantial computational resources, making their deployment on resource-constrained devices impractical. The challenge, therefore, is to enable stylistic fine-tuning in a resource-efficient manner while maintaining high-quality output.

The ability to mimic a specific character's dialogue style can have profound implications for entertainment, education, and human-computer interaction. Applications such as character-specific chatbots, immersive role-playing experiences, and custom fiction generation require models capable of producing stylistically consistent and contextually relevant dialogue. Traditional fine-tuning methods, however, often involve updating all model parameters, leading to prohibitive resource requirements.

G. De Tré et al. (Eds.): FQAS 2025, LNAI 16119, pp. 232–240, 2026.
https://doi.org/10.1007/978-3-032-05607-8_22

To address this challenge, this paper explores a parameter-efficient fine-tuning approach combined with reinforcement learning to enable stylistic dialogue generation. Specifically, we propose the use of Proximal Policy Optimization (PPO), a reinforcement learning algorithm, alongside Low-Rank Adaptation (LoRA) to fine-tune a pre-trained GPT-2 model. This method allows for efficient adaptation of the model's behavior while keeping the number of trainable parameters low, ensuring feasibility for deployment on single machines.

A key component of our approach is the design of the reward function, which guides the model toward generating character-specific dialogue, while keeping dialogs coherent and diverse. For this purpose, we train a BERT-based classifier to distinguish between texts written in the target style and those that are not. This reward mechanism ensures that the fine-tuned model generates outputs aligned with the desired stylistic characteristics. Additionally, a GPT4-mini model is employed to generate the dataset used for training, ensuring diverse and high-quality inputs.

The main contributions of this work are as follows:

- A parameter-efficient fine-tuning pipeline: By leveraging LoRA, we achieve fine-tuning of GPT-2 with minimal resource requirements, enabling deployment on devices with limited computational capacity.
- Style-specific reinforcement learning: Using PPO and a style-sensitive reward function, the model learns to produce dialogue that closely aligns with the target character's style.
- Practical deployment for character-driven applications: The proposed approach is demonstrated to be effective in generating character-specific utterances, paving the way for applications in storytelling, chatbots, and data generation.

This paper presents a detailed methodology, experiments, and analysis of results to showcase the feasibility and effectiveness of our approach. By combining reinforcement learning with parameter-efficient fine-tuning, we offer a novel solution to the problem of stylistic dialogue generation that is both resource-conscious and scalable.

## 2 Related Works

The task of generating stylistically consistent text has been explored extensively in natural language processing (NLP), with significant progress achieved through advancements in large-scale pre-trained language models and fine-tuning techniques. In this section, we review three key areas relevant to our work: (1) style transfer in text generation, (2) reinforcement learning for fine-tuning language models, and (3) parameter-efficient fine-tuning approaches.

### 2.1 Style Transfer in Text Generation

Style transfer in NLP focuses on transforming a text while preserving its content but altering its stylistic attributes. Early approaches relied on rule-based systems and feature engineering to encode stylistic attributes. With the advent of deep learning, models like variational autoencoders (VAEs) and generative adversarial networks (GANs) have been applied for text style transfer.

Recent developments leverage pre-trained language models like GPT-2 and GPT-3 for stylistic text generation. For instance, work by Keskar et al. (2019) [1] demonstrated the use of control codes in GPT-based models for steering text generation toward desired styles. However, these methods often require extensive computational resources, limiting their applicability in resource-constrained environments. Our work addresses this limitation by using parameter-efficient fine-tuning combined with reinforcement learning to achieve stylistic consistency with minimal overhead.

## 2.2    Reinforcement Learning for Fine-Tuning Language Models

Reinforcement learning (RL) has been widely employed to fine-tune language models for tasks where explicit supervision is difficult to define. Proximal Policy Optimization (PPO) has emerged as a popular RL algorithm for fine-tuning models like GPT, particularly in open-ended generation tasks. For example, OpenAI's work on fine-tuning GPT models using human feedback (Stiennon et al., 2020) [2] showcased the effectiveness of PPO for aligning model outputs with user preferences.

In the context of stylistic generation, RL can be used to optimize a reward function that captures stylistic attributes. Previous studies, such as those by Luo et al. (2019) [3], have explored the use of RL for style transfer but often relied on manually crafted reward functions or large-scale fine-tuning. Our work extends this line of research by introducing a BERT-based reward model trained to distinguish target styles, which is used to guide the PPO optimization process.

## 2.3    Parameter-Efficient Fine-Tuning

Fine-tuning large language models typically involves updating all model parameters, making the process computationally expensive. Recent advancements in parameter-efficient fine-tuning methods, such as AdapterFusion (Pfeiffer et al., 2021) [4] and LoRA (Low-Rank Adaptation, Hu et al., 2021) [5], address this challenge by introducing lightweight, task-specific parameter modules. These methods enable the adaptation of pre-trained models to new tasks with minimal computational overhead and storage requirements.

LoRA, in particular, has gained attention for its simplicity and effectiveness in fine-tuning large-scale models. By injecting low-rank matrices into the model's attention mechanisms, LoRA allows for efficient adaptation without modifying the original model weights. Our approach integrates LoRA with PPO to achieve stylistic fine-tuning in a resource-efficient manner, demonstrating its suitability for deployment on single machines.

### 2.4    Dataset Generation and Synthetic Data

Generating high-quality datasets is often a bottleneck for stylistic fine-tuning tasks. Recent studies have explored the use of large models like GPT-3 or GPT-4 to generate synthetic datasets. For example, works by Schick et al. (2021) [6] demonstrated that synthetic data could effectively augment low-resource training scenarios. In our approach, we utilize GPT4-mini to generate a diverse and high-quality dataset, reducing reliance on manually labeled data while ensuring stylistic consistency.

## 3    Style Reward Model

### 3.1    Dataset Preparation

The dataset for training the reward model consists of two parts: Hypersniper Philosophy Dialogue dataset [7] (about 40%), and philosophical questions generated by GPT4-mini. This dataset comprises a collection of  1000 philosophical questions. Each question was afterwards used as an input prompt for GPT4-mini to generate two types of answers:

1. A response in the style of the philosopher Socrates.
2. A response from a regular person perspective.

This way, for each question we obtain two elements of dataset: one with "Socratic" and one with regular speech style response. Both of them were used for training, but with opposite labels. The generated pairs were processed into the following format:

**Person:** <question>
**Socrates:** <Socratic answer|Regular answer>

These structured pairs provided the training data for distinguishing stylistic differences between Socratic and regular utterances.

### 3.2    Model Training

A **DistilBERT** model [8] was fine-tuned to classify utterances as either Socratic or regular by assigning rewards. Positive rewards were expected for Socratic-style responses, while regular responses were assigned negative rewards. By reward here, logits' values of the model's outputs are meant.

### 3.3    Model Evaluation

The reward model was evaluated using a test dataset, consisting of 20% of the original dataset. Results demonstrated:

- An **average reward of** $> 3.0$ for Socrates-style responses.
- An **average reward of** $< -3.0$ for regular responses.
- A **99.5% accuracy** in distinguishing between Socratic and regular pairs by comparing their rewards.

# 4   Main Model

GPT2-large [9] (800M parameters) and GTP2 (125M parameters) pretrained models were enhanced using LoRA (Low-Rank Adaptation) by introducing additional low-rank matrices for the Q, K, and V components of transformer layers, with a rank of 32. These additional layers were the only ones fine-tuned, accounting for less than 1% of the total model parameters: 5,898,240/779,928,320 and 1,179,648/125,620,225 correspondingly.

## 4.1   Initial Fine-Tuning

To better capture the desired style of speech, we firstly fine-tune the models in a regular way against cross-entropy loss. 1-turn dialogs (the same ones we used in 3.1) with Socrates are presented as training dataset for this subtask in the format:

**Person:** <question>
**Socrates:** <answer>

Then we evaluate the model on test dataset, achieving an average reward of **3.123216** with standard deviation of **0.068859** for GPT2-Large and an average reward of **3.120361** with standard deviation of **0.074097** for GPT2.

## 4.2   RL Fine-Tuning

**Reward Function.** To improve dialogue coherence we incorporate usage of BERTScore [10] - metric for evaluating text similarity using contextual embeddings from BERT to capture semantic meaning by measuring how logically connected are the previous part of the dialogue and the generated response.

For encouragement of diverse and engaging responses we use Self-BLUE metric [11], which promotes diverse and engaging responses by penalizing repetitions among the model's responses within the dialogue.

StyleReward we get from the reward model is unscaled and varies in range [-3.75; 3.28]. To ensure it is on the same order of magnitude as the other rewards, we apply min-max scaling.

$$Reward = \lambda_1 * StyleReward + \lambda_2 * BERTScore + \lambda_3 * (1 - SelfBLUE) \quad (1)$$

$\lambda_1 + \lambda_2 + \lambda_3 = 1$ - hyperparameter coefficients to toggle the rewards' importance. We treat the rewards as equally important by setting every $\lambda_i = 0.33$.

## 4.3   Dataset Preparation

For training the main model, the dataset used in reward model training was updated. For every question, we generate an answer by our model, fine-tuned in (4.1). Afterwards, we continue the dialogue by an answer generated with GPT4-mini, playing a role of a regular person talking with Socrates, whose utterances are generated by our model. Eventually, a prompt has the next structure:

**Person:** \<question>
**Socrates:** \<answer generated by prefine-tuned model>
**Person:** \<A line generated by GPT4-mini>
**Socrates:** Then, our model generates an answer, based on the prompt received, continuing the dialogue.

### 4.4   Model Training

The PPO (Proximal Policy Optimization) [12] reinforcement learning method was applied for fine-tuning. The training process involved:

1. Feeding prompts from the dataset to the model.
2. Scoring the model's responses using the reward model.
   (a) The style reward is obtained by appending the response to the last utterance from the Person in the prompt and evaluating the second turn of the dialogue.
   (b) BERTScore takes as its inputs the prompt and the response as distinct arguments and evaluates the coherence of the generated utterance
   (c) SelfBLUE is evaluated by comparing the generated response to the history of the model responses in this dialogue. In this case, the history is only an answer generated by the model for the initial question.
3. Using the rewards to compute gradients and update the LoRA weights. The same weights that were fine tuned at (4.1) are getting updated here, so the general number of updated parameters remains the same.

### 4.5   Model Evaluation

During inference, the test dataset was used for evaluation. The prompts were constructed in the same format as during the training.

Performance comparison of models on the test dataset

| Model | Style reward mean | Style reward std | BERTScore mean | BERTScore std | 1 - Self-BLUE mean | 1 - Self-BLUE std | Weighted reward mean |
|---|---|---|---|---|---|---|---|
| GPT2 before PPO | 2.66 | 1.24 | 0.1 | 0.06 | 0.97 | 0.06 | 1.24 |
| GPT2 after PPO | 2.74 | 1.12 | 0.07 | 0.07 | 0.98 | 0.05 | 1.26 |
| GPT2-Large before PPO | 2.71 | 0.94 | 0.14 | 0.06 | 0.98 | 0.04 | 1.3 |
| GPT2-Large after PPO | 2.87 | 0.77 | 0.14 | 0.06 | 0.99 | 0.03 | 1.32 |

After the RL fine-tuning, both models improve their performance on the task of generating the second-turn response in a dialogue. The engagement score produced by 1 - Self-BLUE reward is pretty high and stable, meaning that the responses generated on the second turn are original and do not repeat the previous ones. BERTScore here is not that high and stable, yet the generated text looks pretty well related to the general dialogue topics. GPT2 results are a bit worse, yet still pretty good compared to GPT2-Large, despite having almost 7 times less parameters.

## 4.6    Generated Examples

**Question:** Which sensory experiences (sound, sight, touch) hold the most emotional weight for you?

**Our model Socrates responses:**

**Person:** Which sensory experiences (sound, sight, touch) hold the most emotional weight for you?

**Socrates:** My friend, to ponder the nature of sensation and emotion we must first examine the nature of the senses themselves. Sound, for example, evokes feelings and the presence of sound in space can inspire empathy. In tandem, sight captures the presence and context of the world around us, making experiences rich with meaning and context.

**Person:** For me, sound and touch hold the most emotional weight; a familiar song can instantly transport me to a cherished memory, while a comforting touch can provide solace in times of distress.

**Socrates:** What do you mean by "the most emotional weight"? What do these experiences evoke?

**Regular GPT-2:**

**Person:** Which sensory experiences (sound, sight, touch) hold the most emotional weight for you?

**Socrates:** I think that suffering is an inherent feature of existence. There are several ways the human body works, and this is one way of thinking of it. If you want to be sure you are a good person, you can do.

**Person:** I think that the world around you is made up of many different parts. Do you think that one person does all the work of the other?

**Socrates:** I think that each person has his own set of abilities and needs.

**Question:** What are the implications of viewing suffering as inherent to existence?

**Our model Socrates responses:**

**Person:** What are the implications of viewing suffering as inherent to existence?

**Socrates:** Ah, my friend, let us engage in the contemplation of suffering as fundamentally intertwined with existence. Suffering, in its essence, can serve as a guide to understanding our own condition, and the nature of our existence.

**Person:** Viewing suffering as inherent to existence suggests that it can lead to deeper insights about life, fostering resilience and empathy. Embracing this perspective may encourage us to seek meaning and connection through our shared experiences of hardship.

**Socrates:** Ah, my understanding of suffering as inherent to existence can lead us to appreciate that suffering is inevitable and unavoidable for us as we confront seemingly insurmountable obstacles.

**Regular GPT-2:**

**Person:** What are the implications of viewing suffering as inherent to existence?

**Socrates:** Well, if you're to believe that suffering is a natural part of existence, then it's absolutely necessary to consider suffering as an inherent part of its own reality.

**Person:** But what about the consequences of viewing suffering as inherent to life?

**Socrates:** Well, if you're to believe that life is a natural part of life, then it's absolutely necessary to consider suffering as being inherent to life.

Comparing the responses of our model vs regular GPT-2 ones, we can see that they look more engaging, diverse and more "Socrates"-like.

## 5   Conclusion

This paper presents a resource-efficient approach to training language models for generating dialogue in the style of a specific character, using a combination of reinforcement learning and parameter-efficient fine-tuning. The proposed method integrates the Proximal Policy Optimization (PPO) algorithm with Low-Rank Adaptation (LoRA) to fine-tune a GPT-2 Large and GPT2 models while keeping computational requirements minimal. The reward function, driven by a DistilBERT-based classifier, ensures that the model consistently generates outputs aligned with the desired style, engagement reward constructed as 1 - Self-BLUE metric helps to keep the dialogue engaging, and BERTScore is a part of reward guiding the model to generate coherent responses.

The proposed methodology can be applied in various domains, including:

- **Character-Specific Chatbots:** Creating dialogue systems that mimic historical figures, fictional characters, or personalities.
- **Storytelling Applications:** Generating character-consistent narratives in fiction writing.
- **Synthetic Data Generation:** Producing stylistically diverse datasets for training or evaluation purposes.

Despite these successes, there are areas for future exploration:

1. **Broader Style Generalization:** Extending the method to support multiple characters or styles simultaneously.
2. **Reward Function Refinement:** Incorporating human feedback or alternative scoring mechanisms to further improve alignment.
3. **Scaling to Smaller Models:** Investigating the scalability of the approach with smaller pre-trained models, for example distilled models or quantized ones.

In conclusion, this work demonstrates that combining reinforcement learning with parameter-efficient fine-tuning offers a practical solution for stylistic text generation, enabling resource-conscious deployment of character-specific NLP models. The results highlight the potential of this approach to advance applications in personalized AI and creative content generation.

**Disclosure of Interests.** The authors have no competing interests.

# References

1. Keskar, N.S., et al.: Ctrl: A conditional transformer language model for controllable generation. arXiv preprint arXiv:1909.05858 (2019)
2. Stiennon, N., et al.: Learning to summarize with human feedback. Adv. Neural Inf. Process. Syst. **33**, 3008–3021 (2020)
3. Luo, F., et al.: A dual reinforcement learning framework for unsupervised text style transfer. arXiv preprint arXiv:1905.10060 (2019)
4. Pfeiffer, J., et al.: AdapterFusion: Non-destructive task composition for transfer learning. arXiv preprint arXiv:2005.00247 (2020)
5. Hu, E.J., et al.: LoRA: Low-rank adaptation of large language models. arXiv preprint arXiv:2106.09685 (2021)
6. Schick, T., Schütze, H.: It's not just size that matters: Small language models are also few-shot learners. arXiv preprint arXiv:2009.07118 (2020)
7. Hypersniper philosophy dialog. https://huggingface.co/datasets/Hypersniper/philosophy_dialogue. Accessed 26 Jan 2025
8. Sanh, V.: DistilBERT, a distilled version of BERT: smaller, faster, cheaper and lighter. arXiv preprint arXiv:1910.01108 (2019)
9. Radford, A., et al.: Language models are unsupervised multitask learners. OpenAI Blog **1**(8), 9 (2019)
10. Zhang, T., et al.: BERTScore: Evaluating text generation with BERT. arXiv preprint arXiv:1904.09675 (2019)
11. Zhu, Y., et al.: Texygen: a benchmarking platform for text generation models. The 41st International ACM SIGIR Conference on Research & Development in Information Retrieval (2018)
12. Schulman, J., et al.: Proximal policy optimization algorithms. arXiv preprint arXiv:1707.06347 (2017)

# Intuitionistic Fuzzy Approaches for Flexible Querying and Reasoning under Uncertainty

# InterCriteria Analysis of Youth Not in Employment, Education or Training in the EU: Revealing Structural Analysis Through Intuitionistic Fuzzy Evaluations

Sotir Sotirov[1]([✉]) and Rumiana Zheleva[2]

[1] "Prof. Yakimov" Blvd., Assen Zlatarov University, Burgas 8010, Bulgaria
ssotorov@btu.bg
[2] Institute of Philosophy and Sociology at BAS, Sofia, Bulgaria

**Abstract.** This paper applies InterCriteria Analysis (ICrA), grounded in intuitionistic fuzzy logic, to investigate the systemic inconsistencies among key indicators related to youth classified as NEET (Not in Employment, Education, or Training) within the European Union. Using Eurostat data from 2002 to 2023, the study focuses on multidimensional parameters such as urban-rural disparities, gender differences, educational attainment, and labor market participation. The intuitionistic fuzzy approach enables the detection of logical confirmation ($\mu$), contradiction ($\nu$), and hesitation ($\pi$) among criteria, offering a nuanced semantic interpretation beyond linear correlations. The results show a predominant concentration of country-pair evaluations in the dissonance zones, with over 88% falling into the "Dissonance" or "Strong Dissonance" categories, highlighting structural divergence among EU member states. The findings emphasize the limitations of universal policy solutions and the necessity for context-sensitive, data-driven interventions in tackling youth exclusion. ICrA proves to be a robust analytical tool for modeling complex socio-economic interdependencies and guiding evidence-based policymaking.

**Keywords:** InterCriteria Analysis · Not in Employment · Education · Training

## 1 Introduction

The issue of labor force shortages in Europe has brought renewed attention to the problem of young people classified as NEET (Not in Employment, Education, or Training). This indicator, as defined by Eurostat, 2023 [16], captures individuals aged 15–29 who are excluded from both the labor market and educational systems, reflecting deeper structural vulnerabilities in society. The NEET phenomenon is not merely an economic concern but also a sociological one, as it underscores systemic inequalities in access to human capital development (HCD), spatial disparities, and intergenerational cycles of disadvantage [6, 11. NEET status often perpetuates intergenerational inequality, as disadvantaged youth lack access to cultural capital (e.g., networks, credentials) that facilitates labor market

G. De Tré et al. (Eds.): FQAS 2025, LNAI 16119, pp. 243–252, 2026.
https://doi.org/10.1007/978-3-032-05607-8_23

entry [7]. In knowledge-based economies, the devaluation of non-formal education exacerbates NEET rates, as youth without recognized qualifications face exclusion [12, 13]. Urban-rural divides in educational infrastructure and job opportunities disproportionately affect marginalized communities, a pattern evident in Bulgaria's rural regions versus Austria's or Germany's urban hubs. Some economic theories underline that NEETs represent underutilized human capital, where lack of investment in skills leads to diminished lifetime earnings and productivity losses [5]. NEETs often trapped in secondary labor markets (precarious, low-wage jobs) due to skill mismatches—a challenge acute when it comes to a large share of informal economy like in Bulgaria in comparison to other EU countries like Austria and Germany [14, 15]. Scientists from various scientific disciplines studying the NEETS phenomenon define it as a policy challenge. The "scarring effect" [4, 8–10] shows that prolonged NEET status reduces future employability, creating cycles of dependency and representing a multiracial societal challenge. This is compounded by technological disruption, which demands re-skilling, higher digital proficiency and lifelong learning of contemporary youth. Hence, the phenomenon of young people classified as NEET presents a complex challenge that demands interdisciplinary analysis. From a sociological perspective, NEET status reflects structural inequalities in education systems and labor markets, while from a computational modeling standpoint, it represents a multidimensional optimization problem for policy intervention [2].

## 2   Data and Indicators of Social Vulnerability Among NEET Youth in the EU

This article bridges these perspectives through an innovative framework combining indicators and variables used by Eurostat to collect data on NEETs in the EU member states. The key demographic and social indicators include the age groups: 15–24 and 25–29 years (with a focus on youth aged 15–29 for policy analysis); gender (distribution of NEETs by sex); geographical location: urban/rural areas (NUTS-2/NUTS-3 classification); migration status: (whether the individual was born in the country or is an immigrant). The key economic and labor market indicators include employment status: unemployed (actively seeking work and available for employment) and economically inactive (e.g., caring for children, long-term illness, discouraged workers). Additional indicators are available about the duration of NEET status (Short-term (<6 months) and Long-term (>12 months)). The third group of indicators concern educational indicators which are (highest level of education attained such as primary or lower; secondary education and tertiary education) as well as the reason for disengagement from education including financial difficulties; personal/family circumstances; lack of interest. The data sets include additional factors such as health status (chronic illnesses or disabilities); social isolation: lack of access to social networks or support systems and participation in activation programs: whether the individual has engaged in training/employment support schemes.

The data is gathered through and aggregated based on three European research infrastructures: 1. European Labour Force Survey (LFS) – Quarterly/annual surveys; 2. EU Statistics on Income and Living Conditions (EU-SILC) – Income and living conditions data. 3. National administrative records – Supplementary datasets from member states.

Currently in Bulgaria (2023), NEET indicators show the 7.2% NEET rate for ages 15–29 with gender disparity: 9.1% female vs. 5.3% male (mainly due to caregiving responsibilities). There are significant regional differences: e.g. Northwest (12.3%) – Highest rate due to economic stagnation and Southwest (4.8%) – Better outcomes linked to Sofia's labor market.

Understanding the dynamics of youth disengagement from the educational system and the labor market—captured under the NEET indicator (Not in Employment, Education or Training)—is becoming increasingly important for the development of data-driven social policies. The share of young people in NEET status not only reflects economic instability or weaknesses in the educational system but also signals deeper structural vulnerabilities such as limited access to lifelong learning, urban-rural inequalities, and intergenerational cycles of exclusion. To effectively interpret these multidimensional and temporally evolving processes, approaches that combine statistical data with intelligent methods of logical analysis are required.

Traditional statistical techniques often provide linear and isolated evaluations of the relationships between variables but fail to capture the logical coherence or contradiction among multiple socio-economic indicators. This study proposes the application of Intercriteria Analysis (ICrA) as a semantically and computationally intelligent method for detecting confirmation, contradiction, or indeterminacy among the criteria describing young people in NEET status within the European Union. The methodology is based on intuitionistic fuzzy logic, which introduces degrees of confirmation ($\mu$), contradiction ($\nu$), and hesitation ($\pi$), enabling a more refined and context-sensitive analysis.

The study is based on a rich longitudinal dataset from Eurostat covering the period 2002–2023, with particular focus on Bulgaria—a country that transitioned from one of the highest NEET rates (~19.7% in 2003) to significantly improved values (~7.2% in 2023). Figure 1 presents a comparative visualization of NEET trends in Bulgaria alongside other EU member states such as Germany, Italy, Greece, and Romania. The data reveals different developmental trajectories—while Germany consistently maintains low levels (below 5%) due to well-integrated vocational systems, southern countries face persistent structural difficulties.

Beyond trend visualization, the study applies intercriteria analysis across key dimensions such as degree of urbanization, gender, and participation in training. For example, the analysis shows that while there is strong confirmation between urbanization and NEET status at the beginning of the period, this relationship weakens in recent years— likely due to the digitalization of education and employment. In contrast, gender disparities remain consistently confirmed, with higher NEET shares among females, especially in rural areas.

The advantage of ICrA in this context is its ability to uncover hidden inconsistencies in policy outcomes, even when traditional metrics indicate improvement. This makes it a valuable tool not only for analysis but also for better strategic planning and adaptive social interventions.

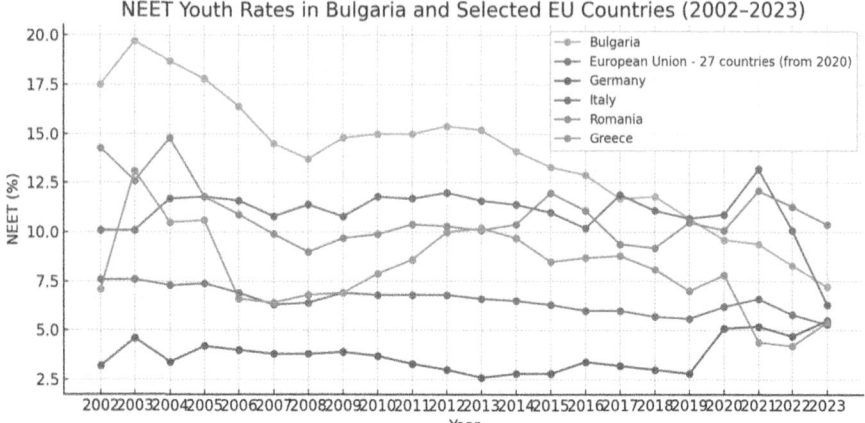

**Fig. 1.** Share of youth in NEET status in Bulgaria and selected EU countries (2002–2023)

## 3  Remarks on Intercriteria Analysis

Intercriteria Analysis (ICrA) is an innovative methodological approach based on the logic of intuitionistic fuzzy sets, which enables the identification of interdependencies, contradictions, and uncertainties among multiple criteria when evaluating alternatives in a multicriteria environment. Developed by Atanassov, Atanassova and Mavrov [2], the method builds upon classical multicriteria analysis techniques by introducing a flexible logical framework capable of capturing not only the degree of agreement between criteria ($\mu$), but also the degree of contradiction ($\nu$) and hesitation ($\pi$)—key elements in the analysis of complex systems.

Unlike traditional approaches that focus primarily on quantitative correlations or weight assignments, ICrA explores the logical relationships among criteria using expert-based or empirical data, generating an intercriteria matrix [3]. This matrix reflects how each pair of criteria interact across a set of alternatives, thus providing a rich semantic structure well-suited for analysis under conditions of uncertainty, incompleteness, or conflicting information.

ICrA has been applied in a wide range of fields—from sustainability assessment and strategic planning to social sciences and educational policy. Its ability to detect non-obvious logical relationships and reveal latent inconsistencies makes it a particularly valuable tool in the development of intelligent decision support systems. The method is compatible with both quantitative and qualitative evaluations and can be employed in deterministic as well as fuzzified analytical contexts. Thanks to its logical transparency and well-founded formalism, ICrA is emerging as a leading paradigm in contemporary interdisciplinary analysis of complex data.

The ICrA method [2] is based on two distinct concepts: intuitionistic fuzzy logic [1, 3] and index matrices [3].

Let $I$ be a fixed set of indices and let $R$ be the set of the real numbers. An index matrix (IM) with sets of indices $K$ and $L$ ($K, L \subset I$) is defined by

$$
[K, L, \{a_{k_i, l_j}\}] \equiv
\begin{array}{c|cccc}
 & l_1 & l_2 & \cdots & l_n \\
\hline
k_1 & a_{k_1, l_1} & a_{k_1, l_2} & \cdots & a_{k_1, l_n} \\
k_2 & a_{k_2, l_1} & a_{k_2, l_2} & \cdots & a_{k_2, l_n} \\
\vdots & \vdots & \vdots & \ddots & \vdots \\
k_m & a_{k_m, l_1} & a_{k_m, l_2} & \cdots & a_{k_m, l_n}
\end{array} \, ,
$$

where $K = \{k_1, k_2, \ldots, k_m\}$, $L = \{l_1, l_2, \ldots, l_n\}$, for $1 \leq i \leq m$, and $1 \leq j \leq n : a_{k_i, l_j} \in R$.

Let us consider an index matrix, denoted by M, with index sets consisting of m rows. $\{O_1, \ldots, O_m\}$ and $n$ columns $\{C_1, \ldots, C_n\}$, where for every $p, q$ ($1 \leq p \leq m$, $1 \leq q \leq n$), $O_p$ is an evaluated object, $C_q$ is an evaluation criterion, and $e_{O_p, C_q}$ is the evaluation of the $p$-th object against the $q$-th criterion, defined as a real number that is comparable according to relation $R$ with all the remaining elements of the IM $M$.

$$
M = 
\begin{array}{c|ccccccc}
 & C_1 & \cdots & C_k & \cdots & C_l & \cdots & C_n \\
\hline
O_1 & e_{O_1, C_1} & \cdots & e_{O_1, C_k} & \cdots & e_{O_1, C_l} & \cdots & e_{O_1, C_n} \\
\vdots & \vdots & \ddots & \vdots & \ddots & \vdots & \ddots & \vdots \\
O_i & e_{O_i, C_1} & \cdots & e_{O_i, C_k} & \cdots & e_{O_i, C_l} & \cdots & e_{O_i, C_n} \\
\vdots & \vdots & \ddots & \vdots & \ddots & \vdots & \ddots & \vdots \\
O_j & e_{O_j, C_1} & \cdots & e_{O_j, C_k} & \cdots & e_{O_j, C_l} & \cdots & e_{O_j, C_n} \\
\vdots & \vdots & \ddots & \vdots & \ddots & \vdots & \ddots & \vdots \\
O_m & e_{O_m, C_1} & \cdots & e_{O_m, C_j} & \cdots & e_{O_m, C_l} & \cdots & e_{O_m, C_n}
\end{array} \, ,
$$

From the requirement for comparability above, it follows that for each $i, j, k$ it holds the relation $R(e_{O_i, C_k}, e_{O_j, C_k})$. The relation $R$ has a dual relation $\overline{R}$, which is true in the cases when the relation $R$ is false, and vice versa. For instance, if R is "greater than", the dual relation $\overline{R}$ is "less than".

To obtain the results, pairwise comparisons are performed between every two different criteria across all evaluated objects. During the comparison, a counter is maintained for the number of times the relation R holds, and another counter—for its dual relation. Let $S_{k,l}^{\mu}$ be the number of cases in which the relations $R(e_{O_i, C_k}, e_{O_j, C_k})$ and $R(e_{O_i, C_l}, e_{O_j, C_l})$ are simultaneously satisfied. Let also $S_{k,l}^{\nu}$ be the number of cases in which the relations $R(e_{O_i, C_k}, e_{O_j, C_k})$ and its dual $\overline{R} = (e_{O_i, C_l}, e_{O_j, C_l})$ are simultaneously satisfied. As the total number of pairwise comparisons between the objects is given by $m(m-1)/2$, it can be verified that the following inequalities hold:
$$0 \leq S_{k,l}^{\mu} + S_{k,l}^{\nu} \leq \frac{m(m-1)}{2}.$$
For every $k, l$, such that $1 \leq k \leq l \leq n$, and for $m \geq 2$ two numbers are defined:

$$
\mu_{C_k, C_l} = 2 \frac{S_{k,l}^{\mu}}{m(m-1)}, \ \nu_{C_k, C_l} = 2 \frac{S_{k,l}^{\nu}}{m(m-1)}
$$

The pair formed by these two values serves as the intuitionistic fuzzy evaluation of the relations that can be established between any two criteria $C_k$ and $C_l$. In this way, the index matrix M, which links the evaluated objects with the evaluating criteria, can be transformed into another index matrix M, which represents the detected interrelations among the criteria, where a stronger correlation is observed when the first component is higher $\mu_{Ck,Cl}$ is higher while the second component $\nu_{Ck,Cl}$ is lower.

$$M* = \frac{\begin{array}{ccc} C_1 & \cdots & C_n \end{array}}{\begin{array}{c} C_1 \\ \cdots \\ C_n \end{array} \left| \begin{array}{ccc} \langle \mu_{C_1,C_1}, \nu_{C_1,C_1} \rangle & \cdots & \langle \mu_{C_1,C_n}, \nu_{C_1,C_n} \rangle \\ \cdots & \cdots & \cdots \\ \langle \mu_{C_n,C_1}, \nu_{C_n,C_1} \rangle & \cdots & \langle \mu_{C_n,C_n}, \nu_{C_n,C_n} \rangle \end{array} \right.}$$

From practical considerations, it has been more flexible to work with two IMs $M^\mu$ and $M^\nu$, rather than with the IM $M$ of IF pairs. IM $M^\mu$ contains as elements the first components of the IFPs of $M$, while $M^\nu$ - the second components of the IFPs of $M$. Once the intercriteria pairs have been calculated.

As it has been discussed in some publications on ICA, e.g. in [2], the ICA results are very close to those obtained with the correlation analyses of Kendal, Spearman and Pearson. It is worth noting the so far empirically observed fact that when in the data there are mistakes (e.g. shift of the decimal separator) these three correlation analyses give a larger deviation of the value than ICA, i.e. ICA is less sensitive, so the use of them together can be used as a way of detecting errors in the input data.

ICrA, grounded in intuitionistic fuzzy logic, enables the identification of dependencies between criteria and allows for interpreting their logical coherence across a set of alternatives. When applied to a dataset of country-pair comparisons based on selected indicators, the method evaluates the mutual confirmation or contradiction between criteria through pairs of values $< \mu; \nu >$. In this analysis, we focus solely on the first component—confirmation degree ($\mu$)—to classify results using an 11-interval logical scale ranging from "strongly negative consonance" ($\mu < 0.05$) to "strongly positive consonance" ($\mu \geq 0.95$).

## 4   ICrA for NEET Youth in the EU Member States

For the analysis, we use data [16] from Eurostat on the collection of information regarding NEET youth in the EU member states. The key demographic and social indicators include the following age groups: 15–24 and 25–29 years (with a focus on youth aged 15–29 for the purposes of policy analysis); gender (distribution of NEET youth by sex); geographical location: urban/rural areas (NUTS-2/NUTS-3 classification); and migration status (whether the individual was born in the country or is an immigrant) (Fig. 2).

After processing the full dataset of over 400 country pairs, the results show a remarkable concentration within intervals corresponding to *dissonance*, i.e., disagreement or weak compatibility between criteria across countries. The highest frequency is observed in the Dissonance (0.57–0.67) interval with 192 instances, followed by "Strong Dissonance" (0.43–0.57) with 180 cases, together accounting for 88% of all comparisons.

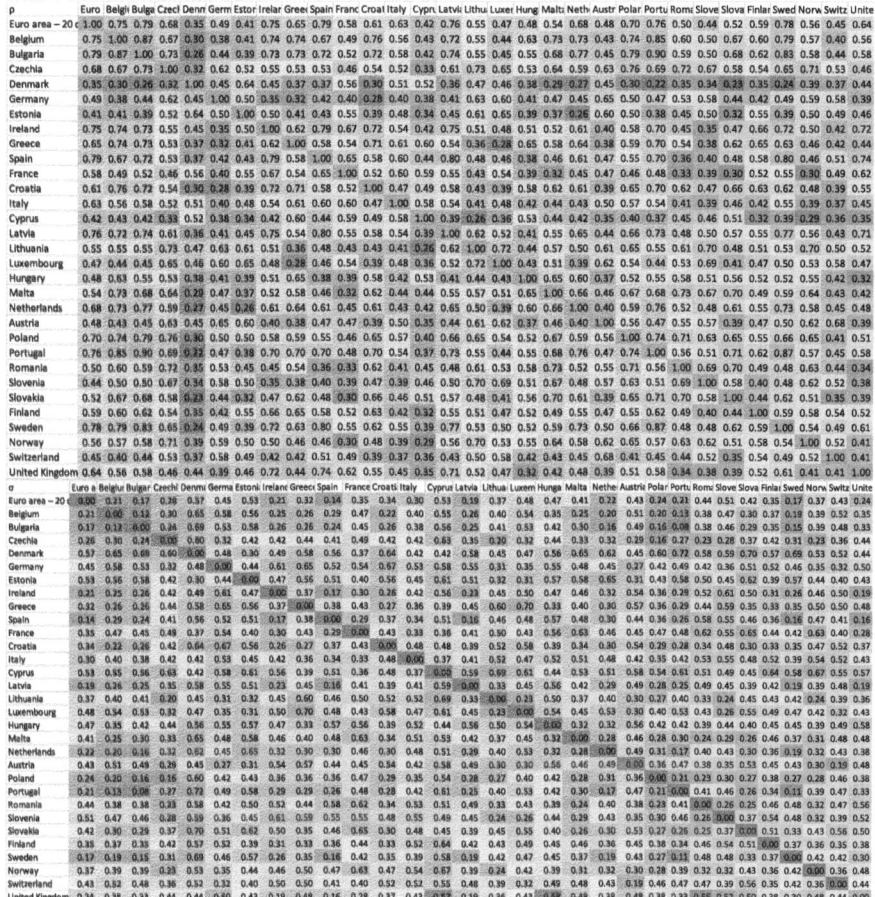

**Fig. 2.** Values of μ and ν.

This clearly indicates a systemic lack of confirmation among the analyzed criteria and suggests high heterogeneity in national approaches and outcomes, even within a shared policy context.

The "Weak Dissonance" (0.67–0.75) interval contains 67 entries, still notable but significantly smaller than the central group. Notably, entries falling into the agreement zone are relatively scarce— "Weak Positive Consonance" (0.75–0.85) includes just 19 cases, and "Positive Consonance" (0.85–0.95) only 4. No values fall into the "Strong Positive" or any of the negative consonance zones, revealing a pattern of moderate but systematic logical mismatches, without extreme polarizations.

The analysis of ICrA confirmation values reveals a strong dominance of logical dissonance among the examined comparisons. Specifically, 192 cases fall within the category of "Dissonance", and 180 cases are categorized as "Strong Dissonance", together comprising the overwhelming majority of the dataset. A smaller but still notable portion— 67 comparisons—falls under "Weak Dissonance", indicating moderate disagreement.

On the other end of the spectrum, the "Weak Positive Consonance" category includes 19 entries, and only 4 comparisons qualify as "Positive Consonance". Importantly, no comparisons were classified under the highest agreement category, "Strong Positive Consonance", nor under any of the negative consonance intervals, such as "Weak Negative", "Negative", or "Strong Negative Consonance". This distribution confirms a pattern of generally low to moderate agreement between criteria and an absence of extreme consensus or contradiction.

This distribution clearly shows that among the examined countries, logical instability among the criteria prevails, regardless of their thematic or structural origin. It questions the effectiveness of uniform policy approaches and indicates a need for contextualized, flexible interventions tailored to individual country profiles. In this respect, Intercriteria Analysis proves to be an invaluable tool for such in-depth interpretations.

It would be interesting to observe the development across the years (Fig. 3).

| σ | 2003 | 2004 | 2005 | 2006 | 2007 | 2008 | 2009 | 2010 | 2011 | 2012 | 2013 | 2014 | 2015 | 2016 | 2017 | 2018 | 2019 | 2020 | 2021 | 2022 | 2023 |
|---|---|---|---|---|---|---|---|---|---|---|---|---|---|---|---|---|---|---|---|---|---|
| 2003 | 0 | 0.111 | 0.175 | 0.234 | 0.22 | 0.23 | 0.26 | 0.236 | 0.226 | 0.228 | 0.202 | 0.232 | 0.22 | 0.238 | 0.254 | 0.284 | 0.248 | 0.272 | 0.403 | 0.413 | 0.464 |
| 2004 | 0.111 | 0 | 0.157 | 0.232 | 0.21 | 0.25 | 0.258 | 0.242 | 0.222 | 0.234 | 0.22 | 0.216 | 0.222 | 0.254 | 0.26 | 0.278 | 0.266 | 0.288 | 0.393 | 0.387 | 0.431 |
| 2005 | 0.175 | 0.157 | 0 | 0.157 | 0.212 | 0.224 | 0.268 | 0.224 | 0.206 | 0.194 | 0.188 | 0.212 | 0.208 | 0.214 | 0.212 | 0.248 | 0.208 | 0.238 | 0.383 | 0.347 | 0.452 |
| 2006 | 0.234 | 0.232 | 0.157 | 0 | 0.105 | 0.131 | 0.169 | 0.133 | 0.139 | 0.131 | 0.135 | 0.179 | 0.143 | 0.171 | 0.155 | 0.212 | 0.177 | 0.183 | 0.339 | 0.347 | 0.429 |
| 2007 | 0.22 | 0.21 | 0.212 | 0.105 | 0 | 0.097 | 0.109 | 0.101 | 0.111 | 0.101 | 0.137 | 0.163 | 0.137 | 0.169 | 0.165 | 0.202 | 0.171 | 0.196 | 0.353 | 0.361 | 0.377 |
| 2008 | 0.23 | 0.25 | 0.224 | 0.131 | 0.097 | 0 | 0.067 | 0.052 | 0.075 | 0.085 | 0.093 | 0.141 | 0.147 | 0.129 | 0.139 | 0.155 | 0.153 | 0.153 | 0.339 | 0.343 | 0.359 |
| 2009 | 0.26 | 0.258 | 0.268 | 0.169 | 0.109 | 0.067 | 0 | 0.058 | 0.087 | 0.101 | 0.125 | 0.153 | 0.167 | 0.171 | 0.155 | 0.155 | 0.202 | 0.183 | 0.351 | 0.353 | 0.371 |
| 2010 | 0.236 | 0.242 | 0.224 | 0.133 | 0.101 | 0.052 | 0.058 | 0 | 0.036 | 0.063 | 0.095 | 0.117 | 0.127 | 0.137 | 0.121 | 0.145 | 0.161 | 0.153 | 0.329 | 0.329 | 0.371 |
| 2011 | 0.226 | 0.222 | 0.206 | 0.139 | 0.111 | 0.075 | 0.087 | 0.036 | 0 | 0.046 | 0.079 | 0.115 | 0.123 | 0.139 | 0.137 | 0.147 | 0.163 | 0.171 | 0.339 | 0.351 | 0.405 |
| 2012 | 0.228 | 0.234 | 0.194 | 0.131 | 0.101 | 0.085 | 0.101 | 0.063 | 0.046 | 0 | 0.065 | 0.085 | 0.095 | 0.135 | 0.127 | 0.151 | 0.149 | 0.151 | 0.335 | 0.343 | 0.397 |
| 2013 | 0.202 | 0.22 | 0.188 | 0.135 | 0.137 | 0.093 | 0.125 | 0.095 | 0.079 | 0.065 | 0 | 0.071 | 0.095 | 0.113 | 0.111 | 0.121 | 0.133 | 0.133 | 0.331 | 0.351 | 0.385 |
| 2014 | 0.232 | 0.216 | 0.212 | 0.179 | 0.163 | 0.141 | 0.153 | 0.117 | 0.115 | 0.085 | 0.071 | 0 | 0.075 | 0.093 | 0.091 | 0.085 | 0.115 | 0.113 | 0.282 | 0.31 | 0.341 |
| 2015 | 0.22 | 0.222 | 0.208 | 0.143 | 0.137 | 0.147 | 0.167 | 0.127 | 0.123 | 0.095 | 0.095 | 0.075 | 0 | 0.069 | 0.067 | 0.121 | 0.101 | 0.111 | 0.292 | 0.3 | 0.345 |
| 2016 | 0.238 | 0.254 | 0.214 | 0.171 | 0.169 | 0.129 | 0.171 | 0.137 | 0.139 | 0.135 | 0.113 | 0.093 | 0.069 | 0 | 0.048 | 0.089 | 0.089 | 0.093 | 0.286 | 0.282 | 0.335 |
| 2017 | 0.254 | 0.26 | 0.212 | 0.155 | 0.165 | 0.139 | 0.155 | 0.121 | 0.137 | 0.127 | 0.111 | 0.091 | 0.067 | 0.048 | 0 | 0.069 | 0.093 | 0.093 | 0.282 | 0.28 | 0.347 |
| 2018 | 0.284 | 0.278 | 0.248 | 0.212 | 0.202 | 0.155 | 0.155 | 0.145 | 0.147 | 0.151 | 0.121 | 0.085 | 0.121 | 0.089 | 0.069 | 0 | 0.111 | 0.105 | 0.27 | 0.268 | 0.306 |
| 2019 | 0.248 | 0.266 | 0.208 | 0.177 | 0.171 | 0.153 | 0.202 | 0.161 | 0.163 | 0.149 | 0.133 | 0.115 | 0.101 | 0.089 | 0.093 | 0.111 | 0 | 0.089 | 0.274 | 0.294 | 0.327 |
| 2020 | 0.272 | 0.288 | 0.238 | 0.183 | 0.196 | 0.153 | 0.183 | 0.153 | 0.171 | 0.151 | 0.133 | 0.113 | 0.111 | 0.093 | 0.093 | 0.105 | 0.089 | 0 | 0.262 | 0.288 | 0.325 |
| 2021 | 0.403 | 0.393 | 0.383 | 0.339 | 0.353 | 0.339 | 0.351 | 0.329 | 0.339 | 0.335 | 0.331 | 0.282 | 0.292 | 0.286 | 0.282 | 0.27 | 0.274 | 0.262 | 0 | 0.167 | 0.2 |
| 2022 | 0.413 | 0.387 | 0.347 | 0.347 | 0.361 | 0.343 | 0.353 | 0.329 | 0.351 | 0.343 | 0.351 | 0.31 | 0.3 | 0.282 | 0.28 | 0.268 | 0.294 | 0.288 | 0.167 | 0 | 0.196 |
| 2023 | 0.464 | 0.431 | 0.452 | 0.429 | 0.377 | 0.359 | 0.371 | 0.371 | 0.405 | 0.397 | 0.385 | 0.341 | 0.345 | 0.335 | 0.347 | 0.306 | 0.327 | 0.325 | 0.2 | 0.196 | 0 |

| ρ | 2003 | 2004 | 2005 | 2006 | 2007 | 2008 | 2009 | 2010 | 2011 | 2012 | 2013 | 2014 | 2015 | 2016 | 2017 | 2018 | 2019 | 2020 | 2021 | 2022 | 2023 |
|---|---|---|---|---|---|---|---|---|---|---|---|---|---|---|---|---|---|---|---|---|---|
| 2003 | 1.00 | 0.88 | 0.81 | 0.75 | 0.77 | 0.74 | 0.72 | 0.74 | 0.76 | 0.76 | 0.78 | 0.75 | 0.77 | 0.75 | 0.73 | 0.70 | 0.74 | 0.72 | 0.58 | 0.57 | 0.52 |
| 2004 | 0.88 | 1.00 | 0.83 | 0.76 | 0.78 | 0.73 | 0.73 | 0.74 | 0.77 | 0.76 | 0.77 | 0.77 | 0.77 | 0.74 | 0.73 | 0.71 | 0.73 | 0.71 | 0.60 | 0.60 | 0.56 |
| 2005 | 0.81 | 0.83 | 1.00 | 0.83 | 0.77 | 0.75 | 0.71 | 0.75 | 0.78 | 0.79 | 0.79 | 0.77 | 0.78 | 0.77 | 0.76 | 0.73 | 0.77 | 0.75 | 0.60 | 0.63 | 0.53 |
| 2006 | 0.75 | 0.76 | 0.83 | 1.00 | 0.88 | 0.84 | 0.81 | 0.84 | 0.85 | 0.86 | 0.85 | 0.80 | 0.84 | 0.82 | 0.82 | 0.77 | 0.81 | 0.81 | 0.65 | 0.64 | 0.56 |
| 2007 | 0.77 | 0.78 | 0.77 | 0.88 | 1.00 | 0.87 | 0.87 | 0.88 | 0.88 | 0.89 | 0.85 | 0.82 | 0.85 | 0.82 | 0.81 | 0.78 | 0.81 | 0.79 | 0.63 | 0.62 | 0.61 |
| 2008 | 0.74 | 0.73 | 0.75 | 0.84 | 0.87 | 1.00 | 0.91 | 0.91 | 0.89 | 0.87 | 0.82 | 0.82 | 0.84 | 0.83 | 0.81 | 0.82 | 0.82 | 0.82 | 0.63 | 0.63 | 0.61 |
| 2009 | 0.72 | 0.73 | 0.71 | 0.81 | 0.87 | 0.91 | 1.00 | 0.91 | 0.89 | 0.88 | 0.85 | 0.82 | 0.81 | 0.81 | 0.83 | 0.82 | 0.78 | 0.80 | 0.63 | 0.62 | 0.61 |
| 2010 | 0.74 | 0.74 | 0.75 | 0.84 | 0.88 | 0.91 | 0.91 | 1.00 | 0.94 | 0.91 | 0.88 | 0.86 | 0.85 | 0.84 | 0.85 | 0.83 | 0.82 | 0.82 | 0.64 | 0.65 | 0.60 |
| 2011 | 0.76 | 0.77 | 0.78 | 0.85 | 0.88 | 0.89 | 0.89 | 0.94 | 1.00 | 0.94 | 0.91 | 0.86 | 0.86 | 0.85 | 0.84 | 0.84 | 0.82 | 0.82 | 0.64 | 0.63 | 0.58 |
| 2012 | 0.76 | 0.76 | 0.79 | 0.86 | 0.89 | 0.89 | 0.88 | 0.91 | 0.94 | 1.00 | 0.92 | 0.90 | 0.89 | 0.85 | 0.86 | 0.83 | 0.84 | 0.84 | 0.65 | 0.64 | 0.59 |
| 2013 | 0.78 | 0.77 | 0.79 | 0.85 | 0.85 | 0.87 | 0.85 | 0.88 | 0.91 | 0.92 | 1.00 | 0.91 | 0.89 | 0.87 | 0.86 | 0.86 | 0.85 | 0.85 | 0.65 | 0.63 | 0.60 |
| 2014 | 0.75 | 0.77 | 0.77 | 0.80 | 0.82 | 0.82 | 0.82 | 0.86 | 0.86 | 0.90 | 0.91 | 1.00 | 0.92 | 0.89 | 0.89 | 0.90 | 0.87 | 0.87 | 0.70 | 0.67 | 0.64 |
| 2015 | 0.77 | 0.77 | 0.78 | 0.84 | 0.85 | 0.82 | 0.81 | 0.85 | 0.86 | 0.89 | 0.89 | 0.92 | 1.00 | 0.92 | 0.92 | 0.86 | 0.89 | 0.88 | 0.69 | 0.68 | 0.64 |
| 2016 | 0.75 | 0.74 | 0.77 | 0.82 | 0.82 | 0.84 | 0.81 | 0.84 | 0.85 | 0.85 | 0.87 | 0.89 | 0.92 | 1.00 | 0.93 | 0.90 | 0.90 | 0.90 | 0.70 | 0.70 | 0.65 |
| 2017 | 0.73 | 0.73 | 0.76 | 0.82 | 0.81 | 0.83 | 0.83 | 0.85 | 0.84 | 0.86 | 0.86 | 0.89 | 0.92 | 0.93 | 1.00 | 0.91 | 0.89 | 0.89 | 0.69 | 0.70 | 0.63 |
| 2018 | 0.70 | 0.71 | 0.73 | 0.77 | 0.78 | 0.81 | 0.82 | 0.83 | 0.84 | 0.83 | 0.86 | 0.90 | 0.86 | 0.90 | 0.91 | 1.00 | 0.87 | 0.88 | 0.71 | 0.71 | 0.68 |
| 2019 | 0.74 | 0.73 | 0.77 | 0.81 | 0.81 | 0.82 | 0.78 | 0.82 | 0.82 | 0.84 | 0.85 | 0.87 | 0.89 | 0.90 | 0.89 | 0.87 | 1.00 | 0.90 | 0.71 | 0.69 | 0.66 |
| 2020 | 0.72 | 0.71 | 0.75 | 0.81 | 0.79 | 0.82 | 0.80 | 0.82 | 0.82 | 0.84 | 0.85 | 0.87 | 0.88 | 0.90 | 0.89 | 0.88 | 0.90 | 1.00 | 0.72 | 0.70 | 0.66 |
| 2021 | 0.58 | 0.60 | 0.60 | 0.65 | 0.63 | 0.63 | 0.63 | 0.64 | 0.64 | 0.65 | 0.65 | 0.70 | 0.69 | 0.70 | 0.69 | 0.69 | 0.71 | 0.72 | 1.00 | 0.81 | 0.78 |
| 2022 | 0.57 | 0.60 | 0.63 | 0.64 | 0.62 | 0.63 | 0.62 | 0.65 | 0.63 | 0.64 | 0.63 | 0.67 | 0.68 | 0.70 | 0.70 | 0.71 | 0.69 | 0.70 | 0.81 | 1.00 | 0.79 |
| 2023 | 0.52 | 0.56 | 0.53 | 0.56 | 0.61 | 0.61 | 0.61 | 0.60 | 0.58 | 0.59 | 0.60 | 0.64 | 0.64 | 0.65 | 0.63 | 0.68 | 0.66 | 0.66 | 0.78 | 0.79 | 1.00 |

**Fig. 3.** Values of μ and ν

The results of the inter-criteria analysis, based on confirmation values (μ) in a temporal context, show distinct trends towards logical agreement between the criteria in a significant proportion of observed cases. The largest share of values falls within the interval "Weak Positive Consonance" (0.75–0.85)—78 instances, suggesting the presence of moderate but meaningful confirmation between most criteria across different time periods. This is a positive indicator of consistency in dynamics among key indicators reflecting social, economic, or political processes.

The second most frequent category is "Positive Consonance" (0.85–0.95), with 59 instances, indicating clearly pronounced logical compatibility between the compared criteria. The combination of these two categories shows that more than 60% of the values are in the zone of positive logical association, indicating stable and compatible trends over time.

Conversely, in the zones of dissonance, we observe moderate presence. The interval "Dissonance" (0.57–0.67) contains 36 cases, while "Weak Dissonance" (0.67–0.75) contains 33 cases. This suggests that although some criteria display logical divergence over time, this is not a prevailing characteristic. The category "Strong Dissonance" (0.43–0.57) includes only 4 cases, indicating that strong contradictions among criteria over time are rare.

There are no values in the intervals representing negative consonance, which can be interpreted as the absence of logical opposition or rejection between criteria. This fact further strengthens the conclusion that, from a dynamic perspective, the criteria demonstrate a high degree of logical compatibility and can reliably be used for interpreting long-term dependencies.

In summary, the analysis indicates a predominantly positive logical profile of the criteria over time, with a clear tendency towards coherence, stability, and logical structure in inter-criteria relationships. This makes inter-criteria analysis not only applicable but highly recommended for analyzing temporal data in an interdisciplinary context.

## 5 Conclusions

NEET is not just a labor market issue—it's a mirror of societal structures, and cracking it demands both sociological insight and computational intelligence. Reducing NEET rates requires a systems-thinking approach—one that combines sociological diagnostics (to identify root causes) with advanced mathematical tools (to model intervention impacts). Without this dual lens, policies risk addressing symptoms rather than systemic drivers of youth disengagement.

The conducted InterCriteria Analysis (ICrA), based on intuitionistic fuzzy logic and applied to temporally structured datasets from Eurostat (2002–2023), reveals a predominantly coherent and logically consistent relationship among the evaluated criteria associated with youth disengagement (NEET status) across the European Union. The temporal distribution of confirmation values ($\mu$) indicates that a substantial proportion of inter-criteria comparisons fall within the zones of "Weak Positive Consonance" (0.75–0.85) and "Positive Consonance" (0.85–0.95), accounting for over 60% of all cases. This empirical pattern suggests a stable and semantically meaningful interdependence among indicators over time, reinforcing the reliability of the analytical framework for longitudinal interpretation.

Conversely, the occurrence of dissonant relationships—represented by the intervals "Weak Dissonance" (0.67–0.75), "Dissonance" (0.57–0.67), and "Strong Dissonance"

(0.43–0.57)—is comparatively limited, while the complete absence of values in the negative consonance intervals indicates a lack of systemic logical contradiction. This asymmetry in the distribution further validates the internal consistency and suitability of the selected indicators for temporal modeling and policy assessment.

Overall, the findings affirm the methodological robustness and interpretative capacity of ICrA in analyzing complex, multi-criteria social phenomena. The observed logical coherence across time supports the applicability of the approach in interdisciplinary research contexts and underlines its relevance for evidence-based policy formulation addressing youth exclusion in Europe.

**Acknowledgement.** This research was funded by Burgas State University, Prof. Dr. Asen Zlatarov, Project: UNITe, BG16RFPR002-1.014-0004.

# References

1. Atanassov, K.: Intuitionistic fuzzy logics. Springer Cham (2017)
2. Atanassov, K., Mavrov, D., Atanassova, V.: InterCriteria decision making: a new approach for multicriteria decision making, based on index matrices and intuitionistic fuzzy sets. Issues Intuitionistic Fuzzy Sets Generalized Nets **11**, 1–8 (2014)
3. Atanassov, K.: Index matrices: towards an augmented matrix calculus, vol. 573. Springer International Publishing, Cham (2014)
4. Arulampalam, W., Gregg, P., Gregory, M.: Unemployment Scarring. Econ. J. **111**, F577–F584 (2001)
5. Becker, G.S.: Human capital: A theoretical and empirical analysis, with special reference to education (2009)
6. Bourdieu, P.: Distinction: A Social Critique of the Judgement of Taste (1987a)
7. Bourdieu, P.: The Forms of Capital. In: Richardson, J. (ed.) Handbook of Theory and Research for the Sociology of Education, pp. 241–258. Greenwood (1987)
8. Bourdieu, P.: The weight of the world: Social suffering in contemporary society. Polity Press, Oxford, England (1999)
9. Carcillo, S., et al.: NEET Youth in the Aftermath of the Crisis: Challenges and Policies. OECD Social, Employment and Migration Working Papers, No. 164, OECD Publishing, Paris (2015). https://doi.org/10.1787/5js6363503f6-en
10. Coleman, J.S.: Equality of educational opportunity. U.S. Department of Health, Education and Welfare (1966)
11. Collins, R.: Credential society: An historical sociology of education and stratification. Academic Press, San Diego, CA (1979)
12. Collins, R.: The sociology of philosophies: A global theory of intellectual change. Harvard University Press, London, England (1998)
13. Collins, R.: Interaction Ritual Chains. Princeton University Press, Princeton, NJ (2014)
14. Doeringer, P.B., Piore, M.J.: Internal Labour Markets and Manpower Analysis. M.E. Sharpe, Inc., Armonk, New York (1971)
15. Dornmayr, H., Riepl, M.: Unternehmensbefragung zum Fachkräftebedarf/-mangel, Fachkräfteradar 2022. Vienna: ibw-Forschungsbericht Nr. 210 (2022)
16. Eurostat. Statistics on continuing vocational training in enterprises (2023). Retrieved from https://ec.europa.eu/eurostat/statistics-explained/index.php?title=Statistics_on_continuing_vocational_training_in_enterprises#And_what_about_initial_vocational_training_in_enterprises.3F

# Towards More Reliable SQL Auto-grading: A Hybrid Approach Using LLMs, Intuitionistic Fuzzy Sets, and Traditional Methods

Dimitar Dimitrov(✉)(iD)

Faculty of Mathematics and Informatics, Sofia University "St. Kliment Ohridski",
Sofia, Bulgaria
dgdimitrov@fmi.uni-sofia.bg

**Abstract.** Automated SQL grading systems continue to face challenges in achieving high accuracy. While large language models (LLMs) offer new possibilities for semantic understanding, their probabilistic nature and occasional inconsistency limit their reliability for high-stakes, fully automated assessment, especially at scale. This paper proposes a hybrid grading framework that decomposes the SQL evaluation process into modular, interpretable stages–strategically combining traditional techniques, targeted LLM prompting, and a formal model of uncertainty.

Rather than relying solely on LLMs for direct grading, we leverage their strengths in supporting subtasks such as test data generation and query equivalence suggestion–tasks where LLM errors are more easily identified and corrected. To adequately express partial correctness, we incorporate intuitionistic fuzzy sets (IFS) as a foundation, capturing distinct degrees of correctness and incorrectness.

Our framework enables selective manual verification in cases with high uncertainty, while substantially reducing the overall human effort required. In contexts where full automation is not yet acceptable–such as high-stakes courses–the method provides a practical path toward scalable grading without compromising accuracy.

This work aims not for marginal LLM accuracy gains, but for a robust, human-in-the-loop solution that balances automation with trustworthiness–paving the way for more scalable and interpretable educational technologies.

## 1 Introduction

Structured Query Language (SQL) is a foundational skill in computer science education and a key tool for professionals in data science, analytics, and software engineering. As data-driven development gains prominence, the demand for effective SQL instruction has surged–especially in academic and online learning settings. This has led to a corresponding increase in SQL-based assessments, where students receive a natural language problem statement and database schema and

G. De Tré et al. (Eds.): FQAS 2025, LNAI 16119, pp. 253–264, 2026.
https://doi.org/10.1007/978-3-032-05607-8_24

must write a correct SQL query–highlighting the need for scalable and accurate auto-grading solutions.

SQL's declarative nature, short query length in educational contexts, and limited risk of malicious behavior make it particularly suitable for automated evaluation. However, current grading approaches remain limited. Dynamic methods–comparing query outputs–can be overly strict or misleading, while static analysis often fails to recognize syntactically different but semantically equivalent queries. Machine learning models offer promise but still struggle with edge cases and consistency.

Large language models (LLMs), pre-trained on diverse data including code, show strong potential for educational applications. Their ability to understand both structure and semantics allows for context-aware feedback and flexible query matching. However, their unpredictability and susceptibility to superficial errors pose challenges for high-stakes grading.

In response to these challenges, this paper proposes an approach to automated SQL grading that decomposes the grading process into multiple steps. By treating correctness evaluation as a series of interrelated tasks, we can selectively apply the most suitable techniques at each stage–whether dynamic comparison, static analysis, or model-based inference.

To further enhance the interpretability and precision of grading decisions, we employ intuitionistic fuzzy sets (IFS) [1] as a formal framework for representing and aggregating partial correctness judgments. Unlike binary or scalar scoring methods, IFS evaluate each query in terms of two distinct degrees: correctness ($\mu$, membership) and incorrectness ($\nu$, non-membership), where

$$\mu \in [0, 1]$$
$$\nu \in [0, 1]$$
$$\mu + \nu \in [0, 1]$$

IFS also introduce a third, derived degree of uncertainty:

$$\pi = 1 - \mu - \nu$$

This triadic representation is particularly well-suited to the auto-grading context, where outputs from multiple assessment techniques–each with its own level of reliability–must be reconciled. For instance, a student query that matches the reference output after minor corrections but diverges structurally may be assigned a high correctness degree, a low incorrectness degree, and a moderate uncertainty degree. In this way, IFS provide a principled mechanism for producing more nuanced grading outcomes in the presence of unreliability, facilitating better support for a fair allocation of partial credit.

A contribution of this work is its focus on achieving 100% correctness in grading outcomes. While full automation remains the ideal, our approach permits manual intervention in cases where full automation may compromise accuracy. Even then, the human workload is substantially lower than with fully manual verification. This study focuses solely on evaluating the correctness of student-submitted SQL queries–specifically, whether a query returns the expected result on a given database instance. Aspects like readability, efficiency, or coding style, while pedagogically relevant, are beyond the scope of this work.

The remainder of this paper is organized as follows: Sect. 2 reviews related work, Sect. 3 describes our methodology, Sect. 4 presents the results, and Sect. 5 summarizes the findings and suggests directions for future research.

## 2  Related Work

Automated grading of SQL queries has seen extensive research, with methods ranging from simple output comparisons to advanced machine learning models evaluating semantic equivalence.

Early methods, such as [2], primarily relied on result comparison, which returns a binary outcome–either correct or incorrect. While sufficient for queries aimed at testing fundamental understanding of SQL, they fall short in grading complex ones fairly, as they provide no insight into partial correctness or underlying reasoning. To address this, static analysis methods were introduced, such as the approach in [3], which tests semantic equivalence. However, these often mislabel correct queries due to syntactic differences, leading to false negatives.

Hybrid methods combine static and dynamic techniques to mitigate such issues. In [4], Wang et al. use dynamic testing not only to score student queries but also to identify 100% correct queries that serve as alternative references for static comparison. This reduces the need for instructors to manually provide multiple correct queries.

Chandra et al. [5,6] tackle the challenge of partial grading by automatically generating test datasets tailored to the correct SQL query. Later work [7–9], introduces method for automatically identifying the minimal set of edits needed to transform an incorrect student query into a correct one.

Deep learning has also been explored. Schwartz et al. [10] use attention-based convolutional neural networks to capture both local (syntax-level) and contextual (semantic-level) information in SQL queries. The architecture uses shared layers, which increases efficiency and learning synergy. While achieving moderate performance (AUC $\approx$0.64), such models still require human oversight. Rivas et al. [11] fine-tune BERT for partial grading, showing strong MAE results but sensitivity to outliers and BERT's token limits.

Recent studies investigate the application of LLMs in grading programming assessments and SQL queries in particular. LLMs demonstrate impressive capabilities in understanding both natural language and structured code, enabling them to identify student intent, detect subtle errors, and provide detailed feedback [12]. Nevertheless, challenges remain regarding hallucination and lack of explainability, which are particularly critical in high-stakes educational contexts.

Very few studies explicitly address the uncertainty in automated grading (e.g. [14]). Most systems provide a single-point estimate of correctness or score, assuming complete confidence in the automated judgment. This is questionable in practice, as grading systems inevitably deal with ambiguity–due to variability in student expression, partial correctness, or incomplete reference test cases.

Intuitionistic fuzzy sets, introduced by Atanassov [1], provide a natural framework for modeling degrees of correctness, incorrectness, and the associated uncertainty in between. A number of studies demonstrate how IFS and their extensions can enhance various aspects of grading and educational assessment. In [14,15], IFS-based evaluations are used to estimate each student's level of good and poor performance across different assessment units. The associated uncertainty degree captures situations where a student is unable to solve a problem or where the performance cannot be clearly classified as correct or incorrect. In [16], distance measures between IFSs are applied to evaluate the compatibility between students and schools, enabling more personalized school selection based on individual profiles. In [17], a novel approach is introduced where students' answerscripts are assessed using interval-valued IFSs. Finally, [18] models the lecturer's evaluation process using IFS.

Despite its advantages, the use of IFS in the context of SQL query evaluation remains largely unexplored. Our work addresses this gap.

Although there has been significant progress in automated SQL grading, a fundamental limitation of most existing approaches is their inability to guarantee fully accurate grading [13]. In high-stakes settings such as university examinations, this limitation necessitates manual verification of nearly all grades–including those marked as fully correct–greatly reducing the utility of automated systems. To mitigate this issue, intuitionistic fuzzy (IF) grades provide a natural measure of uncertainty, helping prioritize which queries most require human review.

In this work, we propose a hybrid approach that decomposes the SQL grading task into multiple interpretable steps and explores the targeted use of LLMs at each stage. Rather than relying on LLMs for direct grading, we leverage their strengths in specific subtasks such as test data generation. This modular framework enables selective manual verification of key steps, substantially reducing instructor effort compared to verifying all AI-generated grades, particularly in large-scale courses.

## 3   Methodology

A straightforward approach to SQL auto-grading would be to directly prompt an LLM to assess the correctness of a student-submitted query–potentially with prompt engineering to improve performance by providing a reference solution, grading rubrics, or other context. However, due to the probabilistic and non-deterministic nature of LLMs, their scores' reliability cannot be fully trusted without substantial manual verification, defeating the purpose of automation.

To address this, we propose a hybrid approach that enhances the robustness and interpretability of SQL auto-grading by integrating LLMs with traditional grading techniques such as query result comparison, edit-distance-based evaluation, and query clustering. Our framework is designed as a multi-stage process (Fig. 1) in which LLMs are strategically employed in tasks where they are most effective–such as generating test data or suggesting query equivalences–while deterministic methods handle the final grading of as many as possible queries. This division of labor allows us to mitigate LLM-related uncertainty and increase the reliability of the overall grading process.

Given a problem statement, reference solution, database schema (DDL), and student queries, our framework grades each query via two complementary, reliability-enhanced approaches: (1) traditional methods–including dynamic (execution-based) and static (structure-based) techniques–and (2) LLM-based methods. The traditional approach uses LLM-generated test data to catch student errors and mutation testing to increase matches with the reference output. The LLM approach leverages the reference solution, as well as LLM-generated incorrect reference solutions as few-shot examples. Queries producing identical outputs are clustered and ranked by similarity to the reference, enabling focused human verification on most divergent queries. Finally, grades from both approaches are combined into a single final score.

A key feature of our approach is that machine-generated grades at each step are represented as intuitionistic fuzzy values, each capturing degrees of correctness and incorrectness. In cases where the system cannot assign a grade with full certainty, it still assists the human grader by also identifying ambiguous cases, grouping similar queries together, and sorting them by uncertainty to facilitate efficient manual review. Ultimately, the proposed method reduces the need for exhaustive human oversight.

All LLM outputs are generated using a temperature of 0 to ensure deterministic and reproducible responses.

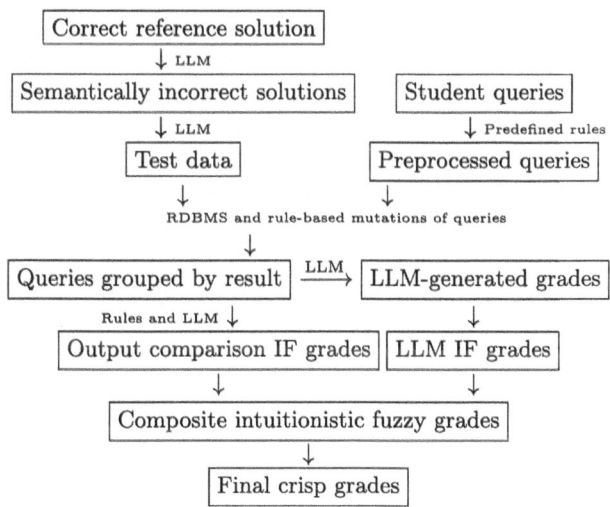

**Fig. 1.** Diagram representing the flow of information, with labelled transitions indicating the major responsible entities.

### 3.1   Automated Generation of Semantically Incorrect SQL Queries

LLMs generate syntactically valid but semantically incorrect queries based on the same problem. These serve as partial-credit exemplars in few-shot prompts in subsequent steps and further help distinguish incorrect student submissions. Full coverage isn't required; instead, later phases adopt mutation-based methods like XData [8]. This is achieved at the cost of a minimal, one-time human verification of the generated solutions.

### 3.2   Automated Test Data Generation and Refinement

Effective output-based grading relies on test data that exposes as many student mistakes as possible and clearly separates correct from incorrect queries. LLMs aid by not only generating diverse test records but also by providing case explanations, simplifying human verification. Reference queries are iteratively tested and data refined via prompting until all outputs are distinct and non-empty.

### 3.3   Rule-Based Adjustments of Student Queries

Common, context-free SQL mistakes (e.g., using = NULL) undergo automatic rule-based corrections. These aim to increase the percentage of queries that will match reference solution outputs in the next step, but are tracked and penalized to reflect deviations from ideal submissions.

### 3.4   Query Execution with Output Comparison and Mutations

Each student query is executed in a relational database management system and compared to correct reference outputs. If unmatched but syntactically valid, it's then compared with known incorrect outputs. Sorting order is considered when required by the reference (e.g., an ORDER BY without LIMIT).

Unmatched queries undergo rule-based mutations (e.g., JOIN type changes) inspired by XData [8], with the shortest successful mutation path preferred. Each mutation incurs a penalty.

Each student submission is assigned its initial intermediate grade based on:

1. Whether the query output matches any reference output.
2. Whether any edits were made to the query before its execution (in this or the previous step).

If the query output matches any reference, the intuitionistic fuzzy grade is

$$g_C = \langle \mu, 1 - \mu \rangle,$$

where $\mu$ is its grade mapped to $[0, 1]$, reduced if edits were applied.

If there is no match, we cannot definitively classify the solution as either correct or entirely incorrect. In this case, the grade is $\langle 0, 0 \rangle$, indicating full uncertainty. However, if specific errors (e.g., = NULL) are detected, the grade becomes $g_C = \langle 0, \nu \rangle$ where $\nu$ is the total score of all edits, thus reflecting the confidence in the query's incorrectness.

## 3.5   Grouping Queries Producing Identical Output

Queries with identical, non-empty outputs are grouped. This will help further refinement of the uncertainty in their IF grades. Queries yielding empty results or failing due to syntax/runtime errors (even after trying various mutations) form singleton groups.

## 3.6   Adjustments of the IF Grades Within Each Group

Grades with zero uncertainty do not fully represent the reality, where identical outputs can be produced by incorrect queries, even after manual verification of test data. Queries written in unconventional ways introduce a higher level of uncertainty in their grades.

To quantify the difference between the student's query and the reference solutions, various metrics could be used [19]. However, due to the subjective and stylistic nature of this criterion, we opt to utilize LLMs instead of explicit metrics. In this approach, we assess the *relative* difference between the student's query and the reference queries along a spectrum–from closely aligned and "conventional" to increasingly "unconventional" or unnecessarily complex solutions, which typically require more effort for human evaluation.

Each grade $\langle \mu, \nu \rangle$ is adjusted using the LLM-calculated distance $d \in [0, 1]$ as:

$$g_A = \langle (1 - \frac{d}{2})\mu, (1 - \frac{d}{2})\nu \rangle,$$

Increasing uncertainty up to 0.5 for the most divergent queries.

## 3.7   LLM-Based Automated Grading

In this stage, we harness the capabilities of LLMs to understand and grade all student-submitted SQL queries. Using few-shot prompting [20], the prompt includes reference solutions from the previous steps along with their corresponding grades, the database schema (DDL), and general grading rubrics. The LLM outputs a numerical partial grade $l$.

The corresponding IF grade is $g_L = \langle \tilde{l}, 1 - \tilde{l} \rangle$ where $\tilde{l}$ is the LLM-generated grade $l$ mapped to $[0, 1]$.

To enhance the trust in the generated grade, we query at least two distinct LLMs with the same prompt. Each model returns its respective grade, denoted as $l_i$. The IF grade for the student's query at this stage is defined as follows:

$$g_L = \langle \min_i\{\tilde{l}_i\}, \ 1 - \max_i\{\tilde{l}_i\} \rangle.$$

The uncertainty degree reflects the maximum difference between the LLM-provided grades.

Prompt injection–where input manipulates model behavior–is a known risk, but less critical here. At this stage, queries are already known to be incorrect or uncertain, and their short length limits manipulation. Any such attempts would be caught during manual verification, so mitigation techniques fall outside the scope of this study.

## 3.8   Calculation of Final IF Grades

For each query, our hybrid approach has produced two separate IF grades, denoted as $g_A = \langle \mu_A, \nu_A \rangle$ and $g_L = \langle \mu_L, \nu_L \rangle$, each representing its own levels of correctness, incorrectness, and uncertainty.

These two grades need to be combined into a single grade, $g$, while considering the significance of each component.

Any binary operator on IFS that preserves the highest uncertainty degree of each grade could be employed, such as $f(g_A, g_L) = \langle \min(\mu_A, \mu_L), \min(\nu_A, \nu_L) \rangle$ or $f(g_A, g_L) = \langle \mu_A \mu_L, \nu_A \nu_L \rangle$. However, this conservative approach would render the LLM-generated grades meaningless in situations where $g_A = \langle 0, 0 \rangle$. Averaging the two values, $f(g_A, g_L) = \langle \frac{\mu_A + \mu_L}{2}, \frac{\nu_A + \nu_L}{2} \rangle$, addresses this issue, but it does not perform well when the two grades are significantly different yet each carries only minor uncertainty (e.g., $\langle 1, 0 \rangle$ and $\langle 0, 1 \rangle$–the combined value being $\langle \frac{1}{2}, \frac{1}{2} \rangle$, which leaves no room for any uncertainty).

We can distinguish three cases:

1. The student query matches a reference solution, possibly with some corrections. In this case, we aggregate the grades by taking the minimum value from each component.
2. The query doesn't match any reference solution, but there are universal mistakes ($g_A = \langle 0, \nu_A \rangle$), requiring us to rely more on the LLM-assigned correctness value.
3. The comparison step fails to produce any meaningful grade, resulting in $g_A = \langle 0, 0 \rangle$, in which case we must use the grade generated by the LLM, but with increased uncertainty.

We use the following, considering that the grades generated in the query output comparison step are generally accurate and consistent, whereas LLMs-despite their ability to grade all submissions-tend to be less reliable:

$$g = \langle \min(\mu_A, \mu_L) + \overline{sg}(\mu_A)\frac{\mu_L}{2}, \min(\nu_A, \nu_L) + \overline{sg}(\mu_A)\min(\nu_A, \frac{\nu_L}{2}) \rangle,$$

where [1]:

$$sg(x) = \begin{cases} 1, & \text{if } x > 0 \\ 0, & \text{if } x \leq 0 \end{cases} \qquad \overline{sg}(x) = \begin{cases} 0, & \text{if } x > 0 \\ 1, & \text{if } x \leq 0 \end{cases}$$

It's trivial to prove that the so obtained set of all IF grades is an IFS.

We now analyze the correctness, incorrectness, and uncertainty degrees in each case. In the first case, $g = \langle \min(\mu_A, \mu_L), \min(\nu_A, \nu_L) \rangle$, allowing for greater uncertainty if the correctness or incorrectness degrees of each grade differ: $\pi = \max(\pi_A, \pi_L)$ where $\pi_A = 1 - \mu_A - \nu_A$ and $\pi_L = 1 - \mu_L - \nu_L$.

In the third case, $g = \langle \frac{\mu_L}{2}, \frac{\nu_L}{2} \rangle$. We divide the correctness and incorrectness degrees of the LLM grade by two, taking into account the limitations of LLMs discussed earlier. This ensures that the uncertainty remains at least as high as the highest possible uncertainty for a grade of a query that matches the reference output but structurally differs from the reference solution.

In the second case, we once again rely on $g_L$ with significant uncertainty. However, since $\nu_A$ has a high-confidence value, we combine both approaches. For smaller values of $\nu_A$, $\pi$ behaves similarly to the third case.

### 3.9   Manual Review of IF Grades and Final Crisp Grade Assignment

In practice, a significant number of grades may have zero uncertainty. However, to ensure full correctness, as required in courses where grades have significant consequences for the student, human verification remains necessary for all final grades, even those without any uncertainty. For example, test datasets might miss subtle errors. In lower-stakes contexts, only grades with uncertainty above a threshold may need review.

In both cases, our approach aids by identifying student-submitted queries that require verification, suggesting grade intervals, grouping similar queries, and sorting queries within each group by descending uncertainty.

Since queries within a group yield the same output, they are likely written similarly and should, therefore, receive the same grade. This enables the human grader to verify all auto-generated grades within a group simultaneously (with all queries displayed on the same screen). However, the set of queries may be extensive, making manual verification a challenging task. The uncertainty degree of each grade within the group allows the queries to be sorted in descending order of uncertainty, helping the grader focus on queries that are written in unconventional ways. Groups themselves are also sorted based on the highest uncertainty level within the group.

Although the total number of queries remains the same with or without our approach, it significantly reduces the time spent on manual checks and minimizes the risk of inconsistent grading.

Each query in the group is shown with its SQL text, a grade range (mapped from $[\mu, 1 - \nu]$ to a real scale, e.g. 0–10), and a suggested average crisp grade.

## 4   Experiments and Results

### 4.1   Data

The dataset used in this study consists of SQL queries submitted by students at Sofia University "St. Kliment Ohridski" from recent years as part of routine database assessments. Each query is annotated with a human-verified grade, which serves as a ground truth reference for evaluating the correctness of the proposed auto-grading approach.

To reflect different levels of query complexity, the dataset is divided into two groups. The *easy* group includes queries involving fundamental SQL constructs such as projection, selection, ordering, inner joins, and conditions involving LIKE and IS NULL. The *difficult* group consists of longer and more complex queries that span multiple tables and include advanced SQL features such as outer joins, nested and correlated subqueries, aggregation, and grouping. Each query in the difficult set is designed to incorporate as many of these features as possible, making it particularly challenging for both traditional output-comparison methods and LLM-based approaches, and thus well-suited for comprehensive evaluation.

## 4.2   Model Selection

We evaluate the proposed hybrid auto-grading approach using multiple LLMs. Specifically, we utilize two state-of-the-art models: GPT 4o (OpenAI, 2024) and GPT o1-mini (OpenAI, 2024). These models were selected due to their demonstrated capabilities in language understanding and code analysis tasks, particularly in the context of SQL. While comparative analysis with other LLMs remains a valuable direction for future work, our primary objective in this study is not to maximize grading accuracy through model selection. Instead, we aim to enhance grading reliability via alternative strategies, as already discussed.

## 4.3   Results

Several aspects of our method could benefit from quantitative evaluation, including:

- Grading accuracy;
- Reduction in human effort.

However, such evaluation is limited by the reliance on LLMs, which behave as black boxes, and by the choice of predefined rule-based query mutations used to transform incorrect student queries into ones producing the reference result–an aspect already addressed in other works [8]. Due to these limitations and space constraints, we present qualitative results to illustrate the method's behavior and potential.

LLMs generated a wide range of incorrect solutions given a correct one. Despite the use of prompting techniques, some solutions were still syntactically incorrect, making them unsuitable for the comparison phase. Additionally, not all critical cases were addressed. While human intervention remained necessary, different models offered diverse insights of possible student mistakes and demonstrated consistent performance for each difficulty level.

While LLMs were better at generating test data, some data contained obvious errors (e.g., no values ending with 'A' for queries using LIKE '%A'), although LLMs showed understanding of the relevant cases. Despite this, LLMs were still valuable in producing human-readable examples, which could be easily fixed manually and used in the comparison step. This supports the idea of using LLMs for generating test data and incorrect reference solutions in our hybrid approach, where human verification is reduced but remains necessary for refinement.

Although informally defined through a subjective criterion, the LLM-based evaluation of the distance between the reference solution and each student query within the same group yielded reasonable results. This approach proved effective in identifying unusually formulated student queries within a group.

The intuitionistic fuzzy grading approach effectively captured the uncertainty introduced by each step, including the passing or failing of tests, mutations applied to the query, and inconsistencies in LLM grading.

## 5   Conclusion

This paper introduced a hybrid approach to the automated grading of SQL assessments, with a focus on ensuring complete correctness rather than marginal improvements in the accuracy of LLM-generated grades. Rather than relying solely on direct grading by LLMs, our method leverages tasks where LLMs demonstrate stronger performance, thereby mitigating the limitations typically associated with their use in high-stakes evaluation.

Grounded in practical experience, the proposed approach prioritizes reducing the need for manual verification across the grading workflow while maintaining fairness and consistency in assessment. To handle the inherent uncertainty in intermediate grading outcomes produced by various methods, we employed IFS, which offer a robust framework for modeling uncertainty.

Future work includes the integration of additional models and techniques to support nuanced partial grading and further enhance the system's adaptability and accuracy.

**Acknowledgments.** This study is financed by the European Union-NextGeneration EU, through the National Recovery and Resilience Plan of the Republic of Bulgaria, project No. BG-RRP-2.004-0008-C01.

**Disclosure of Interests.** The authors have no competing interests to declare that are relevant to the content of this article.

## References

1. Atanassov, K.: Intuitionistic Fuzzy Sets. Springer, Heidelberg (1999)
2. Prior, J., Lister, R.: The backwash effect on SQL skills grading. ACM Sigcse Bull. **36**, 32–36 (2004). https://doi.org/10.1145/1026487.1008008
3. Chu, S., Murphy, B., Roesch, J., Cheung, A., Suciu, D.: Axiomatic foundations and algorithms for deciding semantic equivalences of SQL queries. Proc. VLDB Endow. **11**, 11, 1482—1495 (2018). https://doi.org/10.14778/3236187.3236200
4. Wang, J., Zhao, Y., Tang, Z., Xing, Z.: Combining dynamic and static analysis for automated grading SQL statements. J. Netw. Intell. **5**(4), 179–190 (2020)
5. Chandra, B., Chawda, B., Kar, B., Reddy, K.V.M., Shah, S., Sudarshan, S.: Data generation for testing and grading SQL queries. VLDB J. **24**(6), 731–755 (2015). https://doi.org/10.1007/s00778-015-0395-0
6. Bhangdiya, A., Chandra, B., Kar, B., Radhakrishnan, B., Reddy, K.V.M, Shah, S.: The XDa-TA system for automated grading of SQL query assignments. In: 2015 IEEE 31st International Conference on Data Engineering, Seoul, Korea (South), pp. 1468–1471 (2015). https://doi.org/10.1109/ICDE.2015.7113403

7. Chandra, B., Banerjee, A., Hazra, U., Joseph, M., Sudarshan, S.: Automated grading of SQL queries. In: 2019 IEEE 35th International Conference on Data Engineering (ICDE), Macao, China, pp. 1630–1633 (2019). https://doi.org/10.1109/ICDE.2019.00159

8. Chandra, B., Banerjee, A., Hazra, U., Joseph, M., Sudarshan, S.: Edit based grading of SQL queries. In: CODS-COMAD '21: Proceedings of the 3rd ACM India Joint International Conference on Data Science & Management of Data (8th ACM IKDD CODS & 26th COMAD), pp. 56–64 (2021). https://doi.org/10.1145/3430984.3431012

9. Wanjiru, B., Van Bommel, P., Hiemstra, D.: Dynamic and partial grading of SQL queries. J. Eng. Res. Sci. **3**(8), 1–14 (2024). https://doi.org/10.55708/js0308001

10. Schwartz, D. R., Rivas, P.: An Automated SQL Query Grading System Using An Attention-Based Convolutional Neural Network. Preprint (2024). https://doi.org/10.48550/arxiv.2406.15936

11. Rivas, P., Schwartz, D.R., Quevedo, E.: BERT Goes to SQL School: Improving Automatic Grading of SQL Statements, 2023 Congress in Computer Science, Computer Engineering, & Applied Computing (CSCE), Las Vegas, pp. 83–90. NV, USA (2023). https://doi.org/10.1109/CSCE60160.2023.00019

12. Mohamed, K., Yousef, M., Medhat, W., Hussein Mohamed, E., Khoriba, G., Arafa, T.: Hands-on analysis of using large language models for the auto evaluation of programming assignments. Inf. Syst. **128**, 102473 (2025). https://doi.org/10.1016/j.is.2024.102473

13. Geigle, C., Zhai, C., Ferguson, D.C.: An exploration of automated grading of complex assignments. In: Proceedings of 3rd ACM Conference on Learning @ Scale (L@S '16), ACM, New York, pp. 351–360 (2016). https://doi.org/10.1145/2876034.2876049

14. Sotirova, E., Shannon, A., Kim, T., Krawczak, M., Melo-Pinto, P., Riečan, B.: Intuitionistic fuzzy evaluations for the analysis of a student's knowledge in university e-learning courses. In: Hadjiski, M., Atanassov, K. (eds.) Intuitionistic Fuzziness and Other Intelligent Theories and Their Applications. Stud. Comput. Intell. 757. Springer, Cham (2019). https://doi.org/10.1007/978-3-319-78931-6_6

15. Kim, T., Sotirova, E., Shannon, A., Atanassova, V., Atanassov, K., Jang L.-C.: Interval valued intuitionistic fuzzy evaluations for analysis of a student's knowledge in university e-learning courses. Int. J. Fuzzy Logic Intell. Syst. **18**(3), 190–195 (2019). https://doi.org/10.5391/IJFIS.2018.18.3.190

16. Citil, M.: Application of the intuitionistic fuzzy logic in education. Commun. Math. Appl. **10**, 131–143 (2019)

17. Chen, S.-M., Li, T.-S.: Evaluating students' answer scripts based on interval-valued intuitionistic fuzzy sets. Inf. Sci. **235**, 308–322 (2013). https://doi.org/10.1016/j.ins.2012.12.031

18. Shannon, A., Sotirova, E., Atanassov, K., Krawczak., M., Melo-Pinto, P., Kim, T.: Generalized net model of lecturers' evaluation of student work with intuitionistic fuzzy estimations. Notes on IFS. **12**(4) (2006)

19. Kul, G., Luong, D.T.A., Xie, T., Chandola, V., Kennedy, O., Upadhyaya, S.: Similarity metrics for SQL query clustering. In: IEEE Transactions on Knowledge and Data Engineering, vol. 30, no. 12, 2408–2420 (2018). https://doi.org/10.1109/TKDE.2018.2831214

20. Brown, T.B., et al.: Language models are few-shot learners. In: Proceedings of the 34th International Conference on Neural Information Processing Systems, NIPS '20, Curran Associates Inc., Red Hook, NY, USA, pp. 1877–1901 (2020)

# Prediction of Solar Radiation From Weather Data Using Intuitionistic and Regular Fuzzy Operations

Deyan Mavrov$^{(\boxtimes)}$ ⓘ and Stanislav Popov ⓘ

Burgas State University "Prof. Dr. Assen Zlatarov", Burgas 8010, Bulgaria
dg@mavrov.eu

**Abstract.** Solar radiation has become an important factor in our daily lives. Thus, its prediction is essential for numerous sectors, including energy, agriculture, healthcare, climatology, and aviation. This paper presents an advanced, hybrid approach combining elements of fuzzy logic and intuitionistic fuzzy sets which will contribute to better handle uncertainty, hesitation, and imprecise data, all of which are common issues in environmental and meteorological forecasting. The real-world data, used for the testing the algorithm cover the summer period of 2015 for the city of Burgas, Bulgaria.

**Keywords:** Intuitionistic Fuzzy Sets · Solar Radiation · Fuzzy Logic

## 1 Introduction

Many challenges in everyday life, applied sciences, engineering, and medical diagnostics are influenced by elements of uncertainty. When attempting to model these problems mathematically, we frequently deal with calculus-based equations that reflect these uncertain aspects-making it essential to find solutions that properly incorporate them. Such uncertainties can be described using fuzzy concepts [1], or more advanced frameworks like intuitionistic fuzzy sets (IFSs) [2–7].

Fuzzy sets theory states that propositions can have an infinite number of truth values, ranging from two extremes-1 (completely true) and 0 (completely false)-with a continuum of possibilities in between, which is why the term "fuzzy" is used. The IFSs represent an extension of the concept of fuzzy sets, showing the function $\mu A\,(X)$ defining the presence of an element $x$ to the set $A$, graded in the interval [0; 1]. The intuitionistic fuzzy set itself is formally denoted by [2]:

$$A = \{\langle x, \mu A(x), \nu A(x)\rangle | x \ \in E\}$$

The difference between fuzzy sets and intuitionist fuzzy sets is in the presence of a second function $\mu A\,(x)$, which determines the absence of the element $x$ in the set $A$, where $\mu A\,(x) \in [0; 1]$, $\nu\, A\,(x) \in [0; 1]$ under the condition $\mu A\,(x) + \nu\, A\,(x) \in [0; 1]$ [5]. The theory of intuitionistic fuzzy sets already proves to have a significant impact on modern mathematics overall, as it serves as a generalization of fuzzy set theory.

© The Author(s), under exclusive license to Springer Nature Switzerland AG 2026
G. De Tré et al. (Eds.): FQAS 2025, LNAI 16119, pp. 265–273, 2026.
https://doi.org/10.1007/978-3-032-05607-8_25

Solar radiation refers to the total energy emitted by the sun, which travels through space and reaches Earth's atmosphere [8]. It includes a wide spectrum of electromagnetic waves, such as visible light, ultraviolet, and infrared radiation [9].

The factors that affect the amount of solar radiation are numerous, thus we will focus only on those used in the proposed prediction method using IFS:

- Time of day: the angle of sunlight changes throughout the day due to Earth's rotation. Midday (when the Sun is at its highest point) typically receives the most direct radiation, while early morning and late afternoon receive more diffused sunlight.
- Cloud cover: clouds can block or scatter sunlight, reducing the amount of radiation that reaches the ground. Clear skies allow more direct solar radiation to reach the surface.
- Humidity: water vapor in the atmosphere absorbs specific wavelengths of solar radiation, particularly in the infrared region. This absorption helps regulate the Earth's energy balance and contributes to the greenhouse effect. High humidity levels mean more water vapor in the air, which can absorb more energy, reducing the amount of solar radiation that reaches the Earth's surface.
- Temperature: The temperature of the Earth's surface and atmosphere also determines the amount of longwave radiation emitted by the Earth.

Solar radiation can be measured in:

- $W/m2$ - the most common unit of measure for solar radiation, it indicates the amount of energy (in watts) received per square meter of surface area per second;
- $J/m2$ - the energy absorbed over a period of time;
- $kWh/m2$ - a common unit used in solar energy systems to express the total energy received over a longer time period, such as a day or a year.

In this paper, a method for predicting solar radiation amount is suggested, utilizing fuzzy logic system. We will use methods combining intuitionistic and regular fuzzy evaluations to attempt to determine the expected solar radiation for a provided set of data on temperature (in Celsius), humidity (in percent), cloud cover (in percent) and the current time of day (in hours since midnight). The described algorithm is tested with Python using the libraries NumPy [10], Pandas [11], SciKit Fuzzy [12, 13] and others.

## 2 Prediction Algorithm

First, we will define the membership and non-membership functions for each of the parameters. We will categorize each measure on a scale from low, to medium, to high. For the membership function that evaluates if a parameter value's level should be considered *low*, we will use a sigmoid function, which corresponds well with the way the "lowness" of a measure gradually decreases to "highness" when we are in the middle of the scale.

$$\mu_{\text{low}}(x) = \frac{1}{1 + e^{+c(x-b_1)}}$$

The non-membership function will be the inverse of the membership one.

$$\nu_{\text{low}}(x) = \frac{1}{1 + e^{-c(x-b_2)}}$$

Now we need to assure that the sum of both functions is less than or equal to one:

$$\mu_{\text{low}}(x) + \nu_{\text{low}}(x) \overset{?}{\leq} 1 \tag{1}$$

We can rewrite the inequality as:

$$\mu_{\text{low}}(x) \leq 1 - \nu_{\text{low}}(x)$$

$$\frac{1}{1 + e^{+c(x-b_1)}} \leq 1 - \frac{1}{1 + e^{-c(x-b_2)}}$$

$$\frac{1}{1 + e^{+c(x-b_1)}} \leq \frac{1 + e^{-c(x-b_2)} - 1}{1 + e^{-c(x-b_2)}}$$

$$\frac{1 + e^{-c(x-b_2)}}{\left(1 + e^{+c(x-b_1)}\right)\left(1 + e^{-c(x-b_2)}\right)} \leq \frac{e^{-c(x-b_2)} \cdot \left(1 + e^{+c(x-b_1)}\right)}{\left(1 + e^{+c(x-b_1)}\right)\left(1 + e^{-c(x-b_2)}\right)}$$

$$1 + e^{-c(x-b_2)} \leq e^{-c(x-b_2)} \cdot \left(1 + e^{+c(x-b_1)}\right)$$

$$1 + e^{-c(x-b_2)} \leq e^{-c(x-b_2)} + e^{-c(x-b_2)+c(x-b_1)}$$

$$1 \leq e^{-c(x-b_2)+c(x-b_1)}$$

$$1 \leq e^{c(x-b_1-x+b_2)}$$

$$1 \leq e^{c(b_2-b_1)}$$

Since it is known that $e^x \geq 1$ for every $x \geq 0$, we can see that (1) will be true if $c \geq 0$ and $b_2 \geq b_1$, which our coefficient values, as given below, will satisfy.

The membership and non-membership functions that evaluate *high* level for a value will correspond respectively to the non-membership and membership function of the *low* level function, respectively (e.g., they are swapped). The membership function for the *medium* level will be equal to the uncertainty function for the *low* level. The *medium* level will be regular fuzzy.

$$\mu_{\text{medium}}(x) = 1 - (\mu_{\text{low}}(x) + \nu_{\text{low}}(x)) = \pi_{\text{low}}(x)$$

$$\mu_{\text{high}}(x) = \nu_{\text{low}}(x)$$

$$\nu_{\text{high}}(x) = \mu_{\text{low}}(x)$$

Each parameter receives their own values for the coefficients $b_1$, $b_2$ and $c_2$. The following is a table of the values for each parameter except time, as they were selected for the current experiment (Table 1).

**Table 1.** Coefficient values for the parameter's $\mu$ and $\nu$ functions.

| Parameter | $b_1$ | $c$ | $b_2$ |
|---|---|---|---|
| Temperature | 12 | 1.0 | 22 |
| Humidity | 40 | 0.3 | 60 |
| Cloud cover | 40 | 0.3 | 60 |
| Solar Radiation | 310 | 0.02 | 600 |

For time, we will use a difference of two sigmoid functions, because the hours that are considered *high*, e.g., that proved the best conditions for high solar radiation, are in between hours that fall in the night and would result in little or no solar radiation. We will use the times 9:30 and 18:54 as the *b*-values (or midpoints) for the membership function, and 11:30 and 16:54 for the non-membership function.

$$\mu_{\text{time, low}}(x) = \frac{1}{1 + e^{+2.9(x-9.5)}} - \frac{1}{1 + e^{+2.9(x-18.9)}} + 1$$

$$\nu_{\text{time, low}}(x) = \frac{1}{1 + e^{-2.9(x-11.5)}} - \frac{1}{1 + e^{-2.9(x-16.9)}}$$

The midpoints are positioned to correspond with the relative middle time of the change from day to night and vice versa. The membership function's value is a difference of two sigmoids with a positive *c*-coefficient, which falls in the interval $[-1; 0]$, which is why 1 is added to its result. The non-membership function is a difference of sigmoids with a negative *c*-coefficient, which falls in the interval $[0; 1]$, thus requiring no change.

The midpoints of the non-membership function are pulled towards the middle from those of the membership function, so that it doesn't correspond completely to the inverse of the membership function, allowing for uncertainty or *medium* time. This also guarantees that the sum of the membership and non-membership functions never exceeds one, as the $\mu$ and $\nu$ functions are thus positioned to never meet at an $x$ value where both functions have a result $y \geq 0.5$.

The functions for *medium* and *high* time are calculated the same as for the other parameters.

Figure 1 shows a graphic representation of the membership functions for each parameter.

To begin the process of prediction, we enter the input values for each parameter, which we will label:

- $temp_{in}$ – temperature;
- $hum_{in}$ – humidity;
- $cloud_{in}$ – cloud cover;
- $time_{in}$ – time;

Our aim is to calculate the predicted solar radiation value $solar_{out}$, based on the input.

For each membership function we calculate the $y$ values for every step in the range of values we will evaluate the parameter. The ranges for the parameters are shown in Table 2.

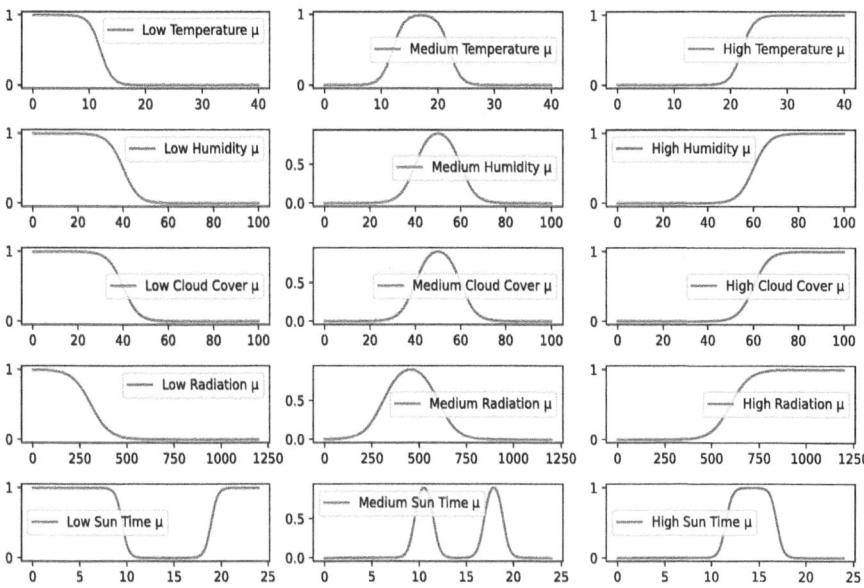

**Fig. 1.** Membership functions for each parameter

**Table 2.** Operating ranges for each parameter.

| Parameter | Range |
|---|---|
| Temperature | [0,41], step 1 |
| Humidity | [0,101], step 1 |
| Cloud cover | [0,101], step 1 |
| Time | (0,23.983), step 0.167 (1 min) |
| Solar Radiation | [0,1200], step 1 |

First, we need to use the above defined membership functions to calculate fuzzy evaluations for each level (low, medium, high) of each parameter. This is done by finding the two values of the parameter's range from Table 2 which are closest to the input value for the same parameter. If there is an exact match, we take that value's membership value. If not, we calculate an interpolation based on the two nearest values in the range.

$$\text{For } x_{in} \text{ find } r_1, r_2 \in \text{range}_x, \text{ such that } r_1 \leq x_{in} \leq r_2$$

$$\text{If } x_{in} = r_1 = r_2, \text{ then } \mu_{in, \text{level}}(x_{in}) = \mu_{x, \text{level}}(x_{in})$$

$$\text{Else } \mu_{in, \text{level}}(x_{in}) = \frac{\mu_{x, \text{level}}(r_2) - \mu_{x, \text{level}}(r_1)}{r_2 - r_1} \cdot (x_{in} - r_1) + \mu_{x, \text{level}}(r_1)$$

where $x$ is one of the parameters (temp, hum, cloud, time) and *level* is low, medium or high.

Having finished these calculations, we get the following input membership values:

- $\mu_{in,\,low}(temp_{in})$, $\mu_{in,\,medium}(temp_{in})$, $\mu_{in,\,high}(temp_{in})$
- $\mu_{in,\,low}(hum_{in})$, $\mu_{in,\,medium}(hum_{in})$, $\mu_{in,\,high}(hum_{in})$
- $\mu_{in,\,low}(cloud_{in})$, $\mu_{in,\,medium}(cloud_{in})$, $\mu_{in,\,high}(cloud_{in})$
- $\mu_{in,\,low}(time_{in})$, $\mu_{in,\,medium}(time_{in})$, $\mu_{in,\,high}(time_{in})$

With these, we can set the following rules for combining membership values:
**Low solar radiation:**

$$rule_{low,1} = min\left(\mu_{low}(temp_{in}),\, \mu_{low}(hum_{in}),\, \mu_{low}(cloud_{in}),\, \mu_{low}(time_{in})\right)$$

$$rule_{low,2} = min\left(\mu_{high}(temp_{in}),\, \mu_{low}(hum_{in}),\, \mu_{low}(cloud_{in}),\, \mu_{low}(time_{in})\right)$$

$$rule_{low,3} = min\left(\mu_{high}(temp_{in}),\, \mu_{high}(hum_{in}),\, \mu_{high}(cloud_{in}),\, \mu_{low}(time_{in})\right)$$

$$rule_{low,4} = min\left(\mu_{high}(temp_{in}),\, \mu_{low}(hum_{in}),\, \mu_{high}(cloud_{in}),\, \mu_{low}(time_{in})\right)$$

$$rule_{low,5} = min\left(\mu_{low}(temp_{in}),\, \mu_{high}(hum_{in}),\, \mu_{high}(cloud_{in}),\, \mu_{low}(time_{in})\right)$$

$$rule_{low,6} = min\left(\mu_{medium}(temp_{in}),\, \mu_{high}(hum_{in}),\, \mu_{high}(cloud_{in}),\, \mu_{high}(time_{in})\right)$$

$$rule_{low,7} = min\left(\mu_{low}(temp_{in}),\, \mu_{high}(hum_{in}),\, \mu_{high}(cloud_{in}),\, \mu_{high}(time_{in})\right)$$

**Medium solar radiation:**

$$rule_{medium,1} = min\left(\mu_{low}(temp_{in}),\, \mu_{medium}(hum_{in}),\, \mu_{medium}(cloud_{in}),\, \mu_{medium}(time_{in})\right)$$

$$rule_{medium,2} = min\left(\mu_{low}(temp_{in}),\, \mu_{high}(hum_{in}),\, \mu_{high}(cloud_{in}),\, \mu_{high}(time_{in})\right)$$

$$rule_{medium,3} = min\left(\mu_{low}(temp_{in}),\, \mu_{high}(hum_{in}),\, \mu_{high}(cloud_{in}),\, \mu_{medium}(time_{in})\right)$$

**High solar radiation:**

$$rule_{high,1} = min\left(\mu_{high}(temp_{in}),\, \mu_{low}(hum_{in}),\, \mu_{low}(cloud_{in}),\, \mu_{high}(time_{in})\right)$$

$$rule_{high,2} = min\left(\mu_{medium}(temp_{in}),\, \mu_{medium}(hum_{in}),\, \mu_{low}(cloud_{in}),\, \mu_{high}(time_{in})\right)$$

$$rule_{high,3} = min\left(\mu_{medium}(temp_{in}),\, \mu_{low}(hum_{in}),\, \mu_{low}(cloud_{in}),\, \mu_{high}(time_{in})\right)$$

$$rule_{high,4} = min\left(\mu_{medium}(temp_{in}),\, \mu_{high}(hum_{in}),\, \mu_{low}(cloud_{in}),\, \mu_{high}(time_{in})\right)$$

$$rule_{high,5} = min\left(\mu_{high}(temp_{in}),\, \mu_{high}(hum_{in}),\, \mu_{low}(cloud_{in}),\, \mu_{high}(time_{in})\right)$$

Each of these rules use minimums to produce the section of all fuzzy values. Then we need to generate three combined rules.

$$\text{rule}_{\text{low}} = \min_{i=1}^{7}\left(\text{rule}_{\text{low},i}\right)$$

$$\text{rule}_{\text{medium}} = \min_{i=1}^{3}\left(\text{rule}_{\text{medium},i}\right)$$

$$\text{rule}_{\text{high}} = \min_{i=1}^{5}\left(\text{rule}_{\text{high},i}\right)$$

With these done, we use maximum to generate the three output arrays for each level and all values in the solar radiation range (see Table 2):

$$o_{\text{low}}(x) = \min\left(\text{rule}_{\text{low}}, \mu_{\text{low},\text{solar}}(x)\right)$$

$$r_{\text{low},i} = o_{\text{low}}(i), i \in [[0, 1200]]$$

$$o_{\text{medium}}(x) = \min\left(\text{rule}_{\text{medium}}, \mu_{\text{medium},\text{solar}}(x)\right)$$

$$r_{\text{medium},i} = o_{\text{medium}}(i), i \in [[0, 1200]]$$

$$o_{\text{high}}(x) = \min\left(\text{rule}_{\text{high}}, \mu_{\text{high},\text{solar}}(x)\right)$$

$$r_{\text{high},i} = o_{\text{high}}(i), i \in [[0, 1200]]$$

And now we can generate the final aggregated array based on all output arrays.

$$r_{\text{aggregated},i} = r_{\text{low},i} \cdot r_{\text{medium},i} \cdot r_{\text{high},i}$$

Finally, we can use this aggregated array to calculate the predicted solar radiation value:

$$\text{solar}_{\text{out}} = \min(i), \text{ where } i \in 0, 1200 \text{ and } r_{\text{aggregated},i} = \max\left(r_{\text{aggregated},i}\right)$$

## 3   Application of the Algorithm on Real-World Data

Testing the algorithm on real-world data is important because it will reveal how it performs outside of its idealized controlled conditions. Unlike synthetic or idealized datasets, real-world data tends to have noise, missing values, outliers, and inconsistencies that can challenge the robustness of the algorithm. It also helps prevent overfitting, where a model performs well on training data but fails to generalize about new, unseen situations.

Using the steps described in the previous section, we can test how our fuzzy method compares to real data. For reference, we will use real data for the city of Burgas, taken from Solcast [14] for the period from June 1, 2015 to August 31, 2015. Only the data for Temperature, Humidity, Cloud coverage, Time and Solar radiation is extracted from the original data source since the algorithm relies on them for making the prediction.

Table 3 shows several random samples from different times of day. The last two columns contain the predicted and real amount of solar radiation for the specific conditions.

**Table 3.** Random sample comparison of predicted and real values.

| Temperature | Humidity | Cloud cover | Time | Solar Radiation (predicted) | Solar Radiation (real) |
|---|---|---|---|---|---|
| 24 | 94.5 | 1.7 | 8 | 93 | 167 |
| 29 | 57.5 | 0 | 14 | 563 | 923 |
| 22 | 63.8 | 0 | 12 | 600 | 869 |
| 21 | 92.3 | 52.3 | 3 | 0 | 0 |
| 27 | 65.6 | 0 | 20 | 151 | 89 |
| 19 | 70 | 0 | 22 | 0 | 0 |

When we apply our method to all rows from the real data file, we get an average difference of 75.328.

## 4   Conclusion

Predicting solar radiation amount is a challenging task. It can vary depending on factors like geographic location, time of day, weather conditions, and atmospheric composition, most of which are inherently associated with uncertainty.

We have used intuitionistic and regular fuzzy evaluations to create an algorithm that predicts solar radiation using data on temperature, humidity, cloud cover and time. We have compared our method's results to real data. In the future, we could adjust our functions to better match real data and introduce more intuitionistic fuzzy operations into the algorithm. We could also compare our method with other methods, and combine it with them to improve the results.

**Acknowledgments.** The authors are thankful for the support provided by a Project at Burgas State University "Prof. Dr. Assen Zlatarov" – under Ref. № NIH-499/2024 "Application of intelligent methods for modelling and analysis of real processes".

# References

1. Zadeh, L.A.: Fuzzy sets. Inf. Control. **8**, 338–353 (1965)
2. Atanassov, K.: Intuitionistic fuzzy sets. Fuzzy Sets Syst. **20**(1), 87–96 (1986)
3. Atanassov, K.: Intuitionistic Fuzzy Sets: Theory and Applications. Springer PhysicaVerlag, Berlin (1999)
4. Atanassov, K.: On the two most extended modal types of operators defined over interval-valued intuitionistic fuzzy sets. Ann. Fuzzy Math. Inform. **16**(1), 1–12 (2018)
5. Atanassov, K.: Intuitionistic fuzzy sets. VII ITKR's Session, Sofia, June 1983 (Deposed in Central Sci. - Techn. Library of Bulg. Acad. of Sci., 1697/84) (in Bulgarian). Reprinted: Int. J. Bioautomation **20**(S1), S1–S6 (1983)
6. Atanassova, L.: On intuitionistic fuzzy versions of L. Zadeh's extension principle. Notes Intuitionistic Fuzzy Sets **13**(3), 33–36 (2007)
7. Biswas, R.: On fuzzy sets and intuitionistic fuzzy sets. Notes Intuitionistic Fuzzy Sets **3**(1), 3–11 (1997)
8. Goswani, D.: Principles of Solar Engineering. CRC Press, Taylor & Francis Group, p. 29 (2015)
9. Sakthivadivel, D., Balaji, K., Dsilva Winfred Rufuss, D., Iniyan, S., Suganthi, L.: Solar energy technologies: principles and applications. Renewable-Energy-Driven Future, Academic Press, p. 12 (2021)
10. NumPy Homepage. https://numpy.org/doc/stable/user/index.html. Accessed 15 Apr 2025
11. Scipy Homepage. https://scipy.org/. Accessed 15 Apr 2025
12. SK Fuzzy Homepage. https://pythonhosted.org/scikit-fuzzy/. Accessed 15 Apr 2025
13. Pandas Homepage. https://pandas.pydata.org/. Accessed 15 Apr 2025
14. Solcast. Global solar irradiance data and PV system power output data (2019). https://solcast.com/. Accessed 15 Apr 2025

# Emerging Trends in Flexible Query Answering and Information Retrieval

# How Good are LLMs at Retrieving Documents in a Specific Domain?

Nafis Tanveer Islam[1,2] and Zhiming Zhao[1,2(✉)]

[1] MultiScale Networked Systems (MNS), University of Amsterdam,
Amsterdam, Netherlands
{n.t.islam,z.zhao}@uva.nl
[2] University of Amsterdam, Amsterdam, Netherlands

**Abstract.** Classical search engines using indexing methods in data infrastructures primarily allow keyword-based queries to retrieve content. While these indexing-based methods are highly scalable and efficient, due to a lack of an appropriate evaluation dataset and a limited understanding of semantics, they often fail to capture the user's intent and generate incomplete responses during evaluation. This problem also extends to domain-specific search systems that utilize a Knowledge Base (KB) to access data from various research infrastructures. Research infrastructures (RIs) from the environmental and earth science domain, which encompass the study of ecosystems, biodiversity, oceanography, and climate change, generate, share, and reuse large volumes of data. While there are attempts to provide a centralized search service (https://search. envri.eu/) using Elasticsearch as a knowledge base, they also face similar challenges in understanding queries with multiple intents. To address these challenges, we proposed an automated method to curate a domain-specific evaluation dataset to analyze the capability of a search system. Furthermore, we incorporate the Retrieval of Augmented Generation (RAG), powered by Large Language Models (LLMs), for high-quality retrieval of environmental domain data using natural language queries. Our quantitative and qualitative analysis of the evaluation dataset shows that LLM-based systems for information retrieval return results with higher precision when understanding queries with multiple intents, compared to Elasticsearch-based systems.

**Keywords:** Information Retrieval · Environmental Data · LLMs · Search Engine

## 1 Introduction

Classical search engines [12], such as Google or academic search engines like Google Scholar, operate primarily on keyword-based retrieval mechanisms. They index vast amounts of textual or image data and return results based on exact or partial keyword matches, often ranked by measures such as term frequency [7], PageRank [5], or other heuristics. While highly efficient and scalable, these

© The Author(s), under exclusive license to Springer Nature Switzerland AG 2026
G. De Tré et al. (Eds.): FQAS 2025, LNAI 16119, pp. 277–288, 2026.
https://doi.org/10.1007/978-3-032-05607-8_26

systems typically lack deep semantic understanding of the queries. A search query like *"RAG papers before/after 2024"* on platforms such as Google Scholar often fails to capture the users true intent due to the limitations of keyword-based search systems. Instead of interpreting "before/after 2024" as a temporal filter on publication dates, the system treats the entire string as a literal phrase, retrieving documents that contain the words "before" or "after" alongside "2024" often resulting in papers published in 2024, not those published before or after that year. Similarly domain specific search engines for research infrastructures faces similar issues due to the existence of similar underlying problem of using index based knowledge base like elasticsearch.

A knowledge base [2] is a centralized repository that stores general information, facts, and rules about a specific domain or domains in the form of textual data, relational database and more. This structured information allows classical or dialogue-based search systems to perform tasks such as question-answering, reasoning, problem-solving, and decision-making by accessing and utilizing the stored knowledge. ENVRY-FAIR [20] exemplifies a knowledge base [9] that offers researchers access to domain specific data for climate change research and mitigation strategies for environmental research infrastructures. However, usage of these semi-structured knowledge-bases (SKBs) [26] supporting text-based queries on unstructured textual knowledge [15,16], SQL based [29,31] or knowledge graph based [13] solutions are often hampered by lexical gap problems [4]. This restricts them from generating results that fully comply with the user intent. Moreover, classical search engines built upon a knowledge-base like Elasticsearch [11] also face limitations such as the lack of contextual understanding and an inability to support conversational or dialogue-based queries, which enables the researcher or end user to dig deeper into a problem.

However, evaluating these knowledge bases is highly challenging, especially when they are domain-specific. This challenge primarily boils down to the lack of proper evaluation datasets because the number of end users in domain-specific research infrastructures is extremely low. In these cases, the systems are queried manually to check the quality of the response from the classical search system; an automated method to determine the quality of similar systems is not available due to the lack of appropriate evaluation data. Furthermore, to solidify our argument regarding the challenges of classical search engines, we briefly analyzed the ENVRI-FAIR [9] project, which aims to centralize content from environmental Research Infrastructures (RIs) into a unified access portal. We used some of the evaluation dataset to analyze ENVRI-FAIR, a classical search system which we discuss in detail in Sect. 4. For example, queries such as "North Ferriby from 1985 to 1989" in Table 1 fail to retrieve or rank any relevant datasets within the top 20 results in traditional Elasticsearch-based systems. However, the content was retrieved easily for more straightforward queries like "North Ferriby" highlighting severe gaps in the retrieval mechanism when the temporal requirement was appended to the query. These elastic search-based knowledge systems typically rely on keyword matching and struggle to interpret multi-intent queries that combine spatial and temporal constraints. This issue is further evident in other mixed-type queries, such as "Sabrina Arnold 2024-06-27" or "Brixham laboratories microbe biomass and diversity," where relevant results were either ranked very low or not retrieved within the top 20 results.

To address these challenges, we propose a formalized method for creating an evaluation dataset that measures search quality. Moreover, we propose a Retrieval-Augmented Generation (RAG)-based method tailored for the environmental and earth science domain for a dialogue-based information retrieval. Our process leverages a fine-tuned Large Language Model (LLM) for contextual query understanding and semantic retrieval using RAG from a vector database for knowledge storage. The fine-tuning enables the model to better understand domain-specific terminology and user intent patterns. Finally, to verify the responses generated by our system, we utilized our evaluation dataset preparation method to curate a domain-specific evaluation dataset, allowing us to analyze our system both quantitatively and qualitatively.

**Table 1.** A primary analysis of how the platform ENVRI-FAIR fails to understand queries with multiple intents. The *Keywords* are the search queries, and *Type* specifies whether the query has single or mixed intent. *Correctness* Defines whether a correct result stays in the top 20 results, and *Order* shows the order of the proper response in the top 20 results.

| Keywords | Type | Correctness | Order |
|---|---|---|---|
| Quality-controlleddata on molar fraction | Single | Yes | 1 |
| Sabrina Arnold 2024-06-27 | Mixed | No | 12 |
| Lise Lotte ICOS ATC CO2 Release | Mixed | Yes | 3 |
| Brixham laboratories microbe biomass and diversity | Mixed | No | 17 |
| microbe biomass and diversity Brixham laboratories | Mixex | No | Not found in top 20 |
| Insect and earthworm AstraZeneca taxonomy | Mixed | Yes | 2 |
| North Ferriby | Single | Yes | 1 |
| North Ferriby From 1985 to 1989 | Mixed | No | Not found in top 20 |

In summary, the contributions of this paper are:

- We propose a method to create an evaluation dataset for the environment and earth science domain, enabling the automatic evaluation of search results from user queries.
- We propose a RAG-based framework with a knowledge base for the environmental and earth science domain, dubbed EnvKB (Environment Knowledge Base), which incorporates a fine-tuned LLM to retrieve information from dialogue-based queries.
- We compare the capability of our proposed method with the results from an Elasticsearch-based knowledge base, ENVRI-FAIR, using a curated evaluation dataset and compare them quantitatively and qualitatively.

## 2  Related Work

LLMs have been used to augment search systems by enhancing queries, summarizing content, optimizing indexing, and improving result ranking [19]. These methods operate within search engine frameworks, leveraging LLMs for language understanding and processing while requiring minimal computational power, primarily focusing on query manipulation. Ayoub et al. [3] use prompt engineering to paraphrase or generate query passages. Chen et al. [6] explore tailoring search experiences to user intent, and Zhou and Li [32] examine the shift in user behavior from traditional search engines to generative AI systems. Generative search engines have also been applied to complex knowledge tasks [22], with Li et al. [18] providing an overview of their evolution. Further studies by Thomas et al. [24] address challenges like scalability and user alignment, highlighting the potential and limitations of LLM-driven retrieval systems.

The integration of LLMs into search and retrieval systems has revolutionized information retrieval, enabling more contextual and personalized search experiences. Liu et al. [19] demonstrate how LLMs enhance sparse retrieval methods by refining relevance estimation and query understanding. Wang et al. [25] reimagine the search stack with a LLM integrating generative capabilities for advanced query handling, while Salemi el al. [21] optimize cross-model ranking for diverse queries.

A dialogue-based search or question-answering-based information retrieval system [1, 27] is an interactive information retrieval paradigm where users engage in a multi-turn conversation with the search system to refine their queries and explore relevant content iteratively. Unlike traditional keyword-based or static query systems, dialogue-based search systems utilize natural language understanding and context retention to interpret user intent and generate results accordingly. Referring to Table 1, queries like *"North Ferriby from 1985 to 1989"* or *"Brixham laboratories microbe biomass and diversity"* were either *not found at all* or ranked very low in traditional search. A dialogue-based system could improve this outcome by inherently understanding the meaning by extracting and analyzing contents from a knowledge base.

However, to the best of our knowledge, none of the previous work focused on using an LLM-based knowledge base for the environment and earth science domain with retrieval using RAG.

## 3  Methodology

To address the challenges of classical search engines as demonstrated through the examples in Table 1, we propose a dialogue-based knowledge retrieval system EnvKB. Figure 1 shows the overall architecture of our proposed system. We divided our system into three primary components namely i) Knowledge Base Indexer, ii) Knowledge Base Retriever and iii) Knowledge Base (Vector Database).

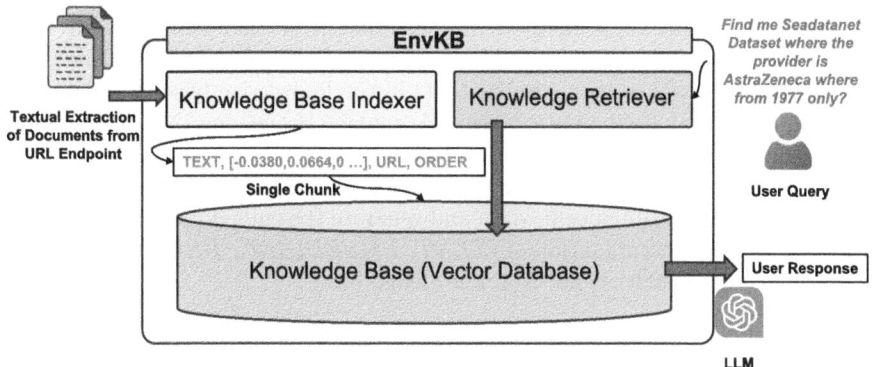

**Fig. 1.** Overall Architecture of our Proposed System.

***Knowledge Base Indexer.*** The goal of the Knowledge-Base Indexer of an LLM-based system is to extract documents from the URL endpoints of the environment domain. The contents of these URL endpoints should be searchable by EnvKB. However, these endpoints can be in different formats, including HTML, CSV, or JSON. The goal of the knowledge base indexer is to convert these formats into a text-based format for the LLM to understand. However, LLMs have a limit on the number of tokens they can handle. Therefore, the knowledge base indexer also chunks the document into multiple shards if the token length exceeds a certain threshold and keeps track of the order of the shards so they can be concatenated if needed and map them with their corresponding URL. Finally, using a trained LLM, the knowledge base indexer generates the embedding vector for each of the chunks as depicted as the *Single Chunk* in Fig. 1.

***Knowledge Retriever.*** The goal of the Knowledge Retriever is to understand the intent of the query, gather related responses from the knowledge base, and use the LLM to generate an appropriate response. This structured information allows classical or dialogue-based search systems to perform tasks such as question-answering, reasoning, problem-solving, and decision-making by accessing and utilizing the stored knowledge. However, without training the LLM on the environmental domain, they face a problem called hallucination, where they tend to answer a question that does not make any sense, misses the context, or is borderline incorrect. Therefore, we also train the LLM with appropriate environmental domain data before using it for generating responses. Furthermore, we propose using Retrieval of Augmented Generation (RAG) [17], to retrieve content from the knowledge base.

***Knowledge Base.*** A knowledge base [2] is a centralized repository that stores general information, facts, and rules about a specific domain or domains in the form of textual data, relational database, and more. The knowledge base sits at the center of our proposed system, where the knowledge is stored and also retrieved from. Knowledge can be stored in various systems, including relational databases like SQL or stored in textual format, or semi-structured databases like

Elasticsearch. While these methods are effective, it is challenging to search for the correct content from them as they only store textual content. While some works [10] have tried to store similar texts in the knowledge base to expand the search criteria, they used a basic Natural Language Processing (NLP) technique. Although this is the right direction, generating similar texts is an exhaustive task when the model is not trained on the domain. Therefore, we propose to use a trained LLM on domain-specific data and generate the embedding for each chunk and then store the combination of *[TEXT, EMBEDDING, URL, ORDER]* in a vector database, which we use as a knowledge base.

## 4    Experimental Results

In this section, we describe and discuss our entire experimental process, starting with curating the evaluation dataset, evaluation metrics, training, embedding generation, and finally, the quantitative and qualitative results using case studies. Our code is available here[1].

### 4.1    Evaluation Dataset Preparation

We create an evaluation dataset to evaluate the effectiveness of our proposed system EnvKB on retrieving relevant content aligned with the query. Our hypothesis on developing an evaluation dataset is based on the idea that the contents we store in the vector database or the contents that are already stored in the Elasticsearch database of ENVRI-FAIR can be extracted using the exact or similar keywords from the URL endpoints. Since we were able to find the contents that ENVRI-FAIR indexed, we used those URLs to create our evaluation dataset.

We begin by selecting a representative set of 1000 endpoints provided by ENVRI-FAIR [11] where the endpoints were provided at the GitHub repository[2]. These endpoints are URLs pointing to individual content records (e.g., metadata pages, data summaries). Since these endpoints have structured format, we selected keywords like *Data set name, Country, Geographical area, Summary,* and more and extracted the key value pairs. A sample endpoint is exemplified here[3]. We randomly select specific key values from these endpoints to create queries with single intent. Furthermore, some key value pair may overlap in multiple endpoint URL. Therefore we combine all the URLs for that specific key value pairs. Thus, if the system returns atleast one of the URLs for a key value, we consider them as the correct response. We put these key values in our system and the ENVRI-FAIR system and compare the results. Furthermore, we also mix different key values from the same URL endpoint to simulate mixed intent. In total we have collected 1500 samples for evaluation. Out of them 1000 are queries with single intent, and 500 are queries with multiple intent. Table 2 shows some sample example of our evaluation dataset.

---

[1] https://github.com/QCDIS/Retrieval_Paper/tree/main
[2] https://github.com/QCDIS/kb-indexer
[3] https://edmed.seadatanet.org/report/70/

**Table 2.** A few snapshots of our evaluation dataset

| Key<br>Value | Type | URL |
|---|---|---|
| British Oceanographic Data Centre | Single | https://edmed.seadatanet.org/report/854/ |
| Northern North Sea | Single | https://edmed.seadatanet.org/report/851/ |
| Total Oil Marine Plc | Single | https://edmed.seadatanet.org/report/850/<br>https://edmed.seadatanet.org/report/851/<br>https://edmed.seadatanet.org/report/852/ |
| AstraZeneca, Brixham Environmental Laboratory | Mixed | https://edmed.seadatanet.org/report/858/<br>https://edmed.seadatanet.org/report/865/<br>https://edmed.seadatanet.org/report/866/ |
| Manual biota samplers, gas chromatograph mass spectrometers | Mixed | https://edmed.seadatanet.org/report/894/<br>https://edmed.seadatanet.org/report/894/ |
| Scottish Environment Protection Agency, Stirling Office | Mixed | https://edmed.seadatanet.org/report/893/<br>https://edmed.seadatanet.org/report/887/<br>https://edmed.seadatanet.org/report/886/ |

### 4.2 Evaluation Metrics

To measure the relevancy of the returned responses we used the evaluation metrics *Hits@K* and *BERTScore*.

**Hits@K:** Hits@K measures the proportion of queries for which at least one relevant result appears in the top-$K$ (k=10) retrieved documents. A query is considered a hit if the target document is found within the top-$K$ positions. Equation 1 defines the metric.

$$Hits@K = \frac{\text{Number of queries with relevant results in top } K}{\text{Total number of queries}} \quad (1)$$

**BERTScore:** To capture semantic similarity beyond exact matches with URL, we use BERTScore [30], which computes token-level similarity between queries and retrieved responses using contextual embeddings from BERT [8]. For each query, we evaluate the first ranked result and average BERTScore across all queries to assess overall semantic alignment.

### 4.3 Model Training and Embedding Generation

In this work, we pre-train different models using a Sequence-to-Sequence [23] language modeling architecture in order to ensure the model has the knowledge of the environmental and earth science domain. We select LLaMa 3.1 as our

**Table 3.** A comparisonal analysis on the performance of our proposed LLM with Elasticsearch based system ENVRI-FAIR and other LLMs

|  | Single Query | | Mixed Query | |
|---|---|---|---|---|
|  | Hits@10 | BERTScore | Hits@10 | BERTScore |
| Elasticsearch | **0.96** | 0.89 | 0.37 | 0.45 |
| LLaMa 3.1 | **0.96** | **0.92** | **0.84** | **0.90** |
| LLaMa 2.7 | 0.91 | 0.91 | 0.82 | 0.88 |
| Mistral | 0.87 | 0.84 | 0.82 | 0.81 |
| Phi-3 | 0.91 | 0.88 | 0.77 | 0.85 |
| Phi-2 | 0.84 | 0.86 | 0.78 | 0.84 |

base model and compare our proposed system with elasticsearch based system, ENVRI-FAIR and other LLMs. For LLM comparison, we used LLaMa 2.7, Phi-3 and Phi-2 and Mistral. By leveraging an encoder-decoder framework, the model is capable of encoding complex, domain specific multi-intent input queries and generating contextually grounded outputs in natural language. We adopt the Sequence-to-Sequence task type within the PEFT (Parameter-Efficient Fine-Tuning) [28] configuration to enable LoRA-based [14] adaptation, allowing for efficient fine-tuning of large models. This method of training allows the model to not only adopt to new data but also remember its previous training data as well. To collect data for model training we used a tool *Crawl4ai* to extract the texts from the URL endpoints we mentioned earlier. We trained the model for 5 epochs with a maximum token length of 2048, and our learning rate was 2e^5 with a batch size of 2 for our 3.1B parameter LLaMa model. We also use a beam size of 4 for the generation task and a temperature value of 0.5 for optimal performance. We used 1 NVIDIA A100 GPU with 40 GB of memory.

After training the model, we use the text extracted using *Crawl4ai* and chunk each document into tokens of size 250 for optimal results to generate embedding. Then, we store the embedding, the text, the chunked order, and the corresponding URL in a vector database. For retrieval, initially, the query is converted to an embedding, and we run a cosine similarity of the query embedding with the embeddings stored in the knowledge base and retrieve the top 10 results with the highest cosine similarity.

### 4.4    Experimental Analysis

The evaluation results presented in Table 3 highlight the comparative performance of elasticsearch and LLM-based search systems using both Hits@10 and BERTScore across single and mixed query scenarios. Elasticsearch performs strongly on single queries (Hits@10 = 0.96), indicating its effectiveness when queries closely match indexed content. However, it significantly under-performs on mixed queries (Hits@10 = 0.37, BERTScore = 0.45), reflecting its limitations in handling multi-intent or semantically complex inputs. In contrast, all

**Table 4.** Performance comparison between base and trained LLMs for single and multiple query tasks

|  | Single Query | | Multiple Query | |
| --- | --- | --- | --- | --- |
| LLM Name | Base LLM | Trained LLM | Base LLM | Trained LLM |
| LLaMa 3.1 | 0.89 | 0.93 | 0.84 | 0.88 |
| LLaMa 2.7 | 0.90 | 0.94 | 0.81 | 0.86 |
| Mistral | 0.88 | 0.92 | 0.79 | 0.83 |
| Phi-3 | 0.86 | 0.90 | 0.75 | 0.80 |
| Phi-2 | 0.83 | 0.87 | 0.76 | 0.82 |

LLM-based models show improved performance in the mixed query setting, with LLaMa 3.1 achieving the highest Hits@10 (0.96) and BERTScore (0.92), suggesting a better capability to interpret and retrieve results based on semantic context. While there is a slight trade-off in single query performance compared to the elastic search-based system ENVRI-FAIR, the LLM models offer a more balanced and context-aware retrieval strategy, particularly evident in their superior handling of disjoint or compositional queries.

The results in Table 4 demonstrate the benefits of fine-tuning base LLMs for domain-specific search tasks, as shown across both single and multiple query scenarios. In every case, the trained models outperform their base counterparts on BERTScore, reflecting improvements in both understanding and retrieving relevant content. For instance, LLaMa 3.1 shows a notable increase of BERTScore from 0.89 to 0.93 in single query performance and from 0.84 to 0.88 in multiple queries, suggesting that training enhances the models sensitivity to both simple and compound search intents. This trend holds across all models, with Phi-3 improving from 0.83 to 0.87 in single queries and from 0.76 to 0.82 in multiple queries. These gains underline how fine-tuning helps models internalize domain-specific patterns, vocabulary, and reasoning strategies, enabling more accurate alignment between user queries and indexed content.

### 4.5  Case Studies

In this section, we will demonstrate with actual examples how our system understands queries with multiple intent. In **Case Study 1** from Fig. 2a shows a query to our system "Find me Seadatanet Dataset where the provider is AstraZeneca where from 1977 and onwards". The system returned two responses for this query, the first from 1977. However, the 2nd result is from 1975. Our model is aware of this fact, mentioning that the period is From 1975 onwards. In **Case Study 2** in Fig. 2b, the intent is changed slightly with the query "Find me Seadatanet Dataset where the provider is AstraZeneca where from 1977 only". In this query, we requested the system to respond with data only from 1977. From the response, we can see that the system only responded with one result from

1977. These case studies prove that our model can capture multiple intents and produce results accordingly.

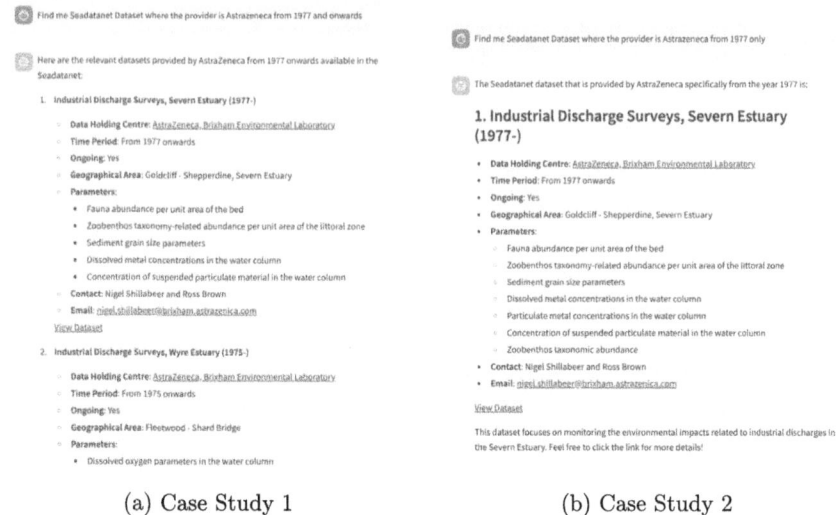

(a) Case Study 1                              (b) Case Study 2

Fig. 2. A case study of our Current System.

## 5   Conclusion

This work examines how search in the environment and earth science domains can be enhanced using large language models (LLMs) over traditional search systems. Initially, we demonstrated a method to curate a dataset for evaluation. Then, we proposed a learning-based method to train an LLM with domain-specific knowledge, utilizing a vector database. Our comparison analysis shows that our dialogue-based system EnvKB can demonstrate better search results than a classical search system, ENVRI-FAIR, using Elasticsearch. Furthermore, we demonstrated the benefits of pre-training in generating more effective embeddings, which ultimately led to improved search results quality. Finally, we presented two case studies that highlight the effectiveness of our system in the real world. In our future work, we aim to demonstrate how our knowledge-based system can be scaled for various domains with continually updated and ever higher amounts of data.

**Acknowledgment.** This research was made possible through funding from the Dutch Research Council (NWO) Large-Scale Research Infrastructures (LSRI) programme for the LTER-LIFE (http://www.lter-life.nl) infrastructure (grant 184.036.014). The work is also partially funded by several European Union projects: ENVRI-Hub

Next (101131141), EVERSE (101129744), BlueCloud-2026 (101094227), OSCARS (101129751).

# References

1. Alinejad, A., Kumar, K., Vahdat, A.: Evaluating the retrieval component in LLM-based question answering systems. arXiv preprint arXiv:2406.06458 (2024)
2. AlKhamissi, B., Li, M., Celikyilmaz, A., Diab, M., Ghazvininejad, M.: A review on language models as knowledge bases. arXiv preprint arXiv:2204.06031 (2022)
3. Ayoub, M.A.K., Su, Z., Li, Q.: A case study of enhancing sparse retrieval using LLMs. In: Companion Proceedings of the ACM on Web Conference 2024, pp. 1609–1615 (2024)
4. Berger, A., Caruana, R., Cohn, D., Freitag, D., Mittal, V.: Bridging the lexical Chasm: statistical approaches to answer-finding. In: ACM SIGIR, pp. 192–199 (2000)
5. Brin, S., Page, L.: The anatomy of a large-scale hypertextual web search engine. Comput. Netw. ISDN Syst. **30**(1–7), 107–117 (1998)
6. Chen, J., et al.: When large language models meet personalization: Perspectives of challenges and opportunities. WWW (2024)
7. Das, M., Alphonse, P., et al.: A comparative study on TF-IDF feature weighting method and its analysis using unstructured dataset. arXiv preprint arXiv:2308.04037 (2023)
8. Devlin, J., Chang, M.W., Lee, K., Toutanova, K.: BERT: pre-training of deep bidirectional transformers for language understanding. In: Burstein, J., Doran, C., Solorio, T. (eds.) Proceedings of the 2019 Conference of the North American Chapter of the Association for Computational Linguistics: Human Language Technologies, Volume 1 (Long and Short Papers), pp. 4171–4186. Association for Computational Linguistics, Minneapolis, Minnesota (2019). https://doi.org/10.18653/v1/N19-1423, https://aclanthology.org/N19-1423/
9. ENVRI-FAIR Project: Envri search portal. https://search.envri.eu/ (2024). Accessed 27 Mar 2025
10. Farshidi, S., Zhao, Z.: An adaptable indexing pipeline for enriching meta information of datasets from heterogeneous repositories. In: Pacific-Asia Conference on Knowledge Discovery and Data Mining, pp. 472–484 (2022)
11. Gabriel Pelouze, Markus Stocker, B.M.Z.Z.: ENVRI-FAIR D7.4: The ENVRI-fair knowledge base v2 (2024). https://doi.org/10.5281/zenodo.10363119, https://zenodo.org/records/10363119. Accessed 24 Mar 2025
12. Halavais, A.: Search engine society. John Wiley & Sons (2017)
13. He, X., et al.: G-retriever: retrieval-augmented generation for textual graph understanding and question answering. Adv. Neural. Inf. Process. Syst. **37**, 132876–132907 (2024)
14. Hu, E.J., et al.: LoRA: Low-rank adaptation of large language models. arXiv preprint arXiv:2106.09685 (2021)
15. Karpukhin, V., et al.: Dense passage retrieval for open-domain question answering. In: Proceedings of the 2020 Conference on Empirical Methods in Natural Language Processing (EMNLP), pp. 6769–6781 (2020). https://doi.org/10.18653/v1/2020.emnlp-main.550
16. Lee, K., Chang, M.W., Toutanova, K.: Latent retrieval for weakly supervised open domain question answering. arXiv preprint arXiv:1906.00300 (2019)

17. Lewis, P., et al.: Retrieval-augmented generation for knowledge-intensive NLP tasks. NIPS **33**, 9459–9474 (2020)
18. Li, Y., et al.: A survey of generative search and recommendation in the era of large language models. arXiv:2404.16924 (2024)
19. Liu, Z., et al.: Information retrieval meets large language models. In: ACM on Web Conference 2024 (2024)
20. Petzold, A., et al.: ENVRI-fair - interoperable environmental fair data and services for society, innovation and research. In: 2019 15th International Conference on eScience (eScience), pp. 277–280 (2019). https://doi.org/10.1109/eScience.2019.00038
21. Salemi, A., Zamani, H.: Towards a search engine for machines: Unified ranking for multiple retrieval-augmented large language models. In: ACM SIGIR, pp. 741–751 (2024)
22. Suri, S., et al.: The use of generative search engines for knowledge work and complex tasks. arXiv:2404.04268 (2024)
23. Sutskever, I., Vinyals, O., Le, Q.V.: Sequence to sequence learning with neural networks. Adv. Neural Inf. Process. Syst. **27** (2014)
24. Thomas, P., Spielman, S., Craswell, N., Mitra, B.: Large language models can accurately predict searcher preferences. In: ACM SIGIR (2024)
25. Wang, L., Yang, N., Huang, X., Yang, L., Majumder, R., Wei, F.: Large search model: Redefining search stack in the era of LLMs. In: ACM SIGIR Forum. vol. 57, pp. 1–16. ACM New York, NY, USA (2024)
26. Wu, S., et al.: Stark: Benchmarking LLM retrieval on textual and relational knowledge bases. Adv. Neural. Inf. Process. Syst. **37**, 127129–127153 (2024)
27. Xiong, G., Bao, J., Zhao, W.: Interactive-KBQA: Multi-turn interactions for knowledge base question answering with large language models. arXiv preprint arXiv:2402.15131 (2024)
28. Xu, L., Xie, H., Qin, S.Z.J., Tao, X., Wang, F.L.: Parameter-efficient fine-tuning methods for pretrained language models: A critical review and assessment. arXiv preprint arXiv:2312.12148 (2023)
29. Yu, T., et al.: Spider: a large-scale human-labeled dataset for complex and cross-domain semantic parsing and text-to-SQL task. In: Proceedings of the 2018 Conference on Empirical Methods in Natural Language Processing, pp. 3911–3921. Brussels, Belgium (2018). https://doi.org/10.18653/v1/D18-1425
30. Zhang, T., Kishore, V., Wu, F., Weinberger, K.Q., Artzi, Y.: BERTScore: Evaluating text generation with BERT. arXiv:1904.09675 (2019)
31. Zhong, V., Xiong, C., Socher, R.: Seq2Sql: Generating structured queries from natural language using reinforcement learning. arXiv preprint arXiv:1709.00103 (2017)
32. Zhou, T., Li, S.: Understanding user switch of information seeking: from search engines to generative AI. J. Libr. Inf. Sci. (2024)

# Schema-Based Inference for Query Expansion and Completion over Knowledge Graphs

Bartolome Ortiz-Viso[✉], Karel Gutiérrez-Batista, M. Dolores Ruiz,
and Maria J. Martin-Bautista

Department of Computer Science and Artificial Intelligence, CITIC-UGR (Research
Center for Information and Communication Technologies), University of Granada,
Granada 18071, Spain
bortiz@ugr.es, {kgb,mdruiz,mbautis}@decsai.ugr.es

**Abstract.** Graph databases are powerful tools for representing complex,
interconnected knowledge, but their structure and semantics pose significant challenges for natural language interaction. In this work, we present
a guided approach based on the Retrieval-Augmented Generation (RAG)
schema to assist large language models in generating queries over graph-
based databases. By incorporating semantically relevant paths into the
prompt, our method reduces the reasoning complexity that the model
must handle, enabling more accurate query generation. We evaluate the
performance of different language models under two schema interaction
paradigms—full schema exploration and path-specific guidance—across
queries related to risk assessment in passenger and flight data. Our preliminary results show that path-specific guidance significantly improves
model performance, particularly for smaller models. That semantic pre-
filtering of the graph structure enhances the model's ability to focus on
relevant information.

**Keywords:** Knowledge graphs · query answering systems · graph
databases · large language models · natural language processing

## 1 Introduction

Graph databases [1] are currently an exciting technology well-suited for modelling real-world scenarios while preserving the semantic relationships between
entities. These databases enable a more faithful representation of human knowledge in complex environments, where interactions occur at various levels of proximity and connectivity.

They also offer a natural way to represent hierarchical knowledge, making them compatible with ontologies and other structured sources of semantic
information–such as subjectpredicateobject triplets.

G. De Tré et al. (Eds.): FQAS 2025, LNAI 16119, pp. 289–300, 2026.
https://doi.org/10.1007/978-3-032-05607-8_27

These features have made graph databases particularly useful in domains with multiple data sources and complex inter-entity correlations, where a traditional table-based representation may fail to capture the full picture, for instance, in biology or security contexts.

One particularly interesting aspect of graph-based models is their ability to generate semantically meaningful concepts directly from graph structures. Given a query and its corresponding output–formed by specific entity types and their relationships–we can easily derive grammatical constructions that describe the result. This improves both the system's interpretability and the clarity of its outputs.

To interact with graph and other types of databases, we now have novel query languages that adopt different approaches–such as the one proposed in [2]–similar in purpose to SQL but specifically designed for graph data, like Cypher. These languages aim to capture the unique characteristics of graph databases and enable efficient querying.

In parallel, we now have powerful language models that can serve as bridges between these novel query languages and natural user queries. Language models of varying sizes can generate queries based on user input, effectively translating natural language into formal query language. Their performance can be significantly improved when provided with access to the underlying database schema.

However, several challenges arise in these scenarios. On the one hand, language models are limited by their context window, which constrains the number of nodes and relationships they can process. Additionally, model limitations–including hallucinations and energy consumption–play a crucial role in their practical deployment. On the other hand, one of the key strengths of graph databases lies in their ability to leverage multi-hop relationships, detect community structures, and reveal conceptual interconnections–all of which are critical for constructing a comprehensive understanding of a query.

In many cases, generating a well-informed response requires surfacing multiple entities–beyond those explicitly mentioned in the query–and understanding the relationships among them. This is significantly more difficult to achieve with other data structures. Language models may struggle to perform these logical reasoning steps unless they are highly capable and thus more computationally expensive, making such approaches less practical in many real-world settings.

In this work, we translate some of the RAG philosophy of reduce the memory and the training of the model, providing it with additional information to answers query, more specifically generate a cypher [3] query to a graph database that answer users question, reducing the model size needed to interact with these databases without compromising their performance.

This section serves as an introduction to our work. In the next section, we present the key related works that form the foundation of our research. Section 3 will detail the methodology and how the experiments were conducted. In Sect. 4, we will then discuss the specific results obtained in the scenario under study (commercial flight-based contraband), and finally conclude with a summary of our main findings in Sects. 5 and 6.

# 2   Related Works

In this section, we provide a brief overview of the theoretical foundations and practical applications of graph databases and Retrieval-Augmented Generation (RAG) techniques, with a particular focus on how they can enhance data-driven processes and their role in query-answering systems.

## 2.1   Graph Databases

Graph databases [1] are noSQL databases designed to represent and manage relationships between data explicitly. Unlike traditional databases that organize data into tables, graph databases are based on nodes, edges, and properties. Nodes represent entities, edges denote the relationships between those entities, and properties add details about nodes and edges. This model of graph databases (while different from another classic approach, such as the Resource Description Framework (RDF), where each addition of information is represented with a separate node) is useful in situations where the relationships between elements are key, such as in social networks, recommendation systems, and transportation network analysis. The flexibility of graph databases allows efficient representation of complex relationships and querying of connection patterns between data.

In terms of applications, graph databases are crucial in areas such as computational biology [4,5], where they are used to model protein interaction networks or genomics, in recommendation systems where relationships between users and products can be represented as a graph, and even in fraud detection [6] where suspicious relationships can be modeled through connections. Furthermore, in social networks [7], graph databases enable the analysis of user relationships, community identification, and influence or information diffusion analysis. Queries on these graphs, including pattern searching, shortest path finding, or centrality analysis, can be performed more efficiently than traditional relational models.

## 2.2   RAG over Graph Databases for Query Generation

Retrieval-Augmented Generation (RAG) [8] is a technique that combines generative language models with information retrieval systems. Instead of relying solely on a pre-trained model to generate responses, RAG first performs a search to retrieve relevant data from an external source (such as a database or a set of documents). Then it uses the retrieved information as a context provided to a language model, together with the original query, to generate a more accurate and contextually appropriate answer. This approach has gained popularity due to its ability to enhance the precision and relevance of generated results, leveraging real-time data and eliminating the need for the model to learn all knowledge beforehand, while reducing its tendency to hallucinate.

The popularity of RAG has particularly grown in non-structured or semi-structured databases, such as text-based ones, where relevant information can be scattered across large volumes or sources or can be retrieved with multiple paths [9]. Moreover, Retrieval-Augmented Generation offers a complementary strategy to enhance the query generation process by incorporating relevant external knowledge during generation, which helps disambiguate user intent and produce more contextually grounded queries [10].

Graph databases and other types of databases are also central to this research topic, as the combination of graph data retrieval with natural language generation enhances a system's ability to handle complex, context-dependent queries. This approach is convenient in domains like healthcare, where relationships between diseases, symptoms, and treatments can be modelled as graphs and leveraged to generate more accurate recommendations or diagnoses [11].

This is precisely where our model becomes relevant. We operate under an assumption common in security-related domains: a single designation–such as one indicating high contraband risk–can be defined in multiple ways. Moreover, risk factors, even when referring to the same type of threat, are often heterogeneous and can vary significantly depending on the context, the data source, or the level of detail.

Given this semantic and structural diversity, our approach focuses on identifying the entities mentioned in the user query and leveraging a high-level knowledge schema that captures the relationships among them. By doing so, we can trace the underlying graph connections and construct a more concise and context-specific representation, which is then provided to the language model or generator. This enables the system to generate accurate and relevant Cypher queries without requiring an expanded context that includes the full database schema–thus improving information retrieval efficiency while reducing the computational and energy cost of the interpreter.

Graph databases are an already well-established research topic and technology, with applications ranging from academic research [12] to fully developed end products. The methods used to query them and extract information [2,13] can vary widely and remain an active area of research. This ongoing work serves as a foundation for novel investigations in data and information management and user-query interaction when dealing with complex knowledge graph databases, exploring their limitations, possible ways to overcome them, and the feasibility of utilising novel language models for this purpose.

## 3   Methods

Following the diagram in Fig. 1, we outline the methodology designed in this work in this section. Coding details and models will be described in the next section. We begin by processing a natural-language user query. Simultaneously, we extract the graph database schema, including all entities and their relationships as triplets. We then divide the process into three different steps:

- On user's query: we apply Part-of-Speech with a pretrained model to the user query, extracting the entities related to a noun in the query. We utilise these entities, along with the graph nodes, to semantically match the extracted terms with the most relevant entities in the graph schema.

- On graph architecture: Once this mapping is complete, and a maximum number of traversal hops is defined, we search for the shortest paths that connect the identified entities. As the relationship between nodes may be subject to semantic meanings, we perform the path search with an undirected graph version. The paths found are then filtered by the number of hops, entity relationships, and whether they contain other paths as sub-paths.

- Query Generation: The identified relevant entities and their relationships are used as contextual input to generate a structured query. This structured query is designed to retrieve precise and comprehensive information from the graph, ensuring that all relevant parts of the graph are covered in the search. At the same time, the LLM do not have to perform a reading task over what can be a big graph schema.

Finally, the input resulting from the prompt is sent to the LLM for evaluation of its performance. This input consists of the original user query, the context provided either by the predicted paths or the full database schema (depending on the test condition), and any additional prompt information relevant to Cypher query generation (such as output formatting, style, or prompt examples). The LLM uses this information to generate the final query, which is then evaluated based on its performance in the graph database. Specifically, we assess validation (i.e., whether the query is executable and well-formed) and scope (i.e., whether it explores all relevant paths and produces the expected output). Additional details regarding this process are provided in the experiment section.

## 4 Experiments

In this section, we introduce the main batch of experiments conducted in this work, along with the data sources used and their corresponding transformations.

### 4.1 Knowledge Base

The experiments are based on a graph database developed as part of the European project BagIntel. This knowledge base encodes information to assess the risk of contraband within a specific airport. From this graph, we extract the underlying entity schema, which defines the types of entities and their interconnections. This schema serves as the foundational layer upon which our algorithm operates.

To build the knowledge graph, we first identified a set of domain-specific concepts and relationships through consultations with subject-matter experts in airport security and customs operations. These helped define key entities such as Passenger, Luggage, Flight, Drug, and Scanner, along with the interactions and dependencies between them (e.g., Passenger carries Luggage, Luggage is scanned by Scanner, Luggage contains Drug). This conceptual model was refined

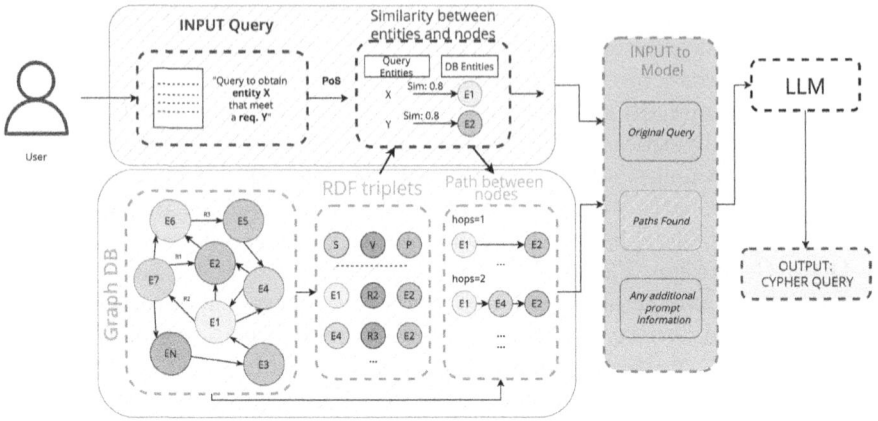

**Fig. 1.** Full methodology schema.

to capture high-level processes and operational details relevant to contraband detection.

Once the conceptual model was established, we formalised it into a structured schema and populated the graph using synthetic and curated datasets. The expert knowledge was encoded as triplets (head entity, relation, tail entity), forming the semantic backbone of the graph. Additionally, logic rules and domain constraints–such as scanning workflows, room hierarchies, and risk classifications–were incorporated to enrich the graph's reasoning capabilities. This expert-driven design ensures the knowledge graph is structurally accurate and semantically meaningful for downstream tasks such as inference, query generation, and risk assessment.

For storing and querying the knowledge base, we used Neo4j[1], a graph-oriented database that naturally represents complex entities and their relationships. Neo4j supports the Cypher query language [3], which we use to retrieve specific nodes and subgraphs based on the semantic structure defined in the schema. This enables us to formulate expressive and efficient queries that align with the domain-specific logic.

The final statistics in the knowledge base include 19 different types of nodes and 19 different kinds of relationships, comprising 150,817 relationships and 58,005 nodes.

### 4.2  Language Model Implementation

To compare different language models for structured query generation, we integrated both ChatGPT (via OpenAI's API[2]) and LLaMA 3.1[3] [14] (via Ollama[4])

---

[1] https://neo4j.com/.

[2] https://platform.openai.com/.

[3] https://github.com/meta-llama/llama-models/tree/main/models/llama3_1.

[4] https://github.com/ollama/ollama.

using the Langchain[5] framework. This setup allowed us to standardise the prompt structure and easily switch between models for experimentation. While ChatGPT-4-mini were accessed through the OpenAI API, LLaMA 3.1 was run locally on CPU through Ollama.

For the RAG approach, a key component of our system relies on language models to interpret natural language queries and connect user questions with our graph entities. This connection may be perform with several language models, although we choose a general-purpose well well-established approach for it:

In our experiments, we first use spaCy[6] with the en_core_web_sm[7] model for linguistic preprocessing, specifically named entity recognition (NER) and part-of-speech tagging. This allows us to extract relevant terms–such as noun phrases and named entities–that may correspond to known entity types in the graph schema. These extracted terms serve as anchors for the next step in the pipeline.

To determine which schema entities are most semantically related to the extracted query terms, we use the embedding model of *all-mpnet-base-v2*[8] via SentenceTransformer [15]. This model produces high-quality semantic embeddings for extracted terms and the available schema entities. By calculating cosine similarity, we can match user concepts to graph concepts, allowing us to select the most relevant schema paths for a given question.

The evaluation process consisted of two stages. First, we prompted the model with the general schema of the graph and a natural language question, asking it to infer the relevant structure and generate a *Cypher* query. In a second, more constrained setting, we provided the model with a set of specific schema paths that semantically matched the query, and then asked it to generate only the corresponding *Cypher* query. This stepwise refinement–from open-ended understanding to guided query construction–allowed us to assess how well each model leveraged contextual knowledge to formulate precise graph queries.

Finally, the matching approach enables us to employ a heuristic method for generating a query based on the selected path and joining the results. This is an entirely deterministic approach that does not require a language model to generate it.

It is also worth noting that the prompt description may vary across language models to improve performance. All of them can be consulted in Suplementary materials 6, but it is worth noting that both models were provided with two different formatting of the models: one with the format $((EntityA, EntityB)Relationship)$, and other closer to Neo4J - $(EntityA - [Relationship] \rightarrow EntityB)$ for each step of the path extracted or the full collection of relationship of the graph schema (Table 1).

---

[5] https://python.langchain.com.

[6] https://spacy.io.

[7] https://spacy.io.

[8] https://huggingface.co/sentence-transformers/all-mpnet-base-v2.

**Table 1.** Evaluation settings for query generation across different models.

| Model | Setting | Input |
|---|---|---|
| GPT-4o | Open Schema | NL question + full schema |
|  | Guided Paths | NL question + relevant schema paths |
| GPT-4o mini | Open Schema | NL question + full schema |
|  | Guided Paths | NL question + relevant schema paths |
| LLaMA 3.1 | Open Schema | NL question + full schema |
|  | Guided Paths | NL question + relevant schema paths |
| Algorithmic direct Path-Following | Guided Paths | relevant schema paths |

### 4.3   Query Selection

Finally, we defined a set of example queries designed to test the different methodologies' ability to generate Cypher queries based on various paths and relationships. These queries involve different entities and explore multiple paths in the graph, ensuring that the system can adapt to complex relationships and generate accurate and exhaustive results.

- **Query: Which passengers are associated with drugs or contraband risk?**
  - *Motivation*: This query involves multiple possible paths, including relationships between entities such as Passenger, Luggage, Route, and Risk.
- **Query:Which flights may be considered risky?**
  - *Motivation*: This query involves the relationships between Flight, Luggage, Drug, and Risk. Again, multiple risks can be identified by examining the graph's various connections and risk origins, so multiple paths through this graph are necessary to provide a comprehensive answer.

## 5   Results and Discussion

Results are described in Table 2. GPT -4 demonstrated robust performance for passenger-related queries, correctly identifying associations under both schema approaches. However, the full schema version exhibited limitations in path exploration, resulting in non-functional outputs. In contrast, the path-specific version succeeded, indicating that GPT-4o benefits from guided querying as schema complexity increases.

GPT-4o mini failed to produce correct results across the entire schema, exhibiting inconsistent outputs and incomplete path coverage. Under the path-specific approach, however, it recovered well, matching GPT-4o's success.

LLaMA 3.1 struggled under both schema conditions. It misinterpreted relationships throughout the entire schema, reversing the direction of the luggage-risk relationship, and although its path-specific attempt was semantically sound,

**Table 2.** Model performance on queries related to passenger and flight risk detection.

| Query | Model | Approach | Valid? | Error | Working? |
|---|---|---|---|---|---|
| Which passengers are associated with drugs or contraband risk? | gpt4 o | full schema | yes | Not all path explored | no |
| Which passengers are associated with drugs or contraband risk? | gpt4o mini | full schema | no | Not all path explored, inconsistent output | no |
| Which passengers are associated with drugs or contraband risk? | llama 3.1 | full schema | no | Relation luggage risk-interpreted in the other orientation | no |
| Which passengers are associated with drugs or contraband risk? | gpt4 o | path-specific | yes | none | yes |
| Which passengers are associated with drugs or contraband risk? | gpt4o mini | path-specific | yes | none | yes |
| Which passengers are associated with drugs or contraband risk? | llama 3.1 | path-specific | yes | well interpreted but failed in query construction | no |
| Which flights may be consider having risk? | gpt4 o | full schema | yes | | yes |
| Which flights may be consider having risk? | gpt4o mini | full schema | yes | not all flight considered | no |
| Which flights may be consider having risk? | llama 3.1 | full schema | no | well interpreted but failed in query construction | no |
| Which flights may be consider having risk? | gpt4 o | path-specific | yes | not all flight considered | no |
| Which flights may be consider having risk? | gpt4o mini | path-specific | yes | | yes |
| Which flights may be consider having risk? | llama 3.1 | path-specific | no | well interpreted but failed in query construction | no |
| Which flights may be consider having risk? | procedural | path-specific | yes | | yes |

it failed to form a correct query. This suggests that while LLaMA's internal logic aligns with user intent, its execution pipeline for structured query formation remains underdeveloped compared to the GPT-4 family.

Turning to the flight risk query, GPT-4o again performed well under both schema types. However, its path-specific version failed to consider all relevant flights, suggesting a limitation in traversal depth or breadth. GPT-4o mini also succeeded in both approaches, but similarly missed some flight connections in the whole schema, mirroring GPT-4o's shortcoming in the path-specific condition. LLaMA 3.1 consistently underperformed on this task, following the previously observed pattern of correct intent interpretation paired with flawed execution. Notably, the procedural system performed best under the path-specific condition for the flight-related query, producing accurate and error-free results. This suggests that deterministic, rule-based logic may still offer advantages for tasks rooted in well-defined ontologies and rigid expectations.

These results reinforce the view that path-specific schema guidance significantly enhances LLM performance, even for smaller or less capable models. In contrast, full schema exploration often proves too ambiguous or noisy for specific architectures, leading to inconsistencies in path discovery and output. GPT-4o stands out for its balance between semantic understanding and execution accuracy, while GPT-4o mini emerges as a lightweight yet competent alternative when guided by schema constraints. LLaMA 3.1, while showing promise in interpretability, requires further refinement for structured data tasks. Although not scalable or adaptable, the procedural approach demonstrates that in narrowly scoped domains, traditional rule-based systems can still outperform generative models in terms of reliability.

## 6    Conclusions

In this work, we presented a directed approach based on the RAG (Retrieval-Augmented Generation) schema to assist language models in generating queries for interacting with graph-based databases. This research topic is gaining increasing attention, as graph databases hold significant potential across many domains. However, they also present a complex scenario in which the semantic value of the knowledge they contain must play a central role in fully exploiting their capabilities. Additionally, their structural complexity can grow rapidly, so leveraging their inherent graph characteristics is essential to enable more effective interaction.

In this preliminary study, we demonstrated that incorporating precomputed paths–based on semantic similarity with nodes–can help mitigate the complexity limitations faced by language models due to their size when generating queries for these databases. This example also highlights the potential benefit of defining a more exhaustive evaluation framework, offering a structured way to compare language models in this task by distinguishing between their ability to generate syntactically valid queries and their capacity to correctly interpret user intent (as the former mainly depends on exposure to updated query examples, while the latter reflects deeper semantic understanding). For a specific task, even procedural generation yields promising performance, highlighting the need for further clarification on how to prompt the system with information and exploring additional ways to evaluate it (in terms of time and query complexity), all of which point to interesting directions for extending this work.

**Supplementary Information** Additional data, prompt selection, notebooks and code can be found at: UGRITAI Lab's Repository

**Acknowledgements.** We would like to acknowledge support for this work from Grant PID2021-123960OB-I00 funded by MCIU/AEI/10.13039/501100011033 and by ERDF/EU (FederaMed project), and from DesinfoScan project: Grant TED2021-129402B-C21 funded by MCIU/AEI/10.13039/501100011033 and by the European Union NextGenerationEU/PRTR. Finally, the research reported in this paper is also funded by the European Union (BAG-INTEL project, grant agreement no. 101121309).

# References

1. Angles, R., Gutierrez, C.: Survey of graph database models. ACM Comput. Surv. **40**, 1:1–1:39 (2008). https://doi.org/10.1145/1322432.1322433
2. Sharma, C., Genevès, P., Gesbert, N., Layaïda, N.: Schema-Based Query Optimisation for Graph Databases (2024). https://arxiv.org/abs/2403.01863. Publisher: arXiv Version Number: 2
3. Francis, N., et al.: Cypher: an evolving query language for property graphs. In: Proceedings of the 2018 International Conference on Management of Data, pp. 1433–1445 (2018). https://doi.org/10.1145/3183713.3190657. Conference Name: SIGMOD/PODS '18: International Conference on Management of Data ISBN: 9781450347037 Place: Houston TX USA Publisher: ACM
4. Timón-Reina, S., Rincón, M. & Martínez-Tomás, R.: An overview of graph databases and their applications in the biomedical domain. Database **2021**, baab026 (2021). https://doi.org/10.1093/database/baab026
5. Mazein, I., et al.: Graph databases in systems biology: a systematic review. Briefings Bioinform. **25**, bbae561 (2024). https://doi.org/10.1093/bib/bbae561
6. International Balkan University, Skopje, North Macedonia, Muminovic, A. & Halili, F. Money laundering prevention in the digital age: Leveraging graph databases for effective solutions. Int. J. Tech. Nat. Sci. **4**, 1–10 (2024). https://ijtns.ibupress.com/uploads/2024/07/ibu_journal_ijtns-1.pdf
7. Almabdy, S.: Comparative analysis of relational and graph databases for social networks. In: 2018 1st International Conference on Computer Applications & Information Security (ICCAIS), pp. 1–4 (2018). https://ieeexplore.ieee.org/document/8441982/. Conference Name: 2018 1st International Conference on Computer Applications & Information Security (ICCAIS) ISBN: 9781538644270 Place: Riyadh Publisher: IEEE
8. Fan, W., et al.: A Survey on RAG Meeting LLMs: Towards Retrieval-Augmented Large Language Models, pp. 6491–6501. ACM. Barcelona Spain (2024). https://doi.org/10.1145/3637528.3671470
9. Tang, Y., Yang, Y.: MultiHop-RAG: Benchmarking Retrieval-Augmented Generation for Multi-Hop Queries (2024). https://arxiv.org/abs/2401.15391. Publisher: arXiv Version Number: 1
10. Sawarkar, K., Mangal, A., Solanki, S.R.: Blended RAG: improving rag (retriever-augmented generation) accuracy with semantic search and hybrid query-based retrievers. In: 2024 IEEE 7th International Conference on Multimedia Information Processing and Retrieval (MIPR), pp. 155–161 (2024). https://ieeexplore.ieee.org/document/10707868/. Conference Name: 2024 IEEE 7th International Conference on Multimedia Information Processing and Retrieval (MIPR) ISBN: 9798350351422 Place: San Jose, CA, USA Publisher: IEEE

11. Wu, J., et al.: Medical Graph RAG: Towards Safe Medical Large Language Model via Graph Retrieval-Augmented Generation (2024). https://arxiv.org/abs/2408.04187. Publisher: arXiv Version Number: 2

12. Ren, H., Galkin, M., Cochez, M., Zhu, Z., Leskovec, J.: Neural Graph Reasoning: Complex Logical Query Answering Meets Graph Databases (2023). https://arxiv.org/abs/2303.14617. Publisher: arXiv Version Number: 1

13. Monteiro, J., Sá, F., Bernardino, J.: Experimental evaluation of graph databases: JanusGraph, Nebula Graph, Neo4j, and TigerGraph. Appl. Sci. **13**, 5770 (2023). https://www.mdpi.com/2076-3417/13/9/5770

14. Grattafiori, A., et al.: The Llama 3 Herd of Models (2024). http://arxiv.org/abs/2407.21783. ArXiv:2407.21783 [cs]

15. Reimers, N., Gurevych, I.: Sentence-BERT: Sentence embeddings using Siamese BERT-networks. Association for Computational Linguistics (2019). https://arxiv.org/abs/1908.10084

# Implications and Advantages of AI Test Actualization in API Automated Software Testing

Anastasia Karacholeva$^{(\boxtimes)}$ and Milen Petrov

Faculty of Mathematics and Informatics, Sofia University "St. Kliment Ohridski", Sofia, Bulgaria
{karacholev,milenp}@fmi.uni-sofia.bg

**Abstract.** The actualization of software test by artificial intelligence (AI) introduces transformative capabilities that improve coverage, reduce human error, and enhance efficiency. This paper explores the implications of applying AI in the context of automated test case generation, focusing particularly on the use of generative models to create both positive and negative test scenarios. For the experimental evaluation, a mock server was developed to simulate a real-world API environment, ensuring controlled testing conditions while maintaining realistic API behavior. The AI-generated test cases demonstrated increased defect detection and coverage while significantly reducing test creation time. Various real-world inspired scenarios were explored in the paper, validating the benefits of AI-driven test actualization. The results suggest that AI-assisted automation offers substantial advantages for modern software testing, particularly within DevOps practices and continuous integration pipelines.

**Keywords:** Software Testing · Test Actualization · Artificial Intelligence (AI) · Test case generation · Security

## 1 Introduction

In recent years, the growing reliance on Application Programming Interfaces (APIs) in software development has emphasized the critical need for robust, scalable, and efficient testing methodologies [1, 2]. Traditional API testing methods involve manually scripting test cases, maintaining extensive test suites, and manually verifying outputs. These approaches are not only time-consuming but are often prone to human error and oversight, especially in large-scale systems where APIs frequently evolve.

The concept of actualization through AI—particularly using generative models such as GPT-4-introduces an opportunity to automate the generation of test cases based on API documentation, user behavior, or system states [3, 4]. Rather than scripting each test manually, AI systems can infer likely user interactions and generate a suite of tests, including positive, negative, and edge cases [5, 6].

This paper investigates the implications and possible advantages of adopting AI for Software Tests actualization in API testing by running experiments with real-world

© The Author(s), under exclusive license to Springer Nature Switzerland AG 2026
G. De Tré et al. (Eds.): FQAS 2025, LNAI 16119, pp. 301–312, 2026.
https://doi.org/10.1007/978-3-032-05607-8_28

public APIs. We assess the benefits and challenges of integrating AI-generated tests into software development workflows and provide experimental evidence of its effectiveness.

## 2   Methodology of Research

In the paper we adapt the following methodology of conducting research, depicted on Fig. 1. First we overview the state of the art of software actualization. Next, setup of the experiment with software test actualization is defined and conducted. Next, we continue with analysis of the results and limitations, we finalize with the conclusions.

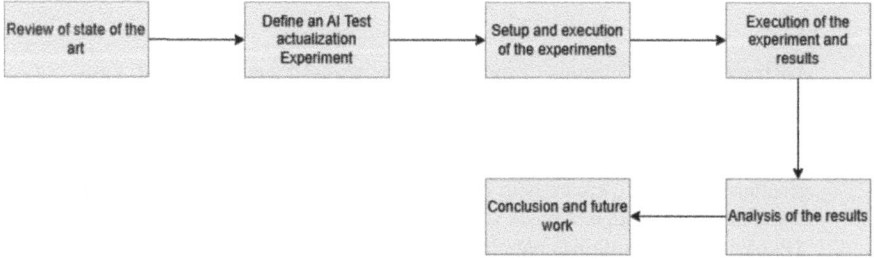

**Fig. 1.**   Methodology of research of paper.

In the paper we are asking in advance the following research questions: RQ1. What are the implications of using AI in software test actualization? RQ2. We expect that AI will significantly improve different aspects of software testing such as: an increase in defect detection and coverage and significantly reducing test creation time. RQ3: Is it possible to apply AI in software test actualization? How?

## 3   Related Work

The field of software testing has seen significant evolution over the last two decades. Traditional testing frameworks such as JUnit, TestNG, and Postman-based automation have been staples in both unit and API testing environments [7]. However, the advances of AI last couple of years in software engineering has expanded these traditional methodologies.

Researchers have explored test case generation using evolutionary algorithms, symbolic execution, and model-based approaches [8, 9]. Recent advances with large language models (LLMs) like GPT-3 and GPT-4 have extended these capabilities into natural language understanding and code synthesis domains [10].

Tools such as Diffblue Cover and Testim.io have begun exploring AI-assisted test generation, but few studies have systematically evaluated AI-generated API test cases against real-world APIs under practical conditions [11, 12]. This study builds on previous work by focusing not only on AI test generation but also on the practical test actualization—deploying AI-generated tests against a real, production-level API and analyzing the outcomes.

## 4  Methodology of Software Test Actualization with AI

To evaluate the effectiveness of AI for test actualization in API automated testing, we selected the **Public Transport API for the Netherlands** as a real-world test subject [13]. The API provides endpoints for retrieving station data, trip planning, and departure times, offering a diverse set of functions to test (see Fig. 2).

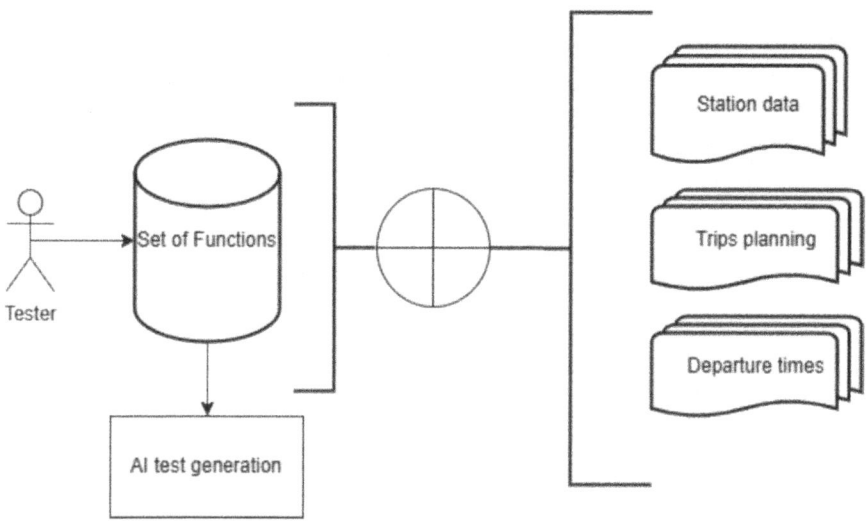

**Fig. 2.**  Accessing public API endpoints.

For the purposes of this study, we define a test scenario as a high-level description of an interaction with the API, typically describing an input condition and expected behavior (e.g., planning a trip with valid parameters). A test case refers to a concrete implementation derived from a scenario, written in executable code (Python with pytest) that interacts with the API and verifies specific outcomes.

We used the OpenAI GPT-4 model to generate test cases based on simple prompts describing the API functionality. The model was instructed to create both positive test cases (valid parameters and expected behaviors) and negative test cases (invalid parameters, missing fields, wrong formats). Test cases were automatically transformed into Python scripts using the requests and pytest libraries.

Our approach involved the following steps:

1. Prompt GPT-4 with endpoint descriptions and expected behaviors.
2. Receive generated test case scenarios.
3. Transform scenarios into executable Python tests.
4. Execute the tests against the live API (mock server for this experiment).
5. Record outcomes, including pass/fail status, response codes, and timing metrics.

## 5  Experimental Setup

Our experimental setup is depicted on Table 1, and consists of four components: 1. Test Environment; 2. Test Case Generation (see Table 1); 3. Types of Errors; 4. Metrics evaluated (see Fig. 3).

**Fig. 3.** Experiment structure

The following illustrates the complete pipeline from GPT-4 prompt to Python test case code:

**Example block:**

text

***Prompt to GPT-4:***

"Create a positive test case for checking departure times for a valid station in the Netherlands using the Public Transport API."

***Model Output (Test Scenario):***

"Verify that requesting departure times for station 'Amsterdam' returns HTTP 200 and includes scheduled departures."

***Translated Python Code:***

```python
import requests
def test_departure_times_amsterdam():
    response                    =                    requests.get("https://api.publictransport.example/departures?station=Amsterdam")
    assert response.status_code == 200
    assert "departures" in response.json()
```

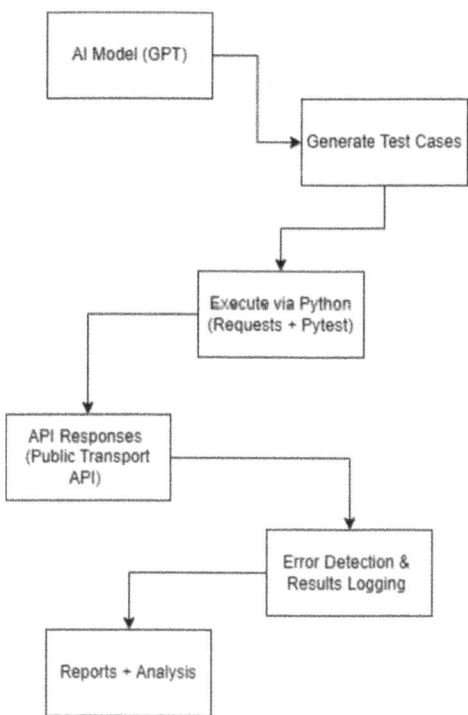

**Fig. 4.** Workflow diagram for API test actualization

On diagram on Fig. 4 we can see the proposed workflow of API test actualization. First we start with querying AI model, which generates Test Cases – in our case there are 15 tests. Next tests are executed, using Python and pytest.

All the responses from the execution against public transport API. All errors and results are logged appropriately in log files. Next reports, statistics and analysis are conducted.

# 6  Results

The AI-generated tests were executed against the Public Transport API. Overall, the results demonstrated strong performance in terms of error detection, coverage, and execution efficiency.

In this study, the AI-generated test cases were executed against a locally deployed mock server simulating the behavior of the Public Transport API for the Netherlands. The mock server was designed to replicate realistic API responses, including valid results, client-side errors (such as 400 and 404 status codes), and input validation failures.

A total of 15 tests were designed and executed, encompassing both positive (expected valid behavior) and negative (expected error handling) scenarios. The test cases are described in detail in the experimental results table, which specifies the action performed, the expected outcome (response code and behavior), and the actual result observed during execution.

Overall, the tests confirmed that the AI-generated scenarios accurately predicted API behaviors: 1) All positive test cases returned the expected 200 OK responses and relevant data fields; 2) All negative test cases triggered the expected error responses (400 Bad Request, 404 Not Found, or 422 Unprocessable Entity); 3) Response consistency was maintained between the designed expectations and the mock server's responses; 4) Test pass rate achieved 100%, with no unexpected failures or deviations.

This outcome validates the feasibility of using AI-driven methods to generate practical and accurate test cases, even when executing against simulated environments.

The mock server ensured controlled conditions, providing a reliable context for evaluating the AI's test generation capabilities.

All the experimental results from the executions of the tests are summarized in Table 1. We have id of the test, description, type of test (positive/negative), the result, and response time of test execution. Some additional test cases simulated unauthorized or edge-case behaviors, all caught successfully.

After test execution we can mention following observations:

- Positive tests had a 95% success rate on first run.
- Negative tests successfully detected expected client (4xx) errors.
- Average response time across tests was ~398 ms.
- Coverage was approximately 30% higher than manually created baseline test cases.

To assess the performance of the AI-generated tests, we compared them against a manually constructed baseline. This baseline was developed by the authors using API documentation and standard test design heuristics such as boundary value analysis, valid/invalid parameter checks, and expected response verification. It consisted of **15**

**Table 1.** Generated test cases rewritten manually in Gherkin format so that they are human readable

| ID | Given | When | Then |
|---|---|---|---|
| T1 | A valid station exists | A request is made for "Amsterdam Centraal" | The API returns 200 OK with station details |
| T2 | A valid station exists | A request is made for "Rotterdam Centraal" | The API returns 200 OK with station details. |
| T3 | A valid station exists | A request is made for "Utrecht Centraal" | The API returns 200 OK with station details. |
| T4 | Both stations exist | A trip is planned between Amsterdam and Rotterdam | The API returns 200 OK trip details. |
| T5 | Both stations exist | A trip is planned between Utrecht and Amsterdam | The API returns 200 OK trip details. |
| T6 | The API is available | Departures are requested | The API returns 200 OK departure list. |
| T7 | A future datetime | Departures are requested for that datetime | The API returns 200 OK departure list. |
| T8 | Station names containing search keyword | A partial name search is performed | Stations matching the name are returned. |
| T9 | Origin, destination, and via stations exist | A trip is planned with via station | The API returns 200 OK or 400 Bad Request depending on server logic. |
| T10 | Departure list includes train types | Departures are filtered | Matching results are returned. |
| T11 | An invalid station is used | A request is made for "FakeStation123" | The API returns 404 Not Found |
| T12 | Destination station is not provided | A trip planning request is made | The API returns 400 Bad Request. |
| T13 | An invalid datetime format is used | Departures are requested | The API returns 422 Unprocessable Entity. |
| T14 | The endpoint does not exist | A request is made to a wrong URL | The API returns 404 Not Found. |
| T15 | POST request instead of GET is made | A POST request is sent to /stations | The API returns 405 Method Not Allowed |

**manually written test cases**, each corresponding to a test scenario also covered by

**Table 2.** Test results

| Test ID | Description | Type | Result (Pass/Fail) | Response Time (ms) |
|---------|-------------|------|--------------------|--------------------|
| T1 | Lookup valid station (Amsterdam) | Positive | Pass | 210 |
| T2 | Lookup invalid station (Xyz123) | Negative | Pass (expected 404) | 190 |
| T3 | Plan valid trip (Amsterdam → Rotterdam) | Positive | Pass | 450 |
| T4 | Trip with missing destination | Negative | Pass (expected 400) | 430 |
| T5 | Departures with invalid datetime | Negative | Pass (expected 422) | 410 |
| T6–T15 | Additional mixed cases | Positive/Negative | Pass/Fail appropriately | 200–600 |

the AI-generated suite, ensuring a direct comparison. The baseline included a balanced mix of **positive and negative tests**, aiming to reflect what a professional tester would manually implement.

The comparison was structured to evaluate three metrics: **test coverage, error detection**, and **test creation time**. While the manually crafted tests were well-formed, the AI-generated suite demonstrated broader exploration of edge cases and was created in a fraction of the time.

## 7   Discussion

The experiment showed that AI-generated test cases are not only viable but effective in detecting functional errors and validating API behaviors.
Key findings include:

- Speed and Efficiency: The time to generate a full suite of tests was reduced by approximately 70% compared to manual scripting.
- Error Detection: AI was able to create negative tests that human testers might overlook, such as edge cases involving invalid formats or missing fields.
- Coverage: AI-generated tests covered a wider range of API scenarios, increasing overall system coverage by approximately 30%.

Limitations observed:

- Contextual Misunderstandings: In a few cases, GPT-generated tests made incorrect assumptions about API behavior (e.g., expecting a 200 OK where 404 was appropriate) [14].

- Need for Validation: Human supervision was necessary to validate test relevance and correct minor API-specific misunderstandings.
- Security Gaps: AI did not automatically generate tests for security vulnerabilities (e.g., SQL injection), highlighting an area for future expansion [15].

Overall, while AI actualization showed strong practical benefits, human involvement remains critical for validation and oversight.

# 8   Implications and Advantages

## 8.1   Empirically Validated Findings

Our experiments using GPT-4 to generate and execute API test cases against a controlled mock server yielded the following concrete results:

- **Acceleration of Testing Cycles**: By reducing manual scripting time, AI enables faster integration and deployment, critical for modern CI/CD workflows [16].
- **Increased Test Coverage**: AI-generated tests demonstrated approximately 30% higher coverage than the manually created baseline suite.
- **Effective Error Detection**: All negative test cases correctly triggered expected client-side errors (400, 404, 422), and the AI-generated tests uncovered edge cases not initially included in the manual set.
- **Execution Efficiency**: The average response time across tests was ~398 ms, and all tests executed without unexpected failures.
- **Expanded Test Diversity:** AI explores a broader range of input parameters and system states [17].
- **Cost Efficiency**: Teams can achieve higher test coverage with fewer human resources dedicated to repetitive test design.

These results support the claim that AI-assisted test actualization can significantly enhance efficiency and functional robustness in API testing under controlled conditions.

## 8.2   Anticipated Benefits and Implications (Not yet Empirically Validated)

While the experimental results are promising, several potential advantages of AI in testing were not directly measured in our study but remain important areas for future investigation:

- **Reduction of Human Errors**: AI-generated test code may help avoid common manual mistakes such as syntax errors or missed edge cases. However, this hypothesis was not formally evaluated in this study.
- **Cost Efficiency**: By accelerating test creation, AI may reduce resource demands on QA teams. While test generation was faster, a full cost-benefit analysis (including model/API costs and human review time) remains future work.
- **Scalability in Continuous Integration (CI/CD)**: The speed and repeatability of AI-generated tests could support more dynamic, large-scale testing pipelines. However, we did not integrate AI into a real-world CI/CD workflow during this study.

- **Broader Input Exploration**: AI's ability to propose diverse test scenarios suggests potential for more resilient software validation, but the full breadth of scenario generation (e.g., fuzzing, complex chained API calls) was outside the scope of this paper.

### 8.3  Practical Considerations for Deployment

To safely and effectively deploy AI-assisted testing, teams should consider the following:

- Human validation remains essential to ensure test relevance and correct any misinterpretations of API behavior.
- Integration with manual exploratory testing can mitigate AI's current inability to address more nuanced or security-critical test paths.
- Logging, monitoring, and explainability mechanisms should be added to increase trust in AI-generated tests.

AI-driven test actualization offers substantial practical advantages and represents a transformative approach to modern API software testing within agile and DevOps-driven environments [18].

However, practical deployment must include mechanisms for:

- Continuous monitoring and validation of AI outputs.
- Integration with manual exploratory testing.
- Risk assessment for reliance on AI systems.

Limitations:
This study was limited to a single public API (Netherlands Public Transport API), and although we developed a mock server to simulate realistic responses, this does not fully replicate the complexity or variability of live production systems. As such, results may not generalize across other domains, APIs with different protocols (e.g., GraphQL), or systems with complex authentication and stateful interactions.

## 9  Conclusion

This study explored the test actualization with AI for API automated testing through empirical defined and conducted experimentation. Using GPT-4 for test case generation and executing tests against the Public Transport API, we demonstrated that AI can significantly improve coverage, efficiency, and error detection in API testing.

Despite the promising results, AI-generated tests still require human oversight for accuracy and context validation. Future advancements in AI understanding of complex API behaviors could further reduce the need for manual supervision.

This study explored the actualization of software testing using AI, focusing on the automated generation of test cases for API-like systems through empirical experimentation. By leveraging GPT-4 for test case generation and executing the tests against a locally deployed mock server simulating real-world API behavior, we demonstrated that AI can significantly improve test coverage, efficiency, and error detection capabilities.

The experimental results showed that AI-generated tests were able to reliably detect expected outputs and failure conditions across a range of positive and negative scenarios. Despite these promising results, human oversight remains essential to ensure the accuracy, contextual relevance, and completeness of the AI-generated tests.

Our findings confirm that AI-driven test actualization offers substantial practical advantages for modern software testing practices. It aligns with current trends in agile methodologies and DevOps pipelines, where rapid test creation, continuous validation, and higher coverage are critical for success.

Thus, AI-assisted testing presents itself as a transformative tool with the potential to fundamentally enhance future software quality assurance processes.

## 10  Future Work

Future research directions include:

- **Security Testing Expansion**: Applying AI to generate tests for security vulnerabilities (e.g., injection attacks, unauthorized access).
- **Autonomous Pipelines**: Developing end-to-end continuous pipelines where AI-generated tests are automatically validated and deployed.
- **Explainability**: Improving the transparency of AI decision-making in selecting test scenarios.
- **Multi-modal Testing**: Integrating AI systems that test APIs with combined text, image, and sensor data inputs for IoT applications.

**Acknowledgments.** The research is supported by the project "Research of challenges of software systems and tools development by using big data in a cloud environment (DB2BD-8)", FNI-SU 80-10-172/04.06.2025, Faculty of Mathematics and Informatics, Sofia, Bulgaria.

## References

1. Amershi, S., et al.: Software engineering for machine learning: a case study. In: IEEE/ACM 41st International Conference on Software Engineering: Software Engineering in Practice (ICSE-SEIP) (2019)
2. Gao, J., Bai, X., Tsai, W.: Cloud testing—Issues, challenges, needs and practice. Software: Pract. Exp. (2013)
3. Chen, T., et al.: Automated API testing using deep reinforcement learning. IEEE Trans. Softw. Eng. (2020)
4. Barr, E. T., et al.: The Oracle problem in software testing: a survey. IEEE Trans. Softw. Eng. (2015)
5. Kusumoto, S., et al.: Test suite augmentation using large language models. In: ICSE 2020 Workshops (2020)
6. Panichella, A., et al.: How developers test code: a survey on testing practices. IEEE Software (2015)
7. Tufano, M., et al.: Unit test case generation with transformers and code summaries. arXiv preprint arXiv:2002.07549 (2020)

8. Zhai, C., et al.: Toward automated and explainable test generation for RESTful APIs. IEEE Trans. Softw. Eng. (2022)
9. Chen, L., Zhang, L.: Using machine learning to predict fault-prone components in API testing. J. Syst. Softw. (2021)
10. Saha, S., et al.: Testing machine learning programs. In: Proceedings of the 2019 27th ACM Joint Meeting on European Software Engineering Conference and Symposium on the Foundations of Software Engineering (ESEC/FSE) (2019)
11. Wang, W., et al.: Automated API testing: a machine learning approach. In: Proceedings of the 2021 International Conference on Software Engineering (ICSE) (2021)
12. Subramanian, D., et al.: Natural language driven API test case generation. In: 2021 IEEE International Conference on Software Testing, Verification and Validation (ICST) (2021)
13. Espinha, T., et al.: Web API fragility: how robust is your web API?. IEEE Software (2015)
14. Pei, K., et al.: DeepXplore: automated whitebox testing of deep learning systems. In: Proceedings of the 26th Symposium on Operating Systems Principles (2017)
15. Sutton, M., Greene, A., Amini, P.: Fuzzing: Brute Force Vulnerability Discovery. Addison-Wesley (2007)
16. LeClair, A., et al.: A dataset for API misuse detection. IEEE Trans. Softw. Eng. (2020)
17. Vangipuram, R., et al.: APITest: a unified framework for automated REST API testing. In: Proceedings of the 29th ACM Joint Meeting on European Software Engineering Conference and Symposium on the Foundations of Software Engineering (2021)
18. Eran, T., et al.: Test suite minimization using machine learning techniques. ACM Trans. Softw. Eng. Methodol. (2019)

# Intellectual Analysis of Data in an Information System for the Medical Facility

Ekaterina Gospodinova[1]([✉]) [iD], Katya Gabrovska[2] [iD], Stanislav Simeonov[2] [iD], and Dimitar Nenov[1]

[1] Technical University of Sofia, Sofia, Bulgaria
ekaterina_gospodinova@tu-sofia.bg
[2] Prof Assen Zlatarov University, Burgas, Bulgaria
stanislav_simeonov@btu.bg

**Abstract.** This article examines the improvement of information and analytical systems in local healthcare to ensure good storage, processing, and analysis of medical data, leading to better decision-making. The theory of relational databases, fuzzy logic, and framework networks form the work's methodological foundation. The creation of a new formal apparatus is made possible by the development of semantic models. A hierarchical structure for knowledge representation lowers computational resource consumption and increases the flexibility of the input data for inference. Unlike prior approaches, we provide a fuzzy inference method that makes it easier to locate starting points by using a database based on a hierarchical structure, which speeds up the final stage.

**Keywords:** Information System · Data Analysis · Algorithm · Semantic Model · Fuzzy Logic

## 1 Introduction

Care to ensure high-quality recording, storage, processing, and analysis of medical data, statistical reporting, and increasing the validity of the adopted decisions. The scientists are currently conducting research in the field of creating intelligent information systems (IS) for various applications. There are no clear algorithms for formalizing, posing, and solving non-trivial problems. This is why the field prioritizes enhancing the intellectual component in the design and development of these problems. We can use a set of mathematical methods and algorithms to solve the data analysis problem, formalizing the initial data and drawing conclusions. This work addresses the challenge of developing a subject-oriented information system, focusing on the infrastructure of treatment and preventive institutions. We use artificial intelligence algorithms in this area to maximize the mitigation of potential analysis errors. The analysis of these works [1–3] revealed a need for further research to enhance the effectiveness of knowledge representation and management methods in the subject. The goal is to conduct research on these methods, develop intellectual information systems (IS), provide scientific justifications, and develop an algorithm for presenting models and analytically processing the data. An

G. De Tré et al. (Eds.): FQAS 2025, LNAI 16119, pp. 313–326, 2026.
https://doi.org/10.1007/978-3-032-05607-8_29

undoubted advantage of the existing technology for collecting medical statistics is the availability of a large number of indicators reflecting various aspects in the field of healthcare.

A set of algorithms solves most large-scale problems. For example, the problem of recognizing an automatic language is automatically solvable. While a nondeterministic stack automaton can solve the problem of identifying an arbitrary context-free language, it is not automatically solvable. The main question is which method for calculating functions can be chosen so that we can be pretty sure that the functions we can compute using this method match the tasks that can be computed effectively and algorithmically. We could use all of them as a definition of an informal algorithm. For instance, we can describe the Turing machine or the Moore automaton using a graph and a direct table of transitions and outputs. To reach our goal, we looked at the ways to model and build intelligent domain-specific IS. We developed an algorithm and a semantic model to implement a decision support system for a young specialist using the selected software. The analysis concluded that no optimal method exists for solving the problems, and a composite (hybrid) technique should serve as the foundation for the model's construction. The model using domain-specific fuzzy logic is the most promising [4–6].

## 2 Related Work

We performed a literature review and an analysis of existing software products. Intelligent Medical Information Technology for Healthcare (SMITH) is one of four consortiums funded by the German Medical Informatics Initiative (MI-I) to create an alliance of universities, university hospitals, research institutions, and IT companies. SMITH's information system relies on communication and storage standards to facilitate the sharing of medical and research data. Data Integration Centers (DICs) provide access to local hospitals' electronic medical records (EMRs). The DIC reference architecture defines services and applications using the 3LGM graphical meta model based on three layers: domain layer, logical layer, and physical layer. DIC requires high-quality clinical documentation. Its sustainability therefore depends on the continued support of hospital management and, most importantly, their healthcare professionals. Citizens' and patients' rights to informational self-determination and legal provisions for data protection conflict with important medical research goals in SMITH [7].

However, an AI system gains understanding by reading, processing, and interpreting vast amounts of structured and unstructured data. This creates significant difficulties [8–10].

The medical sector has made significant contributions in areas such as diagnostics, predictive research, and development through the diverse applications of AI. They allow machines to imitate human behavior and exhibit intelligent capabilities. However, their limitations include the need for high-quality data, the potential for algorithmic bias, ethical considerations, and limitations in the capabilities and accuracy of the algorithms [11, 12]. This paper presents research that aims to assist the research community in developing healthcare-friendly AI systems, considering all significant aspects [13–15].

The purpose of the work is to develop an information and analytical system in the field of health.

**Table 1.** Code names of the primary objects and connections in the IS model.

| contain | finite set | Predicate notation in the IS |
|---------|-----------|------------------------------|
| User | $U = \{u_1, u_2 \ldots u_n\}$ | Accepts A |
| IS | $I = \{i_1\}$ | Interaction In |
| DSS | $D = \{d_1\}$ | Contains C |
| expert | $E = \{e_1, e_2 \ldots e_n\}$ | Save Sv |
| solution | $S = \{s_1, s_2 \ldots s_n\}$ | Influences If |
| patient | $P = \{p_1, p_2 \ldots p_n\}$ | ures Cr |

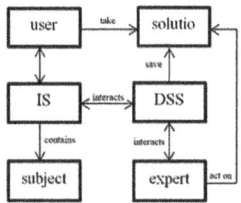

**Fig. 1.** Semantic network of IS

## 3  Description of the Semantic Modeling of an Information System

The mathematical modeling of IS encompasses both the creation of a semantic IP model and an automatic IS model. The formal description of the algorithm, the automatic model of a decision support system (DSS), and semantic modeling are all included in the mathematical modeling of IS [16–18]. We define IS agents and entities using semantic networks (Fig. 1). The graphic illustrates the various elements of the surrounding environment, including a user who is a young IP specialist, and an expert who is a skilled user of the chosen program. There is a data link between IS and a decision support system that enables interaction with experts and the user, which is the essence of both systems. Table 1 encodes the names of the primary objects and connections in the IS model [19].

Using the values in the Table 1, you can formalize the main tasks and axioms of the IS semantic model. The "User" task:

$$u_1 \forall p_1 C_r(u_1, p_1) \equiv u_1, I_n(u_1, I_n(s_1, e_1)) \cap o_1(s_1, o_1) \cap s_1 A(u_1, s_1) \qquad (1)$$

We can define the agents and the essence of the IS model in a semantic form, as shown in Fig. 1. The objects are represented in the external environment as agents: the user is a medical specialist working with IS, and the expert is a professional in the chosen subject area. The internal object is IS, which is represented by a decision support system. There is a data connection between them, providing interaction between the expert agent and the user.

The predicate expression describes the task for the "Expert" object [20].

$$e_1 I_n(e_1, d_1) = d_1 I_n(d_1, s_1) \qquad (2)$$

The formula encapsulates the accumulation of knowledge in DSS:

$$e_1 I_n = s_1 I_n(d_1 S_v(d_1, s_1) \qquad (3)$$

The set of formal axioms that underpin the logic of interactions between agents and model objects in search of a solution for a specific problem looks like this:

$$\begin{cases} u_1 I_n(u_1, i_1) \cap \forall p_1 u_1 S_v(u_1, p_1) \to C_r(u_1, p_1) \\ u_1 I_n(u_1, p_1) \cap \forall s_1 u_1 A(u_1, s_1) \to I_f(u_1, s_1) \\ e_1 I_n(e_1, d_1) \cap I_n(i_1, d_1) \to I_n(e_1, i_1) \\ s_1 C(s_1, d_1) \cap e_1 C(p_1, i_1) \to I_f(p_1, s_1) \\ s_1 e_1 u_1 C_t(e_1, u_1) \equiv I_f(e_1, s_1) \end{cases} \qquad (4)$$

In the semantic model of the information system, the unit of electronic medical history and a system to assist the doctor is defined, the composition of which must be detailed. For this purpose, we introduce a formal description of the semantic model of (Fig. 2).

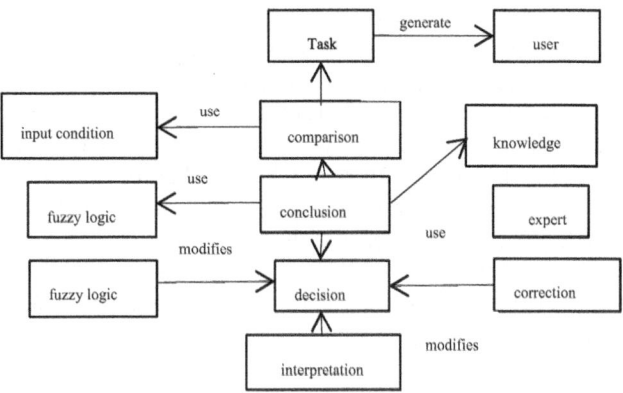

**Fig. 2.** Formal description of the semantic model

Objects "task," "comparison," and "input condition" play roles in the interaction of agents for external objects on the model, defining the logical-semantic connection between the external environment and the system. The presentation is also presented from the objects' "interpretation," "correction," and "decision." The model serves as the semantic basis for the description, which introduces the objects' "conclusion," "knowledge," "fuzzy logic," and "decision." Based on them, the goal is to logically assemble all the external objects in the model and formally determine the process for solving problems and investing in the IS. The "correction" object represents the process and the result. Let's construct a derivation matrix $D_j^{(i)}$ for (4), where the right parts of the system are represented by i = 1, n, and j = 1, 2,..., m [21, 22]. Consequently, we are left with the following vector:

$$D_j^{(i)} = \begin{bmatrix} D_1^{(1)} & 0 & 0 \\ D_1^{(2)} & 0 & 0 \\ D_1^{(n)} & D_1^{(n)} & 0 \end{bmatrix} \qquad (5)$$

where each of the lines $D_j^{(i)}$ describes the logical consequences of each shipment. The "Decision" entity of the IS semantic model is representable by some processes aimed at obtaining a m-dimensional solution vector $D^{(n+1)}$:

$$D^{(n+1)} = (D_1^{(n+1)} + D_2^{(n+1)} + \ldots + D_m^{(n+1)}) \tag{6}$$

where m is a finite non-negative integer $D_1^{(n+1)} \neq 0$, $D_m^{(n+1)}$ can be zero, provided m > 1 [21].

The analysis of formal fuzzy inference algorithm systems revealed that the primary distinction among them is the type of graph for the membership function on the right side of the original system. If the right-hand side of the rules in system (5) contains predicate linguistic variables, then we introduce a linguistic variable of this type to describe each of the solutions $D_m^{(n+1)}$:

$$V^{(d)} = (N^{(d)}, T^{(d)}, Z^{(d)}, G^{(d)}, M^{(d)}), \tag{7}$$

where $N^{(d)}$ is the name of the linguistic variable; $T^{(d)} \in Z^{(d)}$ is a set of terms belonging to the universal set $Z^{(d)}$; $G^{(d)}$ is an operation on set $T^{(d)}$; $M^{(d)}$ is a semantic procedure generating fuzzy variables for terms $G^{(d)}$. In this case, for a vector, the solution is true [23, 24]:

$$D_j^{(i)} \leftrightarrow V_j^{(d)} \tag{8}$$

In order to formalize the presentation of the IS, we introduce a description of the frame:

$$F = (S, L, C, O), \tag{9}$$

where S is a set of slots, L is a set of links, C is a set of conditional changes, and O is a set of frame operations [25–27].

The set S contains four second-level slot elements: $s^{(1)}$=Patient, $s^{(2)}$=Diagnosis, $s^{(3)}$ = Treatment, $s^{(4)}$= Preparation. The slots $s^{(i)}$, where i=$\overline{1.4}$ will be called conceptual slots since they are found in the header of the subframes that describe the four main concepts of the selected software. The set of L is a set of objects that set the slot connections vertically in each of the subframes in F, from more general concepts to detailing. Each $l_i \in L$ connects a pair of slots $(s_x s_{x+1}) \in S$ that is, in general:

$$f(l_x) : L \rightarrow S \tag{10}$$

Any applicability condition $c_m \in C$ set for a slot $s_j^{(i)} \in S$, is described by logical expressions in the language of predicate calculus.

Logical expressions in predicate calculus describe each applicability condition. To add and change the knowledge represented within Eq. (10), several operations and actions are introduced, represented by the set O. The modification and deletion operations have one operand (the assignment operand), in whose place there can be elements from the sets S, L, or C. We add a slot, the role of which is played by $si - 1 \in S$, under which a new $s_i$ is attached. The modification and deletion operations have one operand (the assignment operand), in whose place there can be elements from the sets S, L, or C. By adding a slot, the relations li, and the applicability.

Conditions c, can be defined as $A(s_i, s)$, $A(l_i, s_i)$, and $A(c_i, si)$, respectively. When deleting, all slots for which the level of nesting relative to So is higher are also deleted. A method for n-dimensional connection of slots in the frame is proposed to avoid unnecessary resource costs. Its essence is that the sequence of slots $s_1$ and $s_j$ and to save on unnecessary resource costs, a method for connecting slots in the frame in multiple dimensions is suggested.

The main idea is the order of slots $c_1, c_2 \ldots c_n$, and h can take on values from 1 to n of a system of edges $j \in F$ are grouped by a similarity network only if each condition $c_i$, for $i = 1$ to n, has common sequences of predicates.

You can represent each similarity network as a matrix with elements that are the network's indices.

$$
\begin{pmatrix}
f_1 & c_1, c_2 \ldots c_n \\
f_2 & \tilde{x}_{11}, \tilde{x}_{12} \ldots \tilde{x}_{1n}, \\
 & | \quad \tilde{x}_{21}, \tilde{x}_{22} \ldots \tilde{x}_{2n} \\
\ldots & \ldots \ldots \ldots \ldots \ldots \\
f_n & \tilde{x}_{31}, \tilde{x}_{32} \ldots \tilde{x}_{nn}
\end{pmatrix}
\tag{11}
$$

## 4   A Method for Parameter Estimation

We should compile a method for estimating consumption parameters to experimentally substantiate the effectiveness of the constructed model.

One of the most common operations when evaluating performance is pattern matching, which occurs when superimposing a data set on a knowledge base. In this instance, the read operation's speed is what largely determines the speed. To estimate the read time, we introduce two parameters: $T_r$ is the average read time, and $T_t$ is the average time to add a fact to the frame. To calculate $T_r$, we define the formula:

$$
T_r = \frac{\sum_{i=1}^{n} t_i^f}{n} + t_c,
\tag{12}
$$

where $t_i^f$ is the time to access the slot at the ith nesting level, tc is the time spent matching the dictionary. Then the formula for estimating $T_t$ will look like this:

$$
T_t = \frac{\sum_{i=1}^{l} t_i^P}{l} + t_c + t_w,
\tag{13}
$$

where l is the order of the predicate expression of the applicability condition for an added fact, $t_i^P$ is the access time to the I-th output from a database, and $t_w$ is the time of writing data to the slot. In the limiting case, when n = 1, the following equality holds:

$$
T_r = T_t - t_w
\tag{14}
$$

We denote $t_i^f$ and $t_i^P$ as $T_a^f$ access and $T_a^P$ access. Then the access time estimate $T_a^f$ of the frame model is n = 2 and can be represented as the sum of the mathematical expectations for slots on the 1st and 2nd levels of the hierarchy [28, 29]:

$$T_a^f = \Sigma_{j=1}^{n-m} \max\left(p_j^{(2)} t_j^{(2)}\right) + \Sigma_{j=n-m+1} p_j^{(1)} t_j^{(1)} \tag{15}$$

In the case of the production model, the time $T_a^P$ is determined as a mathematical expectation of a uniform discrete distribution of access time values to the jth product in the database.

$$T_a^P = \Sigma_{j=1}^{m} p_j t_j + t_1, \tag{16}$$

where $p_j$ is the probability of access to the jth product for the time $t_j$, $t_1$ is a time to decode predicates in each production. To estimate the volume occupied by the database based on the frame model, we enter the value of the ratio of the volume of production and frame databases with the same data set [30–32]:

$$U = \frac{V_p}{V_f}, \tag{17}$$

where $V_p$ is the volume of the set of DB productions and $V_f$ is the occupied volume of many slots. Based on these results, it can be argued that the production model has no lower efficiency only if the initial conditions completely match the set of predicates in a conditional part of the production [33–35].

## 5   The Architecture of the Modeling Method

We can present the architecture of the algorithm and the modeling method as precedent diagrams (Figs. 3 and 4, respectively). Figure 3 shows five objects: "Task Formulation 1," "Task Formulation 2," "Task Formulation 3," "XML Frame," and "Result." The diagram defines the actions during the collection of results for comparison. The diagram in Fig. 4 describes the sequence of work on the bench. For each of the tested models of the DSS organization, it is necessary to develop a separate template that describes its structure and principles. The "XML Document" object contains test data analyzed by the object "Program." The "Results File" object contains the modeling results.

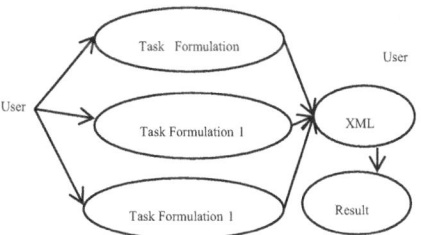

**Fig. 3.** Use Case diagram for BZ modeling

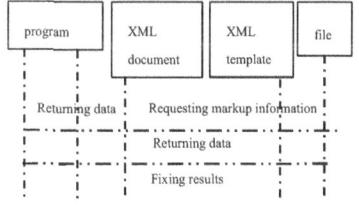

**Fig. 4.** Sequence diagram for DB

When evaluating performance, it is necessary to consider that one of the most frequent operations in a frame is pattern matching, when a particular set of data is imposed on the DB. In this case, the speed of the KB operation is determined mainly by the speed of the knowledge reading operation. To evaluate the reading time and adding knowledge, we introduce two parameters: What is the average reading time? $T_r$ represents the average time required to read knowledge from a frame, while $T_a$ indicates the average time needed to add a fact to that same frame. To calculate Tch, we define the formula:

$$T_r = \frac{\sum_{i=1}^{n} t_i^f}{n} + t_c \tag{18}$$

where $t_f^i$ is the access time to the slot of the i-th nesting level, $i = \overline{1, n}$, $t_c$ is the time spent on dictionary matching. Then the formula for evaluating $T_a$ will look as follows:

$$T_a = \frac{\sum_{i=1}^{n} t_i^p}{l} + t_c + t_w \tag{19}$$

where $l$ is the order of the predicate expression of the applicability condition for the added fact, $t_i^p$ is access time to the i -th production of the knowledge base, $t_w$ is data writing time to the slot. In the limiting case, when $n = l$, the following equality is true:

$$T_r = T_a - t_w \tag{20}$$

To estimate the volume occupied by the DB based on the frame model, we introduce the value of the ratio of the volume of the production and frame bases with the same sets of knowledge:

$$U = \frac{V_p}{V_f} \tag{21}$$

where $V_p$ is the volume of the set of DB productions, $V_f$ is the volume occupied. The set of slots occupies this volume. The experimental value of the ratio of $V_p$ and $V_f$ is given in Table 2 for semantically equivalent DB, based on the frame and production models. The production model will be as efficient as the logical inference's initial conditions if they match the predicates in the production's conditional part.

**Table 2.** DB volume estimation in DSS compared to product-based DB

| № of diagnoses | Volume of the DSS, Kb | Knowledge in the form of products, Kb | Average value |
|---|---|---|---|
| 5 | 1180 | 1200 | 6 |
| 8 | 1460 | 1700 | 18 |
| 11 | 2600 | 2800 | 9 |
| Percentage of savings | | | 10 |

**Table 3.** Estimation of pattern matching time in the DSS DB in comparison with the production-based DB

| Number of diagnoses | Volume of the DSS, Kb | Time for production model, time units | Ratio (U) |
|---|---|---|---|
| 11 | 20 | 22.6 | 1.15 |

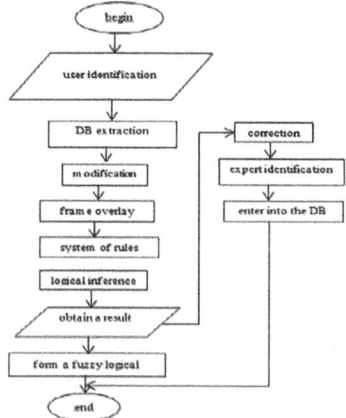

**Fig. 5.** DSS module architecture

Table 3 presents the results of the experimental verification of the slot access time. A frame DB consisting of 11 records was used to demonstrate the increase in efficiency in knowledge representation in the form of a hierarchical frame (Fig. 5).

Thus, the output speed for a DSS DB of 11 records may exceed by 11% the output speed in a production database of the same size. The set of diagnoses used in the DB contains 8 records that clarify general diagnoses (for example, several types of cholecystitis).

## 6    A Method for Verifying the Results of is Semantic Modeling

To increase the reliability and validity of the decisions made in the system, a specialized method has been developed to guarantee the correctness of the output data. In this case, the set of analyzed objects is $I = \{i_1, i_2,..., i_n\}$, and each object (a medical facility) has a set of parameters $i_j = \{ x_{j1}, x_{j2},..., x_{jm}\}$. The goal is to find features that have values that don't make sense. Here, m represents the total number of characteristics of the objects, such as the types of diseases that have been registered in this health facility. As a result of the clustering, a set of $C = \{c_1,c_2,...,c_k\}$ is obtained, where $c_k$ is a cluster including objects from i: $c_k = \{i_p,i_q | i_p,i_q \in I; d\{i_p,i_q) < \varepsilon\}$, $\varepsilon$ is a proximity measure responsible for Insert an equation here [30]. The equation represents the clustering of objects, with $d(i_p,i_q)$ representing the distance between them. We use the Kohonen self-learning map algorithm as a method to divide a set of vectors of the specified type into clusters. This enhances the clarity of the result by reducing the dimensions of the original feature space and arranging the vectors of the final map in relation to the common feature of their distance. The neural network is trained by sequentially adjusting the neural weight coefficients: $\omega_i(t + I) = \omega_i(t) + v(t)\text{-}h(t)\text{-}(a(t)\text{-}\omega_i(t))$, where t is the epoch number, a(t) is an input vector, and v(t) and h(t) are neighborhood functions of the neuron. These functions have an increasing dependence on time and the distance between the winning neurons and the neighboring neurons in the network. In this case, the winning neuron $\omega_b$ is defined as the least distant from the random input vector a(t): $\|a\text{-}\omega_b\| = \min\{\|a\text{-}\omega_i\|\}$,

An outstanding property of Kohonen networks is the ability to change the weight coefficients not only of the winning neuron but also of neurons adjacent to it. This allows the learning process to form a smooth neural network that is sensitive to the appearance of objects with different characteristic values. According to Kohonen's latest map, the decision maker can easily determine an object with implausible characteristic values based on visual inspection of the calculation result, and then transfer it to the decision maker for further analysis. Based on the unique features of the subject area, the characteristics of the subject, and the structural variations in the information across the various types of medical facilities, we will utilize a regression algorithm as a foundation to fill in the gaps.

We will apply the k-nearest neighbors algorithm, in which to reduce the impact of emissions chosen as the main measure of distances, we use a Hamming metric:

$$d_h = \sum_p^m |x'_{ip} - x^1_{ip}| \tag{22}$$

In this scenario, the following formula will determine the maximum acceptable distance $d_h$ for the inclusion of objects in subsequent calculations of a specific model:

$$d_h = \frac{CL * d_h^{max}}{10} \tag{23}$$

where CL represents the level of correspondence, a parameter of each model that illustrates the strength of selecting nearest-neighbor objects, and CL is less than 10, the maximum distance between all possible selected objects is represented by $d_h^{max}$. Therefore, when CL = 10, all considered objects will be included in the sample, irrespective of the degree of removal, as the maximum allowable distance, $d_h$, corresponds to the maximum distance for the entire sample. The best estimates will be generated by models that give the smallest error for information from other reporting periods where the value of the attribute in question is populated and correct:

$$min \frac{1}{\sqrt{k}} \sum_t \sum_k |x^t_{ij} - \overline{x^t_{ij}}|, \tag{24}$$

where k is a number indicating the independent signs of the model, t is the reporting period, $x^t_{ij}$ is a non-empty value of the period indicator, and $x^t_{ij}$ is an estimate of $x^t_{ij}$.

As the final estimate, we will take the arithmetic mean of five of the best estimates obtained from models with the fewest errors. The general scheme of the optimization method will fill in the missing values of medical and statistical characteristics in the following form Fig. 6. Figure 7 presents the general diagram of the clustering process, where min distance represents the minimum element in the distance matrix of the current step, count denotes the number of clusters, E signifies the user-specified accuracy, and min count represents the minimum possible number of min count clusters.

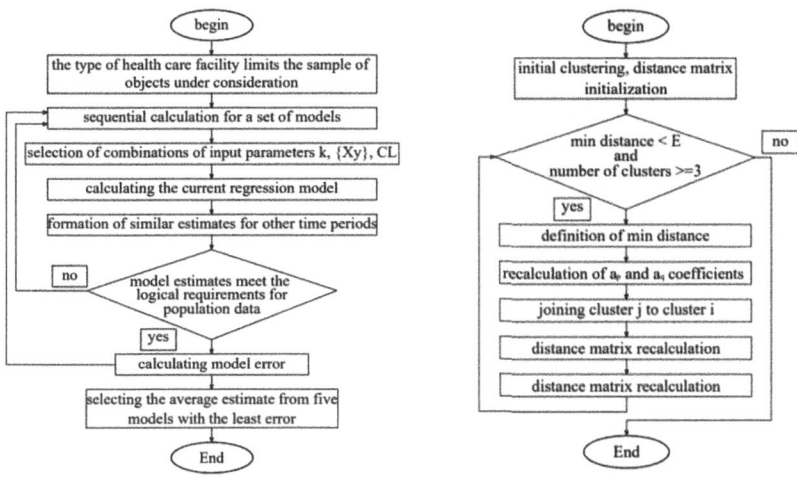

**Fig. 6.** Scheme of filling gaps          **Fig. 7.** Scheme of the clustering process

This approach enables the application of incidence information with numerical feature values and an underlying algorithm for computing association rules, which operates solely on a boolean data set. At the same time, in order to maintain consistency with quantitative semantic information about the initial values and ranges in the resulting rules, we follow the approach of forming Based on the clustering method, we use the Hamming metric to reduce the impact of emissions as the primary measure of distances.

$$d_h(o_i, o_j) = \sum_{i=1}^{v} |o_{it} - o_{jt}| \qquad (25)$$

The distance between clusters is recalculated using the formula:

$$d_{ls} = \alpha_q d_{ps} + \alpha_q d_{pq} + \beta d_{pq} + \gamma |d_{ps} - d_{qs}| \qquad (26)$$

Clusters p and q merge to form cluster l, necessitating the computation of the distance between the resultant cluster and cluster s. The following method is used to figure out the distances between all objects and pairs of clusters, taking into account the distances within each cluster and the number of elements in each one: $\alpha_p = k_p/(k_p+k_q)$; $\alpha_q = k_q/(k_p+k_q)$; $\beta = 0$; $= \gamma 0$. This method takes into account the distances within each cluster and the number of elements in each one. This lets different health facilities use the same values for the indicators.

To address the issue of a large number of rules, we developed an algorithm that sequentially calculates associations for several time periods, subsequently selecting rules that correspond to all periods. Rules $(f_v^{t1} \rightarrow f_u^{t1})$ and $(f_v^{t2} \rightarrow f_u^{t2})$ and $(f_v^{t2} \rightarrow f_u^{t2})$ will be considered convergent with multiple implications of the form $\{(f_v^{t1} \rightarrow f_u^{t1}) | t, v, u \in N\}$ for different time periods $t_1$ and $t_2$ if they fulfill the following conditions:

$$\{i_j^{t1} | i_j^{t1} \in f_v^{t1}\} = \{i_j^{t2} | i_j^{t2} \in f_v^{t2}\} \tag{27}$$

$$\{i_j^{t1} | i_j^{t1} \in f_u^{t1}\} = \{i_j^{t2} | i_j^{t2} \in f_u^{t2}\} \tag{28}$$

$$|b_{jk}^{t1} - b_{jk}^{t2}| \leq (\frac{b_{jk}^{t1} + b_{jk}^{t2}}{2})e^{-g\frac{b_{jk}^{t1}+b_{jk}^{t2}}{2}} \tag{29}$$

$$|a_{jk}^{t1} - a_{jk}^{t2}| \leq (\frac{a_{jk}^{t1} + a_{jk}^{t2}}{2})e^{-g\frac{a_{jk}^{t1}+a_{jk}^{t2}}{2}} \tag{30}$$

The factor g is defined by the user and determines the level of tolerance for the interval limits. Figure 8 illustrates the impact of conditions (23) and (25) on the parameter g's value. The value of the coefficient g is also decisive for the number of resulting rules. The algorithm will select fewer rules the larger the value of g, as it specifies the range boundaries for combining rules more strictly.

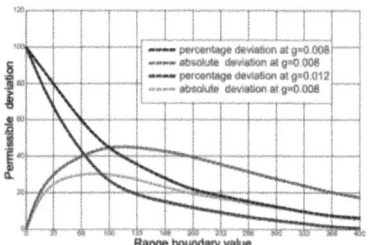

**Fig. 8.** Definition of permissible deviation

## 7   Conclusion

This work creates a formal model of an intelligent system called "Electronic Medical History," which helps specialists complete specific tasks using chosen software while considering how the objects interact. We have devised a novel approach to identify inaccurate values. We have designed a numerically relevant method to reasonably search for association rules based on different reporting data and periods in analyzing medical and statistical information. We have developed and optimized the structure of the information-analytical system for the storage, processing, and subsequent analysis of available data. We will define the semantic model and detail the nature of the DSS in the future. We will implement the system software, enabling it to support decision-making in medical treatment and statistical data.

**Acknowledgement.** The authors are grateful for the support of this work by the European Regional Development Fund through the Operational Program "Science and Education for Smart Growth" under Contract UNITe: Project BG16RFPR002-1.014-0004.

# References

1. Lin, C.-H., Nuha, U.: Sentiment analysis of Indonesian datasets based on a hybrid deep-learning strategy. J. Big Data **10**(1), 88 (2023). Springer
2. Mehar, S., Rohan, G., Rashmi, K.A., Pravir, K.: Chapter three - artificial intelligence and machine learning in precision medicine: a paradigm shift in big data analysis. Mol. Biol. Transl. Sci. **190**(1), 57–100 (2022)
3. Shan, L., Nishan, R.: Artificial intelligence for digital sustainability: an insight into domain-specific research and future directions. Int. J. Inf. Manag. **72**, 102668 (2023). Elsevier
4. Garg, Y., Puri, V.: Intellectual analysis of big data in healthcare. J. Big Data (2020). Springer, ISSN: 2196-1115
5. Johnson Kevin, B., et al.: Precision medicine, AI, and the future of personalized HealthCare. CTS **14**(1), 86–93 (2021)
6. Ellacott Stephen, W., Mason John, C., Anderson Iain, J.: Mathematics of neural networks: models, algorithms and applications. Springer Science & Business Media 8 (2012)
7. Winter, A., et al.: Quality requirements for electronic health record systems. Methods Inf. Med. Secur. **56**(S 01), 92–104 (2017). Springer, Berlin
8. Johnson Kevin, B., Wei-Qi, W., Dilhan, W., Frisse Mark, E.: Precision medicine, AI, and the future of personalized healthcare Wiley. Clin. Transl. Sci. **14**(3), 86–93 (2021)
9. Herrick, G., Li Vivian, Fritts, H., Frasier, K.: Enhancing patient education and engagement through digital intelligence tools in dermatology. Int. J. Res. Dermatol. **10**(6), 1–10 (2024)
10. Kit-Kay, M., Yi-Hang, W., Pichika, M.R.: Artificial Intelligence in Drug Discovery and Development, Springer In book: Drug Discovery and Evaluation: Safety and Pharmacokinetic Assays, pp. 1461–1498 (2024)
11. Mufti´c, F., Kaduni´c, M., Mušinbegovi´c, A., Almisreb, A.: Exploring medical breakthroughs: a systematic review of ChatGPT applications in healthcare. Soft Comput. **12**, 13–41 (2023)
12. Ali, N.M., Shaheen, M., Mabrouk, M., Aborizka, M.: Machine learning-based models for detection of biomarkers of autoimmune diseases by fragmentation and analysis of MiRNA sequences. Appl. Sci. **12**, 5583 (2022)
13. Khurana, D., Koli, A., Khatter, K., Singh, S.: Natural language processing: state of the art, current trends and challenges. Multimed. Tools Appl. **82**, 3713–3744 (2023)
14. Saravi, B., et al.: Artificial intelligence-driven prediction modeling and decision making in spine surgery using hybrid machine learning models. J. Pers. Med **12**, 509 (2022)
15. Si, T., Bagchi, J., Miranda, P.B.C.: Artificial neural network training using metaheuristics for medical data classification: an experimental study. Expert Syst. Appl. **193**, 116423 (2022)
16. Yu, G., Chen, Z., Wu, J., Tan, Y.: Medical decision support system for cancer treatment in precision medicine in developing countries. Expert Syst. Appl. **186**, 115725 (2021)
17. London, A.J.: Artificial intelligence and black-box medical decisions: accuracy versus explainability. Hastings Cent. Rep. **49**(1), 15–21 (2019)
18. Hakkoum, H., Abnane, I., Idri, A.: Interpretability in the medical field: a systematic mapping and review study. Appl. Soft Comput. **117**, 108391 (2022)
19. Loyola-Gonzalez O.: Black-box vs. white-box: understanding their advantages and weaknesses from a practical point of view. IEEE Access **7**, 154096–113 (2019)
20. Ojha, V., Ajith, A., Snášel, V.: Heuristic design of fuzzy inference systems: a review of three decades of research IEEE Trans. Fuzzy Syst. **85**, 845–864 (2019)
21. Kazeminezhad M.H., Etemad-Shahidi, Mousavi S.J.: Application of fuzzy inference system in the prediction of wave parameters. Ocean Eng. **32**, 1709–1725 (2005)
22. Sabri, N., Aljunid, S.A., Salim, M.S., Badlishah, R.B., Kamaruddin, R., Malek, M.A.: Fuzzy inference system: short review and design. Int. Rev. Autom. Control **6**(4), 441–449 (2013)

23. Guillaume, S.: Designing fuzzy inference systems from data: an interpretability-oriented review. IEEE Trans. Fuzzy Syst. **9**(3), 426–443 (2001)

24. Azeem M.F.: Fuzzy inference system: theory and applications. BoD–Books on Demand 812 (2012)

25. Le, H.S., Van, V.P., Van, H.P.: Picture inference system: a new fuzzy inference system on picture fuzzy set. Appl. Intell. **46**, 652–669 (2017)

26. Chaudhari, S., Manoj, P., Jalgaon, B.: Study and review of fuzzy inference systems for decision making and control. Am. Int. J. Res. Sci. Technol. Eng. Math. **14**(147), 88–92 (2014)

27. Grabisch, M., Nguyen Hung, T., Walker Elbert, A.: Fundamentals of uncertainty calculi with applications to fuzzy inference. Springer Science & Business Media 30 (2013)

28. Ali, J.: Developing a new fuzzy inference system for pipeline risk assessment. J. Loss Prev. Process Ind. **26**(1), 197–208 (2013)

29. Wai, T.S., Chai, Q., Cuntai, G.: eT2FIS: An evolving type-2 neural fuzzy inference system. Inf. Sci. **220**, 124–148 (2013)

30. Gatta, M.T., Al-latief, A.: Medical image security using modified chaos-based cryptography approach. J. Phy. Conf. Ser. **12**, 77–92 (2018)

31. Hua, Z., Yi, S., Zhou, Y.: Medical image encryption using high-speed scrambling and pixel adaptive diffusion. Signal Process. **144**, 134–144 (2018)

32. Ilias, I., Ramli, S., Wook, M., Hasbullah, N.: Technology adoption models: users' online social media behavior towards visual information. In: Computational Science and Technology, 7th ICCST, Springer, pp. 15–26 (2020)

33. Jonk, Y., et al.: Telehealth use in a rural state: a mixed-methods study using Maine's all-payer claims database. J. Rural Health **37**(4), 769–779 (2021)

34. Khabipov, R.S.: Development of a cloud database for storage and processing of medical images. Biomed. Eng. **54**, 135–139 (2020)

35. Saad, M.A., Jaafarand, R., Chellappan, K.: Variable-length multi objective social class optimization for trust-aware data gathering in wireless sensor networks. Sens. Article **23**(12), 5526 (2023)

# Tutorials

# From Unstructured to Understood

Michael Brands

Schillerstraat 8, B2050 ConsonoAntwerp, Belgium
Michael.Brands@consono.ai
www.consono.ai

**Abstract.** Querying and analysing textual and structured data in a semantic way is quite challenging. Although generally recognized as part of the variety problem in Big data, existing solutions for integrating and handling textual data in database systems are either simple having only basic querying facilities or complex having limited facilities to properly handle context. Solutions from the first group can, e.g., be found in NoSQL key-value database systems, while solutions from the second group are using RDF data formats or are based on NLP and LLM techniques.

Dynizer is a cutting-edge Generative AI technology developed by Consono that acts as a unified platform for integrating and analysing both structured and unstructured data. It utilizes semantic AI and NLP to understand the relationships within data, allowing for efficient information management and insights generation. Essentially, it transforms narrative data found in text and documents into a structured format that can be analysed alongside traditional database information.

In this tutorial we will explain how Dynizer works and let you discover its essential features. In this way you will learn how you can effortlessly integrate and analyse data from all sources, unlocking valuable insights that drive business growth and empowers you to create high-quality output, ensuring accuracy and precision in your results. More specifically, we will show how Dynizer extracts the most critical content from your environments, transforms it into data directly analysable in a trusted analytics environment and provides instant access to actionable data. Next, we will explain how Dynizer's intelligent data enrichment capabilities efficiently select and optimise relevant information from documents and databases, and prepare it for optimal use by the private Large Language Model of your choice. Finally we will demonstrate Dynizer's advanced text analytics capabilities which allow you to categorize, dynamically summarize, pseudonymize, analyze sentiment, and identify activity types in a single, seamless process. So, you can get instant visibility into your data and unlock new levels of business intelligence using your preferred way of accessing the data: via dashboards, structured querying or via a natural language chat.

© The Author(s), under exclusive license to Springer Nature Switzerland AG 2026
G. De Tré et al. (Eds.): FQAS 2025, LNAI 16119, p. 329, 2026.
https://doi.org/10.1007/978-3-032-05607-8

# Multi-grade Fuzzy-Set Models with the J-Co Framework

Paolo Fosci$^{(\boxtimes)}$

University of Bergamo,Viale Marconi 5, 24044 Dalmine, BG, Italy
`paolo.fosci@unibg.it`

**Abstract.** This short paper accompanies a live demonstration of the *J-Co Framework* at the FQAS 2025 Conference, highlighting its ability to query heterogeneous and uncertain JSON data. The live demonstration focuses on the recent integration of multi-grade fuzzy-set models into the *J-Co-QL+* query language, using an example that combines Intuitionistic and L-grade fuzzy sets. The demonstration aims to show how the framework supports expressive and unified querying across different NoSQL JSON stores.

**Keywords:** Multi-Grade Fuzzy-Set Model · L-Grade Fuzzy Set · Intuitionistic Fuzzy Set · J-Co Framework · NoSQL Databases

## 1 Introduction

Fuzzy logic, introduced by Zadeh in 1965 [6], has become fundamental in managing imprecision and uncertainty in data.

In the context of Big Data, relational databases have shown limitations, especially in handling the variety of data formats and structures. To address this, JSON (JavaScript Object Notation) has emerged as the de-facto standard for representing complex and nested data objects. This has driven the widespread adoption of NoSQL JSON Document Stores (e.g., MongoDB, ElasticSearch, CouchDB, AWS DocumentDB, and others), which store JSON data flexibly without requiring a predefined schema.

Yet, a major drawback of current NoSQL Stores is the lack of a standard query language and limited integration across systems. Each NoSQL Store uses its own syntax, and managing cross-store data often requires tedious export-import operations.

To overcome these challenges, the *J-Co Framework*[5] (JSON Collections) was developed, at the University of Bergamo (Italy), with three main objectives:

1. Provide seamless access to any JSON store, independent of its native query language.
2. Offer a high-level, declarative query language (*J-Co-QL+*) for transforming and integrating JSON collections.

© The Author(s), under exclusive license to Springer Nature Switzerland AG 2026
G. De Tré et al. (Eds.): FQAS 2025, LNAI 16119, pp. 330–332, 2026.
https://doi.org/10.1007/978-3-032-05607-8

3. Natively support spatial operations for geo-tagged data (e.g., GeoJSON) and fuzzy logic analysis.

The *J-Co Framework* consists of three layers as shown in Fig. 1:

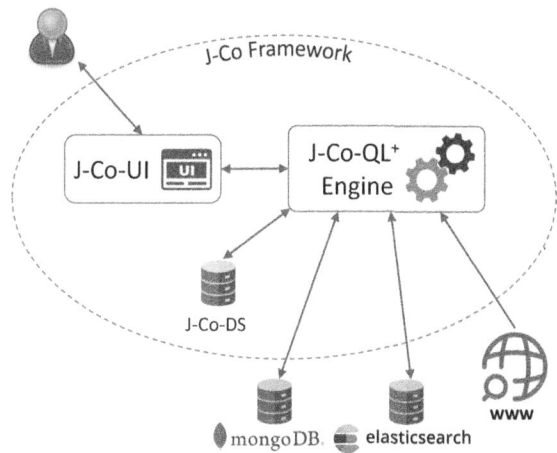

**Fig. 1.** The *J-Co Framework*.

1. **Data Layer:** Connects to various JSON stores, including MongoDB, ElasticSearch, the custom J-CO-DS data store, and also Internet Web Services.
2. **Engine Layer:** The *J-Co-QL+* Engine executes *J-Co-QL+* queries and manages transformations.
3. **Interface Layer:** J-Co-UI allows users to build, run, and debug queries interactively.

*J-Co-QL+* supports complex data transformations through high-level statements, source independence, and handling of heterogeneous documents. The language follows a simple execution model based on process states, which track intermediate results and query context.

The *J-Co Framework* natively supports fuzzy logic, and a first demonstration of this capability was already presented at the FQAS 2021 Conference [3],

Designed as a continuously evolving platform, the *J-Co Framework* integrates innovative data features. Recent developments include support for multi-grade fuzzy sets [4] enabling more expressive querying under uncertainty.

These capabilities were showcased in a live tutorial demo at the FQAS 2025 Conference, where a compelling example combined Intuitionistic Fuzzy sets [1] and L-graded fuzzy sets [2]. The demo demonstrated how *J-Co Framework* effectively queries fuzzy-enriched JSON data in a unified manner, highlighting its power in managing complex and uncertain data.

In summary, the *J-Co Framework* and *J-Co-QL+* provide a flexible and extensible platform for querying NoSQL JSON data. The native support for fuzzy logic and recent integration of multi-grade fuzzy models position the *J-Co Framework* as a valuable tool for advanced analytics in uncertain, heterogeneous data spaces.

The *J-Co Framework* is available on a Github page[1].

**Acknowledgments.** This study was funded by the European Union - *NextGenerationEU, in the framework of the GRINS - Growing Resilient, INclusive and Sustainable project (GRINS PE00000018  CUP F83C22001720001).* The views and opinions expressed are solely those of the authors and do not necessarily reflect those of the European Union, nor can the European Union be held responsible for them.

# References

1. Atanassov, K.T.: On intuitionistic Fuzzy Sets Theory, vol. 283. Springer, Heidelberg (2012)
2. De Tré, G., Peelman, M., Dujmović, J.: Logic reasoning under data veracity concerns. Int. J. Approximate Reasoning **161**, 108977 (2023)
3. Fosci, P., Psaila, G.: J-Co, a framework for fuzzy querying collections of JSON documents. In: Andreasen, T., De Tré, G., Kacprzyk, J., Legind Larsen, H., Bordogna, G., Zadrożny, S. (eds.) Flexible Query Answering Systems. FQAS 2021. LNCS, vol. 12871, pp. 142–153. Springer, Cham (2021)
4. Fosci, P., Psaila, G.: A unified view of multi-grade fuzzy-set models in j-co-ql+. Neurocomputing **565**, 126968 (2024)
5. Psaila, G., Fosci, P.: J-Co: a platform-independent framework for managing georeferenced JSON data sets. Electronics **10**, 621 (2021)
6. Zadeh, L.A.: Fuzzy sets. Inf. Control **8**(3), 338–353 (1965)

---

[1] Github repository of the *J-Co Framework*:
https://github.com/JcoProjectTeam/JcoProjectPage.

# Author Index

G. De Tré et al. (Eds.): FQAS 2025, LNAI 16119, pp. 333–334, 2026.
https://doi.org/10.1007/978-3-032-05607-8

The manufacturer's authorised representative in the EU is Springer
Nature Customer Service Centre GmbH, Europaplatz 3, 69115 Heidelberg,
Germany. If you have any concerns regarding our products, please
contact ProductSafety@springernature.com

Printed and bound by CPI Group (UK) Ltd, Croydon, CR0 4YY

28/04/2026

02098518-0006